The Holocaust and Antisemitism

A SHORT HISTORY

The Holocaust and Antisemitism

A SHORT HISTORY

Jocelyn Hellig

ONEWORLD

OXFORD

THE HOLOCAUST AND ANTISEMITISM: A SHORT HISTORY

Oneworld Publications
(Sales and Editorial)
185 Banbury Road
Oxford OX2 7AR
England
www.oneworld-publications.com

ISBN 1–85168–313–5

Cover design by Design Deluxe
Cover picture of Warsaw Ghetto uprising memorial © Sonia Halliday Photographs
Typeset by LaserScript Ltd, Mitcham, UK
Printed and bound in Britain by Bell & Bain Ltd, Glasgow

Dedicated to South Africa's "Rainbow Nation", *
*whose realism and capacity for compromise
enabled it to overcome the evils of racism, and
allow it both to witness and participate in a
miracle in the making.*

*Phrase coined by Anglican Archbishop Emeritus and Nobel Peace Prize Laureate, Desmond Tutu, to describe South Africa's multicultural and multi-religious people.

Contents

Part II: PRE-CHRISTIAN ANTISEMITISM

Part III: INTER-RELIGIOUS RIVALRY AND ANTISEMITISM

Part IV: THE SECULARISATION OF ANTISEMITISM

Acknowledgements

I owe a debt of gratitude to colleagues and friends who have contributed in some way to this book. The first is Martin Forward, Helena Wackerlin Professor of Religious Studies at Aurora University, Illinois and Executive Director of its Center for Faith and Action, who had the confidence in me to recommend my authorship of this book to Oneworld Publications. I would also like to thank my friend Maja Abramowitch, a survivor of the Holocaust, for reading the draft of chapter 1. Fully aware that I did not go through that hell myself, and therefore of my own limitations in approaching the Holocaust, I wanted to ensure that my theoretical explorations would pass muster for someone who, unfortunately, had. Patrick Hartin, professor of New Testament Studies at Gonzaga University, Spokane, Washington, was of inestimable assistance to me, reading and commenting on chapters 5 and 6, the two chapters on Christian antisemitism that constitute so essential a part of this book. I would also like to acknowledge the input of Leslie Hotz, a medical doctor and friend, who is a well-read layman in matters Jewish. His perusal of most of the manuscript in its early phases – precisely because he shares so few of my perspectives – constituted a valuable testing ground for me. For what I chose to write in the end, however, I take full responsibility.

Particularly deserving of my thanks is Victoria Roddam, Commissioning Editor for Oneworld. She was always there to answer my manifold questions and act as a sounding board as the book took shape, which took far longer than was originally intended as the complexities of the subject gradually unveiled themselves. I am grateful to her for her professionalism, understanding and patience.

Above all, however, I want to express my gratitude to my husband Michael, who pushed me to the boundaries of my confidence, and helped me cope with my anxieties as I worked through the various stages of investigation into this tragic and problematic subject. He certainly honed his culinary skills, an area in which, happily, he has had a long-term interest. While that nourished me physically, his loving support and encouragement gave me the psychological and spiritual sustenance I needed.

When impoverished [the Jews] have been accused of fomenting radicalism, revolution and anarchy.

When enriched, they have stirred the malevolent envy of the dispossessed.

When assimilated, they have been accused of sneakily insinuating themselves into the social and political fabric.

When asserting their ethnic identity, they have been subjected to charges impugning their loyalty and patriotism.

When separating themselves from their neighbors, they have been called rootless.

When concerned for their fellow Jews, they have been denounced as agents of a sinister international conspiracy that respects no borders and honors no national allegiances.

When restricted to a few occupations, they have been condemned as parasites who live off the more conspicuous toil of others.

When released from economic restrictions, they have stimulated jealousy as a by-product of resourcefulness and industriousness.

When practicing their faith, they provoked hostility stemming from myths of Christ-killing and from blood libels.

When distinctive religious customs have been abandoned, an image no less chilling to Gentiles has been projected – the image of a nowhere man who is estranged, uncommitted, the incarnation of those forces of modernization, urbanization and industrialization that have defined our [the twentieth] century.

Steven J. Whitfield

Introduction

Near the beginning of the Jewish ceremonial meal on Passover, the *seder*,[1] the youngest child present asks the question "Why is this night different from all other nights?" The gathering – led usually by the head of the household – then recounts the story of the Exodus, God's wondrous intervention on behalf of the Jewish people, who were brought from slavery to freedom, and, as God's "treasured possession" (Exodus 19:5) were called upon to live life according to his commandments. Each *seder* participant is meant to feel as if he or she personally was redeemed from Egyptian bondage, the eating of unleavened bread, *matzah*, the bread of affliction, reaffirming God's power and compassion. He had taken the Jewish people out of Egypt in so great a hurry that their bread had had no time to rise. The entire evening is dedicated to an exploration and commemoration of freedom to live life based on the gift of the Torah. The annual recounting of this "master story",[2] in a ritual setting, from a special book called the *Haggadah*,[3] keeps Judaism alive by reinforcing it in the memories of adults and introducing it to succeeding generations of Jewish children.

At almost the same time, each year, Christians commemorate the passion and crucifixion of Jesus, the messiah, who was born, lived and died among the Jews, God's chosen people. As both faiths take their authority from the God of Abraham, Easter has historically been a dangerous time for Jews because, though Jesus' cruel death was necessary for the salvation of the world, it was blamed on the Jews. As the deicide people, who had been blind to the real meaning of God's promises and to Jesus as the messiah, they were depicted as wilfully repeating the passion in various forms. The most common slander was the Blood Libel, which asserted that Jews needed the blood of innocent Christian children for use in their rituals, especially in the production of their *matzah*.

All religions have master stories, which scholars call the "mythological dimension". In this context the word "myth" has a meaning very different from the way it is employed colloquially. Although we generally use it to denote something that is *untrue*, scholars take a neutral view to the truth or falsity of the story, seeing "myth" as the charter of a religious community which gives believers the ultimate meaning and purpose of their faith. Myth, the importance of which will be made clear as this book progresses, gives people their understanding of important issues, such as their place in the world, their code of behaviour and their ideas about death and the hereafter. Christianity's mythical dimension is largely dependent on Judaism's, but departs from it in very important ways, seeing Jesus as God incarnate, and offering individual salvation, based on faith in his redeeming death. Judaism is centred on the collective, the *people* of Israel, and seeks not so much salvation, but the hallowing of the everyday act. Both religions are historical, in that Judaism, as we will see in chapter 3, was the first religion in the world to root its mythical dimension in history. Islam was, later, to be founded upon another master story, based on the same tradition, seeing Muhammad as God's last and most perfect prophet. These conflicting stories were decisive in fostering a negative image of the Jews, or antisemitism, and this book will look at each of them, bearing in mind that for almost two thousand years Jews lived as a minority people under either Christian or Muslim hegemony.

As will be made evident in chapter 2, antisemitism is almost impossible to define, but it differs from other forms of group hatred in that it not only dehumanises the Jews, but demonises them. It also endows them with cosmic powers for evil. This kind of hatred, I shall argue in this book, arises out of the rivalry between Judaism and Christianity but, more particularly, out of the way in which the story of Jesus has been told in the New Testament, a story whose repercussions were evident in the Holocaust. Whatever theory is used to explain antisemitism – whether it be psychological, economic or other – there is always a prior negative image of the Jew that requires explanation, and that explanation can only be found in the realm of religion. As William Nicholls (1995, p. xxviii) put it, "The original Christian hostility toward Jews went through a number of formations down the course of western history, acquiring different rationalizations. But all its forms shared one element, the most important – Jews were bad". The basic problem is not Jesus, however. Rather, as Robert McAfee Brown (1983, p. 172) asserts, "it is what Jesus' followers have done with him. Indeed, if Jesus is to be faulted, it would be primarily for not having seen clearly enough that his life and death would be distorted by his followers in ways inimical to his own understanding of his mission". Without the antagonism that was preached in the Christian church about the Jews, the Holocaust could never have happened.

An atrocity that could never have been carried out had not so many ordinary people helped to perpetrate it, the Holocaust has transformed our understanding of antisemitism. Antisemitism can no longer be seen as a marginal problem that has occurred from time to time and from place to place without catastrophic implications. Its deadly potential – now fulfilled – has made abundantly clear how immoral and reprehensible it is, bringing study of it from the margins to the mainstream of scholarship. This led to a revolution in Christian theology, in which Christian scholars, themselves, began to acknowledge that Christianity's "teaching of contempt"[4] for the Jews had to be honestly confronted as a causative factor of the Holocaust. Genocide could never have been accomplished in the absence of European culture's universal understanding of the Jew, and would have been a lot less easy to achieve had the Christian world outside protested. Scholars focused on the negative aspects of the historical relationship between Judaism and Christianity, and the New Testament itself was examined for its culpability in fostering hatred for Jews. Based on their study, I emphasise the positive aspects of Jesus' relations with Jews, indicating how, why and when the picture of a conflictive relationship may have emerged.

How, then, is this book different from the many other books on antisemitism? I believe that it is a difference of emphasis, and arrangement of material. The book has a three-fold thrust. The first is to explain the complex relationship between antisemitism and the Holocaust. The second is the search for the origins of antisemitism, and the tracing of its development. The third is the book's emphasis on a historical approach to antisemitism. This means that each instance of Jew hatred has to be examined within its specific religious, political, social and economic context. Such analysis reveals that the Holocaust was not an inevitable or even logical outcome of Christian antisemitism, in that the church had never wanted to destroy the Jews physically. It was also not a predictable outcome of prior forms of antisemitism. My focus, however, is on *religion*, which offers the only convincing explanation why it is so often the Jews who are the butt of people's hatred.

My particular interpretation can best be explained by telling my own story and that of the genesis of the book itself. Every author approaches his or her work with a history that determines the nature and direction of that work. I lectured on world religions for over twenty years at the University of the Witwatersrand – one of South Africa's most prestigious liberal universities – and always tried to impart to my students the values of the various religions, by putting myself as closely as possible into the shoes of their adherents and emphasising religion's positive influence on the world. But it is impossible to paint a true picture without referring to the negative dynamics between faiths, particularly when they are related to one another. Judaism, Christianity and Islam – the three Abrahamic religions – share a tradition, but differ fundamentally on the way that tradition should be interpreted, and how the promises in it have been, and will be, fulfilled. Though Judaism's basic worldview was adopted, as were some of its prior claims, differences developed, that Judaism found itself unable to share. It began to be viewed as either in error, or inferior, Jews as blind or stubborn, and their degraded status as *deserved*. Over time, an ugly stereotype of the Jew was formed, whose influence endures today. A substantial portion of this book will examine that inter-religious friction.

In the late 1970s, I began research into the thought of Richard L. Rubenstein, Judaism's only "death of God" theologian, which was to be the subject of my Ph.D. thesis. He had come to his radical conclusion in response to the Holocaust, and was later included in – though he had worked independently of – a movement of Christian death-of-God theologians, whose thought hit the scholarly and popular headlines in the mid 1960s. While the Christian death of God theologians celebrated the new era, Rubenstein mourned God's death with a cry of agony. It was a source of pain to Jews that none of those Christian theologians saw fit to include the Holocaust as a reason for God's demise.

As part of his analysis of the question of God and the Holocaust, Rubenstein had focused on the tragic, Antigone-like conflict between the mythic structures of Christianity and Judaism. His insights sharpened perceptions I had already formed, and I was deeply impressed by his discomfort with the Jewish doctrine of chosenness, and the way it relates to antisemitism. He had called for Jews to demythologise it, yet realised how difficult this would be, since both Judaism and Christianity were so dependent on it. As he laconically put it, without the doctrine of chosenness, "the Christ makes absolutely no theological difference".[5]

But Rubenstein's thought took me beyond the question of God and the Holocaust and, indeed, beyond antisemitism itself in the search for causes of the Holocaust. Whereas he had been intent during the 1960s, to examine the Holocaust's implications for Jewish theology, in the mid 1970s, though not abandoning his earlier views, he turned to analysis of the Holocaust's more global implications. He was able to hold in tension antisemitism – as one of the Holocaust's most decisive causes – and "functional rationality", mass killing as a modern problem-solving exercise. He saw this new, modern mindset as the "night side" of biblical thinking. He was, at this stage, working less as a theologian and more as a social theorist. He spoke of God's death in terms of the godless universe in which we live. Jews were targeted by Hitler because of their place in religious history, but they had been *defined* as superfluous, by people who had arrogated to themselves godlike power. Their murder was a strictly modern enterprise. Jews were Hitler's primary victims, but not his only ones, which leads to the question: What exactly *was* the Holocaust, and can we ignore the millions of others who were enslaved, degraded and murdered by the Nazis?

It is with this background that I began this book, which was, originally, to be a book on the history of antisemitism. My overriding instinct was to start with the Holocaust, since it was the ultimate expression of antisemitism in action, and then go back to seek its roots and trace its history. Having barely begun, I was, not so much side-tracked, but lured into the complexities of Holocaust scholarship and the conflicting ways in which the Holocaust is interpreted. We are not always aware of the fact that we only know about the Holocaust in the ways in which it has been told to us, and that every telling – whether it be by a historian, or a survivor, or in the form of a popular film or novel – involves an interpretation. These interpretations give our understanding of it form. Some will emphasise the Holocaust as a specifically Jewish tragedy, with antisemitism as a central causal factor, whereas others – though not denying the importance of antisemitism or the genocide of the Jews – will emphasise the Holocaust as a world tragedy, moving beyond antisemitism in their attempts to explain it. Historiography of the Holocaust is complicated, and in its infancy, and historians, as this book will show, find it difficult to pin down the Holocaust's exact essence.

I was also troubled, not only about the exact meaning of the word "antisemitism" but also about the problematic link between it and the Holocaust. I was struck by the inadequacy and imprecision of the designations we give to these two phenomena that met so tragically in the twentieth century. Though we will elaborate on the semantic problems in the body of the book, the word "Holocaust" is generally used to stand for the brutal and systematic murder of two-thirds of Europe's Jews during the Second World War. The word "antisemitism" has become the popular word for all forms of Jew hatred. The usage of both is hotly debated. Some scholars regard antisemitism as an entirely modern phenomenon and use the word very specifically to denote modern, racially based Jew hatred, whereas others use the word very broadly, to cover all forms of anti-Jewish expression. I shall adopt the latter approach in the conviction that it is too late to attempt to change people's usage of the word, and that most people understand what we mean when we use it, recognising that it is never directed at anyone but Jews. The distinctions implicit in the word "antisemitism" will be clarified in chapter 2 when we discuss the various approaches to this concept. We will see there that, because there is no such thing as a Semite, to whom people could be opposed, the hyphen in the word "anti-Semitism" has largely been dropped in scholarly usage.

The word "Holocaust" is also questionable. First, the designation has been extended to all sorts of social evils – some quite trivial – and, second, its association with religious sacrifice suggests that the Holocaust has some religious meaning. In fact, before the 1960s, there was no name for the tragedy that had befallen the Jewish people. The word "Holocaust" was coined in the early 1960s, by Jews, to denote the murder of six million of their people, who were targeted for destruction for no other reason than that they were Jewish, their murder doing nothing to enhance the German war effort. On the contrary, it hindered it, suggesting to some scholars that Adolf Hitler might have been fighting, in addition to the Second World War, a separate, and for him more ideologically important, war against the Jews.

A biblical word, "Holocaust" derives from the Greek word *holokaustos,* meaning "fully burnt", and was used in the first major translation of the Bible into Greek, the third-century BCE Septuagint. It translated the Hebrew word *olah,* something "brought up" to God in a sacrificial offering made exclusively to him. Selection of it was probably based on the Jews' particular understanding of history as God's chosen people, which will be explained in chapter 3. Focusing particularly on the victims, "Holocaust" was meant to separate this massacre from all other historical instances of murder or genocide, to endow the catastrophe with a religious significance and to point to its incomprehensibility. It implies a universe in which God had a role in – even if it was one merely of allowing – the slaughter of six million of his chosen people, something that many people find repulsive. The murder of Jews had meaning only for the Nazis, who used the term *die Endlösung* "the final solution", for what was to them a mundane solution to a problem. Thus, many now prefer the Hebrew word *Shoah*, meaning "catastrophe" in the sense of a destructive windstorm or other natural disaster.

Shoah stresses the enormity of the event and, also, that its primary victims were Jewish. Use of this designation, as Gabriel Moran (1992, p. 33) suggests, is a strategy to protect the particularity of the disaster, so that it is seen as an atrocity against *Jews* and not as a crime against humanity in general. He warns, however, that this may, in the end, be counter-productive. Isolating the term from English speakers may dilute the relevance of the disaster. In any event, *Shoah*, too, is a biblical word and has, therefore, religious implications. However, it introduces an element of randomness and, maybe, despair. Some people prefer to use the symbol "Auschwitz" to stand for the genocide of the Jews, but, since there were many death camps, this is seen as unfairly selective. Also, as we will see, the Holocaust was more than about death camps, as morally repugnant, final and cruel as they were. It was also more than about Jews and antisemitism. These were part of a wholesale, paranoid restructuring of the world, an important part, but still a *part*. Since no single word is adequate to encapsulate the tragedy, I will employ the generally accepted word "Holocaust" throughout the book. In chapter 1, we will attain a clearer view of what the word "Holocaust" has come to mean to both Jews and non-Jews.

It became important to discuss the elusive way in which the Holocaust relates to antisemitism, and to reveal their complicated relationship. There could not have been a Holocaust without antisemitism, but antisemitism had existed for over two thousand years, and there had never been an attempt to completely obliterate the Jews. What had turned antisemitism into a systematic programme of annihilation? There is a qualitative difference between antisemitism and genocide. Something else had come into the equation that made mass killing of the Jews possible. It became obvious to me that there should be a dual focus in this book. Although it is about antisemitism and its history, it also discusses these other factors. Hence the title: *The Holocaust and Antisemitism: A Short History.*

The first chapter of the book, therefore, considers the various debates that have arisen around the Holocaust, a catastrophe that has thrown up so many problems and so many profound questions, that no one approach is adequate and no final answers are possible. One of the functions of this book is to raise the questions, bearing in mind that in fifty years' time scholars may be posing very different ones. By considering these questions, in no way do I mean to minimise the danger of antisemitism, or to dilute its fundamental immorality; rather, I intend to put it into its historical perspective. The historical approach looks at issues like antisemitism's first manifestation in time – a moment in history that is extraordinarily difficult to locate – and its persistence and continuity, while also noting is protean nature. It indicates the changes that have occurred throughout antisemitism's history, while also pointing to those aspects of it that have remained constant.

THE STRUCTURE OF THE BOOK

The book is divided into four broad sections. The first, comprising of chapters 1 and 2, looks at the theoretical issues underlying antisemitism and its relationship to the Holocaust, as well as discussing the various approaches to the study of antisemitism.

The second section, made up of chapters 3 and 4, deals with pre-Christian antisemitism. Unlike most books on antisemitism, chapter 3 looks at Judaism itself, because it is impossible to understand antisemitism unless we know the basics of what Jews believe about their place in the universe. The way Jews see themselves plays an important role in how others – particularly those who share the fatherhood of Abraham and the promises God made to him – see them. Jews' understanding of their place in God's plan for the world also laid the basis for their particular lifestyle, to which others have responded in various ways, both positive and negative. Chapter 4 considers how the pagan world responded to Jewish claims. Despite intense antagonism, Judaism exerted a profound attraction to gentiles, or non-Jews.

The third section focuses on religiously inspired antisemitism arising out of the inter-religious conflict between the three Abrahamic faiths.

Chapters 5 and 6 discuss the emergence of Christian antisemitism, chapter 5 concentrating on its dynamics, that is, the way it tends to present itself, and chapter 6 on tracing the way it emerged historically. Important here are the implications of Christianity's adoption of the Jewish view of history, which resulted in the Jews becoming the "secret centre" of Christian theology. In reconstructing Christianity's beginnings, in chapter 6, I emphasise the importance, for the future of antisemitism, of an exciting new trend in New Testament scholarship, the reassertion of Jesus' Jewishness. He is increasingly being seen as an observant Jew, who was *not* against his own people, and was executed not at the instigation of the Jews, but by cruel Roman imperial power, on a Roman cross, for a Roman offence. Furthermore, neither he nor Paul is seen as intending to formulate a new religion, the negative image of the Jews in the New Testament being the product of a later period.

Chapter 7 examines the traditional Muslim view of the Jews and Judaism, showing that its antagonism was much milder historically than that of Christendom. The challenge of modernity has, however, resulted in radical changes, so that the current Islamic image of the Jew now rivals its Christian counterpart. This is particularly so among "fundamentalist" Muslims, a contentious designation that will be touched on in that chapter. We also look at anti-Zionism and the interplay of antisemitism with a number of issues, notably the Middle East conflict and Third World ideologies.

The fourth section of the book, chapter 8, covers the secularisation of antisemitism. Religiously inspired antisemitism never resulted in genocide. For that to happen, antisemitism had to be secularised and fused with ideologies like racism. There were moral constraints in Christianity – and later Islam – that disallowed mass killing. Jews had been deemed practitioners of an inferior or incomplete faith, and they had had to live in demeaning conditions as a sign of their stubbornness and error, but they were still seen as *equal* in the eyes of God. Conversion to either Christianity or Islam was always open to them. In fact, Christianity determined that Jews should be kept alive. With the new racial antisemitism, the Jews' evil was now thought to be "in their blood", and conversion was rendered ineffectual. Chapter 8 discusses the amalgamation of the religiously inspired stereotype with new ideologies, like nationalism and romanticism, in the context of a modernising world. It shows how, in accordance with new views about human equality, modern thinkers wanted to make amends to the Jews, but refused to allow them to remain Jews as a collective, thus contradicting those thinkers' own values of freedom and equality.

In the epilogue, I briefly consider the importance of remembering and learning about the Holocaust, and its impact on Jewish self-perception, particularly as it affects the Middle East conflict. I also look at the implications of viewing all of Jewish history through the prism of the Holocaust. Most importantly, I point out that, despite alarming new signs of antisemitism, individuals are *not* doomed by their religions or cultures to antisemitism. Individual choice can make a vital difference.

THE ELUSIVE AND EMOTIVE NATURE OF THE SUBJECT

The reader has probably, at this early stage, perceived how difficult it is to pin down the nature and meaning of the two major phenomena that will be addressed in this book. It may seem flippant to start so serious a work with the advice of the king in *Alice in Wonderland*: "Begin at the beginning ... and go on till you come to the end; then stop". But this was the quotation that constantly popped up in my mind as the work progressed. To this subject, there are neither clear beginnings nor a clear terminus. As I researched and wrote, I barely ever found myself on solid ground. My arguments always seemed to proceed in circular fashion, arriving back at the point at which I had begun. Even the names given to the phenomena are, as we have seen, questionable and misleading, and the phenomena themselves are as elusive as quicksilver. An investigation into either one – on its own – is not only difficult, but emotionally charged. Together, they open a minefield, and misperception, misconception and hurt often ensue. I have tried to keep the text as unrepetitious as possible, and hope that I have succeeded in conveying a highly emotive subject fairly and unemotionally while, at the same time, not giving the impression that the phenomena it involves are any less repulsive.

Covering so broad a canvas, I have had to be selective. Other authors might have chosen other factors in their portrayal of the history of antisemitism. I have tried, throughout, to give the reader a clear idea of the literature that has emerged on the subject over the years, particularly the secondary literature that will make the issues more accessible, and hope that this introductory book will whet the reader's appetite for further reading. I have also shared the way my own South African experience has shaped some of my conclusions, and hope that the examples I have used provoke further thought.

CONVENTIONS

Besides my decision to use the designations "Holocaust" and "anti-semitism" throughout the book, there are other usages that require clarification. "BC" and "AD", indicating the period before and after the birth of Jesus, are replaced with the more neutral notation, "BCE" and "CE", which denote "before the common era" and "the common era", respectively. As will become clear in chapters 5 and 6, the term "Old Testament" has a denigratory ring in that it implies that the "Old" has been superseded by the "New". I have therefore used the title "Hebrew Bible", retaining the term "Old Testament" only when used in a Christian context, where I have generally placed the term in inverted commas. In the light of the negative consequences of the term "Old Testament," there is considerable debate about what the two holy scriptures should be called, some scholars offering totally new designations. Mary Boys, in her valuable 2000 book on Judaism as a source of a new Christian self-understanding, *Has God Only One Blessing?*, suggests that we should replace them with "First" and "Second Testament". Harry James Cargas (1988, p. 305) recommends that we use the terms "Inherited Testament" and "Institutional Testament". The first would acknowledge the Christian debt to Judaism, and the latter would make clear the church's sole role in establishing this particular canon.

I have used the Harvard system of referencing, and elaborated, where necessary, with end notes. Because I have referred to a great number of books, to give the reader an indication of the trends in the various fields of scholarship covered in the book, some of them have not been included in the bibliography. There is enough information, however, for the interested reader to follow up.

I have tried to be consistent about using the New English Bible's translations wherever possible, but have occasionally used more familiar translations where they seem applicable.

Part I

THE HOLOCAUST AND ANTISEMITISM: THEORETICAL ISSUES

1

The Holocaust and antisemitism

One can do without solutions. Only the questions matter. We may share them or turn away from them.

Elie Wiesel

The really pertinent question is not why the Nazis were antisemites but why they committed murder. There is no direct line from antisemitism to the Holocaust for the very simple reason that antisemitism had existed for centuries and yet had never before led to such murderous destruction.

Eberhard Jäckel

INTRODUCING THE PROBLEM

The word "Holocaust" was coined during the 1960s – probably by the survivor and writer Elie Wiesel – to denote the brutal, systematic attempt by the Nazis to annihilate the Jewish people during the Second World War. A word from the Hebrew Bible, "Holocaust" emerged in a specifically Jewish context to denote a pointedly Jewish catastrophe. Its original intention, therefore, was to stand for the murder of two-thirds of Europe's Jews. Immediately after the war, there was a stunned silence. The Jewish people were too shocked by the intensity and universality of the hatred that had allowed such savagery to befall them, and too bereft to speak. It took twenty years to gather enough distance from the event to look back at what had happened and begin to analyse it.

Soon, the word "Holocaust" began to take on other meanings. The Second World War was an enormous and complicated disaster, which unfolded in a global arena. Whole areas were destroyed, and tens of millions had died, not only as the normal lamentable consequence of military activity, but as a result of deliberate murder. Adolf Hitler's particular ideology had led to the enslavement, degradation and death of millions. Many had been callously left out to die by the ravages of weather, overwork, starvation or illness. The six million Jews were the primary victims, but there were millions of others whose fate we cannot ignore. People began to wonder, therefore, whether the word "Holocaust" should not be extended to include all those who had suffered or been murdered during the Second World War. It did not take long before the word began to be used for all sorts of disasters or attempts at social engineering, some of them quite trivial.

With this, it became necessary to remind the world of the central place that Jews had occupied in both Hitler's worldview and the killing machine that he had set up to bring it to fruition. Although many millions of non-Jews also died, Jews saw what happened to them as unique. Never before had there been an attempt to systematically destroy an entire people simply on the basis of their birth and apparently for no practical reason. Attempts at comparison were thought to understate the Jewish tragedy, to trivialise Jewish suffering, and to supplant the memory of what had happened to the Jews with other – and what seemed to be lesser – catastrophes. Such seemed, to Jews, to be a subtle form of antisemitism.

It was only in the 1960s that real analysis of the Holocaust, in the wider context of the Second World War, began. Historiography of the Holocaust emerged as historians began to find ways of explaining the event in terms of its causes, its course and its implications. It became difficult to separate the particularly Jewish aspect of the war from its wider context. Theologians began to ask the questions: "Where was God?" "How had he allowed six million of his chosen people to be so mercilessly destroyed?" "Is there anything in the Jewish–Christian relationship that could have caused so disastrous an outcome for the Jewish people?" Psychologists began to deliberate about Hitler's personality, or the factors that allowed an entire nation to participate – even if it was only by silent consent – in genocide. Sociologists began to look at the kind of world in which such atrocities could be accomplished.

In the early stages, antisemitism, or Jew hatred, seemed to be the primary cause of the Holocaust, and new attention was given to it. Whereas, before, Jews had been persecuted, humiliated and even massacred, there had never been an intention to destroy them utterly. The Holocaust was a *novum* in both Jewish and world history. Yet, the Holocaust had also demonstrated antisemitism's most devastatingly logical outcome. Study of it could no longer be relegated to the sidelines, and it could no longer be viewed as an occasional outburst of hatred that arose from time to time and from place to place. Thus, the Holocaust put the study of antisemitism into the mainstream of scholarship. Realising the contribution that Christianity had made to antisemitism by the negative portrayal of the Jew, both in the New Testament and later, Christian and Jewish scholars began to address the problem. The painful realisation that Christianity, the religion of love, could be linked with so atrocious an outcome led to a revolution in Christian scholarship.

With all the study that was taking place, it soon became clear, however, that antisemitism was not the only cause of the Holocaust. It may not even have been the primary cause. Antisemitism, which had existed for at least two thousand years, had never before ended in genocide of the Jews. There is a qualitative difference between even severe forms of antisemitism – including murder – and an intention to annihilate the Jews, completely. What *was* it, then, that came into the picture to alter it so radically? Was the culprit, perhaps, the modern ethos itself, and did it utilise antisemitism to achieve its aims? Are there other prejudices that could, in other instances, be used in antisemitism's place? Since the Holocaust, there have been other genocides.

From the 1970s, scholars began to look more closely at other developments in the modern world, like bureaucracy, the advance of technology, and a new and brutal kind of rationality that, in seeking to attain specific ends, will stop at nothing – including mass murder – to attain them. Indeed, mass murder might be the most efficient of means. Historians also began to ask whether Hitler intended from early on in his life to destroy the Jews. Those scholars who think that he *did* – known as the Intentionalists – see antisemitism as a primary cause of the Holocaust. Those scholars who hold that he did *not* – known as the Functionalists – give other factors greater weight. They do not deny Hitler's antisemitism. No one could. Even a cursory glance at his autobiographical *Mein Kampf* leaves no doubt of his intense hatred and distrust of Jews. But the Functionalists argue that what he said there does not prove his *intention* to destroy the Jews. He would, they suggest, have been satisfied with their emigration. The decision to murder the Jews came about piecemeal, as the war progressed and new, unforeseen problems emerged. He turned to genocide only when all other methods to get the Jews out of his domain failed.

The link between antisemitism and the Holocaust is, therefore, far from clear. There could have been no Holocaust without antisemitism, but antisemitism does not necessarily lead to genocide. In other words, the Holocaust was not the inevitable outcome of antisemitism. In this chapter, I will flesh out the considerations raised above, and explain in greater detail the various debates that have arisen around them, basing my account on the contrasting viewpoints of a host of scholars. We will see that we know about the Holocaust only in the way that it has been handed down, or told, to us. As each telling is different, we are left with a number of interpretations of it. Some accounts emphasise its specifically Jewish nature, whereas others see it in broader terms. How the Holocaust is defined will determine the place of antisemitism as a causative factor. If the Holocaust is seen as a specifically *Jewish* tragedy, then antisemitism is central. If it is seen as a wider, global catastrophe, then what happened to the Jews presages ominously what can, and does, happen to others. Factors other than, and in addition to, antisemitism will, therefore, assume greater weight. By the end of the chapter we will appreciate that, though there are endless questions, there are no final answers. This should not deter us, however. Given the enormity of the disaster, and the kind of world that we now inhabit, it remains crucial that we continue to pose appropriate and responsible questions, while we grope our way towards understanding.

APPROACHING THE HOLOCAUST

The Holocaust – the systematic murder of one-third of the world's entire Jewish population during the Second World War – was the ultimate manifestation of antisemitism in action. To achieve it, Jews were stripped, by the Nazi government, of their citizenship, their human rights, their dignity and, ultimately, their lives. Discriminatory legislation rendered them totally powerless to change their fate, and the world at large abandoned them. Only a tiny minority of people, at considerable risk to themselves and their families, spoke out for them or helped to save them. Many of these have been honoured, by the Yad Vashem Holocaust memorial in Jerusalem, with the distinction "Righteous Gentile",[1] and one may, today, walk down the peaceful Avenue of the Righteous between the olive trees planted in their name to commemorate their humaneness.

For the most part, ordinary people either participated in the slaughter, or stood by, acquiescing to it by their failure to protest. People both inside Europe and elsewhere had fallen prey to antisemitism, the most ancient and persistent group hatred known to history, a hatred that this book sets out to explain.

Ending little more than a half a century ago, the Holocaust still casts a long shadow over human consciousness. Had Hitler won the war, there is a strong possibility that the Jewish people may not have survived at all. The Jews were targeted for annihilation for the simple reason that they were born Jewish. Their destruction did not aid the Nazis in their war effort. Rather, it impeded them. But, as Nazi power began to crumble in 1944, the programme of annihilation was intensified. Murder of the Jews, at that point, seemed to be the only end that remained for the Nazis. The Nazi act against the Jews, as Michael Berenbaum (1990, p. 32) points out, was unparalleled in its methodology, leaving six million dead, one million of them children, an entire world destroyed, a culture uprooted and humankind with new thresholds of inhumanity.

Given the high profile of the Holocaust in the public consciousness, it is not always obvious that *we only know about it in the ways it has been passed down to us*.[2] It is also not realised that interest in the Holocaust has not always been as fashionable as it is today and that Holocaust historiography is a very young discipline. Little emerged in the first twenty years after the Holocaust. The work of early Holocaust historians, like Raul Hilberg and Yehuda Bauer, constituted a "revolt against silence" (Hilberg 1998, p. 5). Perpetrators did not want to hear what they had done, bystanders did not want to be told of their complicity, and the Jewish community was too shocked to speak. The subject was also deeply sensitive because of some of the accusations against Jewish leadership that were emerging from historical probing. Jewish leaders were seen as having unwittingly collaborated with the enemy through compliance. The early analysts failed to realise the total powerlessness of the Jews under Nazi domination. Historical analysis is offering increasing insight on such issues.

Since the late 1960s, attempts to represent and understand the Holocaust – from historical treatises to popular films and novels – have grown from a trickle to torrent. Although retelling of it is essential in order to keep the memory of the tragedy alive, the growth in coverage has led to suggestions that there is "too much" about the Holocaust. There has also been so much profiteering that the judgement "there is no business like Shoah business" seems hardly out of place. Some accounts of the Holocaust are more responsible and sensitive than others, but every telling is *subject to the interpretation of the teller*. These interpretations, provided they are not denials of the important part that the slaughter of Jews played in the catastrophe – an element of the conflict that has left so much grim historic evidence in its wake – should be given a hearing in our efforts to understand what occurred. As we shape our own picture of the Holocaust, some interpretations will acquire more prominence in our view than others. The idea of differing interpretations of the Holocaust is an important one to the subject of this chapter, because the link we establish between antisemitism and the Holocaust is itself dependent on interpretation.

I refer here – and through most of the book – to the specifically Jewish dimension of the tragedy. But millions of other people were subjugated, tortured, enslaved and killed by the Nazis. The deputy leader of the Nazi Party, Rudolf Hess, once said, "National Socialism is nothing but applied biology."[3] The Nazis were attempting to create an "ideal" social order, by remodelling the pure and noble race of Germans on the basis of new values such as racial purity, racial hygiene, and "good" "clean" living. Some members of "inferior" races had to become slaves to establish and maintain German superiority in Germany's new, expanded domain, and others, who threatened the "wholesomeness" of German life, were deemed to be "unworthy of life" (*unwertes Leben*) altogether. These – among whom the Jews were the prime victims – were targeted for death. Jews, the most hunted and persecuted, constituted one part of an entire "mosaic of victims", to use Michael Berenbaum's apt phrase (1990). Victims included Soviet prisoners of war, Jehovah's Witnesses, mentally retarded, physically handicapped or emotionally unstable Germans, Gypsies (the Roma and Sinti), German male homosexuals, trade unionists, political dissidents, and clergymen who dared to speak out against Nazi policy. We may never know the number of men, women and children of all ages killed by the Nazis in their orgy of violence, said V. R. Berghahn (1996). They left behind a trail of blood and tears – particularly in Eastern Europe – that defies human imagination, hardened as it is by the pictures of cruelty and destruction, flashed across our television screens, of other genocides in places like Bosnia and Rwanda. And this, Berghahn says, "is *before* we contemplate the systematic murder of six million Jews from all over Europe" (italics mine). Jews ranked the lowest in Hitler's racial hierarchy. They were to be hunted down and destroyed without mercy. When the war ended in 1945, fifty to sixty million people were left dead in its wake. The Jews were the primary victims, but not the only ones.

Before the Second World War, antisemitism had, for the most part, been of secondary, or marginal, interest. Despite its periodic intensity, it had never resulted in a programme of genocide. Something new had taken place. Antisemitism now had to be taken seriously because the world had seen its horrible denouement. But was it a question of antisemitism alone? Is there not also a sense in which those particular factors that helped transform antisemitism into active genocide against the Jews were part of a wider trend of human destructiveness?

THE ROLE OF ANTISEMITISM IN THE HOLOCAUST

The Holocaust, as Michael Marrus in his excellent and now classic 1987 overview of Holocaust historiography, *The Holocaust in History*, points out, seems both qualitatively and quantitatively different in kind from other massacres that punctuate history. This has led to the assertion that the Holocaust is unique and that antisemitism should be seen as its chief cause. Although these assertions have some substance, they do not, he says, sit well with the wider community of historians. Informed theories about the centrality of antisemitism in Nazism do *not* claim that anti-Jewish ideology was a predominantly German doctrine or even a constant preoccupation of the leaders of the Third Reich. Research, he avers, suggests the very opposite. Furthermore, antisemitism, on its own, was not enough to cause the Holocaust. Other historic factors determined the way in which antisemitism could be exploited.

If one were asked to name the most antisemitic country in Europe in the 1890s, several scholars suggest, the answer would probably be France, with Czarist Russia coming a close second. The map of European antisemitism then looked different from that of the 1930s and 1940s and, even in the 1930s, though Germany would be a strong contender, it would certainly not be the only one. At the end of the nineteenth century, France, with its severe pogroms,[4] and the trumped up accusations of treason against a Jewish military officer that led to the Dreyfus affair, looked potentially a lot worse than Germany, which had accorded fundamental rights to Jews and where there were no pogroms. Scholars, Marrus suggests, no longer insist with assurance on the "Jewish question" in pre-Nazi Germany. There was undoubtedly antisemitism there, but it is difficult to ascertain its exact source and location. Though the influence of antisemitic parties may have been on the decline, antisemitism had become pervasive in public life. It had become, as Shulamit Volkov (1988) argued, part of a "cultural code", a convenient abbreviation for a broad cluster of ideas, values and norms. Antisemitism was indicative of a broader ideology, of which it was but a part.

Though there was a general tide of antisemitism in Europe in the late nineteenth century, some scholars, like Uriel Tal, and, more recently, Daniel Goldhagen, have made a case for the special intensity of *German* antisemitism. Tal, in his 1975 book, *Christians and Jews in Germany: Religion, Politics and Ideology in the Second Reich, 1879–1914*, argued that there were two strands of anti-Jewish thought in Germany, the traditional and the radical. The first strand was rooted in Christianity and its relationship to Judaism. It was religiously inspired opposition to the Jewish rejection of the Christian majority faith. (An explanation of this sort will constitute much of this book.) The second was a more modern manifestation. It was violently anti-Christian in inspiration, pagan in its models for the ideal society, and *racist* in its definition of Jews. This blend, as we shall see in chapter 8, was much more virulent and uncompromising than the earlier Christian form, and it was this amalgam, with the addition of new ideas, that was to form the basis of Nazi antisemitism.

There is no certainty about the extent to which antisemitism was, from the beginning, a driving force behind the Nazi party. Rubenstein and Roth, in their comprehensive and insightful 1987 introduction to the Holocaust, *Approaches to Auschwitz*, claim that, when the Nazis came to power in 1933, their commitment to antisemitism was clear, but their practical policies towards Jews were not. It is one thing to have antisemitic feelings and quite another to make those feelings effective in a political regime. Hence, it took time for the Nazis to work out a coherent anti-Jewish programme. But this is the nub of the problem. What were the *exact* circumstances that caused genocide to occur, and for the Holocaust to start in Germany and not elsewhere? Antisemitism, as Marrus (1987, p. 9ff) points out, played an uneven role among Nazi leaders and in voting patterns, and it is not even certain how important it was for members of the Nazi party. He suggests that the Nazis shared very few clearly articulated goals, and this applied even to antisemitism. There were times when the Nazi leadership made a determined effort to make the party socially acceptable, by toning down antisemitic rhetoric. At other times, hatred of

Jews was shouted from rooftops. Antisemitism was utilised if viable, and played down or abandoned if not, depending on how politically advantageous it was at any given time or place. Many, Marrus says, were drawn to antisemitism through Nazism and not the other way around. Hitler's antisemitism, on the other hand, formed the very core of his worldview and Jews were a factor in everything that ever concerned him.

It should be noted here that most historians do not see the Holocaust as an inevitable outcome of antisemitism, or even of German antisemitism. A particular set of historic circumstances resulted in its occurrence and it is the weighting of individual components of the broader historic situation that leads to different opinions on what caused the Holocaust. What distinguishes the Holocaust is not antisemitism, but the Nazi programme to annihilate the Jewish people. Without the latter, there would have been a severe case of antisemitism, but no more. Not the least among the factors that enabled the Holocaust to occur was the personality of Hitler. Let us look then at Hitler's antisemitic worldview within the context of European antisemitism at the time. The precise nature of his intentions and his exact role in the Holocaust are subject to dispute, but no reliable historian questions the fact that Hitler had a determinative role.

HITLER'S ANTISEMITIC WORLDVIEW

Hitler, as Robert Wistrich in his well-known 1991 book on the history of antisemitism, *Antisemitism: The Longest Hatred*, pointed out, was heir to an age-old tradition of Christian antisemitism which had, by his time, been transmuted into biological racism. Hitler formulated his own amalgam, however, in a new secular and political "faith" called National Socialism. Although he was anti-Christian, and contemptuous of Christianity, he borrowed motifs freely from Christian precedents that conceived of Judaism as a demonic force. In his early years in Bavaria, he often evoked the myth of the Jews as Christ killers, but claimed messianic status for himself as the militant saviour of the German people. "Thus," he said in *Mein Kampf* (1939, p. 74), "I believe I am acting today in the spirit of the Almighty Creator: by resisting the Jew, I am fighting for the Lord's work". His animus against Christianity was aimed ultimately at Judaism. For example, he disapproved of the fact that Martin Luther had translated the Bible into German, because that had allowed the "Jewish spirit" to permeate the German population.

Jews were an essential part of Hitler's understanding of the historical process, which was, he believed, driven by struggle, hence the name of his frenzied and repetitive autobiography, *Mein Kampf*, or *My Struggle*. He saw his own personal struggle as analogous to that of his people. "The idea of struggle is as old as life itself," he said in a 1928 speech, "for life is only preserved because other living things perish through struggle ... in (which) the stronger, the more able, win, while the less able, the weak, lose." Adopting a crude perversion of Darwin's ideas about biological evolution, natural selection and the survival of the fittest,[5] Hitler conceived of history as a global arena in which peoples, in order to survive, are forever engaged in ruthless competition. The struggle, which is "often very bitter", he said in *Mein Kampf* (1939, p. 36), "kills off human sympathy. One's own painful struggle for existence destroys his feeling for the misery of those it left behind".

He was deeply impressed by the idea that racial mixing would lead to the destruction of civilisation. "Mingling of blood", he said (1939, p. 288), "with the decline in racial level that it causes, is the sole reason for the dying out of old cultures". He saw as the ultimate pollutant the Jew, who was the "most extreme contrast to the Aryan" (1939, p. 292). "Historical experience," he suggested, "offers countless examples" of the fact that the "mingling of Aryan blood with inferior races" will result in the end of the "sustainer of civilization". Such mixing would cause both physical and intellectual retrogression, and mark the beginning of a "slow but sure wasting disease" (1939, p. 279). The "iron logic" of nature, he said (1939, p. 279), was its will to breed life upwards (1939, p. 278). To oppose this was to seek destruction.

For Hitler, Jews were an anti-race with no culture of their own. "The Jew," he said (1939, p. 295), "possesses no civilization-building power; he has not and never did have the idealism without which there can be no upward development of man. Consequently, his intellect is never constructive, but destructive". The Jew, he claimed (1939, p. 293), "has never possessed a culture of his own, the basis for his mental processes has always been furnished by others. In every age his intellect has developed by means of the civilization surrounding him. The reverse of the process has never taken place". Everything Jews had, therefore, like parliamentarianism or democracy, they had taken over from other "sound" races, and perverted. In the process, they weakened these societies and undermined their capacity for struggle, thus becoming the sinister enemies of humankind. "Whatever sham civilization the Jew possesses today is the contribution of other peoples, mostly spoiled under his hands" (1939, p. 294).

By their constant mingling with other peoples, the Jews had corrupted their positive qualities, and poisoned their institutions. Insinuating themselves into other societies, Jews aimed to dissolve them. Marxism was one means they used to achieve this, and capitalism another. Jews were thus seen as a constant threat, both to the world in general and to the German people in particular. As the latter's prophet, Hitler promised to save them from degeneration and lead them to a glorious future. Hitler's beliefs had nothing to do with real Jews, and transcended any real "racial" categories that people may use. Jews, as Steven Katz (1998, p. 61) points out, were the negative pole, the embodiment of evil. In Hitler's myth of a new world, the Jews personified the devil, the vampire, the parasite upon the nations.

When Hitler came to power in 1933, Germany's economy was in crisis, unemployment was rife and the people's national self-confidence was at a low ebb. Hitler diagnosed Germany's degeneration as being directly proportional to the triumph of Jewry, which, as it spread its tentacles, was threatening the world. From early on in his life, he had been deeply influenced by *The Protocols of the Elders of Zion*, the counterfeit minutes of a meeting of the so-called secret Jewish world conspiracy. It had been forged by the Czarist police in 1905, and has since become the "bible" for antisemites. The more it was asserted that these were a forgery, the more this became "proof" for Hitler that they were genuine (1939, p. 299).

The *Protocols*, one of the most sinister and destructive forgeries ever fabricated, achieved worldwide distribution through the motor car magnate Henry Ford's popularisation, *The International Jew*. Serialising it for seven years in his weekly newspaper, *The Dearborn Independent*, Ford helped to spread its nonsensical argument that Jews were conspiring to rule the world. This made the *Protocols* as Norman Cohn (1967) put it, "a warrant for genocide". So impressed was Hitler by Ford's work that he had it widely distributed in German translation, and even had a portrait of Ford in his private office. If the Jews should succeed, Hitler warned, the world would be smothered by "filth and offal" (1939, p. 294). They were a typical parasite, "spreading like a harmful bacillus wherever a suitable medium invites it. And the effect of his existence is also like that of parasites: wherever he occurs, the host nation dies off sooner or later" (1939, p. 296). This being so, Hitler wanted the Jews removed from his ambit. Some suggest that his desire for their removal was so absolute that their physical annihilation would not have been enough. Hitler wanted the destruction of the Jewish angle of vision and the Jewish understanding of history. This was to be replaced by a Nazi reconstruction of Jewish history. Jews would survive only as a museum piece, created in the Nazi image.[6] "Anything in this world that is not of good race," said Hitler (1939, p. 288), "is chaff".

To create a new and "ideal" Nazi world, Hitler needed to expand Germany's territory eastward in order to secure *Lebensraum* (living space) for a perfectly homogeneous German race. To effect this, he had to put up an unrelenting fight against Bolshevism, which for him was a "Jewish" invention. Germany's decay and decadence, he believed, resulted from the triumph of Jewry in the First World War, and the "stab in the back" they delivered to Germany. As they were ready to pounce again, he saw his battle with the Jews in cosmic terms, as a titanic struggle between two races fighting for world domination. It was an either–or situation. Jews represented the totality of evil, and their eradication was the condition for the future development of the German people and the world. This was, as Saul Friedländer (1997) put it, "redemptive antisemitism".

Karl Schleunes, in his lucid and beautifully written classic 1972 book that was to inaugurate what became known as the "Functionalist" position, *The Twisted Road to Auschwitz*, explained how Hitler used the Jews as a weapon in his fight for power. It was "the Jews" who helped to hold Hitler's system together – on the practical as well as the ideological level. The Jew was cast into a variety of different roles, each playing on the fears of a particular social group in Germany. For the working class, he was the wicked financier, responsible for its economic misery. For the bourgeoisie he was the rabid Bolshevik revolutionary about to destroy the foundations of society. Once in power, Hitler had to reconcile the various spectres he had created. But, by steering attention away from genuine economic and social grievances towards the Jews, he was able to ignore the promises he had made to the German people. An ideological retreat would have been impossible.

Antisemitism seems to have been the glue that held together the various elements of Hitler's worldview. He believed that three pillars lay beneath the German people's self-understanding and capacity for struggle: nationalism, the *Führer* principle and militarism. These could be under-mined by their opposites, however, and the German people destroyed.

In one of his sudden flashes of insight, Hitler "discovered" that the three opposing features – internationalism, democracy and pacifism – had been invented and carried by Jews. If the Jews were left to their own devices, not only would they smother the world in filth, but they "would then exterminate one another in embittered battle". With their "lack of willingness for self-sacrifice", however, which Hitler saw as expressed in their cowardice, "they would turn even this battle into a sham" (1939, p. 294). The role Hitler attributed to the Jews, fusing, as it did, the various facets of his worldview, enabled it to constitute, in Eberhard Jäckel's opinion (1972), a blueprint for massacre. If Hitler annihilated the Jews, he would restore meaning to history, give vitality to the German struggle and find living space. If he failed, and there was no struggle for living space, there would be no culture, and all nations would die out.

EXPLAINING HITLER

There have been many attempts to explain Hitler and find the root of his obsession with Jews. Extremely instructive, for our purposes, is Ron Rosenbaum's 1998 book, *Explaining Hitler: The Search for the Origins of His Evil*. Here Rosenbaum attempts, through interviews with a number of scholars who have tried to explain Hitler, to discover the real Hitler, to penetrate his evil and to determine whether it resides in germ form in all of us, or whether Hitler is completely off the human grid. Allied to this is the question of whether Hitler is explicable or not. The real Hitler has been buried beneath a mountain of theories, offered by historians, philosophers, writers and theologians. Rosenbaum identifies three levels of despair of ever being able to explain him. The first is represented by the Holocaust historian Yehuda Bauer, who believes that Hitler is explicable in principle, but that we no longer have enough material to do so. The second may be seen in the work of the Jewish theologian Emil Fackenheim, who suggests that Hitler is beyond explanation. The third is encapsulated in the attitude of the filmmaker Claude Lanzmann, who rejects the very idea of trying to explain Hitler. He forbids such attempts, seeing them as obscene. Lanzmann was particularly outraged by being presented with a picture of Hitler as an infant – an "innocent" Hitler, a Hitler without victims.

The picture each explainer drew of Hitler was different, so different that Rosenbaum jocularly wondered whether the various Hitlers would be able to recognise one another enough to be able to say *"Heil"* in hell.

Each scholar looks at the facts through his or her own personal lenses. Rosenbaum examines these lenses, looking at the factors that constrain or influence the explainers. He thus finds himself "explaining the explainers" and offering, in the process, a valuable and unusual synthesis of Holocaust scholarship, as well as a comment on Western culture. Alan Bullock, for example, sees Hitler as a mountebank, whereas Hugh Trevor Roper believes him to have been "convinced of his own rectitude", that is, genuinely believing that he was killing the Jews for the ultimate benefit of his own people. The philosopher Berel Lang argues that Hitler *wanted* to perpetrate evil, and that he pursued the art of evil. Rosenbaum suggests that the diverse explanations reveal something about our culture's problems in confronting evil. We can hide behind explanations and thus avoid looking down the abyss of absolute evil. Explanation becomes exculpation. For this reason, Rosenbaum rejects many – especially the psychological – explanations. The latter tend to blame irrevocable forces behind Hitler rather than Hitler himself.

Many of the explanations of Hitler have been too rigid, and have allowed no room for evolution in Hitler's ideas. Historians, Marrus points out, tend to be uncomfortable with theories that imply no changes of ideology, or a psychological consistency that lasts for decades and is extended to the whole population. Historians look for change and record it. They prefer to interpret Hitler's personality in interaction with his environment. Hitler was applying his ideas in a real historic situation, promising solutions to real problems. Herein lay Hitler's attraction, and it is in understanding the wider reality in which he operated – the historic context – that the historian's quest lies.

The way Hitler is explained, particularly his exact role in the Holocaust, varies considerably. The more Hitler is distanced from the decision-making process, the more antisemitism seems to be shifted from the centre of the explanation for the Holocaust. Yet, as we know, the fate of the Jews cannot possibly be overlooked. There is no doubt about Hitler's antisemitism. What *is* in doubt is whether he was driven by an insane passion to annihilate Jews, at any cost, or whether antisemitism was part of a cold, calculating search for absolute domination.

RECALLING THE HOLOCAUST

Since we only know about the Holocaust in the ways it has been passed down to us, we are dependent for our knowledge on the way people have told it to us. Because the disaster was one of such enormous proportions, no single account can encapsulate it. Each is conditioned by limitations – like the lapse of time, the circumstances and interests or inclinations of the teller, the fragility of memory, and the message that the teller wishes to convey. This is the case whether the accounts are memoirs of survivors, diaries of victims, historians' interpretations, or even popular works of art, like novels or films. Depending on the interpretation, then, the centrality of the Jewish dimension of the Holocaust shifts from one account to another.

A pertinent example is the contrast between two films on the Holocaust, Alain Resnais' thirty-minute *Night and Fog*, and Claude Lanzmann's nine-and-a-half-hour meditation on the Holocaust, *Shoah*. One of the features that unites them is that both filmmakers achieve their effect by juxtaposing the timeless visual beauty of nature with the Nazi outburst of savagery that cruelly tortured and killed innocent people. The breathtaking loveliness – and innocence – of the countryside of Poland (where the major death camps were located) forms the backdrop to the story of the death camps. Both filmmakers depict the brutality of the perpetrators and the fear, suffering, humiliation and wholesale death of the victims. Both are driven by the moral impulse that post-war generations are obligated to remember a crime that is both unimaginable and inexpressible. Both are telling us of the same event, interweaving the past with the present, and using a technique that shocks us through the use of contrast. Both, as Ilan Avisar (1988, p. 13) put it, make the viewer realise that today's rich green grass rises from soil fertilised by the grey ashes of millions.

But Resnais – though his film uses archival material that obviously contains film clips of Jews in their degradation – does not mention the word "Jew". Lanzmann, on the other hand, focuses solely on the genocide of the Jews – without using any archival material at all. Resnais wants to portray the event as a crime against *humanity*. Lanzmann – largely through the medium of interviews with survivors – concentrates on the Holocaust as a specifically Jewish tragedy. He focuses on the process by which two-thirds of Europe's Jews were destroyed. Both films have become classic records of the Holocaust but, with their different emphases, they leave the viewer with very different messages.

In addition to the problem of individual interpretation, and the limited nature of any single account to do the Holocaust justice, a third problem arises. The events described are so extreme in their horror that they almost defy description. Most of us have been separated from the events by time or historical circumstance. They are so totally outside our experience that their full horror cannot be penetrated or their ultimate significance grasped. The systematic massacre of so many innocents, Marrus points out, is bound to escape our understanding in some profound sense. The Holocaust will, therefore, always be to some extent "unimaginable", and no amount of interpretation or theorising should be permitted to detract from its awesomeness.

Theo Adorno, in his now famous dictum, that "After Auschwitz" the writing of poetry is "barbaric",[7] was using poetry as a metaphor for imaginative literature. He seemed to be saying that we do not have the linguistic conventions through which we can grasp or convey the meaning of the scientific murder of millions, and that it may be obscene to extract aesthetic pleasure from such suffering. There is an intolerable gap between the aesthetic constructions we devise and the loathsome realities of the Holocaust. Thus silence may be the better option. Adorno was pointing to the sheer difficulty and moral peril of dealing with the Holocaust in literature. Lawrence Thomas (1991, p. 371) echoes this difficulty. To speak about the evil suffered by the millions of victims, he says, is profoundly humbling. If we do anything more than reporting the facts, we run the risk of trivialising and distorting and, thereby, desecrating the memory of those who suffered so. Yet, the very telling of the Holocaust involves more than just reporting the facts. So we always have to be aware that we may fail to do it justice. If we do not talk about the Holocaust, however, it will be lost to memory. What we may be able to learn from the dimensions and scale of the tragedy will forever be obscured. Daniel Schwarz (1999, p. 22) suggests, therefore, that "it is barbaric *not* to write poetry" after Auschwitz, because those who perished "rely on us to speak".

WAYS OF RETELLING THE HOLOCAUST

I have divided the various forms of retelling of the Holocaust into five groups. The first category is to be found in diaries and other testimonies of victims who wrote during the war. The second is the constantly growing collection of survivor testimonies – whether on audio or videotape, on film, or in written form. The third lies in the all-important work of historians and the way in which they have reconstructed and explained the Holocaust. These, from the point of view of establishing the link between antisemitism and the Holocaust, constitute the most important category, so we will return to them in greater detail later in this chapter. The fourth consists of popular works of art in which the Holocaust is portrayed either as a primary subject or as forming the historic background to the story told. Novels like André Schwarz-Bart's *The Last of the Just* give us accounts of the Holocaust which emphasise the Jewish aspect of the tragedy, and thus focus on the centrality of antisemitism, whereas William Styron's *Sophie's Choice* has a more universal focus. The last category of recall lies in monuments and museums that, on the one hand, commemorate the event – remembering its victims – and, on the other, serve to convey a message or "lesson" to the public. Let us turn, in a bit more detail, to these five categories.

Victims' testimonies

Diaries and other forms of testimony of victims – like poems or paintings left by the children of Theresienstadt (Terezin) – are often regarded as the truest and purest form of Holocaust testimony. Theresienstadt offers an interesting example of individual reactions because it was ostensibly "better" than other camps. It was a place where the Nazi art of deception was at its highest. Serving as a sort of way station to Auschwitz and other extermination camps, fifteen thousand children passed through its gates between 1942 and 1944. It was a "model" camp that the Nazis used to show foreigners how ostensibly "well treated" Jews were, and was euphemistically called a "ghetto", though every one of its inhabitants was condemned in advance to die. One poem by a child, Pavel Friedmann, conveys the sense of entrapment and pain through the image of a butterfly.

> The last, the very last,
> So richly, brightly, dazzlingly yellow.
> Perhaps if the sun's tears would sing
> Against a white stone ...
> Such, such a yellow
> Is carried lightly 'way up high.
> It went away I'm sure because it wished to
> Kiss the world goodbye.
>
> For seven weeks I've lived here,
> Penned up inside this ghetto
> But I have found my people here.

The dandelions call to me
And the white chestnut candles in the court.
Only I never saw another butterfly.

That butterfly was the last one.
Butterflies don't live here
In the ghetto.[8]

This poem falls into the same category as diaries – like those of Anne Frank, or Moshe Flinker – giving us insight into the conditions to which children and young adults were responding. Anne's and Moshe's diaries give us systematic accounts of how two young Jews were forced to live, and how they handled the onslaught against their people emotionally, spiritually and practically. Anne Frank reflects the predicament of a secularised, fairly assimilated Jewish family in hiding from the Nazis. Moshe Flinker's diary, on the other hand, conveys the innermost thoughts and fears of a young religious Jew during the Holocaust. Together, they help us to form a more comprehensive picture of the Holocaust – even though each is but a fragment of the whole. However, we must remember that neither of them survived. Neither had an idea of what the outcome of the war might be, and whether they would survive to tell the story. This may have moderated their pessimism. We, today, read their accounts, and look at the poems and pictures of the children at Theresienstadt, in the sombre grey light of hindsight.

Survivor testimonies

A second category of Holocaust retelling is survivors' testimony. An increasing number of memoirs are being published and there are several active programmes to record survivors' experiences. The fact that time is passing, and many survivors are no longer alive, has led to a sense of urgency in capturing the recall of those who are left.[9] To the survivors has fallen the frightful task of having to bear witness, to reapproach the unapproachable, to speak of the unspeakable. The systematic attempt to round up every last Jew, the sense of ensnarement as the noose tightened around various communities, the way individuals were caught in the net, their responses and the miraculous ways in which they – the few – escaped their fate are the stuff of these accounts.

They tell of another universe, where madness was sanity, where human compassion was punished and cruelty rewarded. They tell of betrayal by people who had been neighbours for a lifetime. They tell of courage and resilience, but also of the urge to self-preservation, sometimes at the expense of others, and the guilt that is inevitably borne by the survivor in the face of the death of so many others. The memoirists' representation of the full range of human responses is important, because the Jewish victims of the Holocaust need to be seen not as saints, but as people of flesh and blood, who had been degraded and reduced to ciphers. They were ordinary people, with the full range of human emotions, both positive and negative. Victims of the Holocaust are often called martyrs, *kedoshim*. As Bauer points out, however, this implies their death had some meaning, and obscures the fact that their deaths had meaning only for the Nazis. Whereas some of the victims' ancestors had had the "luxury" of choice, and had chosen death instead of forced conversion, thus dying to sanctify God's name, here the element of choice was missing. "They were ordinary people", Bauer (1998, p. 15) insists, "victims of murder; this does not make them holy, it makes them victims of a crime".

But, again, there is no single account of the Holocaust. Elie Wiesel, in his famous memoir, *Night*, mourns the loss – and maybe even the death – of God, whereas for Jerzy Kosinski, in his 1972 book *The Painted Bird*, the Holocaust has nothing to do with God, who, in any case, does not exist. The Holocaust owes itself entirely to human savagery. In addition, each testimony is tinged by the limitations of memory and also by the fact that its content has, perforce, been organised retrospectively. Thus, the event has no clear boundaries. For example, when did the Holocaust begin in a particular survivor's account? With Hitler's rise to power in 1933? With the outbreak of the war in 1939? With the first intrusion of Nazi brutality into his or her own personal life? When did it end? Was it with the liberation of the camps? With entry into a new haven – such as the USA, Israel or South Africa? In the case of recorded interviews, was it when the interviewer felt that the story had been adequately told, or when the tape ran out? Each survivor's account will give different outlines and different meanings to the event. One will emphasise specific details that another does not recall. These differences do not make the one account "right" and the other "wrong". They display the problems confronted by memory when it has to recall a traumatised past. But collectively, these testimonies all confirm the same reality, each one offering a fragment that will help us understand the whole a little more clearly.

The accounts of historians

The third category of retelling is the account of the historians. As far back as the late 1940s, Leon Poliakov, in his book *Harvest of Hate*,[10] gave a reasoned account of what happened during the Holocaust, and an explanation of why it happened. This was to be followed by comprehensive works by Gerard Reitlinger – *The Final Solution: The Attempt to Exterminate the Jews of Europe, 1939–1945* (1953) – and Raul Hilberg – *The Destruction of the European Jews* (1961). Hilberg's book is widely regarded as an unsurpassed survey of the killing process and still represents a milestone in Holocaust studies.

Until the 1960s, there was little public awareness about the Holocaust. Following the trial, in Jerusalem, of Adolf Eichmann, however, world attention was focused on Jewish vulnerability. The Six-Day War in 1967 – with the accompanying worldwide Jewish fear that Israel could possibly be annihilated by the many Arab enemies that encircled it – re-evoked the Holocaust. Since then there has been a torrent of scholarly works, so many, indeed, that it is now impossible for any one scholar to have a full grasp of all of them. Some of the better known ones in the English-speaking world are Nora Levin's 1973 book, *The Holocaust: The Destruction of European Jewry 1933–1945*, Martin Gilbert's 1978 book, *The Holocaust*, and Yehuda Bauer's 1982 book, *A History of the Holocaust*. Bauer is universally acknowledged as one of the doyens of Holocaust history.

The Holocaust presents us with peculiar problems. Some people resist the very idea of subjecting it to historical inquiry. Its vast scale and exceptional dimension, they feel, render it "beyond" history, and they fear the effect of the debates that would automatically ensue from such inquiry. It is also felt that dispassionate scholarly attention might diminish the horror evoked by the Holocaust, or threaten the special place that the trauma of the event has in Jewish experience. It may trivialise the fundamentally evil nature of Nazism. Conversely, there are those to whom the Holocaust is an embarrassment, either because of lingering antipathy towards Jews, on the one hand, or because they believe that extensive historical investigation might lead to accusations of partisanship, on the other. Though these attitudes still prevail, there has been a change, and such inhibitions are losing their force. Marrus's book, *The Holocaust in History*, describes those changes. Elsewhere he points out that Holocaust historiography has since become so sophisticated that it can be used to reveal problems in the historiography of other fields more acutely.

The Holocaust in the popular media

The fourth category of Holocaust recall is the attempt to tell the story through the popular media. Popular films, like Steven Spielberg's *Schindler's List* and Gerald Green's 1978 teledrama *Holocaust*, give us their own individual interpretations. Spielberg centres his account of the Holocaust on the ex-Nazi, Oskar Schindler, who ended up saving Jews and becoming a "righteous gentile". Green bases his rendering on the intimate story of two families, one Jewish and the other German. But there are popular films with yet other agendas. The German film *Heimat*, by Edgar Reitz, mentions the Jews only in passing. It thus bracketed out the trauma of Auschwitz in an attempt to normalise German history, and was designed as an answer to Green's series. Reitz felt that *Holocaust* had robbed the Germans of their own history. Lanzmann's *Shoah* came two years later. His single-minded focus on the destruction of the Jews was, in part, answering Reitz.[11]

There is a great deal of debate as to whether popular representations like *Schindler's List* should be regarded as authoritative. The film provoked controversy for a number of reasons. First, it seemed to defy the accepted limits of representation by making the unimaginable imaginable. Second, being centred on the life of Oskar Schindler, an ex-Nazi who saved about a thousand Jews from Hitler's relentless grasp, it focused on survival rather than on death. Third, Spielberg used actors to re-enact events. Claude Lanzmann, who made no attempt to visually represent the horrors of the Holocaust, condemned Spielberg's approach, maintaining that no actor could conceivably have portrayed, for example, the hunger and emaciation of the camp inmates. A re-enactment is, therefore, by its very nature a falsification. While immortalising the Holocaust in public consciousness, Spielberg had also, through the depiction of a "good Nazi", skewed its entirely malevolent nature. Spielberg was thus seen as taking liberties in representing history. Nevertheless, *Schindler's List* was the first Holocaust film to appeal to a worldwide public audience, and, as Yosefa Loshitsky (1997, p. 7) points out, has since attained the status of a historical document. It has become "the final and undeniable proof of the ultimate catastrophe endured by the Jewish people".

Because of its wide influence, *Schindler's List* has sharpened the debate on whether history – in this case of the Holocaust – should be seen as being the property of professional historians only, or whether there are other, more popular, ways of retelling the past, and of focusing them in public consciousness. Barbie Zelizer (1997) suggests that, in the cultural setting of the West, we tend to give privilege to the voice of historians over that of the creators of popular culture when we shape our history. This, she points out, is out of step with the general trend of the academy, which has been to diversify history-making by listening to voices other than that of the historian. Public discourse has grown more complex and multidimensional, and is dependent on a variety of media technologies. Other spokespeople, she points out, such as politicians, journalists, and the creators of popular culture – including filmmakers, novelists and television screenwriters – have increasingly tried to address events of the past. The images they have created so pervade popular culture that their voice needs admission, because it will allow a better understanding of the variety of ways in which we can relate to the past through its representation.

The distinction, according to Zelizer (1997, p. 30), should be made not so much between the voices of historians and popular culture, but between "the event-as-it-happened and the event-as-it-is-retold". The latter is as far as we can come. Suffice it to say that *Schindler's List*, for all its limitations, has become a milestone in the public memory of the Holocaust. Lawrence Thomas (1991, p. 378) seems to agree with Zelizer. We make, he says, a surprising distinction between fact and fiction. The genocide of the Jews was the supreme aim of the Nazi regime, and fiction serves as an invaluable vehicle for incorporating new judgements into our understanding of this. Though, in Holocaust writing, fact is prior to fiction, we desecrate memory if we treat the Holocaust as a stagnant set of facts. Facts sometimes need a voice, and fiction is of inestimable value in giving them one.

Monuments and museums

The last category of recall is to be found in monuments and museums. This is the area in which the tension between the Holocaust as a uniquely Jewish tragedy and as a world tragedy becomes most obvious. The symbols used to commemorate the Holocaust, and the spaces in which these symbols are placed, raise the question of whether there is any legitimacy in comparing the Holocaust with other genocides or other forms of social engineering. They also raise the question of the message that such symbols are meant to convey. Important examples of this are the United States Holocaust Memorial Museum, which was opened on the Mall in Washington, DC in December 1993, and Yad Vashem in Jerusalem. Both have vibrant research and teaching centres associated with them. But, though in both cases the Jews are clearly the primary victims, the museums have different emphases. Yad Vashem's full name is "Yad Vashem Martyrs and Heroes Remembrance Authority". Being in the Jewish homeland, it focuses on the Jewish fate within the spectrum of Jewish history. It counterpoises the extreme powerlessness of the Jews under Nazism with the heroism of those who resisted, and the long years of diaspora homelessness with the Jewish return to national power. The Washington museum, being on the nation's Mall, has to give a specifically American message, instructing its various minorities through a universal message.

The way we memorialise the Holocaust says much about the way we define it. The word "Holocaust" stands for the genocide of the Jews, but it has since become a symbolic word connoting mass murder and destruction whatever the magnitude. It is now used in a way that includes not only non-Jewish victims of Nazism, but victims of murder – and even oppression – everywhere. Does that dilute the Jewish tragedy? Does the comparison of the Holocaust with other atrocities trivialise it? We will return to these questions later when discussing the uniqueness of the Holocaust. Let us now turn to the formal histories of the Holocaust.

HISTORIOGRAPHY OF THE HOLOCAUST

One would assume that with formal histories one would be on more certain ground, but this is not the case. Study of the subject is fraught with emotion. Histories are based on the belief that the Holocaust is explicable and not beyond history or human understanding, something that many people deny. There are also fears, especially in the Jewish community, that the ultimate trauma of Jewish history will be misrepresented. Marrus (1987) points to three reasons for this. First, the work of the historian is, by its nature, incomplete and always subject to revision. Its provisional nature may make it ring false as a portrayal to those who have experienced the events the historian attempts to describe. Second, there is a fear that even minor inaccuracies serve to "poison" a historian's account, making it a flawed representation of the past. Third, revision of traditional interpretations of Nazism, or the assault on European Jewry, could open the door to apologists for the Third Reich, and thus trivialise the evil nature of the regime. Survivors, Marrus points out, feel especially violated by historians' efforts. These difficulties are inescapable. But, Marrus assures us, once pointed in a scholarly direction, most scholars will forge ahead, hoping to navigate safely, using the customary tools of the trade. Historians do their best, knowing their efforts are imperfect, incomplete and inadequate.

In the same way that the two filmmakers, Resnais and Lanzmann, offered different interpretations of the Holocaust, historians place different weighting on to the almost limitless individual factors that constitute the Holocaust. Histories are an attempt to offer an account of what happened, the steps of procedure, a beginning, an end, and what the present implications of the event may be. They are an attempt to place an event – or series of events – within some framework of meaning. History is, therefore, not a mere catalogue of happenings. The individual historian ranks incidents in importance according to his or her own broader understanding of them. Therefore, every history is also an interpretation and can only be seen as a partial explanation of a complex and far-reaching catastrophe.

In the various histories of the Holocaust, there is a constant tension between the Holocaust as a Jewish tragedy and the Holocaust as a world tragedy, between the decisiveness and adequacy of antisemitism as a causative factor, and the impact of more global forces. Historians' accounts present the problem more acutely, perhaps, than other media, because we rely on historians to give us a balanced, logical and objective account of the Holocaust. Whereas one historian will emphasise the centrality of the genocide of the Jews, another will see this as part of a far wider picture, in which antisemitism plays only a limited role. Some German historians have tried to dilute the unique criminality of the Nazis. There is, as Saul Friedländer (1988) pointed out, an incompatibility between German and Jewish memories. The Nazi past is too massive to be forgotten, and too repellent to be integrated into the normal narrative of memory. So there is a yearning among German historians to normalise the German past. Ernst Nolte, for example, tries to abolish the singularity of the camps by seeing their origin in the Soviet Gulag. The opposite is happening among Jews. In Jewish eyes, the Holocaust is becoming more central – almost a symbol of identification.

Neither Jews nor Germans, says Friedländer, can relate to their own memory without relating to the other's as well. However, whatever centrality the genocide of the Jews is given, no responsible historian would deny the Jewish dimension of the Holocaust. Rather, it is a matter of weighting. When historians try to account for what happened, antisemitism does not always take centre stage. So, although the relationship of antisemitism to the Holocaust is obvious, there is no straightforward link.

To elucidate some of the problems, let us turn to an essay by Dan Michman, in a 1995 edition of the journal *Modern Judaism*, on the methods used by Holocaust historians. Looking back from the vantage point of the mid 1990s, he suggests that Holocaust historiography – though it is still a young discipline – has reached a sufficient state of maturity to allow examination of the manner in which historians look at the past. Because of the complexity of the Holocaust – placed as it is within the Second World War – and the vast body of data, coming out of a seemingly infinite number of relevant documents, Michman uses the Holocaust as representative of the way in which historians analyse other events. He perceives some immediate problems. First, the historian must define what it is he or she is examining. With regard to the Holocaust, definition is particularly problematic. What was the Holocaust? Was it an event in itself, or a detail of a far broader happening? Second, what is the Holocaust's characterising essence – that which makes it distinguishable from other phenomena, like the Second World War? Third, what is its exact time period? Once the answers to these questions have been reached, the historian must offer some sort of explanation of the event and why it occurred. For example, where are the Holocaust's roots to be found? What were the exact historical circumstances that made its happening possible?

Michman chose seven historians on whom to base his study, all of whom were Jewish, and all of whom produced comprehensive studies of the Holocaust.[12] He sees Leon Poliakov, Gerald Reitlinger, Joseph Tenenbaum and Raul Hilberg as constituting the first phase in Holocaust historiography, 1948 to 1961, and Lucy Dawidowicz, Leni Yahil and Arno J. Meyer as constituting a second phase, 1975 to 1991. The second group had far greater access to secondary material and, therefore, more scope for interpretation. Space permits only some of the considerations Michman outlined to be raised. The time period that the various scholars allocate to the Holocaust as a distinct event, for example, differs.

Poliakov and Reitlinger place the dates at 1935–45, starting with the Nuremberg Laws, whereas Hilberg dates the beginning to Hitler's rise to power in 1933. Dawidowicz takes the start back to the late eighteenth century, with the emancipation of the European Jews – the final phase being from 1933 to 1945. Tenenbaum takes the start back to the mid nineteenth century, with the emergence of racist doctrine. Thus, there is no agreement on the time span of the event. The further back it is taken, the less it assumes the form of a discrete event.

The essence of the Holocaust, too, is seen differently. Poliakov, for example, sees the Nazi onslaught in terms of Hitler desiring a new, racist, German religion – with Hitler as its high priest – that would come to fruition through the ultimate destruction of a Satanic Judaism, its polar opposite. The annihilation of the Jews was the culmination of a psychological phenomenon – antisemitic hatred – which Hitler manipulated to provide a scapegoat in order to achieve his ends. The stage of annihilation began with the Nuremberg Laws in 1935, which Poliakov saw as laying the "sacral" basis for Hitler's new faith. Hilberg, on the other hand, though seeing the essence of the Holocaust as the wholesale destruction of the Jews, looks primarily at the bureaucracy that drove the perpetrators. For him, the direction of the process of destruction was already known, and it intensified in a succession of stages – definition, expropriation and concentration. Only with the final phase, annihilation, did the process became irrevocable. The administrative machine, which is the mark of the modern state, was guided by its own logic. It was self-propagating, taking on a life of its own, so that Hitler's role became secondary. Once the process was in motion, Hitler was no longer its centre, nor had he been its prime mover. His coming to power in 1933 simply activated the machinery of destruction. Hilberg does not ignore antisemitism and points out the earlier precedent of Jew hatred in Christianity, drawing parallels between the canon law of the church in restricting Jews, and the Nuremberg Laws. But his analysis suggested that Germans who were part of the machine did not need to hate Jews in order to perform their tasks. Antisemitism has an important place, but it is not central.

Most historians, Michman suggests, look at the Holocaust in terms of what was done *to* Jews. Jews are not seen as playing an active role in the chain of causality. Lucy Dawidowicz, he points out, is an exception. Unlike Hilberg, who examines the Holocaust through the deeds of the perpetrators, she looks at it from the point of view of the experience of the victims. Dawidowicz sees the Holocaust in terms of an active – though negative – interaction between the Jewish and gentile worlds, a clash between Jewish uniqueness and the gentile unwillingness to accept this. She thus perceives a confrontation between Jewish history and general European history. This kind of approach is sometimes used in literary work, a notable example being that of George Steiner. His play *The Portage to San Cristobal of AH*, for example, suggested that Hitler derived some of his ideas, like chosenness, from Judaism. Though Steiner makes some valid points, because he gave Hitler the last word, the ultimate effect was to lay blame on the Jewish mythic structure. This caused an enraged controversy. Such analyses can be, and often are, perceived as "blaming the victim" and shifting the focus to the wrong quarter.[13] But, in all cases, the intentions of the author need to be examined. If these are honest, this can be a valuable approach, and, for all its limitations, is the one used in this book.

All of the historians cited by Michman note two phases of the Nazi policy towards the Jews. The first was the emergence and growth of a clear anti-Jewish policy and the progressive action against and humiliation of Jews, accompanied by the acceptance of emigration as a solution to the "Jewish problem". The second took place only after 1941, when a programme of destruction was implemented. The difference between these two phases is important when we try to pin down the essence of the Holocaust. It is generally perceived as "the Nazi genocidal enterprise as focused on the Jews or Jewish people". But the seven scholars cited do not agree on this basic definition. The fact that genocide emerges only in the later stages of the Third Reich raises other problems that are important to the theme of this book. Was the antisemitic persecution in the early years of Nazi rule – which did not involve genocide – part and parcel of the same "event" as the genocidal enterprise of the 1940s? Is there a common essence in the two stages, or do they differ so basically that they cannot be included as part of the same event? If there is a common essence, what is it, and why was the resulting fate of the Jews so different in the two stages? If there is *no* common essence, how is it that both stages occurred under the same political regime, and within a very short overall period? There is, Michman emphasises, no legitimate debate about the facts of the genocide of the Jews, that Hitler played a role, or of the existence of racism and antisemitism. Rather, the debate centres on the relative weight given to each factor, and its relation to other factors. Reflections on what may be called "the Holocaust era" are so varied and elusive – and perhaps especially so for the historians – Michman concludes, "that we are still distant from a true understanding of this abhorrent episode in Jewish and world history. In other words, we still have not reached a definitive answer to the question: 'What exactly was the Holocaust?'" Without the second phase, we must remember, there would have been little that was qualitatively different from earlier forms of antisemitism.

It seems that Michman could have introduced a third wave of historical reconstruction. Since 1977, there has been a new curiosity on the question of how such a horrific event could actually have been carried out. Issues like the decision-making process in the Third Reich, and the chain of command, have assumed great importance. According to Jäckel (1998, p. 24), it was, for a long time, taken for granted that antisemitism had produced the Holocaust, and that antisemitism must have been particularly severe in Germany. Consequently research was focused on antisemitism. He sees a marked change from 1977, when other causes began to be explored, especially in terms of the decision-making process.

A debate about Hitler's exact role in the process was, ironically, provoked by David Irving,[14] who, in his 1977 book, *Hitler's War*, denied that Hitler ordered the extermination of the Jews. He argued that the programme of annihilation was carried out, behind Hitler's back, by his subordinates, until at least 1943, a view that reverberated in a two-fold direction. His shocking new thesis led, on the one hand, to the questioning by reliable historians of Hitler's precise role in the Holocaust, which resulted in the emergence of a new school of Holocaust historians, known as the "Functionalists"; on the other, it was exploited as "evidence" by Holocaust deniers that there was no programme for annihilating the Jews. A brief excursus on Irving at this point will not be out of place, because it relates to the question of misuse of historical sources and the resultant falsification of history.

By the time *Hitler's War* was published, Irving had already developed a reputation as a maverick historian, who provoked controversy by turning events on their head,[15] and he still, as we will see below, had enough credibility to provoke a scholarly response. He was, however, to move from questioning Hitler's direct role in the murder of the Jews to denial of the Holocaust. This became clear when, in 1988, he issued, under his own imprint, the *Leuchter Report*, a "pseudo-scientific farrago", as David Cesarani (2000b) put it, "proving" that no poisonous gas was used at Auschwitz, a claim that placed a huge question mark over Irving's reliability as a historian. He was not merely interpreting evidence differently, but violating the evidence.

In 1993 Deborah Lipstadt, in her book, *Denying the Holocaust: The Growing Assault on Truth and Memory*, discussed Irving among several Holocaust deniers, regarding him as the most dangerous of them, because he knew how to use historical sources, wrote well, and had established a reputation as a historian. He represented the "respectable face" of Holocaust denial. The 1994 publication of Lipstadt's book in Britain by Penguin, and Irving's crumbling reputation, were what probably prompted him to sue Lipstadt and her British publishers for libel. In Britain, the onus of proof is on the defendant.

Irving's writings, as Cesarani (2000b) points out, had been characterised by three features: a sympathy for Germany accompanied by a minimisation of German crimes; an antipathy for the Allied leadership accompanied by a maximisation of Allied misdemeanours; and the questionable use of historical evidence. Thus, the defence team focused, not on the question of whether or not the Holocaust *occurred*, but on what constitutes reliable interpretation of historical sources. Irving's less than objective motives and his misuse of historical evidence were exposed during the trial and, losing his libel suit, he was branded by Judge Charles Gray as "antisemitic", "racist" and a "neo-Nazi polemecist", engaged in the "vilification of the Jewish race and people". Irving, Judge Gray found, had seriously misrepresented Hitler's views on the Jewish question, which he achieved, in some instances, by misinterpreting and mistranslating documents and, in other instances, by omitting documents or part of them.

When *Hitler's War* first appeared in German, in 1975, the publishers suppressed the more outrageous passages. Irving's reading of Hitler became widely known only in 1977 with the English translation of the book. It provoked a sharp response from Germany's leading historian, Martin Broszat (1977), who completely refuted Irving's ideas about Hitler's innocence. He offered a scathing critique of the way that Irving "normalised" Hitler, reasserting the Hitler of traditional historiography – a man with a fanatical will to annihilate. He did, however, concede that there was no single decision by Hitler. Rather, the murder of the Jews was a policy that developed bit by bit. Thus, the debate was launched that was to grow into two distinct schools of Holocaust historiography, the Intentionalists and the Functionalists.

THE INTENTIONALISTS AND THE FUNCTIONALISTS

The Intentionalists, as their name suggests, believe that Hitler was the driving force behind the Nazi antisemitic policy and that he intended, at an early stage, the destruction of the Jews. They hold that there was, from the beginning, a blueprint for the programme of destruction, a coherent line of thought. Hitler is seen as the sole strategist, with the authority and will to work towards the implementation of the destruction of the Jews. This was his primary aim, and was, therefore, one of the main motivating factors behind the Second World War. Antisemitism in such analyses is an all-important causative factor.

Members of the other school, the Functionalists, suggest that, while antisemitism was always a factor, Hitler's policies against the Jews were worked out piecemeal, as the war progressed and as the Germans faced unforeseen problems. Karl Schleunes was the first to adopt this position, and gave it its clearest articulation; the title of his book *The Twisted Road to Auschwitz* encapsulated his argument. Although Hitler was deeply antisemitic, the programme to make Germany – and indeed the world – *judenrein* (cleansed of Jews) was not charted in advance and there was no straight line leading to annihilation. Annihilation was arrived upon only after the failure of other methods, such as boycott, emigration, legislation and Aryanisation. Proponents of the Functionalist view argue, for example, that the Nazis were content to be rid of the Jews through emigration until as late as 1941. The refusal of most of the rest of the countries of the world to take in the Jews gave Hitler the green light. There is no doubt that, judged from this perspective, antisemitism retains an important place in the Holocaust. The indifference of the world to the Jews' fate must be associated with the negative image people had of Jews, and hence with antisemitism. David Wyman's 1984 book, *The Abandonment of the Jews*, gives a lucid account of the way the United States, for example, failed to mobilise any real opposition to Germany on the question of the Jews. This indifference can be understood only in the light of a widespread negative image of the Jew, or antisemitism.

Christopher Browning was the first to use the word "Functionalist" to describe this school of Holocaust historiography. It sees the Holocaust as resulting from a maze of competing power groups, rival bureaucracies, opposing interests, and ceaseless clashes. Hitler is seen as a brooding, distant leader, ideologically obsessed, but lazy – a man incapable of making long-term plans. The murder of the Jews became a function of the chaos of the system. Hitler's precise role, it is argued, remains hidden in the shadows. Though he was important in the process, and fanatically antisemitic, the murder of the Jews was the result of improvisation rather than deliberate planning. What finally led to the decision of genocide remains a mystery. In the fevered atmosphere that characterised the later phase of the war, a mere nod from Hitler could have sent millions to their deaths. He did not have to give an order. The effect of this type of scholarly approach is to distance the operational importance of the *Führer* and, thus, to broaden the range of culpability. Hilberg, as we have seen, already pointed in this direction when he spoke of the machinery of destruction, whose awesome power ground unrelentingly towards the destruction of its victims, engaging, in the process, an ever-widening circle of perpetrators.

The broadening of responsibility has led to questions about whether there was ever a written order by Hitler to proceed with the annihilation programme. Though the absence of such a document undergirds the claims of the Holocaust deniers, we should not lose perspective. "The Holocaust", Berel Lang reminds us, "was about the extermination of the Jews". Nearly everyone in the Nazi hierarchy, he argues, fully intended the genocide of the Jews. The best evidence we have of a person's intention is not a written expression of it, but the great lengths to which he or she goes in order to perform it and to hide its performance from others. The demand for documentation of intent to exterminate the Jews is, therefore, a charade. Such a document might be helpful, but it is not necessary.[16] Bauer (1998, p. 21) points out that a lot of the most important decisions were *not* written down, because that was the way the Third Reich operated. They were handed down orally and, only by chance are they sometimes corroborated by documentation.

David Bankier (1998, p. 49ff.) gives an interesting explanation of why the intention to destroy the Jews was shouted from the rooftops, whereas the details of their elimination were kept secret, resulting in the need for euphemisms and code language. Germans had to be convinced of the real danger that the Nazis believed the Jews to constitute, but they should not be put off by the gruesome practicalities of the annihilation process, or by Christian morality. Nothing should be allowed to impede the success of the programme. In the last phases of the war, as the Germans increasingly faced the spectre of defeat, a new focus of loyalty was needed. If Germany lost the war, it was argued, the Jews would carry out unspeakable acts of revenge. The Nazi promise to kill all the Jews, therefore, galvanised the people. "There are two things which can unite men", he quotes Hitler as saying in a 1923 speech, "common ideals and common criminality". The promise to exterminate the Jews served to cover up military defeat and divert public attention on to a "positive" aim, while spreading the blame by enforcing collective responsibility. Just enough of the crime was revealed to galvanise the population, enforce adherence and loyalty, and prevent desertion. In the end *all* Germans were responsible, and no one took responsibility for the actual killing.

Lucy Dawidowcz, in her 1975 bestseller, *The War Against the Jews 1933–1945*, encapsulates most clearly the Intentionalist position. The name she gave her book itself implies her conviction that Hitler's most important aim was to rid the world of Jews and Judaism. The war against the Jews was as important ideologically as the war against the Allies and possibly more so. With both scholarly precision and passion, she insisted that Hitler determined as early as 1918 to destroy the Jews. He conceived it as his mission to murder the Jews at the moment he learned of Germany's defeat in the First World War. In one fevered moment, while in a sanatorium in Pasewalk, suffering hysterical blindness after a mustard gas attack, he made up his mind. He was not going merely to drive the Jews out of Germany, nor to expel, harass, exile or defeat them. He determined, at that moment, to annihilate them.

Dawidowcz emphasises (1975, p. 32) how Hitler had, in *Mein Kampf*, dramatised his first confrontation with East European Jews in Vienna. "Once, as I was strolling through the Inner City," he said, "I suddenly encountered an apparition in a black caftan and black hair locks. Is this a Jew? was my first thought. For, to be sure, they had not looked like this in Linz. I observed the man furtively and cautiously, but the longer I stared at this foreign face ... the more my first question assumed a new form: Is this a German?" Looking for answers, he turned to books, buying his first antisemitic pamphlets. But he claimed to have found them unsatisfying, judging their "dull and amazingly unscientific arguments" unconvincing. He thus resorted, he says, to his own slowly rising insights. This picture of the Jew in a black caftan, he says (1939, p. 35), opened his eyes to the connection between Marxism and Jewry and was to become the "rock-ribbed foundation" of all his acts. "I have had to learn a little beyond what I then created; there was nothing I had to change" (p. 35).

One of the important points of departure between the Intentionalists and the Functionalists is the way they interpret Hitler's famous speech of

30 January 1939. "If," he warned, "the international Jewish financiers outside Europe should succeed in plunging the nations once more into a world war, then the result will not be the Bolshevisation of the earth, and the victory of Jewry, but the annihilation of the Jewish race in Europe". The Intentionalists see this as prophetic, while the Functionalists place it in a wider context. They point out that, though one had to take Hitler's statements seriously, so-called "unalterable decisions" were sometimes altered. Furthermore, this was only one small part of a speech – on mainly economic matters – that had rambled on for hours. Only a few minutes were devoted to the Jews (Marrus 1987, p. 37).

Ron Rosenbaum argues that the Functionalists' distancing of Hitler from the annihilation process, in effect, absolves him of the horror of his crimes. There is, Rosenbaum claims, a current fad – for which he particularly indicts Christopher Browning – to represent Hitler as a dithering, Hamlet-like pawn, subject to the forces of the "great abstractions" – like bureaucracy, demography or technology. Rosenbaum opts for Dawidowicz's approach as being the closest to encapsulating the real evil of Hitler, as he deliberately and wilfully – and even laughingly – ordered the destruction of the Jews. He is impressed by Berel Lang's assertion that Hitler had pursued a conscious art of evil. Though Rosenbaum regards antisemitism, itself, as one of the great abstractions, he makes a convincing case for the argument that, as Hitler's intentions are questioned and he is removed from the central decision-making process, antisemitism, as a factor, is minimised.

Despite the extensive debate about Hitler's exact role in the Holocaust, there is no doubt about the importance of his influence. There are conclusions, says Marrus (1987, p. 17f.), that even the outright sceptic must draw. First, Hitler intensely hated the Jews throughout his political career. Jews were seen as a mortal threat to civilisation. Second, he was the principal driving force behind the Nazi movement from the earliest period, setting the ideological tone, and raising his personal antipathy to an affair of state. He alone defined the Jewish menace with the authority, consistency and ruthlessness needed to fix its place for the party and later the Reich. Whether there was a blueprint for the murder of the Jews, or an ill-defined goal, it is widely agreed that he set the course. Antisemitism was central because Hitler determined that it should be so. Opposition to the Jews became a *leitmotif* of the regime, whatever the priority assigned to it in a tactical sense, because, for Hitler, ideological questions were of crucial importance, and they were treated seriously. Beyond this, nothing *required* the killing of the Jews. Antisemitism may have been a necessary condition for the Holocaust, but it was not a sufficient one. In the end, it was Hitler, and his own determination to realise his antisemitic fantasies, that made the difference.

NO HITLER, NO HOLOCAUST

Both Marrus and Rosenbaum were profoundly swayed by a hard-hitting article that was written by Milton Himmelfarb, in *Commentary* magazine (March 1984), to counter the various attempts to distance Hitler from the Holocaust. Himmelfarb's position was summed up in the title he gave the article: "No Hitler, No Holocaust". Hitler killed the Jews not because he had to, but because he wanted to. He might have been moved by a variety of factors, including antisemitism, but he need not have killed the Jews. Although he was affected by antisemitism, he was not determined by it. Hitler, Himmelfarb claims, has been disappearing behind abstractions like geography, demography, technology, socioeconomic stresses and strains, political backwardness, group psychology, religious hatred, racism and new mentalities. None of these, he avers, could have resulted in the Holocaust without the personal will of Hitler, who wanted the Holocaust, ordered it and was obeyed. He was not the sufficient cause, but he was the necessary cause. Although antisemitism, too, was a necessary condition for the Holocaust, it was not a sufficient condition. There was just too great a leap between Christian and Nazi antisemitism. We find it awesome that the power of one man can make such a difference, and would rather conceal this reality from ourselves by hiding behind abstractions and seeing Hitler as a pawn moved by deeper, more profound, forces of history and society that made the Holocaust inevitable. Rosenbaum sees this as resulting in Hitler becoming a product rather than an (im)moral agent.

Himmelfarb directs his polemic against those, like Hyam Maccoby and Henryk Grynberg, who believe that Christian antisemitism led inevitably to the Holocaust. Maccoby, he says, makes Nazi antisemitism indistinguishable from a timeless, unchanging Christianity. Himmelfarb disagrees with Maccoby's conclusion that, because it had for centuries been virtuous for Christians to persecute Jews, the step to genocide was a short one. He is equally insistent that it was not Christian morality that kept Jews alive. No, says Himmelfarb, it was Christian *mythology* that saved the Jews. Under Christianity Jews knew subordination, expulsion, even massacre, but not Holocaust. If one sentence can summarise church law and practice it was: "The Jews are to be allowed to live, but not too well" (1984, p. 38). Christian mythology kept the Jews in a degraded and subordinate position, but kept them alive. It is not Christianity, but its weakening that lies behind the Holocaust. Himmelfarb points to the pagan antisemitism that the Nazis adopted in an attempt to throw off Christianity. Anti-Christian antisemitism, he avers, is descended ideologically from pagan disdain for Jews and emotionally from Christian hatred of Judaism and Jews. Himmelfarb raises points that will be analysed in the rest of this book. In his attempt to expose Hitler by drawing away the veil of the abstractions that have hidden him, he possibly makes another abstraction out of pagan antisemitism.

THE JEWISH–CHRISTIAN RELATIONSHIP AS A CAUSE OF THE HOLOCAUST

It is appropriate, at this point, to briefly introduce another important strand of Holocaust scholarship that will be taken up in greater detail later. That is, the examination of the role that the relationship between Jews and Christians was to play in promoting antisemitism, and the way in which the negative image of Jews became a necessary precondition of the Holocaust. There are several important works in the field, the most prominent being Rosemary Ruether's 1974 book, *Faith and Fratricide*, in which she traces the murderous relationship back to Christian theology itself, namely its Christology, or doctrine about Jesus as the Christ. If Jesus was the messiah promised to the Jews, this constituted, as James Moore (1994, p. 164) put it, a "fulfilment theology", whose immediate implication was the belief that Christianity had supplanted Judaism in God's plan. That Jews continued to exist *as Jews* called this claim into question. Another challenging work is Franklin H. Littell's *The Crucifixion of the Jews* (1975), in which he confronts the credibility crisis facing Christianity in the post-Holocaust world. How was it possible for so many Christians to turn their backs on European Jewry, he asked, and what does this say about Christianity today? Littell was one of the first voices of conscience raised in the post-war period.[17]

Religion, as this book will make clear, was an important underlying factor in the development of antisemitism. Rubenstein and Roth (1987, p. 6) have pointed out that, in any sound approach to the Holocaust, religion must occupy a central place. But it must do so from a perspective that incorporates history, politics, economics and sociology. Such a perspective, they insist, can be developed only by taking very seriously what men and women have, in fact, believed about themselves, their people and their destinies. This, in turn, is intimately associated with what Ninian Smart has termed the "mythical dimension" of religion, to which we will return in chapter 3.

The Holocaust forces us to try to understand the Jewish claim of uniqueness, and the fact that Christianity saw itself as heir to this uniqueness. This resulted in a history of volatile anti-Jewish sentiment in Christianity, which was to become the majority faith in Europe. Without this, the Holocaust could not have happened. The effects of the tragic conflict between Judaism and Christianity escalated, as Rubenstein and Roth (1987, p. 8) point out, until the world reached Auschwitz. The Final Solution is thus a story that is millennia long. Religion has marked it indelibly, creating the makings of catastrophe. One of the main ingredients of the Holocaust was the tension between two groups, one spawned from the other, both of whom see themselves as God's chosen people. Auschwitz has had an indelible impact on the way Jews and Christians – and later Muslims and Jews – think about themselves and one another today. Because of the importance of the religious underpinnings of antisemitism, chapters 5, 6 and 7 will deal with the development of Christian and Muslim antisemitism, and chapter 3 will outline the Jewish mythic structure and Judaism's understanding of history.

It is essential to point out, however, that Jews had lived in Christian Europe for nearly two thousand years and, though they had suffered a great deal of antisemitism – accompanied by persecution, massacres, expulsion and degradation – there had never before been an attempt to annihilate them. On the contrary, there was a theological need, in Christian Europe, to protect the Jewish people and ensure that they were kept alive. This results in two impenetrable questions, which will recur throughout the rest of this book. Was the Holocaust a logical continuation of traditional antisemitism, or was there a radical break with the past? Put differently, did Nazism represent a continuation of Christian antisemitism, or was it a radical overthrow of that outlook? This presents us with a second conundrum: the Holocaust could not have taken place without antisemitism, but was it the inevitable outcome of it? If, as Himmelfarb suggests, Christian antisemitism was one of the "great abstractions", what are the others?

THE GREAT ABSTRACTIONS

Raul Hilberg, as we have seen, focused his attention on the perpetrators rather than on the victims, studying mountains of train schedules and other dry documents to uncover how bureaucratic processes rendered the annihilation of the Jews possible. Once in motion, Hilberg asserted, the bureaucratic machine took on a life of its own. Although his work on the Nazis is unsurpassed for its thoroughness and for the understanding of the death machine that it has given us, his interpretation of German motives and Jewish responses has been questioned. He implies that the Germans did not need to hate Jews, and that the Jews, themselves, unwittingly collaborated with the Nazis as a result of what he sees as the compliant behaviour patterns they had learned over two thousand years of diaspora existence.[18] Hannah Arendt had offered a similar approach. In her 1963 book, *Eichmann in Jerusalem* – which grew originally from her reports on the progress of the Eichmann trial for *The New Yorker* – Arendt significantly diminished the moral responsibility of Eichmann – and hence of other perpetrators – by seeing them as mindless automatons who were "only following orders". Numbed by bureaucracy, they became desk-based killers who performed their grisly tasks without feeling and without any real identification of their victims as human beings. Arendt coined the phrase "the banality of evil".

She was also deeply critical of the Jewish leadership, the *Judenräte*; more so than Hilberg had been. In her account of how they played into the hands of the Nazis she, herself, fell victim to using the antisemitic stereotype. Jacob Katz faults Arendt for "blaming the victims" in a situation in which she, personally, had not been tested. Exploiting the wisdom of hindsight, she failed to appreciate the historic context of the time, and thus assumed a stance of moral superiority. Katz points out that people responded in individual ways to the disaster. Education, religiosity and social and political aspirations made some Jews passive and others active, particularly in the earlier phases of Nazism. He also points out the power of group mentality. People's rootedness in Jewish traditional consciousness helped them to adjust to the new situation and to protect them from despair. The suicide rate was, for example, high in assimilated circles, the orthodox and the Zionists tending to make the best of things. The Zionists were looking to a solution of the "Jewish problem" outside Europe, and were on target in their analysis of the situation that faced European Jews (1975, p. 44).

Arendt's work aroused heated debate. It is germane to our discussion about interpretation to note that a very different picture of Jewish responses to the Nazi onslaught was drawn by the historian Martin Gilbert. In his 1978 book, *The Holocaust*, he emphasised the courage of the victims, and the extent of Jewish resistance under very difficult conditions. There is a problem here of how one should define the term "resistance". Notwithstanding the bias of much of Arendt's work, however, she offers some valuable insights on how economic factors serve to render people superfluous in a social system, and how antisemitism emerges under such conditions.

If we compare Dawidowicz's emphasis with that of Hilberg and Arendt, we see that only for Dawidowicz is antisemitism central. For Hilberg and Arendt – though they do not ignore antisemitism – other forces, like the economy, the advance in technology, and the banality of evil assume more explanatory importance. As the years went by, the focus on antisemitism seemed to diminish. Hitler's personal role in the whole process was questioned. The debate about whether Hitler intended, from the beginning, to annihilate the Jews, or whether genocide was a functional by-product of the war as it developed, tended to shift antisemitism from the centre to the periphery. But there are other "great abstractions". An important one is the human mindset that became dominant in the twentieth century.

Scholars of history, politics and the social sciences have noted that, with modernity, there has been a shift in human thinking patterns and the way human beings evaluate one another in the broader context of the universe. A new way of rationalising, which tends to evaluate human worth in monetary terms, made the Holocaust possible. Issues like the numbing force of bureaucracy and the development of technology are but part of a wider development. That development only came into force in modern times and must, therefore, be seen as a fruit of modernity. Antisemitism was a necessary cause of the Holocaust, but it could not, on its own, have produced it, and was not, therefore, a sufficient cause. A new form of state-inspired problem solving had entered the picture.

Richard Rubenstein, who is intent on exploring the full implications of the destruction of European Jewry for understanding contemporary civilisation, sees the Holocaust as a distinctly *modern* enterprise. Whereas he had in his 1966 work, *After Auschwitz*, focused on the Jewish theological implications of the Holocaust – examining God's complicity in the event – in his 1975 book, *The Cunning of History*, he looks at the Holocaust's more global implications. The Holocaust, he now believes, was not an accidental aberration of modern civilisation, but *part* of it. It was an intrinsic expression of our modern civilisation's problem-solving methods.

He argues that the Holocaust was made possible by the triumph of functional rationality, which, in turn, is based on the biblical way of understanding creation, in which God is not part of the created world and has no rivals. Human beings were given dominion over the world of nature and, because it contains no rival spirits, can feel confident in subduing or harnessing it. This is sometimes referred to as the "demystification" of the world of nature. Taken a step too far, though, God can seem too transcendent. When this happens, human beings lose sight of God's presence and arrogate to themselves godlike decisions such as who is to be allowed to live and who should be allowed to die. What Rubenstein calls "the triumph of functional rationality" is, therefore, the "night-side" of biblical thinking.

Basing his views on the theories of Max Weber, Rubenstein claims that, when governments are confronted with problems raised in the modern period and try to solve them, they use rational means to calculate the value of all things, including people, evaluating everything in monetary terms. When such considerations are paramount, there is no recourse to human dignity or appeal to the sanctity of human life. One of the major problems facing the world since the Industrial Revolution is population explosion, which has resulted in population surplus. Because, in the modern way of reckoning, people have ceased to have human value as children of God, and people themselves are part of the mathematical equation, governments intervene to "solve" the problem, in practical affairs generally, and economic enterprises (whether capitalist or socialist) in particular. *They* decide who is useful and who is not. Methods range from segregation and incarceration, through eviction and expulsion, to outright extermination. These methods have been facilitated by modern means, like technology, and are one of the unanticipated consequences of the growing rule of reason, which Max Weber identified as the central attribute of modernity.[19] The Nazis simply capitalised on these conditions.

They created an ideological campaign against the Jews as enemies, who were seen as causing all of Germany's problems. Jews were thus defined as unnecessary, unwanted and undesirable. This led them to be designated as a surplus population. Most Jews were not impoverished, uneducated, unskilled or unproductive. But they were the group targeted as superfluous. Any population can be defined by a government as superfluous if, for any reason, it can find no viable role in the society where it lives (Rubenstein and Roth 1987, p. 5). In the case of the Holocaust, millennia of anti-Jewish teaching, the particular antisemitic worldview of Hitler, and the historic situation of Germany, along with global forces that brought to power those who found state-sponsored population elimination programmes expedient for solving problems, came together. The Jews occupied such a central place because of the way they have been portrayed in Christian civilisation.

The sociologist Zygmunt Bauman, in his prize-winning 1989 book, *Modernity and the Holocaust*, echoed Rubenstein, emphasising the global forces that were a precondition for the Holocaust. The Holocaust was, indeed, a Jewish tragedy, he says, but Jews were not the only population subjected to special treatment by the Nazi regime. They were, however, the only people marked for total destruction and allotted no place in the new order that Hitler intended to install. Nevertheless, according to Bauman, the Holocaust should be regarded neither simply as a Jewish problem, nor as a problem for Jewish history alone. The Holocaust, he argues, was born and executed in our modern rational society, at a high stage of our civilisation, and at the peak of human cultural achievement. For this reason, it is a problem of *that* society, civilisation and culture.

It is an easy way out, he says, to blame the Germans for their particular bestiality. "The more 'they' are to blame, the more the rest of 'us' are safe, and the less we have to do to defend this safety". The overall effect is to pull the sting out of Holocaust memory. By blaming the Germans, we shift the focus away from the real problems of our society and become complacent. We should, instead, be analysing the ethos of modern Western civilisation – the quality of the institutions we rely on for our safety, the validity of the criteria by which we judge our own conduct, and the patterns of interaction we accept as normal. After all, the Nazis legislated Jews into the position of subhumans, thus denying them any human rights. Had the Nazis been victorious would anything they did have been regarded as technically "illegal"?

Bauman insists that, though considerations such as these may be discussed by scholars, in their ivory towers, they have not entered seriously into contemporary consciousness. They cannot, therefore, affect contemporary practice. The Holocaust was not an aberration of modern society. It was not a failure, but a product of modernity. We have, therefore, to become aware of what social and political mechanisms are capable of when they intersect with antisemitism, or any other inter-group antagonism. On this type of analysis then, emphasis on antisemitism alone is too optimistic and misses the mark. Our society, such scholars believe, has disclosed to us its heretofore unsuspected capacity for violence. We have been taught to respect and admire technical efficiency, good design and material progress, but, in this adulation we are missing something, sorely underestimating modernity's true potential. Citing Rubenstein's *The Cunning of History* (1975, p. 91), Bauman (1989, p. 32) points to the Holocaust as revealing the progressively intensifying night-side of the Judaeo-Christian civilisation. Civilisation may mean medical hygiene, elevated religious ideas, beautiful art and exquisite music, but it *also* means slavery, wars, exploitation and death camps. It is a mistake to imagine that civilisation and savage cruelty are an antithesis. Creation and destruction are inseparable aspects of what we call "civilisation".

HITLER'S WILLING EXECUTIONERS

With this kind of argument – valid though it is – there has been an inevitable distancing from the peculiar Jewish dimension of the Holocaust. Jews feel that their suffering is shunted to the sidelines, their near annihilation ignored, and that the main thrust of Hitler's killing orgy is being obscured. Against this backdrop, and as one of the counterweights to this trend, in 1996, a young Harvard assistant professor, Daniel Jonah Goldhagen, published his Ph.D. thesis under the title *Hitler's Willing Executioners: Ordinary Germans and the Holocaust*. In it, he put antisemitism back on the centre-stage as the primary, if not sole, cause of the Holocaust. According to Samuel Kaplan (1996), some of the great abstractions, like Arendt's "banality of evil", have so penetrated the lay and scholarly mind, that we have lost sight of the importance of antisemitism. Goldhagen's single-minded concentration on it was a timely reminder of its important place.

Believing, as a historian, that the Holocaust is historically explicable, Goldhagen analysed three hitherto relatively uninvestigated agents of the Nazi killing process: police battalions, the camps and the death marches. Exposing the wanton and deliberate cruelty that took place – perpetrated by ordinary men who had been given the choice to behave differently, and would not have suffered unduly if they had refused – he made an excellent case for the argument that ordinary Germans killed and humiliated Jews because they wanted to. They wanted to because they hated them. Germans had become willing participants in mass murder because they were animated by what he called "eliminationist antisemitism", which, under specific conditions, was easily transformed into "exterminationist antisemitism". Besides their hatred of Jews, they genuinely believed them to be a danger to the well-being of Germany. Ordinary Germans, therefore, tortured and killed Jews without scruple and, indeed, with sadistic enjoyment, often going beyond the call of duty in performing their tasks, and photographing their obscenities for the later amusement of friends and family. Antisemitism had allowed them to treat Jews as vermin.

This particularly virulent form of antisemitism, Goldhagen claims, was unique to Germans and had for a long time pervaded German political culture. By the time Adolf Hitler came to power in 1933, the antisemitism of the German people was "already pregnant with murder". Hitler served merely to unleash this antisemetism into practice. Himmelfarb's "No Hitler, no Holocaust" was converted by Goldhagen to "No Germans, no Holocaust". He takes the position, as Jeremy Noakes puts it, of an unreconstructed Intentionalist. Hitler, Goldhagen argued, intended the elimination of the Jews from the start. The German Jews, and all Jews who came under Germany's power, were to be disposed of according to an eminently coherent and goal-directed plan, coordinated from above.

Goldhagen's book was a direct response to Christopher Browning's important 1992 book, *Ordinary Men: Reserve Police Battalion 101 and the Final Solution in Poland*. Browning, the first after Hilberg to consider the motivations of the rank and file rather than focusing on the command structures, argued that ordinary middle-aged men had killed not out of fear of punishment or authority, but primarily because of careerism and peer pressure. Like Goldhagen, he emphasised that they had been given a choice of whether to participate in the mass shootings of Jews, and only a few refused. But Goldhagen's book countered Browning's conclusion, while also arguing against the great abstractions. The killers were not ordinary men, said Goldhagen. They were ordinary *Germans*.

Hitler's Willing Executioners became an immediate bestseller, thus penetrating widely into public consciousness. It presumably confirmed what a great many lay people already believed about German attitudes during the Holocaust. But it provoked a furore in the scholarly world. Despite Goldhagen's disclaimers to the contrary, it seemed to raise antisemitism as the sufficient cause of the Holocaust, thus challenging the several important interpretations that had emerged. Primarily in the footnotes of the book, Goldhagen mounts a polemic against the interpretations of Hilberg, Marrus and several others.

The reviews of the book were mixed, but among them were many extremely hostile ones. Franklin H. Littell, for example, who questioned Christianity's credibility in the post-Holocaust era, regarded the book as out of step with the tenor of our time and the growth of interfaith dialogue. He also saw the book as a hindrance to the growing understanding between Jews and Germans. Littell pointed out that Goldhagen had ignored the most important questions that continue to occupy scholars of the Holocaust. This, indeed, was probably the underlying reason for much of the animosity. Goldhagen had turned on its head decades of responsible historical scholarship. Claiming simultaneously that there was no single cause of the Holocaust and that antisemitism was its sole motivating factor, Goldhagen called for a rethinking of our views on the Holocaust, particularly in its relation to the perpetrators. German antisemitism and German society during the Nazi period, he suggested, need to be looked at afresh if we are to understand the Holocaust. What has already been written about it, and issues that have "generally been considered as settled" need radical revision. "This book," he says, "is that revision" (1996, p. 9).

As we have seen, little has been "settled". Thus, several reviewers have remarked on Goldhagen's arrogant dismissal of the scholars who preceded him and his unnecessary slights on their work. He does not, they point out, demonstrate why previous scholars are wrong. His attack on them, his emotional tone, and the fact that his book became a bestseller – an unusual fate for an academic work – led to a highly emotional attack on Goldhagen, an event that Ron Rosenbaum (1998, p. 337) calls the equivalent of a scholarly "wilding". Shortly after the book's publication, a symposium of major Holocaust scholars was set up at the United States Holocaust Memorial Museum in Washington, DC to discuss it academically. It soon turned into an "impromptu tribunal – with Goldhagen on trial", where not only Goldhagen's thesis but also his character were subjected to an unrelenting assault.

The most valuable part of Goldhagen's book is his considerable research into the attitudes of the perpetrators. Had he acknowledged his undoubted indebtedness to previous scholarship, there is no doubt that his seminal contribution to our knowledge on the Holocaust would have received the scholarly accolades it deserves. His extensive research on various genocidal agencies, said Gordon Craig, should be a model for future scholars working on the Holocaust, but it does not transform our view of the Holocaust. For those who have followed the literature on the subject, he points out, three conclusions are not disputed. There is no doubt that a great many Germans wanted to get rid of the Jews before Hitler came to power, that no one stood up in defence of the Jews when the extermination began, and that the number of participants in the killing is greater than originally supposed. But, as he and other reviewers point out, Goldhagen's theory of antisemitism is not new, and has been better treated by a host of other scholars.

Noakes points out that Goldhagen's focus on one motive, to the virtual exclusion of all other explanations, has produced a reductionist argument. Perhaps the majority of Germans did have negative views about the Jews, and these were strengthened by Nazi propaganda and indoctrination. But, for most, the "Jewish problem" was not, in reality, an issue of great significance, particularly in the middle of the war. People responded to what they knew about the Holocaust in a variety of different ways. Most were uneasy or indifferent – but not enthusiastic, as Goldhagen so boldly asserts. Only within a particular institutional context – governed by its own particular institutional culture and priorities – were people liable to engage in genocidal activities. It was because the regime itself knew this that they kept their operations secret from the general population. This is probably why Himmler, in October 1943, told Nazi leaders, "Later perhaps we can consider whether the German people should be told about this. But I think it is better that we – we together – carry for our people the responsibility ... and then take the secret with us to our graves." Goldhagen's book is *important* but, according to Noakes, is deeply flawed. It is like a case for the prosecution and is written with a barely controlled anger that sits uneasily in a work of scholarship.

By drawing a simple line from antisemitism to the Holocaust, and by offering an all-powerful, all-explaining central model, Goldhagen dulls our sensitivity to the questions raised above, the elusive nature of the event, and the evil that inspired it. Ironically, as Rosenbaum points out, it also has the effect of absolving Hitler, which Rosenbaum finds to be the most dangerous implication of Goldhagen's thesis. Goldhagen's view of antisemitism is so crudely deterministic that Hitler's role is reduced to that of a midwife. Although Goldhagen may narrow the cause of the Holocaust, he does not, according to Rosenbaum, narrow things enough, in that his "eliminationist antisemitism" virtually eliminates Hitler, the really evil force behind the Holocaust. It also has the effect of absolving the German people, who, if they were so beguiled by antisemitism, acted mechanically and therefore did not have to make ethical choices. The surprisingly warm reception of the book in Germany seems to reinforce this view. When the book was translated from English to German, sentences were softened and changed, including in the title itself, where "executioners" became "executors", thus suggesting a far less inflammatory vision of the role of ordinary Germans.

A COUNTER-EXPLANATION

The historian Leon Jick, in a 1998 essay in *Modern Judaism* entitled "Method in Madness", offers a direct counter-explanation. Examining the motivations behind the mass murder of the Jews, he suggests that we misread the Holocaust when we see it as the result merely of hatred or passionate antisemitism. Hitler, he insists, pursued his goals in a cold and calculating way. He aimed at world domination through expansion, annexation and conquest. This would be accompanied by ruthless exploitation. Antisemitism merely served to oil the machinery by which he would bring about his ends. Surplus population acquired in the process of expansion had to be eliminated through forced emigration. Madagascar was seriously considered for the Jews, but the war took a course that precluded them from being sent there.

Had the war ended in 1940, with Germany victorious, Jick seems to suggest, the Jews may have been forcibly deported. Only when Hitler invaded the Soviet Union, in Operation Barbarossa, was there total war. Hitler envisaged a complete transformation of Europe along racial principles and the exploitation of entire populations as potential slave labourers. As there was no place for Jews, they would now have to be murdered. But, as they could also be exploited for slave labour, policy was changed when and where Jews were needed. Jick argues that even the death marches – which many historians see as Germany trying to conceal its crimes – were aimed at returning slave labourers to Germany to work on its V2 rocket, a last-ditch attempt to subdue Russia. So, in 1944, Jews were brought back to a *judenrein* Germany. He concludes with the warning that, whenever the sanctity of human life is compromised and whenever exploitation supersedes humaneness, any evil becomes possible. The Holocaust can be transformed from something unique, into a pattern of history.

According to David Cesarani, the main problem with Goldhagen's book is that it does not make any attempt to consider antisemitism in other countries. Comparisons, he stresses, *are* important because, whether we like to admit it or not, the Holocaust is frequently used as a yardstick by which to measure other atrocities in the hope that we can gain some insight into human motivations. It was not only the Germans who were cruel to Jews. Other perpetrators, too, were heirs to Christian Jew hatred and the Germans found helpers everywhere. The neutral powers and Allies did very little to stop the Germans. How can this be explained in the light of Goldhagen's thesis?

Equally important, why are there continuing genocides? Although Goldhagen's book may give an insight into the role of antisemitism – and that is its greatest achievement – its greatest failure, according to Cesarani, is that it throws no light on the reasons for human cruelty. The Holocaust may be unique in the sense that, as an instrument of state policy, it was prosecuted over an entire continent for a long period of time. Other genocides may be less comprehensive, more erratic and confined, but Germans are human beings and therefore there must be a universal explanation of their actions. To seek this explanation does not derogate one bit from German iniquity or the unique fate of Europe's Jews. By abjuring this quest Goldhagen has compromised his otherwise stupendous achievement and produced, says Cesarani, a mirror image of the demonisation that he so brilliantly exposes.

Consideration of Goldhagen's book serves to illustrate some important aspects of my own book. First, it indicates that with the Holocaust or antisemitism, we are dealing with opaque and emotionally charged subjects. It is difficult to be dispassionate about either, and emotions tend to run high even in academic circles, where objectivity normally reigns. Second, the relationship between the Holocaust and antisemitism, though definite, is not entirely clear. Goldhagen's book, because it is so widely known, has become a benchmark around which current thinking on this relationship can be examined. Third, it highlights the impossibility of arriving at final answers about the Holocaust, a tragedy that throws up greater challenges than any other historical catastrophe. Fourth, it helps to illustrate that there is a difference between events and the recounting of them. The best we can hope for is that we make an adequate distinction between events as they were and events as they have been retold.

Historians of the Holocaust, as we have seen, have reached no agreement on a variety of issues. The current state of play is revealed by an important 1998 collection of essays that arose out of the first conference that took place in conjunction with the United States Holocaust Memorial Museum, in 1993. Its name, *The Holocaust and History: The Known, the Unknown, the Disputed and the Reexamined*, should alert us to the fact that we have no final answers on the Holocaust. Michael Marrus, in one essay in the volume, cautions us that future studies of the Holocaust will not be driven by new sources, but by new questions. "The last thing we would want for Holocaust history is its becoming a broken record, repeating the same agendas over and over again ... theses will generate antitheses ... one way of looking at matters will be challenged by a new approach. Nothing could be worse for Holocaust history than stilling argument and producing an official orthodoxy ... So long as our historical culture is pluralistic and open, so long as our intellectual life is free and challenging, new questions will rain down on Holocaust history. Count on the next generation to frame different problems even for the sources we have already examined ... they will wonder why we even bothered with our own quarrels of any given moment" (1998, p. 34).

We must remember, however, that the Holocaust was about murder and, as Marrus reminds us, *no amount of imaginative reconstruction* will ever change that fundamental reality. "Nevertheless," he continues, "there is a sense in which our view of the matter has altered, has become more shaded, and our vision has acquired greater complexity" (1998, p. 6). But, as time progresses and academic inquiries increase, we may be forced to demystify the Holocaust, and though this might serve to inflict new pain, the alternative is silence. Before leaving this troubled terrain, it is necessary to look at one last issue, the uniqueness of the Holocaust, and to what extent it is valid to compare it with other atrocities.

THE UNIQUENESS OF THE HOLOCAUST

The debate about whether the Holocaust is unique arises out of a justifiable Jewish anxiety that, if the murder of the Jews is not singled out, it will disappear under the general heading of "crimes against humanity", and be forgotten. The uniqueness debate is, therefore, inextricably linked with the role of antisemitism in the Holocaust. People who insist on the Holocaust's uniqueness fear that, by comparing the Jewish fate with any other atrocity, or by extending the meaning of the word "Holocaust" to other groups who suffered during the Second World War, what happened to the Jews will be trivialised. They tend to see such comparison, itself, as a subtle form of antisemitism. The debate centres on three interlinked axes. The first is whether one can include under the event "the Holocaust" the suffering of other peoples during the Second World War. The second is whether one can compare the fate of the Jews with that of other genocides, or even lesser categories of brutality and oppression, like apartheid in South Africa. The third is the extent to which victimhood has become a marker for cultural identity.

There is no doubt that, as the word "Holocaust" enters more widely into public discourse, it will be likened to all sorts of things. For the media and other interest communities, as Hilberg (1998, p. 11) points out, the word "Holocaust" has opened the door to any killing, direct or indirect, of any group, including animals. One of history's most terrible and complex events, as Eva Hoffman (2000) puts it, has become the world's "short-hand for atrocity". The word is used to refer to issues like the availability of abortions or the oppression of the Cubans under Fidel Castro. As a result, there have been attempts to prove the Holocaust's uniqueness.

The most comprehensive argument for the Holocaust's uniqueness is Steven Katz's *The Holocaust in Historical Context* (1994). The first volume in a proposed three-volume treatment of the subject, it is widely acknowledged as a profound work of scholarship, supported by a vast range of carefully researched material. It will, undoubtedly, become a classic in Holocaust scholarship. The method Katz uses is to offer a definition of genocide, and then test whether other catastrophes in history qualify under his definition. He compares the fate of the Jews with a whole range of historical events that people have regarded as genocide, and finds them all wanting. In no other instance was the intention so specific as the Nazi plan to annihilate the Jews. The Jews, alone, were the "victims of genocide". The Holocaust is unique by virtue of the fact that never before had a state set out, as a matter of intentional principle and actualised policy, to annihilate every man, woman and child belonging to a specific people. Whereas for other scholars there have been several genocides, but only one Holocaust, Katz argues that there has been only a single genocide, the Holocaust.

This raises the question of what exactly we mean by the word "uniqueness". We have already seen that scholars are not entirely sure about what exactly constitutes the Holocaust, and whether it is a specifically Jewish tragedy. The word "uniqueness" is also elusive and ambiguous. In a monograph devoted entirely to this concept, Gabriel Moran has shown that the word "uniqueness" can mean two opposing things. It can describe something that is an entirely isolated monad and displays no similarity to anything else. But the question arises, if this thing is so separate, and there is nothing to which it compares, how do we know that it is unique? And if it is unique, what difference does it make, since it is so outside our experience? The word "unique", Moran suggests, can also describe something that shares most of its character-istics with other things. The more closely it shares characteristics with other events, the more that which is different stands out. The thing's uniqueness becomes one of inclusion rather than of exclusion. Moran believes that the Holocaust cannot be isolated from other atrocities and genocides. In order to define it, we need to examine to what extent it is like other genocides and to what extent it differs. The more inclusive our sense of uniqueness, the more pertinent the message we can derive from the Holocaust. This inclusiveness is important because the Holocaust is an abiding challenge. Moran suggests that the Jewish preference for the Hebrew designation, *Shoah*, though it may separate the Holocaust from all other genocides and preserve its uniqueness, might also remove the event from people's consciousness, thus obscuring the lessons that may be learned from it.

Several scholars oppose the idea of insisting on the Holocaust's uniqueness. Cesarani (1996), for example, points out that comparing the Holocaust with other acts of genocide in no way diminishes what happened to the Jews and that we need to make such comparisons to find commonalities in human cruelty. Berel Lang agrees. "So what," he asks, "if the Holocaust is unique? ... Nothing in the enormity of the Nazi genocide would change if that series of acts turned out to be the second – or fifth – instance of its kind."[20] Peter Novick (2001, p. 9) regards the whole attempt to assert the Holocaust's uniqueness as both fatuous and offensive. Any war or catastrophe, he points out, will have some features that it shares with others and some that differentiate it. Insistence on uniqueness ends up by trivialising the features it shares and elevating those it does not. The assertion that the Holocaust is unique – like the claim that it is singularly incomprehensible or unrepresentable – is, he suggests, deeply offensive in practice. What else can all of this possibly mean except "your catastrophe, unlike ours, is ordinary; unlike ours is comprehensible, unlike ours is representable"? What we are doing, he says, is wringing acknowledgement of superior victimisation from another contender.

THE HOLOCAUST AND APARTHEID

The issue of the Holocaust's uniqueness is pertinent in South Africa today, as people come to terms with the country's racist past. There are, understandably, frequent attempts by black South Africans to compare the atrocities of apartheid with the Holocaust. Jews, equally under-standably, point out that there was never an attempt to annihilate the black community. Although comparisons are valid up to a point – in that both were systems of degradation based on race – apartheid stopped far short of genocide. The acrimony that emerges from these claims erupts from time to time in letters to the editor in local newspapers or on radio chat shows. Jews see this comparison as an attempt to universalise and "steal" the Holocaust, and as a slight on their suffering. Though millions of others were killed during the Second World War, they argue, and though millions of others have suffered since, the thrust of the Holocaust was against the Jews. If we regard the Holocaust as a crime against humanity at large, the persistence and continuing threat of antisemitism may be forgotten. Blindness to the specificity of the victims of genocide may allow a similar fate to befall another people earmarked for destruction by a ruling elite. So, universalising the Holocaust is seen to diminish, rather than enlarge, its significance.

But it is precisely at this point, or at the refusal to compare the Holocaust with other calamities, that South African blacks are riled. The assumption drawn is that, because Jews claim that the Holocaust is unique, they also claim a monopoly on suffering – something that in the light of history is unwarranted. To gain insight into the bitterness of the debate, we need to take a look at the South African context.

The Nobel Laureate Archbishop Emeritus Desmond Tutu frequently compares the Holocaust with apartheid: "We don't have gas chambers," he said, "but if you put people in ... resettlement camps where they will starve and children die every day, it's the same sort of thing ... maybe less tidy".[21] As a result, he has often been accused of being antisemitic. But, when South African blacks use the Holocaust as an analogy to their suffering, they usually do so to emphasise the enormity of that suffering rather than to trivialise or undervalue it – the very opposite of Holocaust denial. The intention of the apartheid regime was never identical to that of Nazism, but there was a basic parallel in that both were systems of humiliation based on race. The suffering, indignity and death brought about by apartheid might have been less intentional than that of the Nazi programme, but its effect was devastating. Critics of the comparison are generally not sufficiently sensitive to this. Barry Rubin (1990, p. 90) has suggested that, from a Third World African perspective, praise even of Hitler may not seem as horrific as it does from a Western viewpoint. The Holocaust's uniqueness may seem alien to those who have, themselves, endured centuries of persecution. Suffering and genocide may be part of their own newly emerging self-image.

This means that we have to hold in tension the Holocaust as the particular fate of the Jews and the Holocaust as a world problem. Human suffering, wherever it is, can legitimately be measured against the Holocaust insofar as the Holocaust's uniqueness embraces it. It is worth noting that the South African Jewish Board of Deputies tacitly allows apartheid to be identified somehow with the Holocaust. Holocaust exhibitions that come to South Africa contain references to apartheid and black schoolchildren are bussed in to see them.

This problem also arises in other contexts elsewhere in the world. One of the most obvious foci is the United States Holocaust Memorial Museum in Washington, DC. Some, as Michael Berenbaum has pointed out, opposed its establishment because they saw the "alien tale" of Jewish suffering in Europe as a possible magnet for antisemitism. Others felt that, by placing the genocide of the Jews in the context of a wider set of victims, the specific fate of the Jews was trivialised and denied. Being a government project, Berenbaum avers, the museum cannot be insulated from the political context in which it operates. Its message has to be a universal, and not an exclusively Jewish, one. There are, he points out, private memorials, like the New York Holocaust Memorial (The Museum of the Jewish Heritage). Together, these will define the Holocaust for the American public. We cannot prevent people from conceiving of the Holocaust in the way they choose to. Once it entered international consciousness, it became fair game for all those who wish to use it. Some will be bound to dilute and misrepresent it. But Jews cannot have it both ways, says Berenbaum (1990, p. 25). They "cannot simultaneously maintain that the Holocaust was a horribly sanctified and inviolate topic while complaining that the world is ignorant of its occurrence".

Berenbaum (1990) suggests an inclusive definition of uniqueness, in which the Jewish experience is contrasted with the horrendous plight of others. Whereas the Poles were consigned to subservience, and their intelligentsia was annihilated so that Polish culture could be dominated, *all* Jews were condemned to death. Whereas Gypsies shared some of the horrors assigned to the Jews, others were not imposed on them. They were killed in some countries, and not in others. Those in the rural areas suffered a different fate from those in the urban environment. Murder of Jews was a priority in every country. These comparisons are made not to diminish the suffering of any of the groups, but to isolate those dimensions of the Holocaust that are unique. It is intellectually, historically and pedagogically necessary, says Berenbaum, to make such comparisons in order to arrive at the truth. They should serve to unite ethnic minorities who wish to remember their dead together with the Jewish survivors.

Berenbaum cites *The Other Holocaust: The Many Circles of Hell*, by Bohdan Wytowycky. Like the hell described in Dante's *Inferno*, the hell of the Holocaust was made up of concentric circles with the Jews at the centre. We need to study the ripple effects of their specific place in the Nazi orgy of cruelty and death. Such inclusion will serve to unite rather than divide. World indifference to the Armenian genocide, for example – when the Young Turks, under cover of the First World War, found that the most cost-efficient way to homogenise a modernised Turkey was to annihilate a minority group – facilitated the Holocaust and enabled Hitler to move without too much opposition. The Holocaust needs, according to Berenbaum, to become *the* symbolic orienting event that could prevent a recurrence. Provided that our analogies retain relevance, the Holocaust will be neither trivialised nor de-Judaised.

Yosefa Loshitzky (1997, p. 7) explains that the frequent jibes by African Americans against the Holocaust museum in Washington, DC or against films like *Schindler's List*, should be seen in terms of frustration. The high-profile emphasis on the Holocaust seems unfair because it seems to eclipse the black experience of suffering and this can cause resentment. Racism should be confronted head on, and not as part of a "victim contest". Citing Charles Maier, Loshitzky points out that, in America, victimhood has become part of ethnic or post-ethnic identity, and the Holocaust has been transformed into a new focus of identity.

Closing the circle and bringing us back to both antisemitism and religion, Richard Rubenstein (1990, p. 11) points out that when the question of uniqueness is raised, very few deal with the one aspect of the Holocaust that was absolutely unique. "In no other instance of genocide in the twentieth century," he says, "was the fate of the victims so profoundly linked to the religiomythic inheritance of the perpetrators." In Christianity, the Jews are not simply one of the many peoples of the world. They were, we are told in the Christian scriptures, the people in whose midst God incarnated himself and who, instead of being the first to recognise this supreme act of God's grace, rejected Christ and were blamed for his painful death. "Alone among the victims of genocide, the Jews are depicted as the God-bearing and God-murdering people par excellence. No other religion is as horribly defamed in the classical literature of a rival tradition as is Judaism." In response, Jewish suffering has been interpreted as just punishment of a sinful Israel. The practical consequence of this, to use Helen Fein's apt phrase, has been the removal of the Jews from the common universe of moral obligation.

Jacob Katz (1983, p. 44) warns us, therefore, that, although comparisons with other people's suffering and other genocides are legitimate up to a point, the suffering of no other nation can compare with the uniqueness of the Jewish experience, and not just in the Nazi period. It is not merely the amount of suffering, but its frightening recurrence over time, which lends it the quality of inescapability. To close our eyes to the peculiar, historically conditioned fate of the Jews is tantamount to ignoring its lesson for the present – the realisation of Jewish vulnerability, which seems to be the unavoidable legacy of the Jewish past. With these cautionary words in mind, let us turn to a discussion of the problems relating to the study of antisemitism.

2

Approaching the study of antisemitism

If antisemitism had not achieved its ends in Europe, one would not have to insist on its study; its study must therefore begin with an acknowledgement of its success.

Ruth Wisse

ANTISEMITISM: THE BAFFLING OBSESSION[1]

The basic meaning of the word "antisemitism" is dislike of Jews. Beyond this initial assertion, however, we are faced with a variety of difficulties. One of these is that the word is used to apply to a whole variety of attitudes to Jews, from vague feelings of unease to outright murder, and the whole spectrum of feelings and actions that fall between those two extremes. So, though it is usual, when opening a discussion on a subject, to start by offering a definition and explanation of what the subject is, moving on thereafter to locate its origin in history and chart its progression, the study of antisemitism resists such an approach. In this chapter – a largely theoretical one – we will look at the problems associated with antisemitism, problems that will be elaborated in various ways in the rest of the book. The first, as has already been indicated, is the inadequacy and imprecision of the word "antisemitism" itself and the fact that this term has a history of its own. It is a relatively recent word, coined in the late nineteenth century to denote the idea of the Jews as a race, and has come to stand for a millennia-old phenomenon – hatred of Jews. According to Zygmunt Bauman (1989, p. 34) – to offer but one definition at this point – antisemitism "stands for the resentment of Jews.

It refers to the conception of the Jews as an alien, hostile and undesirable group, and to the practices that derive from, and support, such a conception."

But we immediately stumble on a problem. As Hyam Maccoby (1987) points out, the word "antisemitism" is used sometimes to denote antagonism to Judaism as a religion, and at other times to denote antagonism to Jews as people; in its severest forms, both. In Nazism, for example, the Jews themselves were deemed to be, by nature, inferior and dangerous; Judaism, as a poisonous worldview, was secondary. One can have a negative view of Judaism without being antisemitic, as those who defend the church against the charge of antisemitism, might claim. One can also be antisemitic without knowing about Judaism or being negatively disposed towards the religion *per se*. In almost all forms of antisemitism, however, Judaism is the subject of adverse comment, but it is not always clear whether Jews are considered evil because of their religion, or whether their religion is regarded as evil because of them.

This should lead us to appreciate that antisemitism is not based on what Jews are, but on what they are perceived to be. When discussing antisemitism, then, we are dealing with the image that people have constructed of Jews and the stereotypes that are created over time – which raises another problem. Does antisemitism have anything to do with what Jews do or do not do? A very sensitive issue. Especially since the Holocaust, any suggestion that Jewish behaviour may lie at the root of antisemitism is seen to imply that Jews deserve the hatred that is directed against them, and it becomes a case of "blaming" the victim. As a result, scholars have tended to view antisemitism as a non-Jewish or gentile[2] phenomenon that has nothing whatsoever to do with Jews. This, too, is an over-simplification and historically off-target because it is equally wrong to suggest that Jews and Judaism have nothing to do with antisemitism. Jews are often resented because of real historic factors, like their tendency to live as an identifiably separate community, or the economic role in which they have functioned – frequently as middlemen. Such resentments explain antisemitism on only a very superficial level, however. They are rationalisations of hatred rather than the root cause of it, which, as this book will show, lies in the interface between religions and the way they are perceived. Jewish separateness, as we will see in chapter 3, is part and parcel of Jewish belief and practice, but may have served to complicate relationships between Jews and the outside world.

It could just as easily be argued, however, that what Jews do or do not do is irrelevant. Emil Fackenheim (1986) has observed that antisemitism is the only hatred in which the targets are despised for both their virtues *and* their vices. Whereas the Hebrew Bible, which became the Christian "Old Testament", was interpreted as constantly deriding the Jews for the failure to keep the commandments, the church father John Chrysostom faults them for the very opposite, for observing the law. Fackenheim suggests that when a minority group is hated in this way, there is more to the hatred than is immediately apparent. Only antisemitism, which is more than routine prejudice, can sustain this level of contradiction. Although it must, obviously, be included among the various forms of group prejudice, there is a sense in which it transcends "prejudice," whose real meaning is "judgment before knowledge". Not only does antisemitism not disappear when new knowledge about Jews is attained, but it intensifies. Thus, argues Fackenheim, antisemitism has peculiarities that call for philosophical reflection and head-on confrontation. The Holocaust has made it impossible to take refuge behind ideologies or abstractions. We need to take accurate account of antisemitism's incredible persistence over time, its immense capacity to mutate, and the way it escalates from one period to another. Before proceeding, however, it is necessary to look at the emergence of the term "antisemitism" within its historic context.

THE EMERGENCE OF THE WORD "ANTISEMITISM"

"Antisemitism" is a relatively recent designation that was coined, probably in 1879, by a radically antisemitic German nationalist, Wilhelm Marr, to replace the German word *Judenhass*, or "Jew hatred". Unlike the German word, the new one had a scientific sound to it and said nothing about Jews. Living after the European Enlightenment, Marr was a champion of modernisation and its emphasis on human reason. Accordingly, he was hostile to religion and, whereas previously the Jews' threat was perceived as lying in their religion, he now located it in their ostensible racial character. Marr saw the Jews as a menace to the purity of the Germanic (Aryan) race and its strivings for supremacy. Nationalism, as we will see in chapter 8, was a powerful factor in promoting antisemitism, particularly in its Nazi form.

In his pamphlet, *The Victory of Jewry over Germandom* – the first antisemitic bestseller in history – Marr outlined this threat, drawing upon the prevailing mindset of the nineteenth century, in which racial theories pervaded the way in which the various sciences of the day were understood. As part of their inborn racial nature, Jews were believed to have a destructive mission in history to subjugate and undermine German society. The fact that Jews are given so central a role in secular thought is not surprising when one considers that they were cast as the secret centre of world history in Christian theology. As Steven Katz (1994b, p. 240) points out, the intensity of Jew-hatred is directly proportional to the importance of the role assigned to Jews in a particular culture's larger worldview. If Jews are not assigned any special historical or cosmic role, significant levels of anti-Jewish sentiment do not result, as was the case in China and India. In other words, Jews have to be endowed with a significance that makes them "worth hating", as is the situation in the West. But Marr needed a new, neutral, scientific-sounding word that seemed unconnected to outdated religious concepts, if his ideas were to be persuasive in the modern climate. "Antisemitism" fitted his purposes admirably. It was "Jew hatred" sanitised.

Before the Enlightenment, Jews had lived as separate self-governing groups within the larger society in Europe. But Enlightenment thought, in its general optimism about human potential, affirmed the equality of all people and asserted that rationality and education could bring an end to hatred and superstition. Many felt that it was time for Jews to be emancipated and become citizens of their native lands. They should, for example, be primarily Germans, or Frenchmen, or Austrians, whose religious affiliation and practice were a private matter, determined by personal opinion. They would thus be Germans or Frenchmen or Austrians "of the Mosaic persuasion" and, in the world at large, look and behave no differently than those around them. What underlay the Enlightenment was the conviction that, with human equality, the Jews, as a collective entity, should be eliminated. The outcome of this will be examined in chapter 8, where we will see that a fundamental contradiction lay at the heart of the Enlightenment. It did not result in freedom of religion for Jews and went against its own ideals in its treatment of them.

Jews, as we will see later, had always been perceived as an alien element in Christian Europe. Because their religion had given birth to Christianity and they had not accepted the Christian way as valid for them, their collective presence had been a constant reminder of their rejection of the Christian message. As the chosen people, they were the original bearers of the promise that, for Christians, found fulfilment in Jesus. Their continued presence *as Jews* raised perpetual doubt about the truth of the Christian religious position, presenting Christians with a situation of cognitive dissonance. Nothing had really changed with the emancipation. Marr had wanted a secular society, with complete separation between church and state. Jews, still so overtly involved with Judaism, were seen as hindering the work to liberate society from the quagmire of religious tradition. Secularised Christians were still carrying with them the demonic image of the Jew imbibed in earlier times.

Though regarded as the "patriarch of antisemitism", Marr was but one of many representatives of a new and decisive phase in the history of Jew hatred. He, and those with whom he was in agreement, despised Christianity, but denigrated Judaism even more as the vehicle that, by "inventing" Christianity, imposed the alien Semitic yoke of moral restraint upon European culture. Starting in Germany, the antisemitic movement spread to other European countries, but the practical results that it was aiming for, namely the removal of the Jews as a collective, did not materialise, even though Jews had gone a long way towards cultural and social assimilation. With their refusal to go away, other factors were brought into the equation. The Jews' difference was now perceived to be "in the blood". Conversion to Christianity would, therefore, be ineffectual. Because they could not escape their purported evil nature, their assimilation and integration into the surrounding culture were now rendered impossible. They were trapped. The new nationalist, and strongly anti-Christian, charge that Jews were inferior because they were biologically different marks the beginning of the genocidal strain in antisemitism. Before that, conversion was not only a means of escape, but an ultimate aim of the church. As we will see in chapter 6, there were theological reasons why the church needed to keep the Jews alive.

The irony of it all is that the term "antisemitism" is meaningless. This results from the spurious nature of the notion of race that undergirded it. The new racial theories, as we will see in chapter 8, appealed to prior linguistic ones to give them an aura of scientific support. Hebrew, a language closely identified with Jews because it is the holy language in which their scriptures are written and in which they pray, had been classified as part of the group of "Semitic" languages. The Germanic languages, on the other hand, were classified as "Aryan". On this basis, a leap was made to argue that the Jews were an alien, and inferior, race living with a predominantly Aryan race in Europe. There is, in reality, no such thing as a "Semite" to whom antisemites can be opposed. The common English hyphenation of the word "anti-Semitism" (which has no hyphen in the original German or in Hebrew) thus exacerbates the problem, and the capital "S" endows it with an importance it ill deserves. It has thus become more correct today to write the word without a hyphen.

James Parkes, a pioneer in the investigation into the Christian roots of antisemitism, was the first to drop the hyphen. He used the word "antisemitism" as the equivalent of the German word *Judenhass*. There is, after all, no ambiguity in what we mean when we use the word "antisemitism". We do so to denote opposition not to Semites, but to Jews, and no one else. The argument often proffered by Arabs that they cannot be antisemitic because they themselves are Semites, is, therefore, rendered invalid. Though Arabs too were classified as "Semites", the term "antisemitism" is never seriously applied to them and was not taken seriously even by the theorists of racial antisemitism. Arab antagonism to Jews and opposition to the concept of Jewish sovereignty in Israel may correctly, according to Maccoby (1987), be termed "antisemitism". The term, he says, may legitimately be used to refer to all hatred of Jews that is at a paranoid level and is accompanied by an inclination to attribute a wide range of evils to the activities and influence of Jews.

USING THE TERM "ANTISEMITISM"

The suitablility of the term "antisemitism" is debated for a variety of reasons. For one thing, there are judgemental overtones implicit in its use. Since the Holocaust, the word has become taboo even among antisemites themselves. Today, as Yehuda Bauer (1984, p. 14) wryly observes, "there are no antisemites in the world ... Nobody says, 'I am antisemitic.' You cannot, after Hitler. The word has gone out of fashion." Other terms, like "anti-Zionist", have taken its place. Because "antisemitism" is a recently coined designation for a nineteenth-century phenomenon, some scholars, like Shaye Cohen (1986) and Nicholas de Lange (1991), limit their use of it to the modern period. Bauer (1994, p. 12) long resisted use of the word as an umbrella term, warning us that lumping all the varying expressions of Jew hatred together as "antisemitism", blurs the differences in manifestation over time and clouds our understanding of Jew hatred. But the word has now entered the English lexicon, and accepted usage of it ranges from the narrow (opposition to and denigration of the Jews as a racial group) to the very broad (any type of anti-Jewish behaviour or attitude). Bauer has bowed to the popular trend, pointedly noting, however, that the word is "unscientific, inaccurate, confusing and misleading".

David Kertzer, in his controversial 2002 book *Unholy War*, offers an opposing argument. In tracing Vatican teaching on the Jews from the early nineteenth century to the present, he argues that there is a continuity between the Church's attitude to Jews and what was later preached by the Nazis. To call the former attitude "anti-Judaism" and reserve the designation "antisemitism" for the latter creates the impression that there is little connection between the two, and falsifies history. The Vatican, Kertzer suggests, encourages this separation because it is ambivalent about confronting its anti-Jewish past. Desiring to make amends to the Jews for past oppression, it does not want to be saddled with responsibility for the Holocaust. Although it is prepared to admit past injustices, it refuses to accept that "religious" antipathy to Jews has wider economic, cultural and political ramifications. Annihilation of the Jews as a harmful influence, he correctly argues, could never have been attempted without the hatred inspired by the church's teaching about them.

There is another, related issue that I pointed to in the opening words of this chapter, the difficulty in defining the phenomenon that we call "antisemitism". The word is used to refer to an entire spectrum of attitudes, from inchoate feelings of discomfort about Jews, to the systematic attempt during the Second World War to annihilate them. As the only factor that unites these two extremes is "dislike of Jews", and anything between them also falls under the rubric of "antisemitism", there is a definite imprecision as to what we mean when we use the term. We find, for example, that a "genteel" antisemitism exists in most societies. Michael Marrus, in a 1982 essay on the differences between the theory and practice of antisemitism, illustrates this widespread sense of uneasiness. He does so with a graffito that appeared during the Second World War in Amsterdam – the capital of a country that did a good deal to save its Jews: "Hitler – take your dirty hands off our dirty Jews." Marrus points out that this attitude does not sanction a necessary limitation on the lives or aspirations of Jews, let alone murder of them. Specific constellations of factors are necessary for antisemitism to move from a theoretical to a practical level – where it affects the lives of Jews and thus becomes more threatening – and from there to genocide. The historian has to differentiate clearly between these levels.

Shulamit Volkov (1988) puts it differently. Defining antisemitism on two levels, she differentiates between prejudice against Jews, either individually or collectively, and antisemitism as an element of an ideology. Only when it is part of an entire worldview does it become dangerous. We must bear in mind, however, that it is individuals and their prejudices that enable ideologies to be acted out. As Bauer (1988, p. 340) points out, "a regime doesn't murder; people murder". This makes him cautious about evaluating public opinion polls and the significance of a decline in popular antisemitism.

There is also no agreement on how old the phenomenon of antisemitism is. Some see it as going back to the origins of Judaism itself, whereas others date it back only to the nineteenth century, when the word "antisemitism", with its racial undertones, was coined. Most, however, see it as emerging somewhere between these two extremes. We will see that the age of the phenomenon, or the time that a particular scholar might ascribe to its origins, is intertwined with what that scholar assumes antisemitism to be.

Another difficulty lies in the multi-faceted ways in which antisemitism has manifested itself over time. As Moshe Davis (1988, p. 3) put it, "Antisemitism is a chameleon, changing color and form, climbing walls and creeping into unexpected corners." Because each manifestation is different, each has to be studied against its own particular historic backdrop. Yet another problem is the contradictory way in which antisemites picture Jews in their imaginations. There is also the problem of pinning down antisemitism's precise nature. And so on, *ad infinitum*. One question simply gives rise to another. What I hope to achieve in this chapter is to give the reader some insight into what antisemitism is, while allowing him or her to recognise that, apart from denoting dislike of Jews, there are no definitive answers. I will begin by indicating antisemitism's contradictory nature.

ANTISEMITISM'S CONTRADICTORY NATURE

Michael Curtis (1986, p. 4) has pointed out that no other group of people in the world has been charged simultaneously with:

- alienation from society and cosmopolitanism;
- being capitalist exploiters and agents of international finance, and also revolutionary agitators;

- having a materialist mentality and being people of the Book;
- acting as militant aggressors, yet being cowardly pacifists;
- adhering to a superstitious religion and being agents of modernism;
- upholding a rigid law while also being morally decadent;
- being a chosen people, yet having an inferior human nature;
- being both arrogant and timid;
- emphasising individualism and yet upholding communal adherence;
- being guilty of the crucifixion of Christ, yet blamed for the invention of Christianity.

This catalogue of contradictory accusations cannot possibly be true and no single people could feasibly have such a total monopoly on evil. But it is this very multi-faceted nature of antisemitism that helps to distinguish it from other forms of prejudice. It is the wide range of arguments that cast Jews as peripheral at best and destructive monsters at worst that gives antisemitism its peculiar character.

Though irrationality of this nature is difficult to explain, Fackenheim (1986, p. 22) offers us a valuable clue when he cites Reinhold Niehbuhr: "When a minority group is hated for its virtues and its vices, and when its vices are hated not so much because they are vices, but because they bear the stamp of uniqueness, we are obviously dealing with a collective psychology that is not easily altered by a little more enlightenment." With this statement, Niebuhr takes us into the realm of religion, where antisemitism finds its most influential roots. As this book will show, the mythic structure of Judaism conflicted, initially, with pagan ideas. This same mythic structure was later adopted into Christianity, whose rival interpretation of it cast Jews as Christianity's eternal enemies. Although Christianity's central myth was at odds with Judaism's mythological dimension, it also remained deeply dependent on it. The use of the word "myth" will be explained in the next chapter.

With the emergence of a third religion based on the same under-standing of history and tradition, Islam, a new dimension of antisemitism was to emerge. Though not initially as potentially harmful as Christianity's image of the Jew, the image of the Jews in the Muslim world has taken on a problematic form since the return of the Jewish people to the land of Israel, and especially to independent Jewish statehood. This will be discussed in chapter 7, along with anti-Zionism, the form in which Muslim animosity is usually expressed. Islamic attitudes, it will be shown, did not initially demonise the Jew. That dimension came into the Muslim world in the nineteenth century, as an import with European imperialism, and became manifest in the period of European imperialism and the attendant decline of Islam. The traditional Christian stereotype of the Jew was adopted to answer new questions spawned by the modern situation. Other hatreds may be as strong and as passionate as antisemitism, but they lack, in addition to the other peculiarities noted above, its religious base and its horrible denouement.

THEORIES TO EXPLAIN ANTISEMITISM

The inter-religious aspect of antisemitism is one, but the most important, avenue to understanding the phenomenon. Niebuhr, as we have seen, also pointed to the psychology of antisemitism, which is another avenue of investigation and the more popular of two basic approaches, that explain antisemitism in terms of the exploitation of the negative image of the Jew. The second is the sociopolitical explanation. A third explanation suggests that antisemitism results from specific ideologies, one of the most important being the ideology of race. The first two, which are intimately intertwined, revolve around the idea that in-groups react negatively to out-groups that are both different and identifiable. The in-group transposes on to the out-group aggressions that derive from internal, often unconscious, drives and anxieties, factors that are activated by crises in the external world. It is easier, theorists argue, to cast blame on another, outside oneself, than it is to confront personal motives or to remedy the actual ills that beset society.

Psycho-social theories

Specifically psychological theories of antisemitism are particularly popular because psychology is seen by many to account for nearly all of human behaviour. They explain antisemitism in terms of neuroses that arise to resolve conflict and are "comforting" in that they tend to regard antisemitism as pathological, thus suggesting that it is "abnormal" and subject to cure. As Prager and Telushkin (1983, p. 77) point out, they also offer comfort in that Jews are seen as one among many objects of prejudice. It is thus in the "abnormality of the antisemites" rather than in the "Jewishness of the Jews" that the cause of Jew hatred is to be found. By so de-Judaising antisemitism, however, these theories explain prejudice in general, rather than the specific hatred of Jews. They fail to answer the question of why Jews are so universally and persistently singled out as the object of scorn and contempt.

Psycho-social theories often make use of the scapegoat idea, which suggests that leaders, in order to deflect social discontent away from their own inadequacies, create a scapegoat upon which people can project their frustration, anger and fears. Propagandists exploit the resentment gentiles often feel about the Jews' minority status and separateness, and they focus on those factors that seem to confirm the notion of Jews as different or alien, factors that, for centuries, enabled immediate identification of Jews. In the modern period, when Jews tended to abandon their overtly Jewish appearance and lifestyle, anxiety was exacerbated. The ascendant Jew thus became a particularly potent symbol of threat. But, again, as Prager and Telushkin (1983, p. 73) point out, the scapegoat theory does not answer the question "Why the Jews?" Jews have certainly been used as scapegoats throughout history, but the theory explains why, when, or how people use antisemitism, rather than antisemitism itself.

Not long after the Second World War, the American Jewish Committee commissioned a group of scholars, led by Theo Adorno, to undertake a study of antisemitism, and this resulted in the publication in 1950 of *The Authoritarian Personality*. The book became the basis of research and theorising for years. The authors observed a close correlation between a number of deep-rooted personality traits and overt prejudice (Adorno 1950, p. vi). Seeking the underlying dynamics of Nazi rule – the most extreme form of antisemitism – they found it in a particular type of individual, one whose personality succumbed obediently to the stronger, unscrupulous and often cruel personality who was manipulative of the weak. Nazism was cruel because the Nazis were cruel. Nazis were cruel because cruel people tended to become Nazis. This circular argument was rooted in personality determinants of potential fascism and ethnocentrism, in isolation from contemporary conditions. This had the effect, as Bauman (1989, p. 153) points out, of absolving the rest of humankind. It divided the world into born proto-Nazis and their victims. The dismal knowledge that gentle people can turn cruel, if given a chance, was suppressed, as was the idea that victims can also behave in less than altruistic ways.

This thesis was challenged by Stanley Milgram, who asserted in his 1974 book, *Obedience to Authority*, that cruelty is not committed by necessarily cruel individuals, but by ordinary men and women in the course of their ordinary daily duties. Cruelty, he observed, does not correlate nearly as well with personal characteristics of its perpetrators as it does to the relationship between authority and subordination. People whose convictions may normally dictate otherwise, will perform acts relatively easily when commanded by authority. Behaviour that would be unthinkable when acting on one's own, can, he found, be executed without qualm when carried out under orders. Milgram offered strong proof that inhumanity is a matter of social relationships. As these are rationalised and technically perfected, so is the capacity and efficiency of the social production of inhumanity. He also found that it was far easier to perpetrate atrocities upon a victim who was distant than on one one had to look in the eye.[3] Milgram's research undoubtedly must have facilitated the arguments of those who view the Holocaust not only in terms of antisemitism, but as a catastrophe inherent in Western civilisation. Cruelty correlates with certain patterns of social interaction much more closely than it does with personality features or other individual idiosyncrasies of the perpetrators.

In 1988, Samuel and Pearl Oliner published *The Altruistic Personality*. Considering the many Christians who helped Jews during the Holocaust, at considerable risk to themselves and their families, they tried to pinpoint the social and psychological factors that had influenced them. They did this in the hope of helping the world to use these insights in moulding personalities who are concerned about the fate of others.

Psychological theory is more convincing when looked at in combination with other factors, as here, where it is located in a sociological context. On its own, the psychological approach can be taken to extremes, as in the case of the philosopher Jean Paul Sartre, who went as far as to suggest that antisemitism had nothing to do with Jews. Jews, he suggested, are neither the cause nor the object of antisemitism in that the antisemite is a man who is afraid. Afraid of himself, of his consciousness, of his liberty, of everything but Jews, he invents the Jew who is made to feel "Jewish" and whose links with other Jews are forged by an antisemitic animus. The Jew is therefore a person whom other people consider to be a Jew. Although Sartre undoubtedly uncovered a truth, he erred in his assessment in that he did not look at antisemitism historically.[4] He also so de-Judaised antisemitism that he rendered his argument almost meaningless. As Prager and Telushkin (1985) point out, it is impossible to understand antisemitism if one isolates it from the Jews and Judaism. Though psychological theories undoubtedly give insight into the causes of antisemitism, they explain only how people use the stereotype of the Jews, and not the stereotype's origin. One can be psychologically normal while being an antisemite, and psychological disease is not always associated with antisemitism.

The thrust of this book is that the source and persistence of antisemitism lie in religion, and it seems that Sigmund Freud, the founder of psychoanalysis, made some important observations on the matter, despite the fact that his theories about the origin of religion have been largely discredited. Freud, as a Jew, was himself the butt of antisemitism, as was the movement he founded. His suggestions that unconscious sexual strivings motivate human behaviour led to outrage among the more conservative that he was undermining the morals of Viennese society. Psychoanalysis was seen as a "Jewish" movement, and attracted hostility not only from those uncomfortable with the challenge to sexual mores, but from those opposed to change in general. Jews were, at that time, entering mainstream society, and psychoanalysts, many of whom were Jews, were seen – along with other Jews – as presumptuously crossing borders. Resistance to cultural change and to Jews being emancipated into the wider society went hand in hand, mutually reinforcing one another. As Mortimer Ostow (1989, p. 613) points out, psychoanalysis was a democratising movement. It posited the idea that, underlying all apparent boundaries, there was a universal psychology. "The veneer of inherited nobility, power, and wealth concealed the same hypocrisies, sordid and shameful sexual fantasies, and secrets as those that prevailed among both the lower social and economic classes, and the unwelcome newly liberated Jews, and other outsiders."

In response, Freud offered his own theory of antisemitism's origins. In *Totem and Taboo* (1913 [1960]), and *Moses and Monotheism* (1939 [1951]), he applied his psychoanalytic theory to religion and its origins, seeing religion as arising out of the "Oedipal complex". His "primal crime" hypothesis asserted that the primal horde killed the primordial father, the archetype of God, in an attempt to gain access to the mother, and that religion arises from the subsequent need to placate the dead father. Positing an ambivalence in all human beings – a constant oscillation between obedience to the father and hatred for his remembered image – Freud suggests that there remains a deep desire to dispense with God, not only to assuage guilt, but to be rid of his moral demands. Christianity served to assuage the guilt through the atoning death of Christ, but the blame for the dark deed was projected on to the

Jews, who are now forced to bear the guilt on behalf of all. Furthermore, opposition to Christianity was displaced on to its matrix, Judaism. "Under the thin veneer of Christianity," says Freud (1951, p. 147), Christians "have remained what their ancestors were, barbarically polytheistic. They have not yet overcome their grudge against the new religion which was forced on them, and they have projected it on to the source from which Christianity came to them. The facts [sic] that the Gospels tell a story which is enacted among Jews, and in truth treats only of Jews, has facilitated such a projection. The hatred for Judaism is at bottom a hatred for Christianity, and it is not surprising that in the German National-Socialist revolution this close connection of the two monotheistic religions finds such clear expression in the hostile treatment of *both*" (emphasis mine). One of the persistent features of antisemitism, as we shall see, is the deicide accusation against the Jews, the charge that they killed God.

Freud cited also the Jews' stubborn survival, despite all attempts to eradicate them, as well as unconscious acceptance that the Jews are in fact the chosen people, which results in the operation of sibling rivalry, on the one hand, and an aloofness or separation from other people, on the other. Circumcision, one of the most obvious customs that mark Jews off from others, makes, according to Freud, a disagreeable and uncanny impression on others, reminding them of the dreaded castration idea and of things in their primeval past that they would rather forget (1951, p. 147). Freud was on target, since these features, not necessarily requiring his Oedipal explanation, can be observed at various phases of the history of antisemitism. But it was Freud's amalgamation of psychoanalytic insights with religion that pointed to an answer to the question "Why the Jews?"

Sociopolitical and Socioeconomic theories

These theories ascribe the outbreak of antisemitism to social tensions prevailing in gentile society in the wake of crises, such as economic or political upheaval. They may, perhaps, be more on target than the psychological theories, in that they are based on genuine tensions and conflicts of interest between Jews and other classes. Economic circumstances can cause crisis situations that provide a *pretext* for Jew hatred. The middle class, for example, frequently hates Jews as merchants and middlemen. They are seen as exploiting labour, while not labouring themselves. Theories like that of Hannah Arendt place a great deal of emphasis on economic issues. They claim that Jews, by the time of the Holocaust, had ceased to be an economically complementary minority. They thus became superfluous. One modern way of dealing with population redundancy, claim theorists like Rubenstein and Roth, is mass murder. But any people can be defined by a government as superfluous. Jews, because of their particular role in Christian theology, had already been defined as outsiders, and were easily cast out of the universe of moral obligation.

The trouble with these theories is that they establish an artificial connection between antisemitism and any other social tension. Rubenstein and Roth, as we have seen, needed to turn to religion to find the link. So, though the socioeconomic approach has some validity, it does not, on its own, answer the basic question. Social tension may provide the occasion for antisemitism, but does not supply the cause. A negative image, historians of antisemitism observe, always *precedes* the actual social tensions that ensue. People did not object to the many lawyers, scientists and artists who emerged in nineteenth-century Germany, Shmuel Ettinger (1988) points out. It was only when the number of Jews in these fields began to rise that animosity was aroused. Economic conditions cannot, alone, explain the emergence of modern antisemitism. Ettinger emphasises the fact that modern antisemitism arose in Europe coinciding not with the ostensible wealth of the Jews but with their pauperisation on most of the continent – which forces us back to other explanations. Underlying the antipathy, uncovered by the psycho-social and socioeconomic theories, are cultural attitudes that themselves demand explanation. There had to be a pre-existent image of the Jews as an undesirable group. Where, when and why this image arose is debated.

Ideological theories

A third school of thought explains antisemitism – especially its Nazi version – in terms of ideology, particularly racial ideology. Most radical antisemites, it is argued, believed Jews were racially inferior and the concept of race supplied them with justification for programmes of social exclusion and legal discrimination, which led finally to annihilation. With the spread of reason as a value in modern times, anti-Jewish sentiments lost their theological grounding but retained their elementary force. They needed a secondary justification to support them. Antisemitism, according to Jacob Katz (1983, p. 3), had shown a tendency to link up with any system of thought or set of ideas that offered it ideological shelter. The theory of race is just one example of such ideological fusion, though it was the one that would have the weightiest consequences. Antisemitism fused with other political philosophies, like conservatism, where Jews were condemned as innovators, or socialism, where Jews were detested for their role in capitalism, or liberalism, where Judaism was denigrated as obsolete tribalism, vastly inferior to the ethical Christianity that had superseded it. Nevertheless, argues Katz, ideology no more results in murder than the murderous effect of a knife can be imputed to its inventor. Racial theory played a part in European thinking long before Jews became a factor in the discussion. Even in the nineteenth century, when Comte Joseph-Arthur de Gobineau turned race into a central concept in historical interpretation, his formulas did not yield any specific anti-Jewish animus. He did not see Jews as noble, but they did not get the worst rating either. So, the notion of race, *per se*, did not automatically imply a derogatory judgement of others, and racial thinking did not necessarily imply a destructive attitude to Jews. Race alone cannot account for the radical turn that antisemitism took under Hitler.

The Nazi drive to annihilate the Jews was fed by the prior radical negation of Jewish existence. Racial theory is often a pretext for people arrogating to themselves a high position in the human hierarchy, and for subjugating others, enslaving sectors of their population or decimating their leadership – as the Nazis did to the Poles. But total extermination was singled out for Jews alone. There must, therefore, be another factor to account for the severe consequences that racial ideology entailed for Jews. This factor can only be discovered through the historical approach to the study of antisemitism.

THE HISTORICAL APPROACH TO ANTISEMITISM

The historical approach analyses each manifestation of antisemitism as unique in its own terms, against the backdrop of its specific historic context. With the historical approach we can, for example, make sense of some of the racial theories and how, why and when they amalgamated with an already negative image of the Jew. Katz shows that this took place for the first time with Ernest Renan in the 1850s. He was the first, as we will see in greater detail in chapter 8, to make the link between the alleged vices of the Jewish character and the Jews' racial heritage. In his linguistic studies, he hit on a distinction between the Semitic and Aryan races and proceeded to elaborate this distinction into a system. All positive qualities he attributed to the so-called Aryans, all negative ones to the so-called Semites. Though he did not refer to Jews in particular, the same characteristics he gave to Semites had already been used for Jews by Voltaire a century earlier. What Voltaire saw as the distinguishing traits of a collective Jewish mentality, Renan transformed into racially conditioned characteristics common to all Semites, knowing that the only relevant example was that of the Jews. Renan's views coalesced with Voltaire's at a specific point on the historic spectrum. Without Voltaire and the type of thought he espoused, it would not have taken on the same significance. Voltaire's thought, in turn, would not have taken the form it did without the prior negative teaching about the Jews that had manifested itself in Christianity.

The historical approach seeks to discover why the Jews are so often the butt of people's animosity. Looking at the variety of forms that antisemitism has taken over its long history, scholars have noted that, because each manifestation of it has been different, there is a tension between the continuity of antisemitism and the protean ways in which it manifests itself. It thus becomes difficult to ascertain whether there is any common denominator between the various periods of Jew hatred. Is there, for example, any similarity between pagan antipathy against Jews, and later Christian attitudes, which developed as the early Christian community began to differentiate itself from Judaism, later developing a truly frightening stereotype of the Jew? How do these two forms of Jew hatred, in turn, compare with the lowly position of Jews under Islam? What connection is there between all these and modern antisemitism, and how does modern antisemitism relate to Nazi antisemitism? In other words, are we talking about the same thing when we look at Christian and Nazi antisemitism? Is there a common essence that unites them and, if so, what is it? If not, is it legitimate to call both of them "antisemitism"?

This raises the question of the way in which this hatred has been transmitted from generation to generation. Why did it take on vicious forms at some times and not at others? What were the specific causes of its eruption at specific points in history? How was it rationalised and exploited, and for what purposes? Modern antisemitism is thus a blend of a variety of factors, and any proper history must consist of a careful tracing of the processes whereby anti-Jewish beliefs, dating back a long time, were successfully combined with a variety of modern ideologies. We need to follow all the stages *en route* – showing how ideological fusions and transformations helped to shelter antisemitism and allow its survival. The effect of antisemitism, says Katz (1983, p. 43), changes according to circumstances, such as individual personalities of anti-semites, economic conditions, social processes at work in a given situation, or psychological factors. The totality of these needs to be examined for proper historical insight.

The historical approach to antisemitism, according to Yehuda Bauer (1994, p. 12), centres on three interrelated questions: When did antisemitism begin? Is there any overarching explanation of it? How and why is it transmitted from generation to generation? Theorists have exploited a variety of disciplines in search of answers, but have not been entirely successful. An overarching explanation remains elusive. A great deal of this book will be taken up by the search for origins, for only when this question is given some type of answer, do the other two questions begin to fall into place.

HOW OLD IS ANTISEMITISM?

Robert Wistrich has justifiably called antisemitism "the longest hatred".[5] And yet, one can make such a statement with confidence only if one adopts a broad definition of antisemitism as including all forms of Jew hatred. Dislike of Jews is very old, but its character has kept changing. When we use the term "antisemitism", therefore, we find that the way we define it, and what we are prepared to apply the word to, will determine our views on how far it goes back, and vice versa. Because antisemitism is a new word, coined to denote a new and specific form of Jew hatred that emerged in the nineteenth century, some scholars, as we have already observed, will only use the designation "antisemitism" to apply to modern, secular, and racial, forms of Jew-hatred. When used more broadly, to denote Jew-hatred in general, however, antisemitism may be extended further back in history. Some date it back to the very beginnings of Judaism and give antisemitism an "eternal" quality – as does traditional Judaism and some scholars, like Prager and Telushkin. Others perceive it as emerging in a later period of Jewish history. Most scholars date it back to some time during the diaspora period, after

586 BCE, when, for whatever reason, a substantial number of Jews began to live outside the land of Israel. Having been exiled to Babylon, Jews were to develop an important centre there. The diaspora spread as Jews became dispersed more widely throughout the world. There is no consensus on exactly when, during this particular period, antisemitism emerged, though most scholars date it no further back than the Hellenistic period which began with the sweeping conquests of Alexander the Great from about 332 BCE.

Those who argue for the earlier emergence of antisemitism in the diaspora suggest that it arose when Jews first attracted attention as being different from the society that surrounded them. They point, for example, to the book of Esther, where the existence of a vicious form of antisemitism is indicated. "There is a certain people, dispersed among the many peoples in all the provinces of your kingdom," says the antagonist of the Jews, Haman, to the king of Persia, "who keep themselves apart. Their laws are different from those of every other people; they do not keep your majesty's laws. It does not befit your majesty to tolerate them. If it please your majesty, let an order be made in writing for their destruction" (Esther 3:8). Although this looks like the first call for the genocide of the Jews, its historic accuracy has been questioned because the Persian period was marked by tolerance of religious minorities. What it does indicate, however, was that there were fears of such a possibility in the minds of some Jews, which suggests the possibility of the existence of some tension.

It is generally believed that antisemitism, in its broadest sense, emerged during the Hellenistic period, though some scholars narrow down the time span to the Hasmonean kingdom, immediately after the Maccabean revolt, in 167 BCE, when the Jews had a brief period of independence. But it is also widely held that true antisemitism emerged only with Christianity. Only then, it is argued, were the Jews demonised and endowed with cosmic powers of evil. This identification of the Jews with an occult power beyond themselves marks, according to many, the emergence of true antisemitism, or what Joel Carmichael (1992) calls "mystical antisemitism".

Antisemitism, as the word is used in this book, goes back a long time and has continued to the present day. Over this long period, it has demonstrated an almost limitless capacity of the human imagination to invent negative images. Despite the contradictions, however, there is a strange recurrence of familiar themes. Nonetheless, antisemitism, according to Robert Chazan (1986, p. 50), is not a constant that simply expresses itself in modified patterns from era to era and from place to place. Rather, it manifests itself in shifting patterns of anti-Jewish thinking and behaviour, which are created by the combination of particular constellations of historical circumstances. One factor in this constellation is the nature of the majority among whom a particular group of Jews resides – including the legacy of anti-Jewish stereotypes that that majority may have inherited. The other is the pattern of life of the Jewish minority in question. The specific political-social-economic-religious contexts in which these two interact can result in hostile perception of Jews and the formation of new interactions as conditions change. These then result in new stereotypes, which are bequeathed from one generation to another, a development that can only be revealed through the historical approach.

THE SEARCH FOR THE "PRIOR" NEGATIVE IMAGE

The brutal elimination of one-third of the world's Jews rendered it impossible to look at antisemitism as an isolated hatred that has occurred here and there, from time to time, without practical ramifications. The initial reaction to the Holocaust, according to Shmuel Ettinger, was emotional. Jews were deeply shocked by the depth of Nazi hatred and by the way in which they had become the primary target of widespread murder, and the victims of genocide. The first line of approach was to look at the role of the immediate perpetrators, the German people. The question then moved to the responsibility of those, like the Poles, on whose territories the slaughter was carried out. It was a short move, from this point, to an examination of the responses of the victims. The Jewish leaders' actions, before and during the Nazi period, were scrutinised in order to assess whether, with different attitudinal responses, they could have foreseen the disaster, or acted differently while the war was in progress in order to minimise its impact. It took time for a wider, more universal, historical perspective on antisemitism to emerge.

We have already noted theories such as the psychological and socioeconomic ones, but these, as we saw, do not address the question "Why the Jews?" They force one back to more primal questions, one of these being whether Jews and Judaism play any role in generating hostility, or whether antisemitism should be seen as a gentile problem that has little or nothing to do with Jews. Is antisemitism, therefore, a problem of European history or a problem of Jewish history? If Jews and Judaism do play a role, how extensive is it?

Theories that "blame the victim"

A number of scholars see Jews themselves as responsible for the persistence of antisemitism. In 1894, when simmering antisemitism in France burst into the open in the Dreyfus affair, the Jewish scholar Bernard-Lazare attempted to explain Jew hatred by saying that wherever there were Jews, hostility was aroused. "The general causes of antisemitism", he claimed, "have always resided in Israel itself and not with those who oppose them. This is not to affirm that the persecutors of the Jews always had right on their side ... but to suggest that, in principle, Jews are responsible – at least in part – for their misery."[6] Needless to say, Bernard-Lazare's history of antisemitism has been a controversial one. Composed over a long period of time, it was hastily published to coincide with the Dreyfus trial. Although his thought went through several phases, from assimilationist to Zionist, Bernard-Lazare was always deeply concerned for the fate of the Jewish people. He had, for example, devoted a great deal of his energy to proving Dreyfus's innocence because he sincerely wanted to deprive modern antisemitism of a replacement symbol for Judas Iscariot, who, as the betrayer of Jesus, had served to identify, for future generations, the Jew with treachery.[7] Bernard-Lazare had promised to revise his work on antisemitism, but, because of his early death, aged thirty-eight, he never did. Predictably, his ideas have been exploited by antisemites ever since. Theories can thus present dangers in themselves.

This theory emerged before the Holocaust. Now, in our post-Holocaust age, as James Parkes emphasises, such theories are hopelessly inadequate. They may no longer be advanced without a very careful look at the history of the emergence of antisemitism, particularly in regard to the hostility that developed between Judaism and Christianity. The idea that there was any Jewish share in responsibility for the Holocaust, Parkes insists, provides no basis for the creation of so evil a thing as Nazi beliefs or activities. "The *Jude* of Nazi pornography was entirely a creature of Nazi pornographic imagination."[8]

Hannah Arendt is the most obvious post-Holocaust proponent of the view that Jews, themselves, help to promote antisemitism. But her analysis cannot be separated from socioeconomic or psycho-social theories of antisemitism. In her book *The Origins of Totalitarianism*, (1951), in which she compared the two terror regimes of Nazism and Communism, she saw the conflict between Jews and other social classes in economic terms. Jews, she asserted, had, before the emancipation era, played an important role as court Jews and bankers for the rulers of the early nation-state, becoming, in the process, too closely allied to them. Ceasing, with the rise of industrialisation, to perform an economic function, Jews lost their social function as well. Retaining only their wealth and their status, they became more visible and thus the target of hostility and resentment. Had the Jews not been blind to this process of alienation, she suggests, the Holocaust would have taken on less immense proportions. In a later book, *Eichmann in Jerusalem* (1963), Arendt dealt specifically with the Holocaust. Jewish leaders, both before and during the Nazi period, she suggested, had betrayed their people. By cooperating with the Nazis' bureaucratic demands – giving them, for example, information about their doomed communities – they had led the Jews to be complicit in their own annihilation. The book – with its scoffing and derisory tone – excited controversy more for this suggestion than for its central theme, the portrayal of Adolph Eichmann as a mechanised bureaucrat who performed his tasks without passion or personal responsibility.

In the light of their experience, Jews are, understandably, sensitive to views that veer in the direction of blaming the victim. These are most often simplistic and, as we have seen in the case of Bernard-Lazare, can be used against the Jews. Such views, therefore, open themselves up to attack. But great care needs to be taken in assessing the intention of the scholar who uses such explanatory devices. Scholars who adopt this approach often provoke considerable controversy and even ire. One example is Albert S. Lindemann's 1997 book *Esau's Tears*, which argued that antisemitism is not merely a disembodied fantasy that occurs in isolation from real Jews, but that it developed, in its modern form, as a negative response to the rise of the Jews to prominence. Though originating ultimately in the imagination of the antisemite, negative perceptions, Lindemann argues, have a locus in reality. His aim is not to indulge in moral blame, but to examine the interplay between fantasy and reality in the way people perceive Jews. Understandably, his book received mixed reviews, and some were hostile to the point of character assassination. I, however, found it a fascinating study, by an author who is deeply aware of the hideous repercussions of antisemitism, reveals no personal hostility to Jews and, above all, regards Jewish influence on the world as fundamentally positive.

It is not unusual for scholars, for example Arthur Hertzberg and George Steiner, to regard the way the Jews see themselves, according to their own myths of origin, as exacerbating antisemitism. There is a complex dynamic between the Christian and Jewish mythic structure which plays a part in the problem. Furthermore, this mythic structure was taken over and manipulated by the Nazis. As Rubenstein and Roth (1987, p. 9) affirm, antisemitism should not be analysed as a one-sided visitation from an irrational gentile world upon Jews as passive objects. Rather, the historic situation should be viewed as a seething conflict involving active parties on both sides. Rubenstein and Roth are careful to disentangle "blame" from historical analysis and stress both the objective innocence of the Jewish victims of the Holocaust, and the hideous disparity between the merit of Jewish life, and its treatment by non-Jews in the West. Jews and Christians, they point out, could not but disconfirm each other's religious traditions. The results of that tragic fact escalated until the world reached Auschwitz. These theories, it must be stressed, do not condone antisemitism. A clear separation should be made between those who blame the Jews in order to justify antisemitic opinions and actions, and those who are trying to investigate all dimensions of the problem to understand it. *Understanding* antisemitism should not be confused with *condoning* it.

The traditional Jewish response to antisemitism

The traditional Jewish response to antisemitism is not entirely separable from what has just been said above. It holds that there is nothing new about the Holocaust other than its scale and organisation. Antisemitism, according to Jewish tradition, is the eternal hatred of the eternal people. It is part of the fabric of the Jews' interaction with the wider world. Jewish tradition tells us that God offered the Torah to many nations, but only the Jews accepted it. When God revealed himself at Sinai and entered into a covenant with them as his "treasured people", a *midrash*, or oral interpolation of the Hebrew Bible,[9] which plays on the Hebrew words, tells us that he also gave the gentile world *Sin'at Yisrael*, hatred of Israel. The very existence of the Jewish people, with their special vocation and destiny, arouses gentile animosity, which thus becomes an inescapable part of their fate. This animosity was later, as we will see in chapter 3, embodied in the conflict between Esau and Jacob (Israel). Attempts to destroy the Jews have been part of the relationship from the beginning. This theory is seen to be validated by the many massacres and disruptions that have characterised Jewish life. With the persistence of antisemitism, especially in relation to the conflict in the Middle East, the theory continues to convince. Prager and Telushkin, in their short but feisty 1985 book, *Why the Jews?*, have offered a modern elaboration of the traditional explanation of antisemitism. They see it as arising inevitably from Judaism itself. Judaism's claims and the Jews' superior living conditions have resulted in unavoidable hatred. Thus, antisemitism will persist for as long as Jews continue to exist. They may well be right, but endowing antisemitism with an eternal quality, as Wistrich (1991) points out, though tempting, tends to replace history with myth, and is contradicted by a great deal of positivity in Jewish experience.

It should be noted, at this point, that not very far from, though ideologically the opposite of, this view is the theory of intrinsic antisemitism, a theory that comes from antisemites themselves. In order to justify their hatred, these antisemites claim that, since there has been antisemitism throughout history, there must be something inherently despicable in Jews and Judaism themselves. In other words, Jews deserve to be hated because they are, and always have been, hateful. Going back to pagan animosity against Jews, they argue in circular fashion that, because antisemitism has endured in so many places, times and circumstances, there must be some justification for it. Such a theory may be eliminated because the intention of its formulators is so malignant, but its existence should alert us to the complexity of the subject and the need for full historical investigation.

The first denial of Jewish worth: paganism or Christianity?

An important part of the historical approach to antisemitism is to locate the exact moment at which, as Shmuel Ettinger (1988, p. 9) put it, "the conceptual denial of Jewish worth" began. Most scholars find it either in the classical world or in the relationship between Judaism and Christianity. They are engaged, as Norman Ravitch (1982) points out, in a never-ending and finally irresolvable dispute about the relative importance of pagan antisemitism in the Graeco-Roman world and the antisemitic theology of the emergent church. Some scholars place the responsibility squarely on Christian teaching and tend, therefore, to regard pagan antisemitism as an occasional expression of wonder and distaste at the unique features of Jewish life. Others point to the virulence of pagan antisemitism because they wish to exculpate the church from the horrible fruits of antisemitism. There was a considerable amount of hatred for Jews in the ancient world, which will be discussed in chapter 4, but there is also a broad consensus among scholars that Christianity played the decisive role in fostering the demonic image of the Jew. Chapters 5 and 6 will be devoted to an exploration of this Christian image of the Jew. As David Berger (1986, p. 5) points out, "if ancient paganism had been replaced by a religion or ideology without an internal anti-Jewish dynamic, it is likely that the anti-Semitism of the classical world would have gradually faded. Instead, it was reinforced. The old pedestrian causes of anti-Jewish animus were replaced by a new, powerful myth of extraordinary force and vitality."

The problem, as I have already indicated, lies in the relationship of the mythic structure of Christianity to Judaism, and the fact that the two religions are based on the same Abrahamic tradition. Christianity is deeply ambivalent about Jews and Judaism, and offers both negative and positive evaluations. Because Christians, understandably, assume the exclusive religious truth of Christianity, Jews are, at the simplest level, viewed as religiously wrong. This, according to Robert Chazan (1986), would be true for any other non-Christians, but Jews were for centuries the only significant group of non-Christians in Europe. When Christianity became the official religion of the Roman Empire in the fourth century, the church was able to pass laws that legislated Jews into an inferior position, a situation that might have been less problematic in a more heterogeneous setting.

The particular position of the Jews was, however, exacerbated by the fact that Christianity not only evolved from a Jewish matrix, but shared the Jews' sacred literature, the Hebrew Bible. Asserting Jewish stubbornness in refusing to accept Jesus as the messiah promised in the Hebrew Bible, and blaming them for his death, the Christians called the Jewish scriptures the "Old Testament" and regarded the New Testament as its only legitimate fulfilment.

Anti-Jewish animus thus lies in the very centre of the drama of Christian salvation. Christian animosity against the Jew is thus seen by many as the basis for all forms of modern antisemitism, and continues to reinforce antisemitism through the reservoir of anti-Jewish images that it has accumulated and constantly disseminates through education, the liturgy and art. This is accompanied by the persistent notion of the Jew as the outsider – the "other" – who had rejected Christ's revelation, and who, by continuing to do so – by merely surviving – perpetually raises doubt about the ultimate truth of Christian teaching. This results in a duality in the world's perception of Jews. They are, on the one hand, the pariah people, the despised and demeaned witness of Christianity's final triumph. On the other, they are powerful conspiratorial demons who killed Christ, a crime that they are accused of re-enacting through ritual murder. The latter dimension is repeatedly expressed in conspiracy theories that continue to plague our world.

Despite the rootedness of antisemitism in Christianity, however, there was also a counter doctrine that asserted the right of the Jews to lead a tolerated, though limited, existence in the Christian world. Chapters 5 and 6 will explore these developments and show how, by making the Jews the "secret centre" of world history, the church was able to see the avenging hand of God in all Jewish catastrophes, which led to the "justification" of Jewish suffering up to and including the Holocaust. But chapter 6 will also show how the church consistently rejected a genocidal solution.

THE HOLOCAUST: A "TWISTED DEPENDENCY" ON CHRISTIAN TEACHING

One of the most difficult problems when discussing the relationship of antisemitism to the Holocaust is the question of continuity. When the church came to power in the fourth century, Jews were pushed to the margins of society, where they became an economic social class that evoked hatred over and above their religious difference. The church thus set up a precedent for treating the Jews as lesser people. However, as Steven Katz (1994b) suggests, despite lapses and inconsistencies, the church never wanted a genocidal solution to the Jewish–Christian conflict. Though it might have wished to see the end of the Jews, this would only come about through their conversion to Christianity. Physical genocide must therefore be seen as a rejection and overthrow of this underlying Christian understanding of the Jew, and not as its fulfilment. This does not mean that Katz denies that the millennia of Christian violence against Jews were crucial to creating the matrix for the rise of Nazism, but that there was a "twisted dependency" that is far more complex than previous analyses have allowed. This issue will be explored in chapter 8.

We are left with a conundrum: Is the historic series of Christian anti-Jewish actions – like ostracism, legal and economic disability, theological and sociological devaluation, physical abuse, pogroms, ghettoisation and exile – "completed" by Auschwitz? Or does genocide, rather than complete the series, totally alter it? All forms of antisemitism before the Holocaust, Katz points out, took place within parameters that recognised Jews as fellow human beings who made a moral claim upon Christian society. Christianity always acknowledged that Jews and Christians were children of the same God and were created equal, both possessing ultimate value in God's sight. However alienated from him they may presently be, the Jews are redeemable, even if only at "the end of days". The Holocaust, by contrast, arose out of the very negation of these two normative beliefs. For Nazism there was no moral boundary constraining aggressive action against the Jew. Its basic assertion was that the Jew is inherently corrupt and ultimately irredeemable. This helps to explain why antisemitism worsened as religion's influence declined.

ALLOSEMITISM

The placement of the Jews at the centre of world history, first by Jews themselves, and then by Christianity, and their distinctive lifestyle resulted in the Jew being seen as "other", as an "oddity" that persistently eludes categorisation. Because the concepts and treatments that apply to other peoples seem inadequate for describing and comprehending Jews, Zygmunt Bauman (1995, p. 207) has resurrected the term "allosemitism", coined by the Polish literary historian and critic Arthur Sandauer. *Allus* is the Latin word for "otherness", and "allosemitism" refers to the practice of setting the Jews apart as people radically different from all others. It is, however, a neutral term in that it is non-committal in regard to love or hate of Jews. Bauman suggests, therefore, that antisemitism should be placed within the wider concept of "allosemitism", which forms the ground out of which both antisemitism and philosemitism arise. Containing the seeds of both, allosemitism assures that, whichever of the two emerges, it is bound to be intense and extreme. Because it is part of the legacy of Christendom, Bauman sees allosemitism as endemic to Western civilisation. The fact that Jews are unassimilable into, yet indispensable to the church resulted in it bequeathing to later ages two notions. The first was that the Jews were cast as the embodiment of ambivalence and, hence, disorder. The second was the abstract Jew, the *concept* in place of the empirical Jew, which means that the Jew has remained perpetually distant, and immune to new information that experience may provide. Thus there is an unbridgeable divide between the Jew as an abstraction and the Jew "next door".

Bauman (1995) links allosemitism with the Holocaust in that he sees the latter as arising out of a modern obsession with order and perfection, and the power of elites to remove anything or anyone that disturbs the desired equilibrium or threatens the "health" of the "ideal" society. Basically, modern society finds it difficult to handle otherness and diversity. We are living, he says, in the "Age of Gardening" (1995, p. 218), a time when society is treated as a garden needing design and cultivation. An indispensable part of cultivation, he points out, is weeding, which he defines as "the protection of plants which fit the design against the voraciousness and poisonous impact of such as do not" (1995, p. 219). When society is turned into a garden, he says, the idea of *unwertes Leben* (being unworthy of life) will occupy as central a place in any blueprint of a better society as does the fight against weeds and parasites in every good gardening manual. Modernity inherited the Jews in their role of ambivalence incarnate. As such, they were predestined for the role of the quintessential "weed". Making modern Europe was synonymous, he insists, with allosemitism veering towards its antisemitic pole.

"JUSTIFYING" ANTISEMITISM

Each period of antisemitism had to supply its own justifications for Jew hatred. The church fathers put great stress on the idea of the Jews as killers of God. As deicides, Jews were perceived as an unscrupulous people who deserved to be forsaken. The Middle Ages added usury, black magic and ties with the devil. Over time, as Ettinger (1988) points out, some features were dropped and others adapted or replaced. With these additions, the negative Christian image of the Jews became central to the conceptual world of Europe. Through the practice of Christianity – its rituals, liturgy, biblical lessons and artistic representation of the Jew – antagonism towards Jews was reinforced, enabling it to penetrate where no Jews lived. In the modern era, the focus shifted to the sciences to justify an ancient negative image. This was subsequently exploited in the political arena for political and social ends, but ideological justification was always needed.

There are, as we have seen, many problems in offering any definitive answers to the variety of questions around the study of antisemitism. But we have also observed how important it is to understand antisemitism if there is to be any hope of fighting it. This will involve a great deal more research into the phenomenon. As Yehudah Bauer (1994, p. 21) points out, antisemitism's ubiquity underscores its danger. Though it may be "a disease of the non-Jewish world" *everyone* has to fight it. The last time a major country adopted antisemitism as its official policy, it resulted in a war in which tens of millions of lives were lost – most of them not Jews. This, in itself, is reason enough for all to oppose antisemitism.

Let us now turn to a discussion of Judaism, not in order to apportion "blame", but to ascertain how Jews have perceived themselves in God's economy, and how this may have affected the perceptions of those among whom they have lived. William Nicholls (1995, p. xviii) cautions us that "the origins of antisemitism are to be sought not in Jews but in antisemites. Antisemitism is causeless hatred. The reasons given for it are always rationalizations of a hate *already* in the mind of the antisemite . . . We should never be trapped into taking these justifications seriously, trying to see if there was anything in Jewish behavior that might have provided a basis for them" (emphasis mine). It is with this word of caution in mind that I proceed.

Part II

PRE-CHRISTIAN ANTISEMITISM

3

Jewish history and self-understanding

If Herodotus was the father of history, the fathers of meaning in history were the Jews.

Yosef Hayim Yerushalmi

It's Hebrew tradition that forefathers are referred to as "we," not "they." "When we were delivered from Egypt ..." This encourages empathy and responsibility to the past but, more important, it collapses time. The Jew is forever leaving Egypt. A good way to teach ethics. If moral choices are eternal, individual actions take on immense significance no matter how small; not for this life only.

Anne Michaels

INTRODUCTION: WHY JUDAISM?

It may seem odd to start an investigation into the history of antisemitism by discussing Judaism. Some may even regard it as offensive, in that to do so appears to "blame" the victim. But, as we have already seen, it is impossible to understand antisemitism in isolation from Judaism itself, and some scholars, like Prager and Telushkin (1985), see antisemitism entirely as a response to Judaism, its beliefs, rituals and the lifestyle it demands from its adherents. One cannot understand pagan antisemitism without examining the phenomenon to which it was objecting. Moreover, Judaism was the ground from which Christianity and Islam sprang. They shared its understanding of God as the God who acts in history, but departed from it in ways that led to inter-religious conflict and the denigration of Judaism. This chapter will therefore examine the basics of Jewish belief. It will show how that belief is rooted in a specific understanding of history. It will also explain that certain practices required by Judaism's holy law, the Torah, mark the Jews off as separate from the outside world. Examples of these are the dietary laws and circumcision, practices that, as we will see later, were much resented by the non-Jewish world.

Judaism's fundamental aim is the hallowing of the everyday act. Every action, such as the simple act of eating, is preceded by a blessing in which God is acknowledged as the creator, the bountiful giver of all that is necessary to sustain life. Such ritual raises simple everyday acts to holiness by acknowledging human creatureliness in the face of the glory and goodness of God. The hallowing of the everyday act emerged out of rabbinic Judaism after the destruction of the second temple in 70 CE. We will see below that an essential aspect of Judaism is the promise of the land of Israel. With the failure of the revolt against the Romans from 66 to 70 CE, Jews entered into a two-thousand-year period of homelessness. Although there were many ways of being Jewish at the time – or many Judaisms, as Jacob Neusner (1989) puts it – one sect, the Pharisees, survived. They had stressed the importance of interpreting the Torah through an oral tradition, and were the forefathers of the rabbis who, using oral interpretation, offered meaning to the tragedy by seeing it in terms of exile. The rabbis formulated a holy way of life that would keep Judaism alive in the absence of a homeland and temple. Through their reinterpretation of the biblical understanding of history, which will be discussed below, they were to lay the basis of Judaism as it exists today. All modern forms of Judaism are heirs to rabbinic Judaism, even if only in the sense of opposing it.

The underlying reason for Jews living by a specific divinely commanded lifestyle, as we will see in greater detail later, is that they were the first to assert the existence of only one God, the creator of all, who chose them for some special purpose in bringing about his ends. For Jews, God is the Lord of history. He reveals himself at specific moments in time to guide his creation toward a messianic deliverance when history will be consummated and peace will reign on earth. The Jews are to be God's helpers in bringing this about. This was to create a tension in Judaism. Why would one universal God focus on one particular people to bring about his divine purpose? If all humans are equal, is that not favouritism? What are the obligations and fate of non-Jews? Judaism is thus in tension between particularism and universality. What happens to Jews is intimately bound up with what will ultimately happen to the entire world, which, since God is good, will eventually be redeemed. First, the Jewish people will be returned to their homeland. Thereafter, a global transformation will take place.

Jewish life is based on the Jews' fundamental conviction about how God had chosen to deal with them in history. The story behind that conviction appears in the Torah, the holiest of the Jewish scriptures. The Torah, which means "instruction" or "teaching", guides every aspect of the Jew's life, from cradle to grave. According to tradition, it was revealed on Mount Sinai to Moses, who wrote it down. It was later subjected to oral interpretation, or *midrash* (of which more later), which was designed to mine the profound meaning that was hidden below the written word. It was revealed in all its profundity to Moses who, according to rabbinic Judaism, was given both the written and the oral Torah, the latter being passed down orally through the generations, ultimately to be written down in the *Mishnah* and the Talmud. The task of future generations was to study the Torah in order to keep alive the memory of what God had done for his people, to mine its depths so that they may discover its jewels, and to use these to illumine their lives.

Jews, like people of all religions, have an underlying story that relates their origins, gives their lives meaning and determines their place in the world. Scholars, as we will see below, call this the mythical dimension of religion. Jews tell a story of their intimate relationship with God and record their experience of both his mercy and justice. God had originally made a promise to the forefather of the Jews, Abraham. He called upon Abraham (Genesis 12:1) to leave his father's house and everything that was familiar to him, and go to a land that would be shown to him. Abraham was also promised that he would one day be the father of a great nation, and that the land in question would be given to that nation, the people Israel. Abraham obediently followed God's command, passing through the land, where he sojourned for a while, and soon migrating down[1] to Egypt in search of food. There, his descendants became slaves whom God – faithful to his promise – redeemed to live a free life in their own land. This was known as the Exodus from Egypt.

The Exodus, an unmerited act of divine grace, was to be the foundation of Judaism. But why the Jews? They were not bigger, mightier or more important than any other people. Rather, they were to live a life of special responsibility. They were to be bound by a special agreement –

or covenant (*berit*) – to live a life of holiness under God's commandments (*mitzvot*). So awed were they by God's merciful intervention on their behalf that they could come to no other conclusion than that they must have been chosen. But, to be ready to live a free life under God's command, they had to remain in the wilderness for forty years before being allowed to settle in the promised land. While they were still in transit, God appeared to Moses, in front of the entire people, and gave them the Torah. As a mark of their indebtedness to God for his merciful deliverance of them, the Jewish people were to live the life that God commanded of them. If they were faithful to the covenant, they would remain safely in their land. If they were not, they would be exiled. Jews based their confidence in God and their hopes for the future on the paradigm of what he had already done for them, in a past they were obligated to remember.

Though the Jews gave the world meaning in history, the emergence of rabbinic Judaism saw a new interpretation of how God worked in history. Unconcerned with historiography, as we today understand it, the rabbis saw the Bible as laying down a pattern of history, a pattern that had to be remembered and relived. In the wealth of oral interpretations of the Torah – which became the Jews' portable homeland – time was collapsed, the characters in it being as alive and influential in every age as they were in their own lifetime. What would happen in the future would depend on the Jews' faithfulness to the memory of God's grace and in fulfilling his commandments. Thus, there is a sense in which rabbinic Judaism side-stepped history. It was not the great nations who were the makers of history, said the rabbis, but God, and the nations would be the tools by which he would bring about his purpose for Israel and, ultimately, the world. If the Jews were faithful to the memory of their past, and to the way that past obligated them to live, God could be trusted to send the messiah to bring about their final redemption. Only then would their steadfastness and suffering be vindicated, when all of humanity would come to recognise the one God and to realise that Israel had borne tribulations on their behalf. In the interim, hatred of Jews was seen as an inextricable part of Jewish existence.

At the root of Jewish self-understanding then is the Judaic view of God and the way he acted with his people within history. Jews gave the world meaning in history in that they were the first people to invest their story of origin with historical importance. This new understanding of history arose in a pagan setting, where it evoked a variety of responses, from admiration to hostility. When it was taken up by Christianity and, later, Islam, conflict arose. This will be discussed in chapters 5, 6 and 7. Underlying all this, however, are the stories we tell about ourselves, our myths. So let us now turn to a discussion of Judaism's mythical dimension within the context of world religion.

THE "MYTHICAL" AS A DIMENSION OF RELIGION

The word "myth" is used in common parlance to denote something that is untrue, but scholars of religion use it very differently. Because religion is extraordinarily difficult to define, and its boundaries are often vague, some scholars assert that ideologies like Marxism can be included as religions. To decide whether such ideologies qualify, however, one has to determine the criteria that should define their inclusion or exclusion. Ninian Smart (1984) offers a comprehensive way of defining religion, which looks at the common components of all religions, or their "anatomy". He identifies six of these, calling them "dimensions". All have to be present if a particular phenomenon is to qualify as a "religion". Of these, the mythical dimension will be the most important for our purposes.

The first is the ritual dimension, a variety of outward observances – from intimate private prayers and meditations, to large ceremonial services. These actions, the most immediately observable feature of religion, are based on a second dimension, the mythological, which locates the believer and the rituals he or she performs within a wider context of meaning. The mythological dimension is constituted by one or more stories, which tell the believer about the religion's origin and purpose. Scholars use the word "myth" in a way that takes a neutral view of the truth or falsity of the story in question. William Nicholls (1995, p. 3) suggests that a myth is a story or group of images in which religious energy and emotion are invested. The story tells the members of the community who they are, by giving the group its identity and distinguishing it from other religious groups. The myth is "the charter of a religious community", the energy centre by which it lives. It usually explains ultimate mysteries, such as the creation of the world, the struggle between good and evil, and the way human beings can be saved in the future. "Without myths," he says, "we would not have religions." Michael Goldberg (1995) concurs. We live, he says, in a "story-shaped world". The mythical dimension, or "master story", of a religion provides the model for understanding the world and a guide for how to act in it. Master stories thus both form and inform us. They provide a background text within which a community's convictions about itself and the world gain their sense and significance.

The mythological dimension of religion taps into the deep, archetypal layers of the mind from which profound religious experiences arise. Religions constantly re-enact symbolically the power of the myth through prayer and other rituals. Myth, together with ritual, helps to unite members of a religious community and to express, more clearly than any other of the dimensions, how believers feel about the world and other people. There are also secular myths possessed by nations and political movements, which are equally strong, such as Nazism, with its ideas of racism and struggle. Though such myths have a profound influence on people's behaviour, they lack the other dimensions that would make them into religions.

The third dimension is the doctrinal one, which is not easy to differentiate from the mythical dimension. It is an attempt to give system, clarity and intellectual power to the story, or myth, and determines how that story should be enacted in ritual. The doctrinal dimension articulates what a particular religion formally teaches about issues like creation, God and the predicament of humanity. In recounting the story of Adam and Eve, for example, Christianity posited the idea of "original sin", which Judaism did not. Simply put, in Christianity people sin *because* Adam sinned. In Judaism they sin *as* Adam did. Arising out of the same myth in this instance, the doctrines, or formal teachings, of the two religions differ markedly.

The fourth dimension, the ethical dimension, tells members of a particular religion what their moral obligations to their fellow human beings are, particularly to those less fortunate than they. Failure to observe the ethical commandments of a particular religion has social consequences, such as a gap between rich and poor, or neglect of widows and orphans. This dimension expresses the ideal way that people should relate to one another, but it is people's actual behaviour that shapes the lifestyles and institutions of society, which constitute the fifth, or social, dimension of religion.

The last dimension is the experiential one, and represents the feelings people experience as part of their religious expression. Emotions – such as hope, fear, confidence, joy, tranquillity – are experienced by individuals or groups. This is what keeps the other dimensions alive and meaningful. The experiential dimension concerns the feeling that derives out of contact with some kind of invisible world. It is the absence of this experience in ideologies like Marxism or Nazism that, according to Smart, disqualifies them as religions. The experiential dimension is so vital, according to Smart, that he has called his excellent introduction to world religions *The Religious Experience of Mankind*.

It is difficult to separate the various dimensions in any religion, and this is the case also with Judaism. The mythological dimension constitutes the basis of what it means to be a Jew. Out of the story of the people's origin, with the Exodus from Egypt, all else flows. Like any other religion, Judaism is not a monolith and has not remained static. The principles that have remained constant, however, all find their origins in Judaism's mythical dimension. As we will see, the hostility to Jews in the Hellenistic pagan world was intricately tied in with Jewish monotheism and the fact that it demanded a distinct separation of Jews from the larger society.

JUDAISM'S UNDERSTANDING OF HISTORY

The Jews' mythical dimension, or master story, is the Exodus from Egypt, in which God chose a small band of slaves as his "treasured possession" (Exodus 19:5), delivered them from bondage and called upon them to live by his commandments. The Jews' story is, however, linked to a larger world-encompassing one in that it promises to bring about a transformation of the entire world. All the world's people will be brought into the service of the one God when he establishes his Kingdom on earth. The whole of Jewish history – and indeed world history, from the Jewish perspective – pivots around this central event.

As Goldberg points out, when we try to explain Jewish survival today we can only do so by telling a story. It is through the telling of a story that Jews keep alive their tradition and pass it on from one generation to the next. The Torah, the holy book of the Jews, calls upon Jewish parents to explain to their children, on the festival of Passover, the origins of the Jewish people through telling the story of the Exodus. "On that day you shall tell your child, 'This commemorates what the Lord did for *me* when I came out of Egypt'" (Exodus 13:8). Every Jew is to experience anew each year the wonder of freedom and the gratitude he or she personally owes to God for the unmerited miracle that he wrought for the people. The mythological dimension is thus kept alive through ritual.

The Exodus is a fulfilment of a promise made much earlier to Abraham that he would be the father of a great nation and that his descendants would live in the land that God had promised him (Genesis 12). Only with the Exodus from Egypt, in about 1250 BCE, were the Jewish people formed; God later entered into a covenant (*berit*) with them that would make them a kingdom of priests and a holy nation (Exodus 19:5–6). Holiness in Judaism, *kadosh*, means "set apart". The Jews were to be holy because their God was holy. Just as he, the only power in the world worthy of worship, was different from all else in the world, so they would have to live a lifestyle that was different from that of all other peoples. By living in this manner, the Jews would be a constant witness to God's power. God would keep them alive so that he could bring about his ultimate purpose for the world. By the same token, as Goldberg (1995, p. 94) perceptively points out, by witnessing to God's actions in history, the Jewish people would keep alive, in the world at large, God's reputation as the God of infinite mercy and power.

Jews know God through the series of covenantal promises that he has made to them, and his reputation stands or falls by whether he keeps those promises. Jews have suffered enormously throughout history, the most catastrophic event to have befallen them being the Holocaust. This led to the most important question for modern Jewish theology: Where was God while six million of his chosen people were being mercilessly slaughtered? If God is the Lord of history, how did he allow this to happen? Should so great a disaster not result in doubt about God's power and goodness? A pertinent response to this, with regard to our present discussion, is offered by Michael Goldberg (1995, p. 16). The fact that Jews have survived against the most impossible of odds, he suggests, serves to demonstrate God's power. It is not the individual Jew that God promised to keep alive, but the community. "You are my servant, Israel, through whom I shall win glory" (Isaiah 43:9–12). God ensures the ultimate survival of the Jewish people because his own survival in the world depends on it. The task of the Jews is to live by God's commandments, to remember his great acts and to tell the story faithfully.

Just as all events before the Exodus make sense only in relation to the historical redemption of the Jews from slavery in Egypt, all later events derive their meaning from the covenant that followed. The prophets retell the story, constantly calling the Jewish people back to loyalty to God's commandments. What makes the Jewish myth unique among religious myths is that it took place within history, investing time with meaning. Because the Jewish mythological dimension was, with considerable adaptation, taken over by Christianity, it affected the entire Western world and its conception of time. "History", as Yosef Hayim Yerushalmi points out, is usually seen as being in direct contradiction to "myth". But in Judaism the two are fused because, through their particular understanding of myth, the Jews were the first people to give historic time significance.

Primal societies regard mythic, rather than historical, time as "real". Mythic time is the time of primeval beginnings and paradigmatic first acts, the "dreamtime" when the world was new, suffering unknown, and humans consorted with the gods. The present historical moment has little value in such societies, and achieves meaning only through ritual or the re-enactment of myth. During ritual performance, the present time is transcended and the participant is able to experience, very briefly, the "true" time of origins and archetypes.

For Jews, all meaning is based ultimately on their understanding of God as the God who acts in history. According to Huston Smith (1958, p. 272), Judaism is characterised by its search for meaning in every aspect of existence, and it is precisely this that lifted the Jews from obscurity to permanent religious greatness. Through the master story of the Exodus from Egypt, the Jews gave the world monotheism, the belief not only in God's oneness, but in his goodness. It is the nature of God that invests his oneness with ultimate significance. Other peoples may have their gods, but only one is worthy of worship: the creator of all, the almighty power in the world, the God who is concerned for the well-being of his creation. He is a personal God with whom human beings can enter into a relationship and Jews affirm his greatness constantly. The central conviction of Judaism is encapsulated in the *shema*:[2] "Hear O Israel, the Lord our God, the Lord is one" (Deuteronomy 6:4). Forming the basic credo of Judaism, these words are read in formal prayer twice daily. The *shema* is the first prayer a child learns, and should be the last words on the lips of a Jew at death. It is also the passage that is contained in the *mezzuzah*, which is affixed to the doorposts of Jewish homes to remind Jews of God's goodness and their obligation to him on that account.

In his 2001 book, *Radical Then, Radical Now*, the chief rabbi of Great Britain, Jonathan Sacks, pointed out that the genius of the Jews lies in the fact that they introduced a radically new concept of God that would change the world forever. Through the Exodus, God had shown himself to be on the side of the oppressed. Whereas, before, in what Sacks calls "the world of myth" – using the word "myth" very differently from the way in which it is used in this book – the gods were capricious and spiteful, warring with one another for power, the God of the Jews is the single supreme will, who desires the freedom and dignity of all human beings. Whereas, before, kings were privileged, with lesser humans being subject to their whims, now, all were under God's command, and entitled to equal justice. The emphasis was now on those whom the usual channels of power generally shunt to the sidelines; the poor, the widow and the orphan. Implicit in the Jews' understanding of God is that the world is not as it ought to be, and can only be brought to perfection through human effort in faithfulness to God's will, and that faith is born, not in harmony, but in dissonance. Rather than ziggurats and pyramids, Jews built monuments to life: the family, education, the conversation between the generations, and places of study and prayer, finding eternity in simple things.[3]

As the merciful redeemer, God is working, through the limitations of history, to bring about history's consummation, but the Jews have a special role in this process. They were chosen as God's partners to bring about a total transformation of the world from a place of strife to one of peace. In Jewish prophetic understanding, the world would be so altered at the end of time, or in the messianic age, that the lion would lie down with the lamb, nations would forge their swords into ploughshares, and peace would reign. Everyone would come to recognise the greatness and mercy of the one God and the Jews' vision would be vindicated. As the God who acts in history, as Smith (1958, p. 238) points out, God reveals himself in events that are unique, particular and unrepeatable. History is thus the arena of God's purposive activity.

The Exodus, therefore, is the central event in the Bible, which, as Yerushalmi (1999) points out, records only those facts believed to be important. Though a book of history, it does not conform to modern historiography. In accounts about kings like Omri, for example, all we are told is that they did evil in God's eyes. Judged by political standards, Omri was a capable king, but in the Bible the only thing worthy of note was his disobedience. God's acts of intervention in history and how the Jewish people responded to them – challenge and response – are what constitute history. Hardly a catalogue of heroic deeds, as Yerushalmi points out, much of biblical history seems designed to deflate national pride.

THE ESSENTIALS OF BIBLICAL HISTORY

The essential facts of biblical history start with the wanderings of the patriarchs – Abraham, Isaac and Jacob – in the ancient Middle East during the second millennium BCE and their subsequent descent to the land of Egypt. There their descendants (the Jewish people) became slaves and were redeemed by God. Acting through his prophet Moses, God took them out of Egypt and led them to a land that he had already promised to the patriarchs. During a forty-year period of wandering in the desert, God entered into a covenant with them. They then settled in the land, forming the covenant community around the twelve tribes of Israel. A monarchy subsequently arose, with a succession of three kings – Saul, David and Solomon. Solomon built the first temple in Jerusalem. It was considered to be God's dwelling place, but in a spiritual sense only, since it was devoid of images. A meeting place and rallying point for the Jewish people, it was also the place where sacrifices to God were performed.

After Solomon's death, the kingdom split into two, the northern Kingdom of Israel and the southern Kingdom of Judah. The first was conquered by the Assyrians in 721 BCE and its population – later to become known as the Ten Lost Tribes of Israel – was deported. The Kingdom of Judah was sacked by the Babylonians in 586 BCE, but this time only the leadership was deported. Although this brought about the first exile to Babylon, it also permitted the possibility of a return. When the Persians conquered the Babylonians in 538 BCE, under King Cyrus, the Jews were encouraged to return to Judah and rebuild their temple. But the Jews in Babylon had settled down there, and only a few made the arduous journey back. Thus, a diaspora (Greek for "dispersion") was formed, which persists until this day. In about 332 BCE Alexander the Great conquered the Persians. Because of the return to Judea under Cyrus, Jews now lived both in the diaspora and on their own land in Judea, Samaria and Galilee. At this point, the biblical account ends. Jewish history does not, of course, stop there and for the purposes of this chapter we need to take it further into the post-biblical period, particularly the Hellenistic period, of which there will be more later. Let us return to the master story of the Exodus from Egypt, to tease out its meaning.

THE MEANING OF THE EXODUS

The Exodus, as the "root experience"[4] of Judaism, against which all other events derive their meaning, is made up of a complex of interconnected ideas. Because God had responded to their pain by mercifully delivering them, the Jews concluded that they had been chosen. Having nothing to do with racial superiority or privilege, the Jewish doctrine of chosenness places upon Jews special accountability – to live by the rules of the covenant that God was to enter into with them. Moses came, not in the name of the creator of heaven and earth, but in the name of the God of the fathers, Abraham, Isaac and Jacob – the God who had already revealed himself in history. He was now interacting intimately with a specific people, even though he was creator of all life.

Moses was to lead the people out, a task made more difficult by the fact that God had hardened Pharaoh's heart, making him resistant to letting them go. This led to God bringing upon the Egyptians the ten plagues, the last of which, the slaying of the first-born, forced Pharaoh's hand. The angel of death passed over Jewish homes, whose doorways had been marked with the blood of the paschal lamb (Exodus 12:13), but the Egyptian first-born were slain. When Pharaoh later changed his mind, the sea opened for the Jews, but the pursuing Egyptians were drowned. Throughout, God is the hero of the story, the mounting drama of which, affirms God's glory and might, so that the Egyptians, too, would know that he was Lord (Exodus14:4). God's mercy was reserved for the Jews. As we will see in chapter 4, this portrayal of the Egyptians as the negative butt of the Jewish myth of origin was to result in a virulent form of pagan antisemitism, of specifically Egyptian provenance.

During a forty-year sojourn in the desert, God appeared to the people in a frightening theophany on Mount Sinai. He introduced himself to the entire people in terms of what he had already done for them: "I am the Lord who brought you out of the land of Egypt" (Exodus 20:2). God now commanded them to *remember* these deeds and to show their indebtedness to him by observing the commandments that he was about to give them. Memory of God's deliverance of the people thus became crucial to Israel's faith and existence. Jews are the only people, as Yerushalmi points out, who are commanded by God to remember (*zakhor*). The core of the Jews' memory was their slave origin and the recognition that their present position was owed only to God's mercy. That memory was to become the foundation of Jewish ethics. "The stranger who sojourns with you shall be to you as the native among you, and you shall love him as yourself; for you were strangers in the land of Egypt" (Leviticus 19:34).

The concept of chosenness is inseparable from the Jewish understanding of covenant. God entered into an agreement with the whole people that they would keep their part of the bargain in the new land to which he would lead them. Commanded to live by the dictates of the Torah, the Jews were to be holy in the same way that God is holy. They were thus set apart from other peoples in the world, living by particular commandments, known as *mitzvot*. The word "Torah" means "instruction"; its separate *mitzvot* instruct the lives of the Jewish people. The words "Torah" and "covenant" are interchangeable. The Jews are not to worship anyone or anything other than God, and should not make graven images of him. Idolatry, in Judaism, is more than the mere worship of images, however. It is the raising of any relative value to ultimacy.

Traditional Judaism does not make a distinction between the moral and the ritual, or ceremonial, *mitzvot*. Both must be observed with equal seriousness in order to make manifest God's holy character in the world. Judaism is thus intimately involved with "duties" rather than "rights", emphasising the collective rather than the individual. Because the redemption of the Jews will bring about the redemption of the entire world, what Jews do is important to history as a whole. As Huston Smith (1958, p. 269) put it, history is "in tension between its divine potentialities and its present frustrations. There is a profound disharmony between God's will and the existing social order." Jews are meant to be God's co-workers in helping to make the world aware of his will, and thus in changing the world for the better.

The Jewish people see themselves as constituting one big family – not fragmented and alienated individuals, but an organic whole – made up of individual families. These are the building blocks of the big Jewish "family", whose distinct duty and particular lifestyle are based on its own peculiar historic experience and intimate relationship with God. Members of the Jewish family are connected in both time and space, their bonds extending backwards to Abraham and forwards to all future Jews. The prayers that are uttered by Jews on one side of the world are the same as those offered, on the same day, by Jews on the other, some of them, in essence, going back almost two millennia. Jews generally pray not as individuals, but as a community. When praying on the day of

Atonement, for example, Jews confess their sins in the first person plural, repenting and asking forgiveness for the sins "we" have committed. God gave the covenant to the people as a whole, into the public, not the private sphere. The Jew does not, therefore, look for God in the private sphere. The shared experience is primary.

Associated with the ideas of chosenness, covenant and promise of land are the concepts of reward and punishment. If the Jewish people were faithful to God's commandments, they would live safely in their land. If not, they would be exiled from it. Thus, defeat – or the loss of the land – was understood in terms of divine punishment. The Holy Land is God's possession; Jews have been given tenancy in it. Even outside their land, however, God's covenant with his people remains eternal.

The doctrine of chosenness, as we will see, has had some problematic results. Though anything but a notion of racial superiority, it has been misinterpreted and mimicked over time; the most dangerous instance was Hitler's claim that the Germans were the chosen people. Already in pagan times, the doctrine was seen as ethnocentric. With the emergence of Christianity, it resulted in friction that is reminiscent of sibling rivalry. This will be discussed in chapters 5 and 6. The separateness that was engendered by the Jewish belief in chosenness was, however, to have more immediate consequences in the pagan world.

THE JEWS IN EXILE

Jews have spent more time outside their promised land than in it. Enforced living outside the land is understood as exile, or *galut*. But God, too, is in exile. His divine presence is with the people and he suffers alongside them. As indicated above, there have been two major exiles and, after the second one, in 70 CE, the Jewish people were dispersed throughout the world. For almost two thousand years, until the re-establishment of the state of Israel in 1948, they lived as a minority people in other lands. Jews lived under a series of powers: first the Babylonians, then the Persians, the Greeks and the Romans.

The Babylonian exile was formative for the Jewish people. Distinct patterns of faith were established that reinforced their separateness. Particular emphasis was placed on circumcision, sabbath observance, keeping the dietary laws and marrying within the faith. One of the institutions that arose at this time was the synagogue, or "place of assembly" for worship, study and fellowship. It took over as Judaism's most vital institution after the destruction of the second temple. Babylon later became an important centre of Jewish learning, where the Babylonian Talmud – or *Talmud Bavli* – was produced. Persian rule, as we have noted, tended to be tolerant of religious minorities and it was the Persian king Cyrus who allowed the Jews to build the second temple – at the expense of the royal treasury. In this period, the scriptures began to be collected. During the exile Ezra had renewed the oral tradition of reading and interpreting the Torah, enabling Judaism to survive in the absence of a temple and a territorial homeland.

The Hellenistic period was inaugurated by the conquests of Alexander the Great (365–323 BCE). He established great cities and encouraged the Jews to settle in them. The Egyptian city of Alexandria, which he named after himself, became an important cultural centre of Hellenism, soon replacing Athens in importance. But it also became an important Jewish centre: at one stage, forty per cent of its population were Jewish. By the time of Alexander, Jews were famed for their antiquity, a quality respected by the Greeks and later the Romans. Alexander opened up the Middle East, encouraging the growth of trade between the new cities. The Jews of the diaspora made up an important part of the population, constituting some ten to twelve per cent of Hellenistic society as a whole.

The word "Hellenism" refers to the form of Greek civilisation that spread through the Middle East and Mediterranean countries after Alexander's conquests and persisted well into the period of the Roman Empire. With Hellenism, the Jews were confronted with the tidal wave of a universal society revolving around Greek language and culture. As Joel Carmichael (1992, p. 2) points out, under previous Babylonian and Persian hegemony, there were congeries of relatively isolated states and societies. Absorption into Babylonian society made one merely a Babylonian. Absorption into Greek culture, on the other hand, made one a citizen of the world. The Hellenistic period was thus characterised by the clash of two universal cultures.

The idea that God chose the Jewish people results in a tension in Judaism between God's universality and the particular mission of the Jewish people. Only the Jews are obliged to live according to the laws of the covenant. The rest of the world, if it lived according to the seven Noachide commandments[5] – an attempt at ecumenism by rabbinic Judaism – would inherit the world to come. From the beginning, Jews differentiated between themselves as the children of Israel and the gentiles, or *goyim* (the nations). Although people are inclined to see this as ethnocentrism, it should be understood as an essential part of the Jews' myth of their origin as a people. The Jews conceived of their emergence and their relationship with God in terms of a close familial relationship – like father to son, or husband to wife. Only when the notion of chosenness became universalised by Christianity and later Islam, as Henri Atlan (1987) points out, did the idea of singling out a particular people become a scandal. However, Judaism's universal claims had already clashed with the universal culture of the Greeks.

Many Jews found Hellenistic culture profoundly seductive, while others rejected all that Hellenism stood for. There was also a reciprocal attraction to Judaism among some pagans. Others, however, were indifferent and, occasionally, hostile. Because so many Jews were attracted to Greek culture, some, like the philosopher Philo of Alexandria (50 BCE to 20 CE) or the historian Flavius Josephus, tried to reconcile Judaism with Greek thought. Philo did this by using allegory, producing ideas, like the divine *Logos* (Word), as the mediator through which the world was created. He was trying to emphasise the universal and spiritual aspects of Judaism that could demonstrate its attractiveness to gentiles. Some of these Hellenising ideas were later incorporated into Christianity, such as Christ as the divine *Logos*, as well as ideas such as circumcision of the heart rather than of the flesh.

There is a broad consensus that Judaism was at that time an actively proselytising religion, though a few scholars challenged this in the 1990s.[6] Not all who were attracted to it became full converts, however. There were many gentile God-fearers who observed many of the Jewish laws and customs and clustered around the synagogues, but who did not necessarily follow the dietary laws or submit to circumcision. The situation of the Jews under Hellenism was paradoxical. It was a paradigmatic instance of the capacity of Judaism to enrich itself through contact with and absorption of Greek ideas, but without losing itself.

For those pagans who were not attracted to Judaism, it was not the issue of one God that was strange – polytheism allowed people any number of gods. Rather, it was the barrier created by the demands of Jewish ritual that made social intercourse difficult. The "Jewish cluster of beliefs and customs", as Carmichael (1992, p. 3) points out, "seemed a kind of bizarre arrogance, the bodiless God a form of atheism, the observance of the Sabbath, incomprehensible to the ancient world, a proof of morbid indolence". Greek culture was regarded as the standard for humane existence, and the Jews' refusal to become completely assimilated was somewhat insulting. But the damage was limited because the Jewish worldview was not taken seriously and was not seen to have any bearing on the destiny of other peoples.

The reshaping of Judaism after the Babylonian exile had allowed the Jews to retain their religious beliefs and practices in a strange land. Unlike the many other people who were displaced by wars and deportations and, mingling with the surrounding populations, disappeared into them, Jews retained their identity. A number of religious practices kept them a distinct group. Many of the laws were, from the beginning, designed to distinguish them from other people and to physically separate them. Circumcision and the observance of the sabbath made them obviously different from the rest of society. They had to observe certain dietary laws that forced them to eat separately. They did not intermarry with pagans. Some of their important festivals – like Passover, Pentecost and Tabernacles – were both religious and national. Wherever they lived, Jews continued to make an annual contribution to the temple in Jerusalem, and to accept the Jerusalem authorities as their religious and, in a sense, political leaders.

THE BACKLASH AGAINST HELLENISM

Although Hellenism exerted a profound attraction on some Jews, the very fact that it did so created a backlash among Jewish pietists. The Maccabean uprising of 167 BCE was, in fact, a civil war against Antiochus IV Epiphanes, who had tried to force Hellenism on the Jews and, thereby, to homogenise the population under his control. The miracle that the oil to keep a flame burning in the temple sufficient for one day lasted for eight is still celebrated by Jews on the festival of *Hanukah*, the festival of Lights. The Jewish aristocracy played along with Antiochus because they wanted to rid themselves of their separateness. The Maccabees, for whom these were apostates, wrested Judea from the Greek dynasty, the Seleucids, to which Antiochus belonged, and restored the Jewish national state, which was then governed independently for about a century by the Hasmoneans. It was from this century or so of self-government, according to Carmichael, that actively malicious legends about Jews began to circulate. This will be explained in the next chapter on pagan antisemitism.

The Hasmonean state was soon overshadowed by the rise of the Roman Empire, and passed into the hands of the Romans in 63 BCE when

Pompey marched into Jerusalem. Roman culture, too, was universal. It absorbed Greek culture, becoming its channel, but adding to it military and administrative apparatus that absorbed whole peoples. The Romans, like the Greeks, recognised the antiquity of the Jewish scriptures, which warranted Judaism being given the status of a *religio licita*, a permitted, or officially franchised, religion. They were generally disinterested in the religions of their subjects, provided the latter did not challenge Roman political power, something that the Jews were later to do on three separate occasions.

SECOND TEMPLE JUDAISM

What we call "second temple Judaism" was coterminous with the second temple that was destroyed in 70 CE, after the first rebellion of the Jews against Rome that started in 66 CE. There is clear evidence of pagan animosity against Jews, but it was also in second temple times that Christianity emerged from the matrix of Judaism and began to conflict with it. Neither development can be understood in isolation from what may be called the "Kingdom of God activists", Jewish groups who believed that only by armed rebellion could Roman occupation be ended and the messianic era inaugurated. They were trying to force God to re-enter history, or to "hasten the end" through armed struggle. Pagan and Christian hostility to Jews must have been shaped by this revolutionary activity, but it must also have been influenced by the nature of Judaism at that time, and how it may have been perceived. In trying to ascertain this, however, we are presented with a number of difficulties. The main one is that the rabbis – who arose out of the Pharisees and were the only sect to survive the rebellion – did not record the history of their times. As Yerushalmi points out, although the Bible was a historic document, post-biblical Judaism was not interested in historiography, the accurate recording of historic events. What we do know is that, during Hellenistic times, several Jewish sects emerged in response to Hellenism. Josephus notes the existence of the Pharisees, the Saduccees, the Essenes and the Zealots, which shows that there were several ways of being Jewish. Another was by being a Jewish Christian, a Jew who accepted that Jesus was the messiah. It was only after 70 CE, with the second exile, that rabbinic Judaism took the lead and became the dominant strain in Judaism. This form of Judaism was dominant for almost two millennia. As we shall see in chapter 8, it was challenged by post-Enlightenment

Jewish thought, from which new forms of Judaism, like reform and conservative Judaism, emerged. Thereafter, rabbinic Judaism became known as "orthodox" Judaism. The modern movements have developed different ideas on key issues from those outlined below. Reform Judaism, for example, introduced the idea of a messianic age, rather than a messianic figure, and emphasised ethical over ritual commandments. In its initial phases, it did not deem it desirable for Jews to emphasise a national element and a return to Zion. Rather, they should become more like than unlike the society that surrounded them. Orthodoxy emphasises the idea of the Jews as the "suffering servant" (Isaiah 53), the people "who dwell alone and shall not be reckoned among the nations" (Numbers 23:9) and whose vision will ultimately be vindicated when the world recognises the one true God. Reform's idea of chosenness stresses the idea of the Jews being more integrated into the wider society and becoming a moral "light unto the nations" (Isaiah 42:6).

We have already seen that Jews are commanded to remember, but they are not expected to remember everything. It is *what* they are commanded to remember and the *way* it is remembered that are important. Their memory centres on their experience of God as he acted on their behalf in history, and the manner by which they remember is through ritual and recitation. A superlative example is the declaration from Deuteronomy 26 that the Jew makes at the giving of the first fruits, or in recalling the Exodus from Egypt at the festival of Passover:

> A wandering Aramean was my father, and he went down into Egypt, and sojourned there, few in number; and he became there a nation, great, mighty, and populous. And the Egyptians dealt ill with us, and afflicted us, and laid upon us hard bondage. And we cried unto the Lord, the God of our fathers, and the Lord heard our voice, and saw our affliction, and our toil, and our oppression. And the Lord brought us forth out of Egypt with a mighty hand, and with an outstretched arm, and with great terribleness, and with signs, and with wonders. And He has brought us into this place, and has given us this land, a land flowing with milk and honey.
>
> Deuteronomy 25:5–9

Here, in what Yerushalmi calls "capsule history at its best", all the essentials of Jewish memory appear in one ritualised formula, which tells of the historic emergence of the people within the limitations of time.

The Jews' obligation to remember overflowed into a historical text, the Bible. Written over about a millennium, by a succession of anonymous authors, it became the most distinguished corpus of historical writing in the ancient Middle East. Though the account tells of the actions of men and women, the deeds of Israel, and the nations, the true hero of Jewish history is God. History was a theophany, and all events were interpreted in the light of Jews' response. The result is not theology, says Yerushalmi, but history on an unprecedented scale. Judaism's mythic dimension is embedded in historic concreteness. One incident is not blurred with another and discrepancies are allowed to remain. Biblical characters emerge as individuals, not as types and chronology is respected throughout. Although the Bible may not be factual history in the modern sense of the word, it is not fictitious either. It is a legitimate means of understanding and interpreting events. According to Yerushalmi (1999, p. 14), the Bible links meaning in history, memory of the past, and the writing of history in a web of delicate and reciprocal relationships. In post-biblical Judaism, however, these are pulled asunder.

A REVEALED PATTERN OF HISTORY

For the rabbis, whose task it was to keep Jews and Judaism alive in the absence of a land and a temple, the Bible was not only a repository of the past history, but a revealed pattern of the whole of history. Knowing the scriptures intimately, and basing their beliefs on them, the rabbis knew that history had a purpose, which was the establishment of the Kingdom of God on earth. The Jewish people had a pivotal role to play in the process. Though Jews had often rebelled against God's will, and suffered the consequences, the true pulse of history, the rabbis affirmed, beat beneath the manifest surface of events. There was, as Yerushalmi (1999, p. 21) points out, an invisible history more real than what the world, deceived by more strident outward rhythms of power, could recognise. The Jews' particular responsibility remains central and they continue to constitute the centre of world history.

It was not the great powers – like Assyria and Rome – that were the makers of history, but God. The former were merely the instruments of his divine wrath against Israel, though they themselves may not have realised it at the time. Jerusalem had fallen not because of Nebuchadnezzar's might, but because Israel had sinned. God had allowed it to fall. The triumphalism of the nations, the rabbis taught, would be rebuked by the presence of the "suffering servant" of Israel, who one day would be redeemed by the messiah, and the Kingdom of God instituted. As the rabbis understood it, present events were illuminated by the Bible. Just as the exile of 586 BCE owed to sin, so did the catastrophe of 70 CE. The rabbis needed no new view of history to accommodate either Rome or any subsequent conqueror. The new situation of landlessness was given meaning by the idea that the Roman triumph would not endure for ever. With the coming of the messiah, the return of the Jews to their homeland, and the world itself redeemed, the affairs of Rome would be inconsequential.

The Bible, for the rabbis, constituted a constantly renewable lease on life for the Jewish people. For the first time, the history of a people became part of its sacred scripture. From rabbinic times until the present, the Torah has been interpreted orally by an unbroken chain of scholars. Though it was recorded long ago – in a constantly receding past – that past remains ever relevant. The Torah was to become the patrimony of the whole Jewish people for all time. It is read aloud in the synagogue from beginning to end during the course of a year, and is copied faithfully by hand by properly qualified scribes. With the closure of canon in about 100 CE, Jews stopped writing history. The last historian to write was Josephus, who wrote up until about 94 CE. The future belonged to the rabbis. It was fifteen centuries before another Jew would call himself a historian.[7] The impulse to historiography had ceased.

Yerushalmi suggests that the commandment to remember has kept Jews alive in global dispersion for almost two thousand years. If history is real, events happen only once. There was only one Sinai, but the covenant given there endures for ever. It was delivered both for those who were present *and* for those who were not (Deuteronomy 29:13–14). For those not there that day, the memory of what transpired has had to be faithfully transmitted. Though rabbinic thought may seem to be a flight from history, it is saturated with history.

RABBINIC *MIDRASH*

The method used by the rabbis to mine the treasures buried beneath the surface of the Torah is known as *midrash*, a word that means "to seek out" or "to enquire about" the meaning underlying the written text. There are two types of rabbinic *midrash*: *halakhic* (or legal) extrapolations and *aggadic* (or narrative) explications. An example of the former is the entire body of laws concerning the separation of milk from meat products, which grew out of a single line – stated on three occasions – in the Torah: "You shall not boil a kid in the milk of its mother."[8] Consuming milk and meat together was associated with idolatry, but the rabbis also saw the prohibition as an ethical injunction. They interpreted it to refer to any mixing of milk and meat, and thus formulated a whole body of oral laws that prohibited the two from being cooked together, eaten together or served from the same plates. Utensils used for meat may not even be washed together with those used for milk. The oral laws thus served to specify details when such details were absent in the written Torah.

The *aggadic midrashim* are narrative speculations on the nature of God, creation and the world. They are philosophical musings that establish the theological and ethical framework in which the *halakhot* (laws) are to be performed. An example is the answer that derives from the question: "Why was man created on the sixth day (after the creation of all other creatures)?" We are told that man was created at this stage "so that, should he become overbearing, he can be told, 'The gnat was created before you were.'" Another striking example is the *midrash* on the line from the Song of Songs, "Open to me my love, my dove" (5:2). The rabbis interpreted this erotic invitation, in a frank love poem, as "Open to me the gate of repentance as much as the eye of a needle, and I will open for you gates (of forgiveness) wide enough for carriages and wagons to pass through." It was this type of interpretation that enabled the Song of Songs to be included in the canon at all, because it was interpreted as an expression of the intimate, loving relationship between God and his people Israel.

In the Talmud,[9] the later compilation of the oral Torah, Yerushalmi stresses, the rabbis were on very different ground from the biblical authors. Now they entered freely into discussions on the pre-creation period, speculating about mythical monsters and the like. They fleshed out the characters of the Bible, discussing their fears, hopes and motivations. In the process, the rabbis played with time as though it was an accordion, expanding and collapsing it at will. The Talmud is filled with anachronisms, like the patriarchs instituting the three daily prayer services that were, in fact, only finalised millennia later. For example, in their elaboration of the story of the rape of Dinah, she is represented as going out to see the daughters of the land (Genesis 34:1) while her father and brothers were studying in the *yeshiva*, the most hallowed of duties, as it later came to be in rabbinic Judaism. The *yeshiva*, where Jews sit and study the Torah through its oral interpretations, was a rabbinic, and not a biblical, institution. Biblical events are thus placed in an ever fluid dialogue with one another, and characters who lived millennia ago are brought into the living present. Similarly, elements of biblical history can be telescoped into legendary dimensions with no compromise of the past as recorded in the Bible. As Pinchas Hacohen Peli (1991, p. 105) points out, the enchanted world of *aggadah* transcends time and space. In the "creative historiography" of the *midrash*, Abraham can easily strike up a conversation with Queen Esther, since they both inhabit the biblical universe. Likewise, Moses can carry on a dialogue with King David, and what is so remarkable is that we can listen in.

Thus, the patriarchs are alive today as part of the family of Jews and they serve as contemporary models for Jewish practice. The rabbis knew very well what an anachronism was and they were anything but naïve. They were able to sustain and reconcile historical contradictions, the study of the Talmud probably being one of the finest aids to lateral thinking. The biblical text, itself, remained inviolate. The rabbis had always to return to it before their next flight of *aggadic* imagination. But the events in the Bible could be retold and reinterpreted in a multiplicity of different ways so that they could speak to the present situation.

Although we can discern the history of the biblical period in the Bible itself, and much of it has been confirmed by archaeology, we cannot discern the history of the talmudic period in the Talmud, since it is ahistorical. The rabbis paid little attention to post-biblical events and did not take up history where the Bible left off. The Talmud was never intended as history. The rabbis already had the history of the biblical period and did not set out to repeat it. What they did seek to do was to interpret it for their generation and all the generations of Jews that followed. The law about an eye for an eye and a tooth for a tooth, or the *lex talionis*, for example, was interpreted in terms of monetary compensation. Only in this form is the law binding, since both the oral and the written Torah, according to rabbinic Judaism, were revealed to Moses. By dating their interpretation back to Sinai, the rabbis were giving it legitimacy for all time.

Prophecy had ceased, but the rabbis saw themselves as the legitimate heirs to and interpreters of the prophets. They made the prophetic worldview their own. Just as the prophets had interpreted their own contemporary history, the rabbis, though silent on the actual events that took place in their own time, were interpreting them in terms of the wider meaning of history, locating them within a larger paradigm of redemption and exile. The rabbis viewed the mundane events of their time against a wider canvas. When they canonised the Bible about thirty years after the destruction of the second temple, they retained its historical books and gave them immortality. The Bible was, for them, an organic whole, which contained the Torah, the Prophets and other writings, including the most recent of all its books, the book of Daniel. Certain books were seen as inconsistent with the general message, so they were excluded. Regarded as the "hidden" books, they became known as the Apocrypha. Among them were historical works, like the Maccabees.

OTHER FORMS OF *MIDRASH*

The idea of *midrash*, or oral interpretation, thus assumes vital importance in Judaism, but it is vital to Christianity as well, particularly from the perspective of the development of antisemitism. Whereas the *midrash* on the Bible for Judaism is found in the Talmud, the *midrash* for Christianity on the same basic text, now called the "Old Testament", is found in the New Testament. Thus Judaism and Christianity offer two very different interpretations through which the written text is understood. This, as we will see in chapters 5 and 6, is one of the main reasons for the denigration of the Jews.

But there were many different kinds of *midrash* in second temple times. The various sectarian movements that existed in Judaism at the time each had their own ways of interpreting the text. These can be broadly grouped into three different orientations. The first, rabbinic *midrash*, we have already discussed. Of the other two, one arose out of an attraction to Hellenism and tried to reconcile traditional Jewish views with it – as had Philo. The other arose out of opposition to Hellenistic ideas. The first, according to Rosemary Ruether, can be categorised as "spiritualising *midrash*". Emphasising the universal aspects of Judaism, it saw Judaism's monotheism and ethics as compatible with Greek thought. Midrash of the second type was strongly influenced by Iranian dualism, which posited ideas of an impending cataclysm and a final struggle between good and evil. An important group favouring this latter approach was made up of those who believed that the end of days would only come about through violent armed rebellion against Rome.

Known also as the Kingdom of God activists, they wanted to hasten the coming of the messiah by overthrowing foreign rule. This motivation lay behind the Jewish rebellion of 66–70 CE and the Bar Kochba revolt of 132–135 CE.

The first group of *midrashim*, according to Ruether, were allegorical, whereas the latter were typological, moving from historical types in the past, towards culmination in messianic fulfilment. Although rabbinic interpretation does not differ from this category in terms of the expectation of a messiah, its reinterpretation of history resulted in the discouragement of any revolutionary action that would hasten the end. One of the reasons for the triumph of the Pharisaic party that grew into rabbinic Judaism, Ruether claims, was the fact that Christianity had utilised the Hellenistic, spiritualising *midrash* so extensively. The rabbis had to use all the means at their disposal to defend their people's religious identity and give them meaning in the face of the crushing defeats they had endured. One means was to keep out heretical teaching that could threaten the cohesion and survival of the Jewish community. The rabbis' particular interpretation of the Torah, to which we will now turn, was paramount, and was not to be diluted by beliefs that seemed to challenge monotheism, like the emerging belief in Jesus as the divine Word, or *Logos*, which to them suggested a "second god". It is in this light that one should see the *birkat ha-minim*, the curse – euphemistically called "blessing" – against heretics, that the rabbis instituted to try to exclude Christians – and other groups regarded as heretical, like the Zealots and Sadducees – from participating in synagogue worship. Formulated in about 85 CE, the curse was included with the "Eighteen Blessings", or *amidah*, which form an important part of every prayer service, as a nineteenth blessing. The *amidah* is the silent prayer of praise and supplication offered by the individual Jew, and then repeated aloud in congregation. It would have been impossible for Jewish Christians to lead the prayers in the synagogue, because they would have had to curse themselves. The curse did not imply loss of Jewish status to heretics, but prevented them making their beliefs public in the synagogue. They would have to either abandon their heresy or form their own congregations. It is, therefore, as William Nicholls (1995, p. 158) points out, inaccurate to say that Jews "expelled" Christians from the synagogue. The growth of gentile Christianity and the deteriorating situation between Jews and Christians was, however, to lead to intense rivalry between them. Protection of the rabbinic message, along with discouraging hastening the end, would serve to preserve the Jewish people. Three failed rebellions and the fact that rabbinic Judaism was formed in a mood of post-revolt consolidation encouraged pacifist teaching.

THE HALLOWING OF THE EVERYDAY ACT

The rabbis were confident that the messiah would come, but were not certain about *when*. Some believed that repentance and obedience would bring the messiah. Others said the event would take place independently, at the inscrutable initiative of the divine will. The question that remained was: how were Jews to live in the interim? Through their interpretation of scripture, the rabbis were offering not only meaning to the troubled times in which Jews were living, but a programme of life that would ensure Jewish survival in exile. With the aim of making Jews able to respond fully to the challenge of becoming a holy people, they established a society based entirely on rabbinic understanding of the Torah. This involved the study of the oral law – the fount of Jewish life – and the enacting of the fruits of such study through the hallowing of the everyday act. Each small action in everyday life was to be raised to holiness through appropriate prayers and rituals. The sacrifices that had been performed in the temple were thus replaced. The table, with its detailed commandments about *kashrut* (dietary laws), became the altar. Noteworthy for antisemitism's later development is the injunction prohibiting the ingestion of blood (Leviticus 17:10–14), which requires meat to be soaked and then salted before it is fit for consumption.

Jacob Neusner (1989) suggests that the *Mishnah*, the first body of oral laws to be written down, was a rabbinic response to the crisis of the fall of Jerusalem and the birth of Christianity. Its intricate and highly ordered wording patterns, for example, helped to express order in the face of the wider chaos, and its programme for life was vested in the family as the building block of Jewish society. Offering no history of the second temple period, the rabbis carefully kept the details of the temple ritual, because they believed the temple would soon be restored.

The *Mishnah*, which was finalised in about 200 CE, some 130 years after the destruction of the temple, demonstrated the rabbis' disinterest in current history: it was written as if the temple still stood. Not concerned with the history of Rome itself, the rabbis chose to remember Hadrian and the martyrdom of the Jewish scholars that had taken place under his rule at the time of the Bar Kochba rebellion, 132–5 CE.

This was the last hard-fought revolt by the Jews against the Romans, who had considerable difficulty in quelling it. The Roman casualties were so high that the emperor Hadrian, in his report to the Roman Senate, omitted the customary formula that he and his troops were well. Probably ignited by Hadrian's attempt to Hellenise the area, the revolt had messianic overtones in that it was a last attempt to overthrow Roman rule, regain the Holy Land and rebuild the temple. After the rebellion Hadrian barred the Jews from the city of Aelia Capitolina – built on the site of Jerusalem – outlawed Judaism in the Holy Land and executed the sages who had supported the revolt. Rabbi Akiva (who had hailed Bar Kochba as the messiah) was tortured to death, becoming, along with other scholars punished in this way, the prototype of the Jewish martyr, dying in honour of God's holy name.

Violence had failed to bring any fruit. The future, therefore, could wait. What was needed now was faithfulness to the *mitzvot* that would make God's character manifest in the world: trust, patience and prayer. God would ultimately restore the people to their land, and their temple would be rebuilt. With this, the entire world would be transformed.

RABBINIC RESPONSES TO HOSTILITY

Aggadic midrash allowed scope for endless speculation and flights of fantasy about the historic situation of the Jewish people and its two negative foci, the destruction of the temple, and the ongoing hostility of the gentiles. The *midrash* allowed the creation of another world, the "real" world, that interacts with the mundane world of history and struggle. Though history may continue in its bungling way, the events and characters in the Bible remain constant; typological elaboration upon them explaining current happenings. Though the temple had been destroyed as a result of Israel's sin, the exile and ongoing conflict would, with the coming of the messiah, end. Israel's faith would be vindicated.

The Jews were not alone in formulating commentary on why the Roman victory, the destruction of the temple and the dispersion of the Jews had taken place in 70 CE. Various interpretations were offered of the meaning of the event and what it implied for the future. As we will see in later chapters, the Romans saw it as just recompense for a rebellious people and as discrediting the Jewish God. The emerging Christian community interpreted it as punishment for rejecting Jesus as the messiah and, more especially, for the crime of deicide, discrediting not God, but the Jewish people. The Jews, too, saw the event as a result of sin, but they differed radically on the nature of the sin. According to the Christians, God had rejected the unrepentant Israel. The Jews were homeless and scattered because they deserved to be, and, until such time as they came to see their error, they would remain in this reprobate condition.

The rabbis wanted a positive message. The end of the temple resulted in the proclamation of the primacy of the Torah over the sacrificial cult. They gave no reply to the Christian conviction that the Jews had been punished. Suffering may have come from sin, but the church's interpretation was not the correct one. In some ways, as Norman Ravitch (1982) points out, life was more favourable for the Jews *after* the defeat of the Kingdom of God activists, those who believed that God's kingdom could be brought about only through violent overthrow of the Roman oppressors. The destruction of the temple was not given a central role by the rabbis, as Christian apologists had done. It was only with the establishment of Christianity as the imperial religion in the fourth century that the Jewish position began to deteriorate. In the non-Roman world, the Jews did not perceive their situation as unfavourable until the coming of Islam to the Babylonian heartland. The centrality of the destruction of the temple and discussion of the "woes of Israel", as Ravitch (1982, p. 44) points out, had long been a Christian theme, but was not a Jewish one.

The rabbis explained the ongoing hostility from the gentile world in the same way that they explained everything, in the form of the *midrash*. On the basis of the typological reasoning described above they tended to see the Romans as evil and persecutory. As we will see in the next chapter, on pagan antisemitism, however, this was not necessarily the case. The Jews were not treated more harshly than any other people under Roman hegemony. The Romans clamped down on the Jews specifically as a response to their rebellions and had, at times, tried to homogenise the culture of their subjects as an element of their statecraft. Thus, it is difficult to separate the rabbis' responses to antisemitism from accounts in which they describe their political occupiers.

The rabbinic response to gentile antagonism to Jews was not uniform. Different sages responded differently, and sometimes there was a shift in the approach of an individual sage. Though subtle and complex, rabbinic responses tended to see anti-Jewish animosity as eternal and inevitable. Jewish existence, they suggested, arouses, of itself, gentile hatred.

THE CONFLICT BETWEEN JACOB AND ESAU

A paradigm for all forms of anti-Jewish hostility was the conflict between Jacob and Esau, the warring twin brothers born to Isaac and Rebecca, whose original story is told in the book of Genesis. Jacob emerged from the womb after Esau, grasping his heel. Jacob, who was later renamed Israel – the one who struggles and will overcome – was mild and smooth skinned and did not go outside the camp. Esau, who was identified with Edom, an enemy of Israel, was wild, hairy, and an expert hunter. Isaac favoured Esau, whereas Rebecca favoured Jacob. Even in the womb they were in conflict, but two later incidents confirmed their rivalry so that it took on eternal proportions. The first was when Jacob, the younger twin, exploited his starving older brother's hunger by buying his birthright with a pot of lentils. The second was when Jacob, spurred on by his mother, deceived his aged and blind father by pretending to be Esau and obtaining Isaac's final blessing. Esau implored his father, "Have you only one blessing? Bless me, me also, father!" But it was too late. So "Esau lifted up his voice and wept" (Genesis 27:38). Ever after, "Esau hated Jacob" (33:4) and Jacob had to flee to escape Esau's murderous enmity.

The many trials that Jacob suffered thereafter became symbolic of those endured by the Jewish people. Years later, when the brothers came together, Esau ran to meet Jacob, fell on his neck, and they kissed and wept. The biblical account seems to end reasonably happily when the two brothers then go their separate ways. But the rabbinic *midrash* saw their conflict as eternal. In the biblical account, Rebecca, feeling their struggle in her womb, anxiously went to inquire of God. His answer described the relationship not so much of two brothers, but of two peoples, the Israelites and the Edomites. Thus each boy was to be a progenitor of a nation. The relationship between Jacob and Esau was spun out into a drama that started with their birth, and was taken, through the present, to the remote messianic future, when the conflict will be resolved and Esau's tears dried. Between these two poles in history, the rabbis predict an ongoing confrontation between Jews and gentiles, typologically represented by Jacob and Esau.

Esau was the direct grandfather of Amalek, who is cast as the enemy of Israel from as far back as the Exodus, where he was inexplicably present, blocking Israel's way (Exodus 17:8–16). The Amalekites were an ancient nomadic people who lived in the Sinai desert, and who viciously attacked the Jews while they were wandering in the desert on their way to the promised land. Whenever the Jews failed to abide by the covenant, Amalek is said to have prevailed over them. In this way, Esau became eponymous for any anti-Jewish regime, especially Christianity. Only with the messiah would the struggle between the two peoples come to an end and the last remnants of Amalek be destroyed. The model of Jacob–Esau, Israel–Amalek, was continually brought up to date to explain contemporary circumstances.

Pinchas Hacohen Peli (1991) points out that the rabbis do not see antisemitism as a deplorable one-sided act, committed by gentiles who are out to attack or destroy Israel. Rather, they treat it as an inevitable reality that Jews must learn to endure without either giving up in despair or trying in vain to address its causes. Part of the method of learning to live with the conflict is not to accept it passively, but to retaliate somehow. Since Jews did not have the armamentarium to retaliate physically, they responded on other, more psychological, levels. Moshe Davidowitz (1978) suggests that Jews dealt with the rage they must have felt at their degraded status by means of historical analogies, like the defeat of Pharoah in the Passover ceremony and the demise of Haman on Purim. Fully aware of the vicious attacks against their people, the rabbis saw the church, the Romans or indeed any oppressor as Esau/Edom/Amalek. Through the *midrash*, says Peli, they could offer a response that was proud, controlled and self-assured. Judaism *itself* was powerful. Its God would overcome all obstacles. Thus the Jews and Judaism never disintegrated under the indescribable pressures of irrational animosity.

4

Pagan antisemitism

Almost every note in the cacophony of medieval and modern antisemitism was sounded by the chorus of ancient writers.

Salo Baron

Not all the ancient charges have modern analogues and not all the modern charges have ancient roots.

Shaye Cohen

The last chapter spanned a long period, from the first religious claims of the Jewish people, and their settlement in their own homeland, to the inauguration of a two-thousand-year period of homelessness that started after the defeat of the Jewish rebellion from 66–70 CE. It described the complex background to the emergence of both Christianity and rabbinic Judaism. There were many streams of thought and religious ideas. Some pagans were attracted to Judaism, others to Christianity and yet others to any one of a whole range of ideas about salvation, including pagan mystery religion and gnosticism. Judaism, itself, was far from monolithic. There were, as Jacob Neusner frequently points out, several Judaisms rather than one unified Judaism, each sect believing itself to have the religious answer in troubled political times. Some of them had an apocalyptic worldview and were preparing the way for the messianic triumph and ingathering of the devoted community at the end of days. They expected a violent cataclysm between the forces of good and the forces of evil – an idea long borrowed from Persian dualism – and believed that the crisis era, ruled by evil powers, was soon to come to an end. The view of these messianic sects, from which Christianity was to emerge, was very different from the prophetic, historical future hope that eventually triumphed in rabbinic Judaism.

The last chapter also indicated that the Jews' religious perception of themselves has resulted in antagonism on a number of levels. The Jews, as Rubenstein and Roth (1987, p. 24) point out, affirmed that it was God who accounted for their existence. The fact that they continued to exist as a separate people, who "fell under Hitler's threat three thousand years later *does*", these authors assert (1987, p. 26), "depend on the tradition that God acted in history in the Exodus and at Sinai" (my emphasis). That action "singled out a people whose destiny would not only be linked with the land of Israel but also would set them apart from every other human group that has walked the face of the earth. With Moses, if not with God, the world received 'the Jewish question'. Nothing was ever the same again" (1987, p. 26).

Judged from this perspective, the roots of Jew hatred lie in Jewish religious claims themselves. But, though this indicates that anti-Jewish sentiment goes back a long time, it does not address Ettinger's question: when did the first "fundamental denial of Jewish worth" take place? Put differently, at what precise point were Jews first seen as lesser human beings? In this chapter I aim to discuss pre-Christian antisemitism to see how extensive it was, and how threatening. Most importantly, I will try to pin down its exact nature. We have already observed that, though antisemitism is difficult to define, it has an underlying quality that goes beyond mere denigration or even persecution. All forms of prejudice are dehumanising, in that they treat a targeted group as a monolith and endow all its members with permanent – usually negative – characteristics. But it is the demonisation of the Jews, and the attribution to them of a quality of cosmic and eternal evil that mark antisemitism. Though some scholars, like Peter Schafer (1997), see this kind of hatred as emerging in pagan times, there is a wider consensus that it arose only with Christianity. The problem, according to Gager (1983, p. 13), revolves around three axes:

- the relationship between pagan and Christian attitudes in early Christian times;
- the extent to which Judaism exerted a cultural force on the ancient world;
- the precise character and extent of pre-Christian antisemitism.

We noted in chapter 3 that Judaism exerted an attraction in the ancient world. We must wait until chapters 5 and 6 to get some clarity on the relationship between pagan and Christian antipathy to Jews. Let us now turn to the third of these axes.

IS PAGAN ANIMOSITY "ANTISEMITISM"?

Related to the division among scholars as to whether pagan or Christian antagonism laid the foundation for antisemitism is the question of whether it is legitimate to call resentment of Jews in the pagan world "antisemitism". The designation a particular scholar chooses is likely to correspond with the weight he or she gives to the influence of pagan attitudes on later antisemitism, and with the nature of the anti-Jewish animus that was expressed at the time. Shaye Cohen (1986, p. 43), for example, resists the designation "antisemitism" for the Jew hatred of antiquity. He cautions us that there are large gaps in our knowledge of antiquity because of a paucity of documents. More seriously, though, we tend to look at the past in terms of modern conditions, and to retroject the latter on to our understanding of the past, thus distorting it.

We are inclined to look for racial criteria as well as economic explanations for early Jew hatred. But there is general agreement among scholars that classical antisemitism was neither economic nor racial. They see it as a sociological reaction to the social consequences of Jewish law. They argue that pagan intellectuals, from whom most of the antisemitic writing derives, do not cite economic reasons for the intense hatred of the mob. There are also no specific sources on Jewish wealth, nor criticism of the Jews becoming affluent. Both Feldman (1986, p. 26) and Carmichael (1992, p. 3) suggest that the hatred of the mob had nothing to do with economics. Jews were widely perceived as paupers and beggars, they point out, and it was very often in this role that they were targeted by Jew haters. The slander that Jews were beggars probably derived from Judaism's emphasis on the giving of charity, but this same emphasis, in turn, attracted converts to Judaism, and such conversions themselves became a source of antagonism to Jews. Yet, the first-century CE Jewish historian Josephus did note that hatred, fear and greed for plunder motivated the mob. He saw Jews as superior in wealth and status. Economic issues may have had some bearing on anti-Jewish sentiment, but they do not explain it. Use of the term "antisemitism" to describe the pagan attitudes of antiquity, Cohen

(1986, p. 45) points out, is both anachronistic and misleading. It conjures up a vision of an irrational and deep-seated hatred of Jews, and it is far from certain that such an attitude existed in antiquity. Cohen, like many others, sees the term as describing a distinctly modern phenomenon.

Though not far removed in general sentiment, John Gager (1983, p. 8), is willing to call pagan anti-Judaism "antisemitism". Although the main thrust of his work is to reveal the complexity of Christianity's background and the wide range of attitudes to Jews in pagan antiquity, Gager sees distinct parallels between ancient and modern antisemitism. Both forms of hatred, claims Gager, were expressed by complete outsiders who were ignorant of Judaism, and in each case animosity was based on sweeping generalisations. He cautions us, however, that the negative views about Jews in the pagan world must be contrasted with the considerable admiration for Judaism that was shown in antiquity, and with the strong evidence that Judaism was, at that time, an actively proselytising religion. Indeed, so attractive was Judaism that Tacitus, Seneca and Juvenal saw it as a threat to pagan values and the pagan lifestyle.

Tacitus, who represents the highpoint of Roman literary antisemitism, particularly resented Jewish proselytism. In Book 5 of his *Historiae*, composed in the first decade of the second century CE, Tacitus called Jewish customs "base and abominable", owing their persistence to the Jews' "depravity". The first lesson converts to Judaism learn, Tacitus claimed, was "to despise the gods, to disown their country, and to regard their parents, children, and brothers as of little account". He was probably alluding to the fact that, according to Jewish law, a convert to Judaism, having joined the household of Israel, is regarded as one who has no relatives. Tacitus suggests that, while Jews are loyal and compassionate to one another, "toward every other people, they feel only hate and enmity".[1] Jewish proselytising, and its attendant "Judaising" of the gentile population, is thus an important factor in pagan polemic against Judaism.

Joel Carmichael (1992), who insists on the Christian origins of antisemitism, pointedly reserves the designation "antisemitism" for Christian antipathy towards Jews. Identified by its "mystical" quality, it has endowed Jews with an evil power way beyond their human status and has, in the process, Satanised them. Pagan attitudes to Jews, no matter how virulent, envenomed or hate filled, says Carmichael (1992,

p. 32), were no more than exaggerations of a real human situation. They resulted from inter-group friction, political rivalries and social irritations. Roman antagonism to the Jews was largely an expression of political outrage. Roman governments perceived and treated Jews as intractably rebellious, which is not surprising, since they were the only subject people to have revolted against Roman authority three times within a century. Jews really were, at that time, intransigently mutinous.

Peter Schafer, in his comprehensive 1997 book, *Judeophobia: Attitudes toward the Jews in the Ancient World*, identifies two basic scholarly approaches to historical hostility to Jews. The one is the essentialist/substantialist approach, which assumes that the unique characteristics of Judaism itself laid the basis for antisemitism, which might then be regarded as a "natural" phenomenon in any society, and would be "as old as Judaism itself" (1997, p. 3). The other is the idea that pagan antipathy to Jews was based not on the essence of Judaism, but on real political conflicts, of which there were basically three: the Syrian-Palestinian, the Egyptian and the Roman.

Schafer sees both models, on their own, as untenable, because religion and politics were seldom separated in the pagan world. Most scholars, in effect, combine these approaches, but emphasising one over the other. The functionalists tend to stress politics over religion, "dissolving the phenomenon" and "in the end explaining it away". The essentialists, on the other hand, assume "an always self-identical anti-Semitism arising out of the very essence of Judaism itself". As a result, they run the risk of "confusing cause with pretext and in the end finding the Jews themselves guilty of what happened to them" (1997, p. 8). "One always needs both components to 'create' anti-Semitism," says Schafer (1997, p. 8). One needs both the antisemite and the Jew. Concrete Jewish peculiarities need to be looked at in combination with the intention of the antisemite who sets about distorting and perverting these peculiarities. Antisemitism happens in the mind of the antisemite but it needs its object, the Jew or Judaism. It is the warped imagination of the antisemite, nourished by real Jews as well as by the antisemite's fantasies about Jews, that creates antisemitism.

THE IRRESOLVABLE DISPUTE

The debate about the suitability of the word "antisemitism" for pagan antipathy to Jews is inseparably intertwined with the question of whether real causes of inter-human resentment can be included as antisemitism, or whether it must be seen in totally irrational terms. Schafer, as we have seen, uses the word "antisemitism"[2] for pagan antipathy, and insists that we have to consider both the nature of Judaism and the contorting attitudes of the antisemite. What remains clear, however, is that if we are to find the first instance of the devaluation of the Jew, we have to go back to a time before the birth of Christianity and examine the turbulent historic matrix out of which both Christianity and rabbinic Judaism emerged. Historians trying to elucidate to what extent Jew hatred existed at the time, and to determine how ultimately decisive such hatred was to be in the long term, have to confront the problem – in addition to those outlined above – that different sectors of the pagan population held and expressed different attitudes about Jews. As we saw in the last chapter, a series of political powers ruled over the Jewish world. We also saw that, although Jews still lived in their own land, there was an extensive diaspora of Jewish communities. The emergence of Christianity complicated and exacerbated a hatred that already existed. The question, however, is to what extent it changed the nature of the Jew hatred it found.

Norman Ravitch (1982) views the dispute about origins that has arisen among scholars as irresolvable. It is almost impossible, he says, to decide whether Christian antisemitism was "merely a legacy from the ancient world, given a new theological gloss", or whether Christian teaching developed its own particular virulence – at a level rarely found in the pagan world. The conclusion a scholar will draw will depend on interpretation and weighting of factors. The individual scholar's under-standing of history – or underlying motives in framing history as he or she does – will affect the choice made. Those who place the responsibility squarely on Christian teaching tend to understate the influence of pagan antisemitism, and perceive it as a sporadic expression of amazement and distaste at the unique features of Jewish life. Others, whose motives may be to exculpate the church by denying its ultimate responsibility for the Holocaust, or to emphasise the Jews' capacity to endure in the face of an "eternal" hatred of Jews and Judaism, point to the virulence of pagan antisemitism.

The evidence of widespread antagonism towards Jews and Judaism in Hellenistic times has led some scholars, like Shmuel Ettinger (1988, p. 9), to locate the foundations of antisemitism in pre-Christian times and, therefore, to date its beginnings to that time. The negative attitude to the

Jews formulated specifically in the Hellenistic era, he argues, forms the basis of antisemitism. When Christianity emerged, it was only the form of competition and the character of the conflict that changed. This stance does not deny that theological polemic against the Jews was vital to Christianity – perhaps more so than to any other religion or culture – but it does suggest that it was not Christianity that laid the primary patterns of antisemitism. Christianity, which spread through the pagan world exploited an existent hostility, these scholars claim. It drew on an already deeply-rooted scorn, capitalising on it to increase Christianity's influence among pagans.

Rosemary Ruether, whom we will consider in much greater detail in the two chapters that follow this one, takes a view that is diametrically opposed to Ettinger's, insisting that antisemitism is not of pagan origin. Those who view it as such, she argues, rest their argument on an unjustified denigration of paganism – or negative stereotype of it – that grew out of monotheistic theology. Christian theological opposition to Judaism was not merely a benign expression of difference. It did not take on a virulent character only when the Christian community assimilated into the pagan world, adopting its negative attitudes. Rather, Christian theology was, itself, fundamentally anti-Jewish in that it rooted itself in the Jewish tradition, but opposed the Jewish interpretation of that tradition. Hatred between groups who have no stake in a common stock of religiously sanctioned identity symbols, says Ruether (1975, p. 30), can scarcely be as virulent as that between groups whose relationship expresses a religious form of sibling rivalry. Pagans may have viewed Jews with puzzlement or contempt, but this, she argues, did not lead to fanatical hatred of Judaism or Jews.

PAGAN PERSPECTIVES

One of the most persuasive reasons for some scholars dating antisemitism back to the pre-Christian pagan world is the appearance, in those early times, of the theme of ritual murder. This motif was echoed over and over again in the Blood Libel of the Middle Ages, with tragic consequences. Apion of Alexandria was the first to make this allegation, but it seems that on this particular occasion it did not provoke mob violence. We know about Apion's charge through the report of the Jewish historian Josephus, who mounted a spirited rebuttal in his tract *Contra Apionem (Against Apion)*. Josephus reports Apion as claiming that when

Antiochus IV Epiphanes entered the temple in Jerusalem, he discovered there a Greek whom the temple attendants were busy fattening up and preparing for sacrifice at an annual ritual. The Greek "fell at the knees of Antiochus", imploring him to set him free. He told his tale of distress "with sighs and tears" and "in pitiful tone".

> While travelling about the province for his livelihood, he [the Greek] was suddenly kidnapped by men of a foreign race and conveyed to the temple; there he was shut up and seen by nobody, but was fattened on feasts of the most lavish description … Finally, on consulting the attendants who waited upon him, he heard of the *unutterable law of the Jews* for the sake of which he was being fed. The practice was repeated annually at a fixed season. They would kidnap a Greek foreigner, fatten him up for a year, and then convey him to a wood, where they slew him, sacrificed his body with their customary ritual, partook of his flesh, and, while immolating the Greek, *swore an oath of hostility to the Greeks*. The remains of their victim were then thrown into a pit … The man stated that he had now but a few days left to live, and implored the king, out of respect for the gods of Greece, to defeat this *Jewish plot* upon his life-blood and to deliver him from his miserable predicament.
>
> *Contra Apionem* 2, pp. 94–6, emphasis mine

This, the first ritual murder charge against Jews known to history, inaugurated themes that would be picked up later. But it is important to evaluate such writings in their contemporary context and not to overlay them with present concerns. It must be remembered that most of the hostility against the Jews in pagan times was expressed in the writings of Hellenistic intellectuals and there seems to have been a wide gulf between the intellectuals and the masses, the former openly despising, and having scant influence on, the mobs. Other important accusations by the Hellenistic intellectuals can be grouped, according to Louis Feldman (1986, pp. 30–6), under five categories. Jews were deemed to hate the rest of humankind, to be embarrassingly credulous and to be beggars. They were also accused of dual political loyalty and over-zealousness in proselytising. No single author displays all of these accusations, but they appear often enough to constitute a pattern; an author would sometimes express one of them in an account that seems otherwise favourable to Jews and Judaism.

Hecataeus of Abdera, who visited Egypt around 300 BCE, and who is generally thought to have been otherwise well disposed to Jews – an assumption that Shafer (1997) questions – characterised the Jewish way of life as unsociable and hostile to foreigners. The word he used was *misoxenon*. He believed that the Jews had been expelled from Egypt, an idea frequently encountered in the writing of the ancients. Whereas several authors – like Apion, Lysimachus and Chaeremon – were deeply hostile, attributing such expulsion to disease, Hecataeus seemed to sympathise with the Jews rather than to blame them for their putative expulsion. He admired Moses, noting that "the sacrifices that he established differ from those of other nations as does their way of living, for as a result of their own expulsion from Egypt, he introduced an unsocial and intolerant mode of life" (*Aegyptiaca* 40:3).

As part of their asocial tendencies, Jews were seen by other authors as reluctant to convert the uncircumcised into their faith. Juvenal, for example, condemned the Jews bitterly in his *Saturae* (14:100): "Having been wont to flout the laws of Rome, they learn and practice and revere the Jewish law, and all that Moses handed down in his secret tome, forbidding to point out the way to any not worshipping the same rites, and conducting none but the circumcised to the desired fountain" (Stern 1980, p. 103). "Pointing the way" indicates teaching of the Torah, and the "desired fountain" probably indicates ritual immersion, Juvenal's jibe therefore referring to the Jewish conversion ceremony.

When the Jewish historian Salo Baron claimed that "almost every note echoed in medieval and modern antisemitism was sounded by the chorus of ancient writers", he may have been correct, but such a claim can be overstated. Each negative statement about Jews, historians of antisemitism insist, needs to be examined against its own complex background if we are to avoid inaccurate conclusions. Pagan attitudes to Jews were expressed over a long period of time and over a large geographic area, and came from a variety of sources, constituting a vast literature. Views on Jews are anything but monolithic, reflecting opinions ranging from outright hostility to open admiration.

A major breakthrough in scholarship came with Menahem Stern's monumental three-volume compilation of Greek and Roman texts in the ancient world, *Greek and Latin Authors on Jews and Judaism*, which was published over several years (1976–84). As the most recent and most comprehensive compilation of its kind, it has revolutionised the study of pagan antisemitism. Stern distinguishes between different types of comment about Jews – from positive, through neutral, to negative – and supplies information on the background to each text. He thus prepared the ground for other scholars who would attempt to determine the nature of pagan hostility to Jews and how it compared with Christian attitudes. A notable example is John Gager, who opened a new direction in the study of ancient antisemitism.

The attitudes to Jews in the different sectors of society in antiquity were not uniform. We need, therefore, according to Feldman (1986, p. 15), to analyse separately the positions of the government, the masses and the intellectual elite. Such analysis reveals a more nuanced picture of attitudes to Jews than is commonly presented, ranging from admiration, through toleration born of *Realpolitik*, to outright hostility and hatred. Let us start with government antisemitism in ancient times.

GOVERNMENT ANTISEMITISM

Before the Hellenistic period, the significance of government-inspired antisemitism in the ancient world is difficult to assess. Unless one includes the oppression by Pharaoh at the time of the Exodus – and his threat to kill all Jewish first-born males – as "government antisemitism", there is no record of it until Haman attempted to wipe out the Jews of the Persian Empire in the fifth century BCE, an event whose historicity, as we have seen, is questionable. Carmichael (1992, p. 4) describes ancient Jew hatred as an expression of irritation, occasioned by Jewish separateness, rather than the distinct hatred that was later to characterise antisemitism. Jews lived by their own laws (Esther 3:8), rather than by those of the Persian state, and this was seen as an impediment to Persian statecraft.

According to Wistrich (1991, p. 4), this kind of incident fits the Hellenistic period of the second century BCE more accurately, by which time Jews lived both as distinct minority groups outside their land and as a national group within their own land. In each case, they lived under foreign rule, except for about a century of partial independence under the Hasmoneans. The attitude to Jews displayed by the varying Hellenistic governments was, therefore, important. One of the major centres of Jewish life in pre-Christian times was Alexandria, which was to become the most advanced point of the Hellenised world outside Greece. The Jews had been invited to settle there by Alexander himself and, at one stage, made up as much as forty per cent of the population. It is not surprising, therefore, that a great deal of the antisemitism at the time originated there, though there were also outbreaks of anti-Jewish violence in other cities, such as Antioch and Caesarea. Alexandrian Jews were resented for a number of reasons, which will be detailed below, one of the main ones being their position as middle men between the privileged Greeks and the underprivileged Egyptian natives.

As a universal culture, Hellenism sought to introduce the Greek language and Greek ideas and values to the subject peoples in the areas that had fallen under Hellenistic control. But Alexander had to govern the indigenous inhabitants with tolerance and for this purpose he used the Jews as middlemen, thus forming a "vertical alliance" with them. Jews were given self-rule and were able to enter various fields, including the civil service and the army. They were given certain privileges, such as the freedom to worship their one God exclusively, and sanction to refrain from rituals that would compromise their monotheistic ideals. This situation was inherited by Alexander's successors and continued under the Romans, who admired the Jews for the antiquity of their traditions and treated Judaism, as we saw in the last chapter, as a *religio licita*, under which Jews continued to be granted privileges. The Jews' standing was enhanced under Julius Caesar, who was grateful for the assistance they rendered in his civil war with Pompey.

Though there was no history of virulent antisemitism in Rome itself, the Jews' situation differed under the various emperors according to wider historic circumstances. The rabbis were ambivalent about Rome, regarding it as a wicked kingdom, but balancing this view with some positive evaluations. Although the general tolerance it showed Jews did not go unappreciated, certain Roman oppressors were named as ruthless Jew haters and became the prototypes of gentile oppression. The emperors Titus and Hadrian, especially, are identified with cruel attempts to root out Judaism, the first for crushing the 66–70 CE Jewish rebellion and destroying the second temple, and the second for the cruelties and censorship of Jewish learning associated with the Bar Kochba revolt of 132–5 CE. Titus's victory thrust the Jews into almost two thousand years of homelessness and, even today, no Jew is permitted to stand under the Arch of Titus in Rome, which depicts the Romans removing the holy objects as spoils from the temple. The Seleucid Antiochus IV Epiphanes, who sparked off the Maccabean revolt and the subsequent miracle of the rededication of the temple which is commemorated by Jews in the festival of Lights (*Hanukah*), was also seen as a merciless tyrant.

Looked at from a broad historic perspective, however, none of these men was motivated by the rabid hatred of Jews that the rabbis summed up in their adage "Esau hates Jacob". Most modern scholars would agree, for example, that the Roman destruction of Jerusalem in 70 CE cannot be seen in terms of an antisemitic act, because the Romans had good reason, from their political perspective, to do what they did. The Jews had undertaken a violent rebellion against the state, and the Romans were acting to preserve their empire. As Carmichael (1992) points out, the Antiochan and Hadrianic persecutions of Judaism can be similarly understood, largely as the brutal attempts of the state to repress a rebellion that was motivated primarily by religious zeal. Jewish practice was proscribed not out of hatred, but to help in suppressing rebelliousness. Note that Rome had supported the Maccabees against the Syrian Greeks, its main rival in the Mediterranean.

In this regard Shaye Cohen (1986, p. 46) points to one of the real historic reasons behind the Alexandrian pogroms (about which there will be more later). Apion, the leader of the antisemitic party in Alexandria, was quite justified, in Cohen's view, when he asked, "Why, then, if they (the Jews) are citizens, do they not worship the same gods as the Alexandrians?" (*Contra Apionem* 2:65). Worship of the national gods at that time, he points out, was equivalent to the rallying force of the national flag. The Jews wanted equality with tolerance. They wanted to be allowed to be the same as everyone else while also being different from everyone else. Apion, in Cohen's opinion, rightly refused. Though Cohen finds adequate objective cause for the existence of anti-Jewish animus, he suggests (1986: 46) that there is an elusive point that "separates justifiable hatred from unjustifiable, legitimate opposition from illegitimate, and the 'anti-Jewish' from the 'antisemitic'." To determine whether, or even if, such a line has been crossed requires more knowledge of the historical circumstances than is available to us at present.

Government attitudes were generally determined by pragmatism, though there were isolated instances of oppression. The expulsion of Jews from Rome in 139 BCE and 19 CE resulted from Jewish efforts to attract pagans to Judaism and the Jewish lifestyle. Roman policy was essentially tolerant and reflected the vertical alliance between Jews and the government. It was not, however, an idyllic relationship – as the three bloody Jewish revolts against Rome testify – and among the Romans there was undoubtedly some dislike of the Jews.

According to Moshe David Herr (1988, p. 27), there are indications that the word "Jew" was perceived as an insult in Roman times. This can be inferred, among other instances, by the refusal of Vespasian and Titus to accept the honorific title "Judaicus" after quelling the great revolt of 66–70 CE. Unlike other honorific titles – such as "Africanus", or "Britannicus" – the term was likely to be associated with Judaising, a matter to be considered in chapters 5 and 6. The relationship between Jews and the Roman government, Feldman (1986, p. 21) suggests, was marked by alliance, persecution and revolt. But alliance was dominant. Jews were too numerous in the Roman Empire to risk antagonising, their numbers having swelled to between ten and twelve per cent of the population by the inception of Christianity, as a result of successful proselytism.

POPULAR ANTISEMITISM

A very different picture emerges when we look at the attitudes to Jews among the masses. Their actions supply evidence that popular antisemitism was deep seated and easily triggered to violence. The vertical alliance of Jews with the various governments – Persia, Alexander, the Ptolemies and Seleucids, the Romans – served to restrain the mob on the whole, but it also caused envy. Though we have only fragments of the writings of the masses on papyri – and we may question the direct effect on the masses of the negative writings of the intellectuals – among the masses there was undoubtedly some Jew hatred. This was thrown into bold relief by a series of anti-Jewish riots. The most vicious of these – which have been likened to the antisemitic pogroms and massacre of Jews in seventeenth-century Poland – took place in Alexandria. Mobs pillaged Jewish homes, expressing the pent-up rage that had been provoked by the combination of equal rights and privilege the Jews enjoyed in the Hellenistic world. The marked increase in the number of Jews, as a result of proselytising, added to the mob's fear and suspicion.

A particularly vicious pogrom took place in 38 CE. It arose, the Jewish philosopher Philo reported, from rage against Jews for refusing to obey Caligula's decree that he should be worshipped as a god. But the pogrom was far from inevitable and could have been aborted. It was allowed to take its course because the Roman governor of Egypt, Flaccus, felt insecure about his standing with the emperor in the wake of some administrative changes. The immediate pretext for the riot was the ostentatious visit of the Jewish king Arippa I in all his finery. The mob, whipped up by professional agitators, lampooned him, accusing the Jews of dual loyalty. Flaccus responded by seizing the meeting house of the Jews, depriving them of their civic rights and denouncing them as aliens and foreigners. At one point, he herded the Jews into a tiny quarter of Alexandria, creating the first ghetto in history. The mob was guilty of enormous cruelty, binding Jews, burning them alive and pillaging their homes and shops. Not even their dead bodies were spared from the fury of the masses. Flaccus was later recalled in disgrace for his improper behaviour, banished and eventually executed. He was defended in court by Cicero, who is notorious for the negative statements about the Jews he made in Flaccus's defence.

A second riot followed in Alexandria in 66 CE, coinciding with the Jewish revolt in Palestine, which enabled the antisemites to take cover under the Jews' current profile of unpatriotic rebelliousness. Other riots took place in Palestine and elsewhere. The breakdown of the vertical alliance which resulted from the Jewish rebellion gave the rioters *carte blanche*. The reaction to the Jews' Great Diaspora Revolt against the Romans (115–18 CE) revealed considerable anti-Jewish hostility, but pragmatism won the day, the Roman administration finally taking measures against the Greek trouble-makers to restore law and order.

THE ANTISEMITISM OF THE INTELLECTUALS

Most of the negativity about Jews in ancient times derives from the writings of the intellectuals, but these writings were many and varied and for many centuries did not reflect a preoccupation with the Jews. The first oblique reference to them was by the historian Herodotus in the fifth century BCE in a discussion on circumcision. Menahem Stern has shown that, though extremely negative attitudes to Jews existed, these occupy a small place. Negative views were counterbalanced with admiration of Judaism. So Jews were not universally unpopular.

The writers, themselves, wrote from specific viewpoints and within particular historic circumstances. Cicero's negative comments about Jews in his defence of Flaccus, for example, have to be considered in their contemporary context, which, in this case, was a juridical one. It was customary, at the time, to defame one's opponents in court. Cicero also indicated that his true opinions on Jews may have differed from those he expressed as an attorney. But we do not have records of these other opinions. In his defence of Flaccus, Cicero saw the practice of Jewish sacred rites as being "at variance with the glory of our empire, the dignity of our name, and the customs of our ancestors". He also referred to the Jews as *barbara superstitio*, by which he meant foreign and anti-Roman (*Pro Flacco* 28:67). Other writings come from rhetorical historians or satirists, and are, by their nature, coloured and exaggerated. Furthermore, Jews were not the only people in antiquity to be scorned by intellectuals. Cicero, for one, made similar slurs against other groups in other speeches.

Tacitus, in his *Historiae*, expressed both admiration for the Jews and Judaism, and awe at their uncanny ability to survive in the absence of a homeland. He offers six explanations about the origins of the Jewish people, their religion and customs. Of the six, it is the last – which claims that the Jews had been disfigured by a plague and were, as a result, expelled from Egypt – that set the tone, according to Stern (1980, p. 2). Though the other five may have been more charitable, this explanation was longer than the other five put together, and accords with Tacitus's generally negative sentiments about Jews and Judaism. Tacitus claimed that the Jews' misfortune accounted for many of the religious practices introduced by Moses, who, in order "to establish his influence over this people for all time ... introduced new religious practices, quite opposed to those of all other religions". The Jews, said Tacitus, "regard as profane all that we hold sacred", yet "permit all that we abhor" (*Historiae* 4:1). He accused Jews of being "prone to lust". They abstain from intercourse with foreign women, but "among themselves nothing is unlawful" (*Historiae* 5:2).

Despite such calumnies, however, Stern's examination of the texts, as Feldman (1983, p. 30) points out, reveals that Jews had more contact with non-Jews than is generally assumed, and that of the entire corpus of writings eighteen per cent are substantially favourable, fifty-nine per cent neutral, and only twenty-three per cent substantially unfavourable. Within this relatively small percentage, however, there were some serious charges, that cannot be ignored and which represent two different streams of thought within the Hellenistic world. One derived specifically from Egypt, and the other from elsewhere in the Hellenistic world. The antisemitism of Hellenised Egypt possessed a far more negative tinge than antisemitism elsewhere, and the reason was specifically *religious*.

ANTISEMITISM OF EGYPTIAN PROVENANCE

Egypt had a long-standing anti-Jewish tradition going back to the Persian period, and was the birthplace of most of the ancient traditions hostile to the Jews. The account of the Exodus from Egypt, related in the book of Exodus, had been made available to the Greek reader – Jewish and gentile – through the Septuagint, the third century BCE Greek translation, by Jews, of the Hebrew scriptures, and may have been known to the Egyptian priests even earlier. This pivotal myth of Judaism depicts Egypt as the negative butt of the salvation of the Jews, the Jews having been delivered from their bondage, and led to freedom, at the expense of the Egyptians. The plagues that the Egyptians had been forced to suffer were imposed on them in order to bestow favour upon the Jews. This, according to Stern (1988, p. 16), demanded an Egyptian rebuttal, and the Egyptian priests rose to the challenge, producing counter-myths in which Jews were depicted as sordid, disease-ridden people who had inter-married with the slave population. Far from experiencing a miraculous delivery, they were portrayed as having been driven out of Egypt as lepers. The sabbath, instead of being seen as a day of sanctification and rest, was portrayed as a memento of the Jews' supposedly disease-ridden condition. Having the capacity to travel for only six days, their ill-health forced them to rest on the seventh.

The earliest account of this counter-myth, according to Schafer (1997, p. 15) was to be found in Hecataeus's now lost *Aegyptiaca*, but has come to us through other sources. It was phrased unequivocally, for the first time, however, by the Egyptian high priest Manetho, who seems to have gathered together stories on these themes in the third century BCE, the basic substance of which passed into a general tradition of Hellenistic anthropological and geographical lore. The Jews' putative misanthropy and exclusivism were later treated as fact by historians. One of the most vicious exponents was Apion of Alexandria, but the theme was widely used in Rome, having been taken up, as we saw above, by no less a figure than Tacitus.

Apion, as Stern (1976, p. 389) points out, was a Greek writer and scholar who, though of Egyptian origin, managed to achieve citizenship of Alexandria. He played an important part in the political and cultural life there and was probably the head of the Alexandrian museum. He gained fame in many branches of literature and scholarship, but especially as a Homeric scholar and author of a work on the history of Egypt. Living at the meeting place of the Greek and Egyptian world, he was instrumental in drawing a picture of Egypt's past for educated Greeks and Romans. In the process, however, he also painted a derogatory portrait of the Jews and their past, which was elaborated by later writers.

We are not sure whether Apion devoted a work entirely to the Jews or whether his comments about them were part of his more general history of Egypt. Writers dependent upon Apion suggested the former, but Stern (1976, p. 389) thinks it more probable that he allotted a portion of his history of Egypt – either the third or fourth book – to the story of the Exodus and its consequences. For an account of this, we have to rely on the Jewish historian Josephus, who, in his rebuttal *Contra Apionem* (*Against Apion*), divided Apion's treatment of the Jews into three sections: the Exodus, an attack on the rights of the Alexandrian Jews, and a disparagement of the temple and of Jewish rites and customs.

The Roman emperor Augustus had imposed a tax on non-citizen residents of Alexandria, among them the Jews and the indigenous population. The Jews were keen to become citizens of the city and, in their application for citizenship before the emperor Gaius, were represented by the Jewish philosopher Philo, while Apion represented the Greeks who opposed their application and shared Apion's negative view of the Jews. Apion had considerable influence on the educated classes of his time, though not all treated him with the same respect. He had a flowing style, which is apparent from fragments in other authors, such as Aulus Gellius, and must have been a popular writer. It is therefore not surprising, according to Stern (1976, p. 390), that Josephus singled out Apion as his main target when dealing with antisemitic Graeco-Egyptian writers. "I am doubtful," Josephus said,

> whether the shameless remarks of Apion the grammarian deserve serious refutation. Some of these resemble the allegations made by others, some are very indifferent additions of his own; most of them are pure buffoonery, and, to tell the truth, display the gross ignorance of their author, a man of low character and a charlatan to the end of his days. Yet, since most people are so foolish as to find greater attraction in such compositions than in works of a serious nature, to be charmed by abuse and impatient of praise, I think it incumbent upon me not to pass over without examination even this author, who has written an indictment of us formal enough for a court of law.
>
> *Contra Apionem* 2:2–4

Apion showed an implacable hostility to the Jews throughout his work, which, as Gager (1985, p. 45) puts it, filled the Alexandrian air in the late 30s and early 40s of the first century CE. His account of the Exodus drew on a variety of sources. One such source derived the Jewish sabbath from the Egyptian word for disease of the groin, and stated that Jews had developed this disease during their flight from Egypt. "After six days' march", Josephus quotes him as saying, "they developed tumours in the groin, and that was why, after safely reaching the country now called Judea, they rested on the seventh day, and called that day *sabbaton*, preserving the Egyptian terminology; for disease of the groin in Egypt is called sabbatosis" (*Contra Apionem* 2:21).

A proportion of Apion's diatribe contained original material, for he seems to have had some knowledge of the Jewish scriptures. He knew, for example, that Moses went up Mount Sinai. But when it came to Jewish religious practices, he relied on popular attitudes. He saw Jewish law as unjust, its ceremonies as mistaken, and ridiculed Jewish practices such as circumcision and abstention from pork. Repeating an earlier tale by Mnaseas, about the golden head of an ass having been found in the Jerusalem temple, he added the slander that the Jews worshipped it, as well as making the first accusation of ritual murder, mentioned above.

Second to Apion in antisemitic tendency was the Graeco-Egyptian writer Lysimachus, who is thought to have lived before Apion. He did not deal with the Jews in a separate work, but in his history of Egypt, *Aegyptiaca*. Like Apion, he saw the Exodus in terms of polluted people being driven from Egypt. But he also made the claim that Moses instructed his band of followers "to show goodwill to no man, to offer not the best but the worst advice, and to overthrow any temples and altars of the gods which they found" (*Contra Apionem*, 1:309). Lysimachus claimed that, after crossing the desert, the Jews eventually reached Judea, where they built a city and settled in it. *En route*, when they traversed settled land they plundered the local inhabitants' temples and set them on fire. They also maltreated the existing population. The city in which they settled, he is said to have alleged in *Contra Apionem* (1:311), "was called Hierosyla because of their [the Jews'] sacrilegious propensities. At a later date, when they had arisen to power, they altered the name, to avoid the disgraceful imputation, and called the city Hierosolyma [Jerusalem] and themselves Hierosolymites."

For Apion and his compatriots, the primary motive for this inflammatory rhetoric about Jewish religion and history was the issue of Jewish citizenship. Apion was adamant that Jews had no claim to citizenship of Alexandria. Not only did they refuse to worship the Alexandrian gods or the emperor, but they were, he claimed, outsiders and occupied an undesirable part of the city. "They came", he said (*Contra Apionem* 2:33), "from Syria and settled by a sea without a harbour, close beside the spot where the waves break on the beach." As Josephus (*Contra Apionem* 2:32) affirmed, "The noble Apion's calumny against us is apparently designed as a sort of return to the Alexandrians for the rights of citizenship which they bestowed on him. Knowing their hatred of their Jewish neighbours in Alexandria, he [Apion] has made it his aim to vilify the latter, and has included all the rest of the Jews in his condemnation. In both these attacks, he shows himself as an impudent liar." Josephus regards as stupid Apion's "astonishment at the idea of Jews being called Alexandrians" (*Contra Apionem* 2:38), and sarcastically charges him with having attained his own citizenship unfairly: "Yet Apion displays such noble generosity as to claim for himself privileges from which he was debarred, while he undertakes to calumniate those who have fairly obtained them" (*Contra Apionem* 2:42).

The Jews' attempts to attain citizenship, along with their privileged status, formed the background to the riots of 38–41 CE. The slanders about the Exodus were probably designed to demonstrate that the Jews, whose ancestors had been expelled from Egypt as sacrilegious and polluted renegades, were even less deserving of full civic status than the native Egyptians. Apion took his ideas to Rome and influenced the writings of Seneca, Juvenal and Tacitus.

THE WIDER TRADITION OF HELLENISTIC ANTIPATHY

The wider tradition of anti-Jewish attitudes elsewhere in Hellenistic society seems to have emerged, as indicated above, as a reaction to the religiously sanctioned exclusivity of the Jews. It was a spontaneous reaction to Jewish separation from the cultural manners of others, and to the social consequences of Jewish religious practice. As we have seen, many of the Jewish rituals – such as circumcision, the dietary laws and sabbath observance – set the Jews apart from the people among whom they lived. In addition, Jews did not intermarry with the rest of the population and continued to give an annual contribution to the temple in Jerusalem. Their festivals were national-religious in that they were associated with their promised land and many Jews travelled there on pilgrimage. As a result, these practices were ridiculed, and circumcision, in particular, was regarded as an abomination. Because, as Carmichael (1992) points out, Greek culture was seen as the standard for humane existence, the Jews' refusal to assimilate into it seemed barbarous and insulting. The ensuing slurs against Jews were not racial, however, in that the animosity disappeared if the individual gave up Jewish practice.

Though monotheism was not, in itself, a problem, the Jews' worship of a single, imageless God was incomprehensible. They were seen as excessively credulous, and Horace, in his *Sermones* (1:5, 100), scoffed at their tendency to believe everything. Because they refused to teach gentiles the Torah, they were perceived as following some type of "mystery cult". This led some to the conclusion that Jews hated the rest of humanity. Their belief that they were a chosen people was seen as arrogance, and engendered derision in the light of the conquered and scattered condition in which they found themselves. Their political and military failure indicated that the gods were not favourably disposed to the Jews. Cicero treated Jewish claims to chosenness and divine protection with derision. He wryly commented that the Jewish nation "by its armed resistance has shown what it thinks of our rule; how dear it was to the immortal gods is shown by the fact that it has been conquered, let out for taxes, made a slave". Celsus echoed this by mocking the Jews' "promised land": "We see what *sort* of land it was of which they [the Jews] were thought worthy."[3] But, whereas pagans saw the Jews as punished by the gods, the church saw them as *abandoned* by God. Whereas pagans accused them of pride, the church accused them of blindness.

The exclusivism of Judaism – an inevitable adjunct to its monotheism – was seen as a mark of illiberalism. Jews were perceived as being closed to opposing points of view, and this appeared to deny respect to other religions. Openness to debate, even if it were only theoretical, was a prized value in the Hellenistic world. Jews were seen as unwilling to engage on an equal plane with people of other viewpoints and, hence, as obscurantist. Rational debate was, ostensibly, the key value that underlay Hellenistic intellectualism.

The polytheistic world recognised a wide variety of gods, who sometimes loved and at other times hated human beings. Though the gods governed humans, they occasionally *submitted* to them. The gods could be beneficent, but they could also be cruel and spiteful, withholding the worldly benefits from mortal humans. The hierarchy of the gods reflected those in human society. Bauer (1994, p. 13) points out that, because the pagan gods replicated and legitimated social inequalities, those societies that found them appropriate and necessary found the idea of monotheism threatening. Because it affirmed human equality, monotheism undermined established social structures, with their class distinctions and slaves.

Whether in philosophical or historical writings, Jewish thinkers like Philo and Josephus produced apologetics to counteract the hostility. They tried to show, by biblical interpretation, that Jews are commanded to show respect for others. The Septuagint was as much an apologetic commentary as it was a translation into the Greek vernacular. This was all part of an effort by Jews to accommodate to Greek culture, to synthesise Hebrew ideals with the allure of Greek cosmopolitanism and to reconcile them with Greek rationality. These apologetic writings were propagandist in character, attempting to demonstrate the excellence and superiority of the Jewish laws and teachings. But they made little impression on the Greeks.

The diaspora Jews' maintenance of their ties with their co-religionists in Israel, and the fact that they were an appendage to the homeland, resulted in charges of lack of loyalty to the empire, and maintaining a state within a state. Although it is debated whether this actually resulted in the accusation of "dual loyalty" which was to echo through the centuries,[4] there is no doubt that Jews were accused of sedition, rebelliousness and conspiracy. Apion, as we have seen, focused on the fact that the Alexandrian Jews refused to worship the civic deities. He thus accused them of sedition and questioned their right to citizenship of Alexandria on these grounds.

But, we need to bear Schafer's caution in mind, and not give too much weight to Judaism itself as the ground to antipathy lest we land up "blaming the victim". There is no doubt, says Schafer (1997, p. 209), "that the allegation of Jewish 'separateness' and 'strangeness' does have a *fundamentum in re*, but to argue that it is the *reason* for pagan anti-Semitism is to confuse cause with pretext, to hold the Jews themselves responsible for what others do to them" (emphasis in the original). The crucial question, according to Schafer (1997, p. 210), is "what the Greco-Egyptian and Greek authors *made* of it. They turned Jewish separateness into a monstrous conspiracy against mankind and the values shared by all civilized human beings, and it is therefore [their] attitude that determines anti-Semitism" (my emphasis). This distortion "crosses the line of the unacceptable", as Schafer (1997, p. 206) puts it; the "justifiable" becomes the "unjustifiable", and clear evidence is provided for the existence of virulent antisemitism in the ancient pagan world.

GNOSTICISM

There is another branch of antisemitic thinking that should not be omitted from a discussion of anti-Judaism in the ancient world, and that is gnosticism. This is a system of thought in which the entire Jewish value system is inverted. The Jewish God is seen as an evil, inferior creator of the material world, called the Demiurge.[5] In some gnostic sects, contemporaneous with the birth of Christianity, Jewish religion is regarded as the primary source of evil. Gnosticism arises from a fundamental dualism in which the universe is conceived as the arena of conflict between two powers – one good, one evil. The evil power created the earth and rules over it. He is the God worshipped by the Jews, who are his chosen people and to whom he gave the evil revelation, the Torah. The Jewish religion is the direct expression of evil, from the source of evil. Jews were chosen to act as the representatives of the Demiurge, the evil God, in his struggle against Light. This being so, the good power was the proper vehicle to salvation. This radical form of antisemitism, Maccoby (1987, p. 14) points out, gave the Jews the role of cosmic evil. They are the instruments of a demonic power who, through Judaism, is consolidating his rule over the earth.

No one has succeeded in either defining gnosticism adequately or determining whether it preceded Christianity or grew from it. It is thus difficult to assess its influence on pagan thought. Two central beliefs characterise gnosticism. The first places special emphasis on a particular type of "knowledge" of the divine which, alone, would permit an individual to attain salvation. Hence the name "gnosticism" from Greek *gnosis*, or knowledge. This knowledge, which could be found only in a secret code of truth, transmitted either by word of mouth or by arcane writings, could alter one's destiny. Possession of this knowledge served to unleash a liberating force against the influence of cosmic forces. The second belief was in the existence of two opposing forces in the world, an evil one against a good one, or what we call "dualism".

Until about 1945, when thirteen codices were discovered at Nag Hammadi, in upper Egypt, there was little written evidence of a system of gnosis before the rise of Christianity, and our knowledge of it originates from Christian opponents of the movement, such as Irenaeus and Tertullian, who regarded it as a Christian heresy. Because it came to the world's attention through these polemic writings, it was originally believed that gnosticism arose only in the second century CE as Christian ideas amalgamated with elements from other sources, like Greek philosophy. Later scholars, such as Rudolph Bultmann, however, argued that this system of thought existed well before New Testament times.

Rosemary Ruether (1974, p. 51) argues that a fringe element of Jews themselves may have originated gnosticism, seeking a higher saviour than any on offer, but this is by no means certain. Gnosticism expresses a sense of alienation and an overturning of symbols. It may have come from disaffected Jews or from gentiles who had improperly adopted Jewish symbols. It drew from the same sectarian and syncretistic philosophical materials as Christianity drew on, and arose in the same circles to which Christianity was now appealing, growing rapidly alongside Christianity. It was undeniably a potential source of anti-Judaism. Yet, it was a kind of anti-Judaism repudiated in the New Testament and by the Western church in the second century as a contradiction of the affirmation of the goodness of the material creation that was to become part of orthodox Christianity.

By combining material from diverse sources, it was possible for the gnostics to reconstruct a myth of a Primal Man who descended into this world and was, in some way, imprisoned here, divided into a multitude of sparks of light, which are individual souls. These sparks have to be delivered and reunited by a redeemer from above. The full form of this myth, as Richardson and Bowden in their *New Dictionary of Christian Theology* (1983, p. 226) point out, emerges only in Manichaeism in the third century CE. But that emergence points to the existence of earlier scattered pieces of the myth of which it is both a part and a culmination.

Paul Johnson, in his *History of Christianity* (1982, p. 45), offers an apt image to explain gnosticism, calling it a "spiritual parasite" which used other religions as a "carrier". Christianity fitted this role well. It had a mysterious founder, Jesus, who had conveniently disappeared. He had left behind a collection of sayings that were transmitted by his followers. In addition to his public sayings, there were "secret" ones handed on from generation to generation, by members of gnostic sects. Those gnostics who latched on to Christianity wanted to Hellenise it by cutting it off from its historic Jewish origins. Gnostic sects, with varying forms of ethics, were spreading at the same time as early Christian sects were. Some were ultra-puritan, and others were orgiastic. Some of the latter seized on Paul's apparently negative assessment of the Jewish law, which we will discuss in chapter 6, to preach complete licence. Paul vehemently opposed gnosticism because it invalidated the foundations of Christianity. But he had to fight very hard to combat it because it was hydra headed and constantly changing.

Maccoby (1987) points out that modern forms of antisemitism are no less demonising than gnosticism. Though Nazism and Marxism invoke no cosmic principle, their concepts of underlying reality – of which peoples and religions are only the outward expression – give rise to similar demonising effects when a given community is identified with the retrograde forces of history.

THE CHARM OF JUDAISM

Despite all these negative perceptions about Jews and Judaism, we cannot discount the charm that Judaism held in the pagan world. As we have seen, it was the very appeal of Judaism, and the fact that many pagans became either full Jews or sympathisers with Judaism, that led to much of the hostility. Jews were renowned for their antiquity and their unique religion, whereas Christianity was seen as a parvenu religion and as intolerant as Judaism. Not only this, Christianity was seen as even more offensive in its social exclusiveness. Celsus's attitude to Jews, for example, was conditioned mainly by its connection with Christianity. To disprove the intellectual and religious foundations of the latter, he found it necessary to strike at Judaism first (Stern 1980, p. 226).

Hellenistic thought lacked a theological basis for Jew hatred. Some philosophers, like Aristotle, admired the Jews as possessing the four virtues of wisdom, courage, temperance and justice. But, as a result of the many conversions to Judaism that took place, Jews were accused of aggressive proselytism and of polluting the values of the young. So many pagans were attracted to Judaism that Feldman (1986, p. 37) has offered an interesting scenario. Had the Jews not attempted three bloody revolts against the Romans, he says, and had Christianity not "lowered the price of admission" – presumably by reducing the ritual demands – Judaism might well have become the major religion in the Roman Empire. We thus have a picture of great attraction to Judaism, on the one hand, and intense hatred, on the other.

According to Wistrich (1991, p. 9), ambivalence, rather than hostility, seems to be the more characteristic pagan attitude. Pagan antisemitism remained essentially cultural rather than theological or racist, never developing the institutionalised discrimination, stigmatisation and humiliation of Jews that, as we will see in the next two chapters, became the historic legacy of Christianity. Since our main sources on antisemitism in the pagan world are the writings of intellectuals, and negative statements about Jews form only a small part of the whole corpus of writings that refer to Jews in any way, we must be careful not to over-emphasise the negative. As we have seen, Josephus, in his treatise *Against Apion*, dealt with several Jew haters besides Apion. Had this particular work been lost, suggests Feldman, we would lack a large portion of the most virulent texts. Though heavily dependent on the literary material of the period, we have to take care in drawing any final conclusions from it, because it is certainly not uniformly hostile to Jews. Also, since the writings emerge almost solely from the intellectual elite, they may not reflect accurately the general societal attitude. Unlike the situation that was to develop in Christianity, this societal attitude was neither systematised nor part of a consistent view of reality in which there was a theological underpinning to contempt for Jews.

Nevertheless, hatred seems to have simmered in the mob in protest against Jewish religious separatism and the Jews' equal – yet privileged – status, and was clearly evident in ancient pagan writings. Hatred of Jews was widespread and significant, but has to be seen as part of a varied and complex reality. Depending on how that reality is reconstructed, different scholars draw different conclusions. Whatever their impact at the time, however, these negative statements about Jews by intellectuals had important consequences later. With the rise of the modern antisemitic movement in Germany in the nineteenth century, and its particularly racist quality, which we will discuss in chapter 8, it became fashionable among intellectuals there to cite these ancient authors in order to prove their point. The Jews, these modern antisemites were trying to suggest, embodied inherent characteristics that produced antisemitism wherever they went. What other reason could there have been for the liberal Hellenists to express such virulent antagonism against them? The Jews' instrinsic hatefulness, for modern antisemites, is biologically based, something far removed from even the most negative evaluations of Jews in ancient times. However, modern antisemitism could not have developed without the negative image of the Jew that was to develop in Christendom, a subject to which we now turn.

Part III

INTER-RELIGIOUS RIVALRY AND ANTISEMITISM

5

The dynamics of Christian antisemitism

*It is strange that, after such world-wide success, Christianity ...
still needs the failing of the Jew in order to be able to feel safe in its
own truth.*

Eliezer Berkovits

*Only he who cries out for the Jews has the right to sing Gregorian
chant.*

Dietrich Bonhoeffer

We have seen in the previous chapters that Jew hatred goes back well
before the inception of Christianity and that it was very much in evidence
in the pagan world. But it was sporadic, not widespread, and never
developed into a systematic teaching about Jews. Though pagan
antisemitism may have emerged from the exclusive way in which Jews
observed their religion, it was not inspired by inter-religious rivalry, as is
the case with Judaism and Christianity, or even Judaism and Islam.
However vicious, it remained cultural and was never built into a
theological understanding of reality. It was the singling out of the Jews as
the embodiment of ambivalence and "otherness", or allosemitism,
combined with the fact that they were, in the Christian scriptures,
elevated to a superhuman mythical level, that separated antisemitism
from other hatreds. This combination enabled antisemitism to go beyond
mere denigration or even persecution of Jews, and allows antisemitism to
be expressed in the outrageously contradictory ways I outlined in chapter
2. In this chapter, we will begin considering the way in which Jews have
been turned from ordinary flesh and blood people into mythical beings, a

development that began only with the emergence of Christianity. We will look, here, at the general dynamics of Christian antisemitism and in chapter 6 try to uncover the history of this development. As I have adopted the use of the word "antisemitism" as an umbrella term, it is interchangeable with "anti-Judaism", a word many scholars use for Christian antagonism to Jews.

PUNISHING THE CHRIST KILLERS

There is a haunting scene in Claude Lanzmann's nine-and-a-half-hour film about the Holocaust, *Shoah*, in which a Jewish survivor, Simon Srebnik, is interviewed in Chelmno together with some of the Polish villagers who had known him in his youth. Standing in front of Chelmno's Catholic church, in which the Jews of the various small villages were locked up before being gassed, the villagers animatedly recall how Srebnik was saved from death because, having had a lovely singing voice, he was kept alive as a privileged mascot to entertain the Gestapo. Each villager tries to outdo the other in recalling what happened to the Jews, and why. They died because they were "the richest", we are told, but Poles, too, died. A woman from Grabow tells us that the townswomen there were glad to see the Jewish women go because the Polish men had been attracted to them. Though the Jews "stank" because so many of them were tanners of leather, Jewish women were beautiful. They thought only of beauty and clothes, and had more leisure time for primping. Polish women, on the other hand, worked. Jews had lived in houses on the square, whereas the Poles lived in the courtyards, where the latrines were located. "Jews and Germans ran Polish industry." "Jews are dishonest." "They exploited Poles ... by imposing their prices." "All Poland", we are told, "was in Jewish hands."[1]

What puts all of this into perspective, however, is a rationalisation by one of the men. The Jews of Myndjewyce, near Warsaw, he had learned, had been gathered in a square. Their rabbi, after gaining permission from an SS man, was allowed to speak. "Around two thousand years ago", the rabbi is purported to have advised his community, "the Jews condemned the innocent Christ to death. And when they did that, they cried out: 'Let his blood fall on our heads and on our sons' heads' ... Perhaps the time has come for that, so let us do nothing, let us go, let us do as we're asked."

The villagers enthusiastically fill in the details. Did the witness think the Jews expiated the death of Christ? No. Had Christ sought revenge? No. "The rabbi said it. It was God's will, that's all." A woman then interjects, "So Pilate washed his hands and said: 'Christ is innocent,' and he sent Barabbas. But the Jews cried out: 'Let his blood fall on our heads!' That's all; now you know!"[2]

Until this theological conjecture about the Jews deserving their fate for the crime of deicide, the comments, though vile and profoundly damaging, could have been used in a number of situations of ethnic competition or racism. It is the theological rationale that underlies these other comments that must give us pause. With the accusation that the Jews killed Christ, they are endowed with both superhuman and subhuman qualities. No longer ordinary people of flesh and blood, they are demonised and endowed with cosmic powers for evil.

A brief analysis of this scene, indeed of the film itself, will illustrate much about the emphasis of this book. Like any writer or artist who tries to represent the Holocaust, Lanzmann cannot but be selective about what he chooses to say and what message he intends to deliver. Starting to make his film in the mid 1970s, he took eleven years to make it. From about 240 hours of film, he chose to retain only nine-and-a-half; his emphasis in what he retains is on the victims' pain and the perpetrators' lack of remorse. He concentrates unwaveringly on the Jewish victims of the Holocaust, which he interprets as a specifically Jewish tragedy. He is deeply opposed to the trend that tries to universalise the Holocaust.

As Daniel Schwarz (1999) points out, he is like a district attorney methodically presenting evidence of past crimes against the Jews to the grand jury of his viewers. He does not present a chronological case. Rather, with the death camps as the centre, he explores the killing process in ever-widening concentric circles. The circles are made up of interviews with people who could throw light on the agony of the Jews – victims, perpetrators, bystanders and modern-day analysts. These are filmed either unadorned – with the head and shoulders of the interviewee filling the screen – or against the backdrop of the beauty of the Polish countryside, where the killings took place. Testimony of violent screams is juxtaposed with quietly running rivers, sylvan forests and pretty villages. As Lanzmann uses no archival footage, there is no visual horror in the film. There is so little Jewish presence left in Poland today that he had to work with traces of traces of traces – burial stones, empty buildings, disused railway lines. The visual beauty makes the horror of what occurred more overwhelming. The ordinariness of the lives of the people now bearing testimony to the atrocities they suffered does the same. By centring on interviews, within the interviewees' ordinary life situations, the film presents a complex chorus of voices – all focused on a single problem.

In this way, Lanzmann shows us that history has many voices, and is composed not merely of the actions of the powerful, but of the behaviour of ordinary people and the ways they interpret the past. The sequence cited above gives us an important clue why antisemitism differs from other forms of racism. Ordinary people still find it possible to "explain away" the ghastly fate of the Jews who lived among them as neighbours in terms of "just" punishment for the crime of deicide, the killing of God. In this rationalisation, they cite words that may have come from a Christian preacher's mouth but could certainly never have passed a rabbi's lips.

Rabbis simply do not think in this way. First, the Jewish idea of the messiah, from which the Christian concept of Jesus as the messiah was originally drawn, is associated with a triumphal overthrow of pagan rule and an actual transformation of the world, neither of which occurred after Jesus' death. Second, for Judaism, the messiah neither suffers nor dies. Third, the idea that God could incarnate himself in human form flies in the face of Jewish monotheism, and the killing of God is an impossibility. Fourth, Jesus is not a central figure in Judaism. The tense relationship between Jews and Christians – in a world in which Christianity assumed political power – resulted in a general disinterest in things Christian among Jews, including the person of Jesus. In Jewish experience, Jesus was associated not with loving redemption, but with cruel persecution, particularly during Easter. If Jesus were to be granted any status at all by Jews, it would be no more than as a prophet.

What we see in the Polish villagers' rationalisation is the tendency to theologise history. Because Christianity grew out of Judaism, it shared the Jews' understanding of the way God acts in history. Though rabbinic Judaism does, as we saw in chapter 3, interpret the history of the Jews in terms of reward and punishment, the rabbis' main concern was to focus on the positive. They created a viable way of life that would enable Jews to survive in the absence of their temple, after it was destroyed in 70 CE, whereas Christian theology placed the destruction of the temple at the centre of its understanding of Jews. The Polish villagers are thus offering a lay person's interpretation of Jewish history through Christian eyes.

They are investing a Jewish tragedy with Christian religious significance and, by so doing, are glibly justifying one of the most brutal acts in world history. They are assuming that the Jews deserved what happened to them and that they were expecting to be punished for a crime that they allegedly, and knowingly, had committed two thousand years ago. None of this would be accepted by Jews.

CHRISTIAN THEOLOGISING OF JEWISH HISTORY

The accusation of deicide (the killing of God) has been the most influential factor in the suffering of the Jews. As John Pawlikowski (1986, p. 107) has pointed out, it laid the groundwork for a highly developed theology within Christianity which claimed that Jews, for the remainder of human history, were to be subjected to continual suffering. They were to live in a state of perpetual wandering, without a homeland, as a punishment for this monumental crime. The accusation led to the wide acceptance of the Final Solution to the "Jewish problem". Though not the primary cause, it was the seedbed for the Final Solution's popular acceptance. Christian churches have moved a long way to eliminate it from religious teaching and the liturgy, but as part of Christian culture, both secular and religious, it continues to linger in popular piety. The theologising of history is just one of the many factors that allowed the terrible slaughter to take place, but it leads one to ask what role Christianity played in preparing people's minds and hearts for what was done to the Jews of Europe.

In the Holocaust, six million Jews were murdered in the heart of Christian Europe. Though the Nazis were anti-Christian and hankered after a Teutonic paganism that they ill understood, their philosophy had been moulded within Christian civilisation. Millions of other Europeans, also of Christian background – even if they were no longer practising Christians – passively acquiesced. How do we explain this? Is it not logical to presume a connection with Christian theological teaching about the Jewish people during the last two millennia? A majority of scholars would unhesitatingly answer this question in the affirmative. Two-thirds of Europe's Jews were murdered by baptised Christians, from whom, as Franklin H. Littell (1975, p. 2) tells us, membership in good standing was not – and has not been – withdrawn. The question is not why some Christians may, or may not, become antisemites, but whether Christianity, itself, is the major source of antisemitism.

The new dimension in the image of the Jew that develops with Christianity is intimately bound up with the way in which Judaism and Christianity are linked to one another. Christianity grew out of Judaism, taking over the Jewish view of history, but seeing it as fulfilled in a novel way by a crucified and suffering messiah. With Paul's mission to the gentiles, the conflict transcended this. Now, the very *raison d'être* of Judaism – the obligation to observe the commandments of the Torah – was put into question. Christian anti-Judaism grew out of the inter-religious antagonism spawned by two religions based on the same scriptures and religious tradition. The initial point of departure was the dispute over the messiahship of Jesus and what messiahship constituted. As Rosemary Ruether pointed out, the special virulence that gives rise to diabolising and damnation arises only between groups that pose rival claims to exclusive truth within the same religious symbol system.

The role that Jesus assumes in Christology departs from the Jewish understanding of the messiah. He becomes the Christ, or saviour. In the process, Christianity retains its roots in the Jewish scriptures but distances itself from Jews and Judaism. The Jews, however, remain what Norman Ravitch calls the "secret centre" of Christian mythology and, therefore, the secret centre of world history. This is graphically illustrated in a disturbing encounter between the Jewish theologian Richard L. Rubenstein and a German pastor, Heinrich Grüber of the Evangelical Church of Berlin, in 1961. Grüber was no antisemite, but the logic of his theology forced him to insist that Auschwitz had to be part of God's plan. He regarded Hitler as God's instrument, likening him to Nebuchadnezzar and other "rods of God's anger". Rubenstein was already in the process of developing his "death-of-God" theology, and had had a number of life experiences that were leading to his collapse of faith, but it was Grüber's interpretation of Jewish history that was responsible for the final rupture.

Grüber had almost lost his life at Dachau, where he had been incarcerated for his opposition to the Nazis, and was the only German to go voluntarily to Jerusalem to testify at the Eichmann trial. He had worked hard, since the war, to reconcile German Christians and Jews. Precisely because Rubenstein regarded him as a man of impeccable integrity and religious faith, his unambiguous declaration that God had sent Hitler to exterminate the Jews led Rubenstein to declare the death of God. "If indeed such a God holds the destiny of mankind in his power", wrote Rubenstein (1974, p. 11), "his resort to the death camps to bring about his ends is so obscene that I would rather spend my life in perpetual revolt than render him even the slightest homage." What so deeply troubled Rubenstein was the way in which Christians – even sympathetic Christians – manipulate Jewish religious logic in order to indict the Jewish people. In the shadow of the death camps, Grüber's insistence "dramatized the consequences of accepting the normative Judaeo-Christian theology of history" (Rubenstein 1966a, p. 46). The role assigned to the Jews in the Christian drama of salvation, according to Rubenstein (1966a, p. 48), reveals a logic in Christian theology which, when pushed to the extreme, ends with justification of, if not incitement to, the murder of Jews. The Holocaust of the Second World War was thus "the terminal expression of Christian anti-Semitism".

Norman Ravitch points out that this theologising of history is characteristic of both Roman Catholic and Protestant theologians and that it always presents the danger of justifying Jewish suffering and tragedy – even the Holocaust. This happens when Christians dogmatise abstractly on human themes without testing their conclusions in the crucible of flesh and blood. They are "thinking Jewish"[3] by applying a Christian judgement to Jewish history. Eliezer Berkovits (1978) goes as far as to say that Christian theology justifies Jewish suffering as a "God-pleasing deed". He insists that Christians must face the fact that this is not theology. Jewish suffering is inflicted not by God, but by human beings upon other human beings, for their rejection of Jesus. It is perpetrated as witness to the iniquity of the Jews and the truth of Christianity. This, Berkovits (1978, p. 325) avers, "is nothing but over-bearing Christian conceit". It equates its own will and dark desires with the will of the Almighty. "To ascribe Christian inhumanity against the Jewish people through the ages to the will of God is the ultimate blasphemy."

There is, however, a profound ambiguity in the intimate theological link between Christians and Jews. This connection can, according to Ravitch (1982, p. 52), be dangerous because, though it gives the Jews a place of honour in world history, the obverse of honour – shame and malediction – is always available. On the other hand, the close religious relationship between Jews and Christians serves also to protect them from both mutual and self hatred in a way that no secular ideology can.

In the shadow of the Holocaust, Christianity's "teaching of contempt" for the Jews – as the Jewish scholar Jules Isaac came to call it[4] – stands indicted, says Norman Ravitch. Only convoluted special pleading can even attempt to quash the heinous charge. But the exact responsibility of Christianity remains elusive. Traditional Christianity did not result in genocide. We must therefore distinguish clearly between how far the church was prepared to go in placing opprobrium on the Jews and in acting this out. We must also take note of the total abandonment of constraint that characterised secularised, anti-Christian, versions of Christian faith. The former stopped well short of genocide. The latter were intrinsically murderous.

Christianity's contribution to the antisemitic climate that allowed the Nazis to enact genocide against the Jews, while most of the rest of the world looked on, resulted in study of the Christian roots of antisemitism. Jewish and Christian scholars brought it into the mainstream of scholarship. In Christian circles there has, since the mid-1970s, been a theological revolution. The most pivotal contribution has come from Rosemary Ruether, who located anti-Judaism in the heart of Christian theology, in its Christology – namely, its particular understanding of Jesus as God-Man and saviour. Anti-Judaism thus inevitably found expression in the New Testament itself. Ruether (1974, p. 116) recognises the formal distinction between the terms "anti-Judaism" and "antisemitism", but goes further than previous scholars by linking the two. "Anti-Judaism," she says, "constantly takes social expression in anti-Semitism."

This chapter will consider the way in which, in the light of Ruether's analysis, Christian teaching may be seen to have contributed to antisemitism. It will focus, first, on three areas in Christianity in which anti-Judaism becomes manifest.[5] Then it will offer a brief survey of scholarship on Christian antisemitism and indicate the direction in which it is leading. The next chapter will offer a brief history of the development of Christian antisemitism. The three foci of Christian antisemitism are rooted in: the quarrel over Jesus as the messiah, the doctrine of chosenness, and the accusation of deicide.

THE THREE FOCI OF CHRISTIANITY'S TEACHING OF CONTEMPT FOR THE JEWS

Rejection of Jesus as the messiah

Christian anti-Judaism, argues Ruether, is not peripheral to Christianity, but central. It relates to Christianity's basic understanding about God – that he became flesh incarnate in the form of Jesus, the Christ. Teaching about Christ is known as Christology, and it is here that Ruether finds the core of Christian anti-Judaism. In the Hebrew Bible there is an implicit promise of a messianic age, which, for Christians, was fulfilled with the life, death and resurrection of Jesus. The New Testament clearly makes these connections. It is, according to Ruether, a *midrash* on the Hebrew Bible. This suggests that, in the same way that the Talmud seeks out the deepest meaning of holy writ for Jews, the New Testament does so for Christians. Because the two religions share the same basic scripture, the two *midrashim* contradict one another. Thus, the New Testament sets out to show that the church – not the Jews – was the rightful heir to the promises of God made in the Hebrew Bible. Because the Jews rejected this interpretation, they were seen as punished and rejected by God, and Judaism was discredited. Anti-Judaism is thus built into the Christian *midrash* and becomes the "left hand" of Christology. The term "Old Testament", Ruether suggests, is itself a term of denigration of the Jewish scriptures, since it implies that the Hebrew Bible has been superseded.

Because the Jews seemed unable to see the truth of the Christian claim, it was concluded that they must have been blind to the real meaning of their own scriptures. The church, therefore, developed a polemic against the Jews. It interpreted the "Old Testament" in such a way that it was able to "prove" that Jesus was the messiah predicted in it. If Jews were blind to this, did it not follow that they were also blind to their holy writ's moral demands? Had they not always been blind? This accusation of Jewish blindness was to assume great significance not only with regard to discrediting Judaism's religious law, leadership and worship, but with regard to its history as a whole, dating back to the time of Moses. In order to retain the "Old Testament" – and hence an intimate connection with the Jewish people and their history – the early church had to adopt a "schizophrenic" attitude to the promises and judgements in the Hebrew Bible. The blessings and curses were split from one another. Instead of being applied to one elect people, namely the Jews, they are now applied to two peoples; the Jews and Christians. To the Jews are applied all the curses, and to the Christians all the blessings. Since only one people can be chosen, the Jews become the reprobate people, whereas the church becomes the future elect people of the promise (Ruether 1977, p. 81). As God intended it, it now appeared, there had always been two peoples: the people of faith – the Christians – who are the rightful heirs of the promise to Abraham, and the fallen, disobedient people – the Jews – who never obeyed God or heard the prophets. The church was seen as the true heir of the promises to

Abraham, whereas the Jews were the heirs of an evil history of faithlessness, apostasy and murder. The result is that the Jews are cut off from their divine election as the chosen people. As a punishment, they are destined to be kept alive as witnesses to Christian truths, but they were to live a reprobate existence, outside their promised land and scattered throughout the world. In the process, as Emil Fackenheim (1986, p. 27) points out, two evils were introduced: self-righteousness among Christians, and condemnation of the Jews.

The doctrine of chosenness

An important part of the dynamic described above is the Jewish doctrine of chosenness. Viewed from the perspective of developing Christianity, it became another potent cause of antisemitism. Never regarded by Jews as a doctrine of racial superiority, but rather as one of special *responsibility*, it has resulted in several difficulties. First, it has been consistently misunderstood and distorted by outsiders. Second, it has been emulated throughout the world in order to legitimate a host of racist theories. The most destructive of these is Nazism, an ideology that, according to George Steiner (1967), boomeranged catastrophically against the Jews themselves in a "hideous relationship of parody". Third, in a dynamic not unlike sibling rivalry, it serves to alienate Jews and Christians in that both claim chosenness, and, fourth, it plays an important role in the dehumanisation of Jews, as an expression of allosemitism.

Logically there cannot be two peoples chosen by the same God. The church therefore set out to call itself the "new" or "true" Israel and to abrogate the chosenness of the Jews. This resulted in a myth of "displacement", or "superseding" the "old Israel" with the "new Israel". The idea that the mission of the Jewish people was finished with the coming of Jesus Christ is, for Franklin H. Littell, the cornerstone of Christian antisemitism. This "writing off" of the old Israel, he claims (1975, p. 2), rings a genocidal note. "To teach that a people's mission in God's providence is finished, that they have been relegated to the limbo of history, has murderous implications which murderers will in time spell out."

One of the most destructive entailments of the doctrine of chosenness is that it has thrust the Jews into an unwanted supernatural vocation as central actors in the salvation of the world, making them the "secret centre" of world history. According to Richard Rubenstein, it may be impossible for Christians to remain Christians without regarding the

Jews in mythic, magic and theological categories. "Jews alone of all the people in the world are regarded as actors and participants in the drama of sin and innocence, guilt and salvation, perdition and redemption." The doctrine of chosenness strips the Jews of their humanity because people are unable to conceive of them as ordinary people, capable of the same virtues and vices as others. By condemning the Jews to the realm of the sacred, chosenness places them in a special category of expectation. Either praised as Jesus-like or condemned and murdered as Judas-like, Jews become the objects of decisive hatreds.

So potentially damaging is the doctrine of chosenness that Rubenstein has called for its demythologisation. Yet, this would not be an easy matter, since Judaism and Christianity are equally dependent on its retention. For Arthur Hertzberg (1966, p. 90), the doctrine is so central that he has claimed, "the essence of Judaism is the affirmation that the Jews are the chosen people; all else is commentary". But the chosenness of the Jews is equally central to Christianity. "Unless Jews have a supernatural vocation," avers Rubenstein (1966b, p. 186), "the Christ makes absolutely no theological difference."

The deicide accusation

The dehumanisation engendered by the doctrine of chosenness has been vastly exacerbated by the deicide accusation, which not only dehumanises Jews, but demonises them. Although responsible theologians attempt to spread the blame for killing Christ to all humanity, Matthew 27:25 confirms Jewish guilt for all generations: "His blood be on us and on our children." One who can kill God is not beyond the most heinous of crimes. This slander against the Jewish people acts, as I indicated above, as a justification for the persecution and murder of Jews and was a powerful motivating factor during the Holocaust. Alice L. Eckhardt (1987, p. 33) points out that during the 1930s the German churches emphasised the curse upon Israel. She cites the words of a Protestant bishop in 1936 – the year after the Nuremberg racial laws were issued:

> When the Jews crucified Jesus, they crucified themselves, their revelation and their history. Thus the curse came upon them. Since then that curse works itself out from one generation to another. This people has ... become a fearful and divinely ordained scourge for all nations, leading to hatred and persecution.

Although the deicide accusation was not the cause of the Holocaust, Emil Fackenheim (1987, p. 13) suggests that, "had there been no two-thousand-year-old slander of Jews as a deicide people, the Holocaust could not have happened".

The negative potential of the deicide accusation must be assessed against the power of the myth that encapsulates it. Hyam Maccoby (1982) regards the myth of the crucifixion of Jesus as the most powerful the world has ever known. In a breathtaking drama designed to lift the burden of guilt from those who believe, the Jews do not play the role of the scapegoats, but Jesus himself is the scapegoat who takes upon himself the sins of the world. The function of the Jews was to bring about the necessary death of the scapegoat in order to save humankind from crisis. For Christianity, the cruel, sacrificial death of Jesus was a necessity, and the Jews were the evil instruments by which this was brought about. The Jews are thus the earthly agents of the cosmic powers of evil. They are the deicides who, by their wickedness, unwittingly save the world, but who are doubly damned in that the death of Christ is not efficacious for them. They crown a long career of sin with the greatest of all sins, the murder of God. They become the embodiment of evil, and excite a combination of awe and hate which, as the hallmark of antisemitism, separates it from all other forms of xenophobia.

Because the Jews were cast as cosmic villains in the Christian doctrine of atonement, their role demanded that any sign of happiness or prosperity among them should arouse anxiety for Christians, for if the Jews did not suffer, who would bear the guilt for the sacrifice of Jesus? As antisemitism is so ingrained in the central myth of Christianity, the only solution, according to Maccoby (1982), is the return of the repressed, namely a real understanding of Christendom's irrational prejudice against the Jews and its determination always to think of them in negative terms. It is the idea that Jews are cosmic villains that makes views about world conspiracy, such as *The Protocols of the Elders of Zion*, so plausible. Without the decisive religious significance of Jews in Christianity's central drama, theories about Jews wanting to control and overrun the world would surely be dismissed by rational people as absurd.

Christendom's negative image of the Jews developed over a long period of time, resulting in Jews being perceived and treated as alien in European society. A formidable anti-Jewish stereotype was developed, originally based on religiously inspired antipathy, but later adapting itself around various foci. Christian teaching formed the basis of these developments and has had an ineradicable influence. As Claire Huchet-Bishop (1977) has suggested, the negative image of the Jew fostered by Christian teaching has "permeated our Western culture so thoroughly that even people wholly detached from the church, including atheists, are no longer unbiased in their reactions toward Jews, though they may think they are". This derogatory image thrived for nearly twenty centuries and, given the nature of the human psyche, is not going to vanish overnight. "What Christian teaching has done, it has to undo; and it will take a long time" (1977, p. 180).

A BRIEF REVIEW OF THE SCHOLARSHIP ON THE CHRISTIAN ROOTS OF ANTISEMITISM

Since 1974, scholarship on the Christian roots of antisemitism has been dominated by Rosemary Ruether, and no consideration of the topic can escape the pervading influence of her work. In her 1974 book, *Faith and Fratricide,* she offered the most audacious response to the question of the Christian roots of antisemitism. She exposed the major issues relating to the Christian–Jewish connection so clearly and provocatively, and she was so fearless in stating her claims – despite the possible danger that her work implied for Christianity's survival – that it became *the* text for stating the problem. As we have seen, she regards Christian anti-Judaism as an integral part of the Christian theological message, the "left hand" of Christology. It cannot, therefore, be a superficial or secondary element in Christian thought. Rather, it is an inherent part of Christian exegesis, the New Testament being an anti-Jewish *midrash* on the Jewish scriptures. "For Christianity," according to Ruether (1974, p. 181), "anti-Judaism was not merely a defence against attack, but an intrinsic *need* of Christian self-affirmation" (my emphasis). Tracing the anti-Judaic myth right back to the New Testament, she showed how the theme was taken up and elaborated by the church fathers to become one of the underpinnings of Western culture. Antisemitism, in the sense in which I have used the term throughout this book, thus becomes an inevitable potential for Christian believers.

Ruether's work did not emerge *ex nihilo*, although the scholars that preceded her resisted seeing the New Testament itself as anti-Jewish in intention. In the early decades of the twentieth century, scholars had already begun to analyse some of the New Testament's anti-Jewish themes. Robert Travers Herford (1860–1950), an English theologian, noted the negative prejudice against the Pharisees in the gospels. Forerunners of rabbinic Judaism, they were here depicted as soulless hypocrites. This picture of them has filtered into the liturgy and into textbooks for Christian education. John Pawlikowski (1977) has pointed out, for example, that one basic series of textbooks "depicted the Pharisees in such a distorted fashion that the student would find it virtually impossible to sense any human identification with them, or to believe that they acted out of human motivation". Herford devoted himself to correcting this view of Pharisaic Judaism among Christians and thus to fostering better relations between Jews and Christians.

George Foot Moore (1851–1931), a Harvard professor of history of religion, re-examined Judaism in the first centuries of the Christian era. He challenged the widely held belief that Judaism was a moribund religion, obsessed with dry legalism, and with nothing positive to offer to outsiders. The negative image of the Jews was, by now, being understood as part of the early church's struggle with a *living* Judaism. Moore claimed that Christian interest in Jewish literature had always been "apologetic or polemic rather than historical".[6] Herford and Moore are separated from the scholars who followed them by the Second World War, which had a decisive influence on the study of Christian antisemitism.

Systematic investigation into the way this prejudice transformed itself into hatred, and the disastrous practical consequences that such hatred was later to have, was pioneered by James Parkes, a British Christian scholar, working in 1934, when Hitler had already come to power. He had been asked by the International Student Service to investigate the history of antisemitism. As he worked on his book *The Conflict of the Church and the Synagogue*, Parkes became increasingly convinced that the real roots of antisemitism lay in the conflict between Christianity and Judaism. Though his conclusions were revolutionary at the time, they now appear, as Nicholas de Lange (1991, p. 26) points out, almost banal – because of the Holocaust and the spur it gave to the study of Christianity's responsibility for antisemitism.

Scholarship on the subject was brought from the margins into the mainstream, and was given unprecedented attention by both Jewish and Christian scholars. It was necessary to determine to what extent Christianity was the primary source of antisemitism – not merely in terms of individual Christians who might have added fuel to the hatred, but in terms of whether Christianity itself was, in its essence, and from its beginnings, the primary source of antisemitism in Western culture. This question was not, and is not, easy to answer. As Gager (1983, p. 13) pointed out, it immediately prompted other questions: What was the exact relationship between pagan attitudes to Jews and those of Christians in the Graeco-Roman world? Was Christian antisemitism influenced by pagan antisemitism, or did it bring to the fore something entirely new? What was the precise character of each type of anti-Judaism in the ancient world? What influence did Judaism exert in the Graeco-Roman world, particularly at the time of Christianity's birth and early development? A variety of responses emerged, some continuing to emphasise the pagan roots of antisemitism, but the majority seeing a decisively new expression of anti-Judaism emerging with Christianity.

Modern antisemitism, these scholars argue, can be traced to an anti-Jewish teaching that was consciously and deliberately elaborated in the early church over a number of generations. Anti-Judaism was an inevitable part of the Christian message. They do not deny that there had been prior hostility to Jews in the pagan world, but they see such animosity as limited and as failing to develop into an official, systematised teaching, as it did in the church. As Fackenheim (1986, p. 26) argues, "had the Christian transfiguration of antisemitism not occurred in the ancient world, it would have died with the ancient world. It was, in fact, well on the way to happening." He suggests, by way of example, that the rabbis were, at the time, modifying their opposition to idolatry, and the Graeco-Roman world was demythologising its pagan religion.

The publication in 1948 of *Jesus and Israel* by the French Jewish historian Jules Isaac inaugurated a new era in the study of pagan and Christian views of Judaism. Unlike most scholars, he was forced to pursue his research into Christian antisemitism while in hiding from the Nazis, after they had murdered both his wife and daughter. He was sixty-six years old in 1943, and the last clandestine message smuggled through from his wife was: "Save yourself for your work, the world is waiting." Isaac continued indefatigably until his death in 1963. Stressing Judaism's vitality at the time of Jesus, and the fundamental Jewishness of early Christianity, he laid the blame for antisemitism at the door of Christianity. Through the use of contrasting passages, he showed that Jews have been wrongly blamed for the crime of deicide. He also showed that the Jews of Jesus' time neither rejected nor crucified him, and that

Jesus had not rejected Israel. He later added the premise that antisemitism was not prevalent among pagans in pre-Christian times. Pagan antisemitism, he suggested, was trivial and vulgar compared with Christian antisemitism. Though he saw antisemitism as exclusively Christian, however, coining the phrase "the Christian teaching of contempt", he believed that it resulted from misinterpretation by Christians of their own scriptures and its statements about their founder, Jesus. Antisemitism, he insisted, stands in opposition to the historic origins and basic tenets of Christianity, and its danger lies in the fact that it affects ordinary people, not merely politicians and scholars, and it does so from early childhood. After the war Isaac met with Pope John XXIII, who was sympathetic to his ideas, and Isaac was a prime mover behind the Second Vatican Council, which in 1965, through its document *Nostra Aetate*, absolved the Jews of the crime of deicide.

In 1948, another French Jewish scholar, Marcel Simon, published *Verus Israel*, and his work began to dominate the field. Reaffirming the attractiveness of Judaism at the time of Christianity's birth, he attributed the antisemitism of the early church to the disappointment and resentment felt by nascent Christianity that Judaism "far from converting or collapsing, continued to exert itself even among the ranks of the faithful" (Simon 1948, p. 274).[7] This dynamic of antisemitism has persisted for nearly two thousand years. The fact that Jews insist on remaining Jewish and that they thereby challenge Christianity's dominant dogmas perpetuates antisemitism.[8] Simon felt that it was important to distinguish between the anti-Jewish polemic that was part of the church attempting to identify itself as a separate entity, and Christian antisemitism, which was born of a hatred of Jews arising out of their refusal to accept Christian claims. The latter resulted in hostility to Jews in general.

It fell, however, to Rosemary Ruether to place anti-Judaism in Christology and the New Testament. By doing this, she has redefined the problem. Nevertheless, despite Ruether's bold claims, she lies on a continuum of scholarship from Moore and Parkes, through Simon and Isaac, to the present day. Ruether's main aim was to expose the teaching of contempt and to find possible solutions to the problem. She feels, however, that anti-Judaism may be too deeply embedded in the foundations of Christianity to be rooted out without toppling the entire structure (1974, p. 228).

RUETHER'S INFLUENCE

Before Ruether, most Christian scholars saw the New Testament as devoid of a real antisemitic outlook. They explained its hostility to Jews and Judaism in terms of either a contest for converts or fear of being too closely associated by the Romans with rebellious Jews. The latter reason led to the playing down of Roman responsibility for Jesus' death and the indictment of the Jews for the crime. They also attributed the anti-Jewish tone in Paul's letters to a misunderstanding of what he had in mind concerning the "Judaisers" he was denouncing. Another explanation was that later Christian believers had failed to recognise the negative passages for what they were – a continuation of Jewish prophetic language (often denunciatory), intended for the members of the new community, rather than as a judgement on Judaism itself. Disputes on Jewish law, some scholars point out, had been going on within Judaism at the time. These disputes are reflected here. The anti-Jewish trends were a product of post-biblical distortion. This type of theory continues, as we shall see later, alongside a more open acceptance of the damage done by the New Testament.[9]

Some scholars, like Gregory Baum, had offered explanations of this kind, but Ruether's work forced him, and others, to reverse their previous defences of Christianity. Baum felt compelled to accept Ruether's view that, as long as the Jews – that is, the Jewish religious tradition – continues to reject the Christian interpretation, the validity of the Christian view is in question. The hatred and persecution of the Jewish people is explained by a need to make the Jews realise their error and admit that the church is right. A suffering Israel was, and continues to be, needed by the church for its own self-understanding and justification. But Ruether's book did not go unchallenged. Important works have taken the debate further. One of them is Alan Davies' compilation of a volume of essays, responding to Ruether's thesis, in honour of James Parkes's eightieth birthday, *Anti-Semitism and the Foundations of Christianity* (1979). Another is John Gager's *The Origins of Anti-Semitism* (1983), which marks a distinct turning point in the study of antisemitism.

Though Gager admits that the New Testament deals harshly with Jews, he regards it as reflecting only one side of a complex conflict, and as the voice of the ultimate winners. He shows that the evidence we have for the emergence of antisemitism is scanty and conflicting, and that the conclusions we have based on this evidence are faulty. We have a distorted picture of the nature and universality of Jew hatred at the time of Christianity's birth. The paucity of evidence merely raises other questions.

To make us aware of the variety of religious positions that must have existed at the time of Christianity's emergence, and to reflect the nuances and breadth of the conversation that must have taken place at the time, Gager starts his book with an imaginary argument. He sets the scene in about 138 CE, just after the Romans had decisively crushed the final Jewish revolt in Palestine. In the wake of Bar Kochba's messianically inspired revolt, a Jew, a Christian, a Greek and a Roman each states his religious position. A fifth man listens in silence. He, who is both a Jew and a Christian, finally speaks, throwing all the others into confusion. It is this voice, Gager contends, that is entirely censored from the New Testament.

BROADENING THE CONVERSATION IN EARLY CHRISTIAN TIMES

The Jew starts out Gager's imaginary debate by explaining that he cannot accept Jesus as the messiah. How can Jesus possibly be equal to God? And, in any case, how can one make any such claims without following the commandments? Besides, he argues, the Christian claim is based on the most ridiculous and implausible interpretation of scripture.

The Christian, in his riposte, accuses the Jew of being rebellious and stiff necked. The Jews' teachers had led them astray. If they cannot see what, to Christians, is so obvious, they must surely be blind to the truth of their own holy scriptures. The prophecies had been quite clear, and it is equally clear that Jesus has fulfilled them. The Jews not only killed the prophets, but they have now killed Jesus. God has made Jesus the Lord and Christ for all nations, and the Jews have closed their ears to his universal call for repentance. God has, therefore, abandoned them. The fact that their temple lies in ruins is proof of God's rejection of them. God has replaced the old covenant with a new one, and the commandments are no longer valid. A new covenant, with a new people, has been established by God. The Christians are now the "New Israel".

The Greek debunks both their arguments. Jews, he says, are descended from a motley band of runaway slaves with a charlatan and magician as their leader. True, they have been rebellious. True, they tend to despise the rest of humankind. But the Christians are even worse. Not only have they accepted this nonsense, but they have thrown away the ancestral Jewish customs – worthless as they are – and left themselves with nothing at all!

The Roman then enters the debate. Yes, the Jews have been an extremely rebellious lot, but, now that the Bar Kochba rebellion has been decisively crushed, there is no reason why they cannot calm down and continue to be good neighbours and citizens. Most Jews, he argues, did not really want the rebellion. But one thing troubles him. What is it in Judaism, he asks, that attracts so *many* Romans? Why are there so many converts to Judaism and sympathisers with it? Such interest may well be good for the Jews, but how good is it for the Romans? Yes, Jews do have some valuable ideas – like monotheism and loyalty to God – and their scriptures are certainly ancient enough to warrant admiration and respect, but some of their customs – such as circumcision – are repulsive.

Then the fifth man, who has listened in silence, speaks. He is a Jew *and* a Christian, having converted to Judaism before recognising Jesus as the messiah, and is the son of a local pagan family. He turns to the Jew and says there can be no doubt who Jesus is. It is quite clear that many prophecies have been fulfilled in him. There are just too many correspondences. The Jews must be blind not to see them. And now they have made things worse for themselves by excluding from the synagogues those who accept Jesus as the messiah. He then turns to the Christian and exclaims, "You call us heretics? How can you claim that *you* are now the true Israel when you do not even keep the Mosaic covenant as we do? Jesus came *not* to abolish the law and the prophets, but to *fulfil* them. I know that you call upon the apostle Paul as a witness for your position, but is it not possible that we have misunderstood Paul's teachings?"[10]

The conversation offers a foretaste of the book, in which Gager tries to reflect the multiplicity of voices that have, to some extent, been silenced, while also reinterpreting Paul. In early Christian times several rival factions existed. Judaism was far from monolithic and there were several sects within it. One Jewish sectarian view was highly critical of the others and, as Ruether points out, often saw itself as the "True Israel" at the cost of the others. This was taking place in a situation of messianic fervour and an apocalyptic expectation of the end of days. But, as William Nicholls points out, these factions were all still part of one religion. Jews were riling under Roman domination and there was a section among them that wanted violent overthrow of Roman rule to usher in the messianic era. There were Jews in both Palestine and the diaspora, and in the latter they were a minority. Among the many pagans, or gentiles, many sympathised with Judaism, and many others did not.

In the pagan world, too, there was a great deal of religious ferment. The mystery religions were suggesting new forms of salvation through dying and rising gods. Gnostic ideas, which saw body and soul in dualistic terms, had emerged, possibly among parts of the Jewish community. These were leading to a desire for some kind of superhuman saviour. The earliest Christians were Jews who accepted Jesus as the messiah, while not relinquishing their Judaism. There were also gentiles who were attracted to Christianity. An important group was made up of those, under the leadership of Paul of Tarsus, who felt that one did not have to be bound by Jewish law in order to become Christian, and opposed the so-called "Judaising" tendencies in the early Christian movement. A struggle for legitimacy ensued, and what was to become "orthodox Christianity" won. Judaism, according to Gager, provoked deep internal divisions among both Christians and pagans. Thus, the real debate in Christianity was not between Christians and Jews, but between Christians themselves (1983, p. 269). The anti-Jewish side eventually won, and its ideology is reflected in the New Testament. This view became normative for subsequent Christianity and Western culture.

Gager argues, therefore, that neither pagan nor Christian attitudes to Jews were as uniform and universal as we are inclined to infer. There were positive elements in each that have been suppressed. In addition, the Holocaust has understandably resulted in a focus almost solely on negative attitudes to Jews. Thus the negative has been brought into the mainstream of scholarship and has determined the direction of study. Our perception of early Christianity has been determined by what we today read in the New Testament. The voices of the losers – those who would have accepted Christianity without finding it necessary to repudiate Judaism, and the pagans who saw in Judaism a universal religion for all humankind – have been silenced. In the process, Judaism itself became a loser because of the negative way it has been represented in Christian sources, ancient and modern. Finally, we know so little about the losers, that we, too, are losers. The picture we have has been shaped by selective images from a distant past and is grievously distorted. If we are to gain insight into the roots of antisemitism, a fuller, more nuanced range of attitudes to Jews needs to be exposed. Though Gager has tried to be a dispassionate observer, he admits to having been deeply touched by the Holocaust. He is not so sanguine as to believe that an appreciation of a wider spectrum of attitudes to Jews will eradicate antisemitism, but he suggests that new images may liberate scholars, as well as the culture of which they are part. The images of the past that we carry with us help to shape our present and future.

Gager's book was published twenty years ago, but the attempt to enlarge the conversation continues, one of its important thrusts being to establish what Jesus himself may actually have said. As we will see in the next chapter, the negative story we have been told about Jesus' relationship with the Jews of his time has been extremely damaging. But it is also historically inaccurate. One of the noteworthy current projects to establish what Jesus said is the "Jesus Seminar", a group of New Testament scholars, led by Robert Funk and Dominic Crossan, that arose in the 1980s. Approximately thirty scholars meet at a time, discuss particular passages of the gospels and try to establish, through colour-coded voting, which purported statements of Jesus are reliable within the context of the history we know, and which are not. If we can reconstruct a more accurate picture of Jesus' relationship with the Jews of his time, we can help to create a more harmonious relationship now.

Another group, the International Q Project, is attempting to reconstruct the sources behind the New Testament, especially behind the gospels of Matthew and Luke. It has just completed the text of "Q", a source identified originally by German scholars – from the word *Quelle*, which means "source" – and has been published by Fortress Press, in its Hermeneia Series, under the title *The Q Sayings of Jesus*. I turn now to consider the historical development of the negative Christian image of Jews, attempting to reconstruct events so that we may approximate what really happened, and why the story was told in the way it was.

6

The historical development of Christian antisemitism

Now to the Christian, the Jew is the incomprehensibly obdurate man, who declines to see what has happened; and to the Jew, the Christian is the incomprehensibly daring man, who affirms in an unredeemed world that its redemption has been accomplished.

Martin Buber

It has sunk into the sub-conscious – or unconscious – of Christians that "after all, Jews ought to have become Christians, and, if they don't see it, they can fairly be expected to take the consequences." Their conduct two thousand years ago is constantly brought before us: they are never shown as a normal, contemporary people with a normal contemporary religion.

James Parkes

RECONSTRUCTING EARLY CHRISTIANITY

Although Christianity was to exert a positive force on the world, it also had a destructive potential in the way it represented Jews and Judaism. Though Jesus was a man of extraordinary ability and moral character, whose life has inspired countless noble deeds, the depiction in the gospels of his relations with his own people has had disastrous results. It has led to suspicion and hatred of Jews, and to their persecution and death, a situation without which the Holocaust could not have occurred.

The survey of scholarship in the previous chapter indicated the importance of placing the development of antisemitism within the history of early Christianity and second temple Judaism. Now we will look at the problems of reconstruction and some of the theories about the emergence and development of that negative view. Whereas the previous chapter dealt with the effects of the teaching of contempt for the Jew that started two thousand years ago, this one will try to give an idea of the historic circumstances that gave rise to that teaching. Two millennia of conflict between two religions have obscured the fact that early Christianity was not a new religion. It was part of Judaism. Another fact that is obscured is that Judaism, at the time of Jesus, was a vigorous, and probably actively proselytising, religion that had considerable appeal in the gentile world. The Christian "teaching of contempt", therefore, originally began because Judaism refused to disappear.

To reconstruct the history of early Christianity, information is needed about the historical facts of Jesus' life and how a religion that started with a Jew became so anti-Jewish. The latter development is undoubtedly connected with the apostle Paul and his mission to the gentile world. Paul, who was born a Jew and claimed to have been a Pharisee, did not deem it necessary for gentiles to observe the details of the Torah in order to become part of the covenant people. But there is much disagreement on whether Paul had, himself, become anti-Jewish. Scholars have scoured the pages of the New Testament to ferret out the historical facts, but they stubbornly elude certainty. The first century of Christianity – its most creative period – is also its most historically obscure.

New Testament studies has become a huge and complex field which is reminiscent of detective work in that the slightest clue may lead to new understanding. From internal clues, as they relate to known history, scholars are trying to determine when the various parts of the New Testament were written, for whom, where and why. Who was the author addressing and what message was he trying to convey? Was he the original and only author, or were there various layers of redaction? What was the underlying intention of the entire collection of New Testament writings when they were finally canonised? It is beyond the scope of this book to present even a summary of critical New Testament scholarship but, as we shall see, the above questions have an important bearing on the development of Christian antisemitism.

Most people, while acknowledging that Jesus was a Jew, and that his first followers were Jewish, take it for granted that he was deeply critical of the religion of his people and that he was bringing a new message to replace it. This is the way the New Testament tells the story of Jesus, indicting the Jewish authorities for cunningly bringing about his crucifixion, and depicting the Jews as Jesus' implacable enemies, baying for his blood. None of this, modern critical New Testament scholarship suggests, is historically correct. William Nicholls, in a very scholarly – yet accessible – 1995 summation of recent biblical scholarship, *Christian Antisemitism: A History of Hate*, suggests that we have to "peel back" the layers of the New Testament to reveal the actual history of Jesus. This method must also be followed to throw light on the history of Paul and the early church. The earliest writings in the New Testament are the letters of Paul, and he most probably never met the man Jesus. The New Testament itself thus has a history, and the way this history is reconstructed has an important bearing on the development of Christian anti-Judaism. Peeling back the layers of redaction will help to uncover the true motivation of the writers and show why the New Testament came to depict the Jews in the negative way it did.

The New Testament, as we saw in the last chapter, is a Christian *midrash* on the Hebrew Bible, which Christians now saw as the "Old Testament". Seeking the deepest meaning of the text, the Christian writers began to write their own *midrash*, reading back into the Hebrew scriptures predictions for Jesus as the messiah which are not present in the way Jews understand them. Furthermore, they used the Septuagint, a Greek translation by Hellenistic Jews, which itself had departed from the original meaning through translation. Thus, for example, the Hebrew word in Isaiah 7:14 *almah* is translated in the Greek as "virgin" rather than as "young woman". The reading "a virgin shall conceive" thus supplied a proof text for the doctrine of the virgin birth of Jesus. The "Old Testament" was soon to become a totally different book with totally different intentions, constituting a series of anticipations of the life of Christ. One example of this is Matthew's account of Jesus' parents going down to Egypt to fulfil Hosea's prophecy (11:1): "Out of Egypt I called my son", a statement that, in the Jewish context, refers to the Exodus of the Jews from Egyptian bondage.

The Christian *midrash* gradually moved in a direction that insisted that Jews were in error and their interpretations false. The intention of its original authors may not have been antisemitic, but the layers of redaction became increasingly distanced from Judaism, depicting the Jews as enemies of Jesus and as blind to the purport of their own scriptures. By the time the New Testament was canonised in the fourth century CE, it contained a profoundly anti-Jewish message. This chapter will suggest how this process took shape, and the effects that it had, by looking at some of the turning points in the conflict.

THE GOSPELS AS "HISTORY"

A paucity of information makes Christianity's early history difficult to reconstruct: the main source of facts about Jesus' life is the gospels, which are not history books, but books of faith. William Nicholls reminds us that they were "propaganda" in the original sense of the word, in that they were designed to propagate the new faith. Though they embody authentic historical memories of Jesus, these are used in the service of an entirely new concept of the messiah, different from that of Judaism and embodied in what Nicholls calls "the new salvation myth", of which there will be more later.

Another difficulty facing us today is that there is a tendency for us, in the light of the tragic events of the twentieth century, to read in meanings that were not intended at the time. This is most obviously the case with Paul of Tarsus, whose mission it was to bring the gospel to the gentiles. The intentions of the authors, within their historic situation, may have been different from the way we see them today. Moreover, with the long gap in time, we find difficulty in appreciating the full picture because we have no way of interpreting the silences that must have occurred when pauses in the conversation took place. As E. P. Sanders, in his 1991 biography of Paul points out, for example, we have Paul's letters because a disciple of his collected them in about 90 CE. We probably do not have all that he wrote, but what we do have reveals a man of passion and rage, who is both promoting and defending his mission in the face of a good deal of opposition. What we do not have are the arguments put forward by his opponents which shaped his responses. Reconstruction of Paul's intentions has to be undertaken, therefore, without knowing the exact circumstances that prompted him to answer in the way he did.

It may serve to illustrate how we tend to misread this history by showing how some Christian scholars, particularly those in the German tradition, have looked at the Judaism of Jesus' day. Convinced that Judaism was arid and legalistic, a moribund religion due for replacement in God's plan for the world, these scholars saw Christianity, the vibrant new religion, as supplanting Judaism. The very name they called it, *Spätjudentum,* or "late Judaism", indicated their uncritical acceptance of the idea that, already, Christianity was superseding Judaism. Jesus was a divinely disruptive force within a dying and obsolete Judaism. "In a truer perspective", says Nicholls (1995, p. 12), "the Judaism of Jesus' time was early, not late. It was not destined to be superseded and had an important future ahead of it." We may go even further than has Nicholls. The Judaism of Jesus' time is not even "early" Judaism, since Judaism goes back to the very first experiences of the Jews as a people, the Exodus from Egypt. Rather, it represents a crucial stage in the development of rabbinic Judaism which was going to set the course for all forms of Judaism that have persisted up to the present day. Let us now turn to the central historical figure on which Christianity is based, Jesus of Nazareth.

JESUS

As Christianity is rooted in the Jewish understanding of history, it too is regarded as a historical religion. The central event around which the entire religion pivots is the historical person, Jesus – his life, death and resurrection. As the scholar of world religions Huston Smith (1958, p. 318) reminds us, Jesus was a man of humble Jewish origin, the son of a Jewish carpenter. He was born in a stable and was executed as a criminal at age thirty-three. He never travelled more than ninety miles from his birthplace, owned nothing, attended no college, marshalled no army "and instead of producing books did his only writing in the sand. Nevertheless, his birthday is kept across the world and his death day sets a gallows against almost every skyline."

Despite the enormous influence that Jesus had on the world, we know very little about his actual life because it is difficult to separate the facts of his life from the later teachings about him by the apostle Paul, who, according to several scholars of antisemitism – such as William Nicholls, Hyam Maccoby and Joel Carmichael – began to supplant the Jewish messianic idea, as it moved into the gentile world, with a powerful new salvation myth. A Jewish redeemer, as Jesus was originally thought to have been within the Jewish mythic structure, was now seen as having been born of a virgin and become the personal saviour of all humankind. The pages of the four gospels, Matthew, Mark, Luke and John – the primary source for facts about the historic Jesus – have probably been the most read, studied and analysed texts in all of religious literature. Yet they were written well after Paul's mission, and reflect an absorption of this myth, each with its own unique under-standing. It thus becomes difficult to separate the Jesus of history from the Christ of faith.

It is an extraordinary fact that we have no idea of Jesus' physical appearance. He has been depicted in a variety of ways, but very seldom as Jesus the Jew, with prayer shawl, side locks, and observing the daily rituals of Judaism. One of the very first things that Christians learn about Jesus is that he was Jewish, but there is no real content to this Jewishness. On the contrary, Jesus is traditionally represented as bringing a new religion to replace an obsolescent one, a religion that brings in new ideas, such as a virgin birth and a dying and rising God, ideas alien to Judaism. Most people assume that Jesus was the founder of Christianity and see him as – in his own lifetime – founding a religion that was to be at odds with Judaism. He is presented as the messiah who was promised to the Jewish people, but was spitefully spurned by them because they could not, or would not, heed his message. No sooner did he reach adulthood than he found fault with the Jews around him because of their obsession with dry, pettifogging legalism. They are depicted as intent on the letter of the law rather than on its spirit, and they thus became his enemies. Instead of being open to his message of love, they hypocritically made a show of their own "piety". Because of the threat he presented to their religious way, they are accused of trumping up charges of blasphemy against him and reporting him to the Romans, who crucified him. When given an opportunity to allow Jesus to go free, they, as a blood-thirsty mob, chose the common criminal Barabbas instead.

The latest critical New Testament scholarship shows that this picture of Jesus is no longer credible. The meagre biographical facts of Jesus' life – and they are constantly subject to change – are gradually being supplied by critical New Testament scholarship. Scholars have, for years, searched for the historical Jesus, the man who lived and worked among his own people in Palestine. But to find him has been an almost insurmountable task. Albert Schweitzer made an early attempt that raised profound questions. We know little of Jesus, he said, and what we do know is open to doubt. Jesus was, for example, wrong in his belief that the world was imminently coming to an end. From the perspective of the development of antisemitism, one of the first questions to present itself is how a religion that started with a Jew, and retains the person of Jesus as a central figure, could have developed the anti-Jewish tone that we saw in the last chapter.

FINDING THE HISTORICAL JESUS

The search for the historical Jesus – and thus the *Jewish* Jesus – is dogged by a host of problems.The first is that almost all the evidence lies inside the New Testament – and is, according to Northrop Frye (1982, p. 42), "hermetically sealed within it". A unique literary genre, of abiding artistic power and perennial freshness, the gospels open the New Testament by announcing the good news of the messianic coming. The name "gospel" derives from the word *Godspel*, or "good news". The gospels are not dispassionate histories, but are designed to promote belief through narrative. The details they contain give the impression that they are biographies. But the information in them is often contradictory, because the account of Jesus' life has been embedded within individual perspectives of faith. As religious documents, they are meant to be read through the spectacles of faith, and do not lend themselves readily to historical investigation or detached inquiry.

Second, there is no certainty about the gospels' origins and development in time or space. Although they have, for centuries, been the most read texts in the world, scholars have never managed to establish beyond doubt such simple questions as where, when and for whom they were written. Even the authors of the gospels have not been unambiguously identified. All we have is informed guesswork, based on minute analysis of the text against historic factors that we can establish, which then assesses the evidence the texts offer. There is a general consensus that all the gospels evolved through three stages: first, the preaching of Jesus himself, second, an oral tradition about Jesus which was later written down, and third, the reshaping of the text by the evangelists for their own particular audiences in the light of their particular historical and political situation. If the gospels are not eye witness accounts, and their main concern was not history, their portrayal of Jesus may well tell us more about the Christ of faith than it does about the Jesus of history. Already, then, at the time of writing, the details of Jesus' life had been filtered through decades of developing belief.

Because the picture of Jesus in the first three gospels is drawn from a similar perspective, they are called the "synoptic" gospels. Yet each emphasises different things, contradicting some of the details in the other two. Most New Testament scholars think that the oldest gospel is Mark, and that Matthew and Luke both based their gospels on it, as well as other traditions distinctive to themselves. Some suggest that Matthew and Luke also depended on a source (German *Quelle*) that has since been lost and which is usually referred to as "Q". It is suggested that Mark was written in Rome around 60 CE, Matthew in Antioch around 85 CE, and Luke in Corinth in about 80 CE. John's gospel was probably the latest, written as late as 100 CE, but the late Bishop John Robinson, of *Honest to God* fame, asserted controversially that John was the first of the gospels to be written.

John's gospel stands apart from the three synoptics because it tends to be more theological, offering a belief that Jesus was the pre-existent *Logos* (Word), who had taken on human form and lived among his people – the Incarnation – concealing his true nature from all but those who saw him through the eyes of faith. Ironically, however, John's gospel is sometimes closer to Jesus' actual life circumstances than the synoptic gospels. John, for example, uses the word *opsarion* rather than *ichthus* for "fish". As the former indicates a "smoked fish", it seems to tell us something about the intimate lifestyle of the apostles.[1] More important for the study of antisemitism, John excludes an account of the trial of Jesus which, in the gospels of Mark and Matthew, pictures the Jewish leadership as condemning Jesus for blasphemy and scheming to eliminate him, a scene which, in Luke's gospel, more closely resembles the Jews lynching Jesus. As Nicholls (1995, p. 105) points out, there is adequate historical reason to doubt that a formal trial took place. For one thing, Jesus was ostensibly tried for blasphemy, but blasphemy in Judaism involves the improper use of the name of God the tetragrammaton.[2] Claiming messiahship is not an offence in Jewish law and the identification of Jesus with God is a later development. Also, as Geza Vermes (1983, p. 36) suggested, there were regulations at the time that would have prohibited holding a capital trial by night or on a festival. The synoptic gospels strain our credulity, therefore, by depicting a trial taking place before the full Sanhedrin on the evening of the Passover celebration. We saw, in chapter 3, how sacred that night is to Jews. Although John's gospel is often regarded as the most antisemitic of the gospels, the absence of the trial, which is so damning on the Jews, is probably closer to the historical truth than are the synoptic gospels.

All of the gospels present a negative picture of the Jews and of Jesus' relationship with them. This is particularly true of the Pharisees, the sect to which Jesus, ironically, probably had the closest links. The gospel of Matthew gives a consistently denigrating picture of the Jews, calling them a "viper's brood" and showing them enunciating the terrible curse against themselves, "His blood be upon us and our children" (27:25), which was to echo so appallingly through the centuries. John identifies the Jews as sons of the devil, thus beginning a process of demonisation in a statement, not extant in the other gospels, attributed to Jesus himself:

> "I know that you are descended from Abraham, but you are bent on *killing* me because my teaching makes no headway with you ... That is not how Abraham acted. You are doing your own father's work."
> They said, "We are not base-born; God is our father, and God alone."
> Jesus said, "If God were your father you would love me, for God is the source of my being and from him I come ... Your father is the devil and you choose to carry out your father's desires. He was a murderer from the beginning, and is not rooted in the truth ... You are not God's children that is why you do not listen."
>
> John 8:38ff, New English Bible, emphasis mine

JESUS THE JEW

A new and momentous development in the history of the critical study of the New Testament has been the discovery of Jesus as an observant Jew, not at odds with Judaism, but in harmony with it and with his own people. Modern scholarship is increasingly showing that a new gentile salvation myth was overlaid on the history of Jesus as an observant Jew. On the basis of the Jewish concept of the messiah, the myth was invested with new content that was alien to Jewish understandings of messianism and would have bewildered the real Jesus.

The Jewish messianic expectation is historical and political. It prophesies redemption of the people from pagan rule, through the agency of an anointed king. This will be followed by the inauguration of the Kingdom of God, which will usher in a new, perfected, world and bring about a total transformation of history. The lion will lie down with the lamb, nations will forge their swords into ploughshares and there will be peace on earth. But, as we know, the Romans crucified Jesus, an ignominious death for the messiah, who the Jews believed could not die. The idea of a suffering messiah, who would leave the world unchanged, was not part of Jewish expectation. Thus, Jesus was portrayed in a very different way from which Jews could conceivably have portrayed the messiah. The discovery of Jesus' essential Jewishness has, according to

Nicholls, been the most revolutionary development in the history of the critical study of the New Testament.

Nicholls's book is of great importance to us because it was motivated by what happened to the Jews during the Holocaust, and offers a summary of the scholarship that preceded it. Geza Vermes, David Flusser, E. P. Sanders, James H. Charlesworth and others had analysed the New Testament against the backdrop of a sympathetic – rather than hostile – understanding of Judaism, unearthing an image of Jesus the Jew. Furthermore, Nicholls examines Christian antisemitism in the context of the academic study of religion, that is, within the matrix in which it finds its most convincing roots. He calls for Christians – and Jews – to recognise Jesus' fundamental Jewishness because only in this way can the negative portrayal of Jesus' relationship with the Jews be corrected. Modern scholarship has revealed Jesus as a faithful Jew, not antagonistic to the world of his people. Studied in the context of the Judaism of the second temple period in which he lived, the real Jesus is emerging as a man who, as Nicholls (1995, p. 83) puts it, "belongs essentially to Judaism and only accidentally to Christianity". How, then, did Christianity, with its strong anti-Jewish orientation, grow out of the life and work of Jesus the Jew? Though it stares us in the face, this question is not easy to answer and may never be answered with certainty. The only way to gain insight is to strip off later developments and try to imagine the earliest form of Christianity for what it was – a Jewish messianic movement. Only then will we see how original Jewish beliefs were transformed into the Christian myth, in which Jews appear as enemies of Jesus and as Christ killers. As the new messianic movement spread into the gentile world, the new myth took root. Jesus became the Christ, and Christians began to see his death as a cosmic struggle with the forces of evil. On the cross, Christ defeated the devil and overcame sin and death. With this, in place of observance of the Torah by God's covenant people, faith in the saviour's victory would bring all humankind into God's covenant. Belief in the power of the saviour's victory, as well as participation in the sacraments, would bring the world to salvation.

Getting behind this myth, modern critical methods have made it possible to trace the outlines of a history of Jesus that is surprisingly different from the story that has been familiar to the Western world for two thousand years. They reveal that the idea of Jesus born of a virgin is no longer "gospel truth", and that Jesus was a Jewish teacher who taught from his own direct experience of the nearness of God and his compassion for sinners. What opposition he provoked came from the overly zealous, probably because he attempted to enact, in his own actions, God's nearness and compassion for Israel's sinners, the "lost sheep" of Israel. But he did not himself stray from the Torah that God had given to his people. He may well have criticised some of the religious interpretations and practices of his contemporary Jewish brothers and sisters, much in the way that the biblical prophets castigated their people. But, contrary to the traditional picture, he did not oppose Judaism *per se*. He emphasised God's love and readiness to welcome back repentant sinners, but Judaism had always done this. He may have put more emphasis on the closeness of God, and been acting out this closeness in his own dealings with outcasts and sinners, which some may have seen as scandalous, but he was not bringing a new religion. Although he had gained a reputation among his followers and the crowds for being the messiah, who would deliver his people, he, himself, according to Nicholls, did not make this claim. He saw it as a dangerous illusion, and tried his best to dispel it – but in vain. He lost his life, while still a young man, because of that illusion. The Romans saw him as a pretender and insurgent and crucified him.

Though Jesus, according to Nicholls, did not claim to be the messiah, even if he *had*, such a claim would not have been considered blasphemous by the Jewish community of his time. Thus, there was no formal trial. However, many Jews did believe that he was the messiah. In the light of the Jews' history of rebelliousness under the Romans, and the fact that Jewish messianism centred around the overthrow of pagan rule by a victorious leader, the very association of Jesus with messiahship led to his crucifixion by the Romans as a militant revolutionary.

Jesus' first followers were Jews who believed that Jesus was the long-awaited messiah. Jesus' death caused a crisis, because the notion of a suffering and dying messiah meant nothing to Jews. Soon after Jesus' death, however, there were visions of his resurrection and his earliest followers did as all Jews at the time would have done. They searched their scriptures to find meaning for what had happened, rediscovering biblical allusions to suffering which they could apply to Jesus, like the passages on the Suffering Servant in the book of Isaiah. They were not starting a new religion, and were still part of Judaism. There were several sects at the time, and several ways of being Jewish. This was merely one more. The sects were inclined to see themselves as the "true Israel" and the true inheritors of God's promise, but they were all part of one people.

The new messianic sect believed that Jesus would return soon and that a transformation of the world would come about. The real problem seems to have arisen with the work of the apostle Paul and his call to spread the gospel to the gentiles.

As we know, Jesus did not return and in the meantime the gospel was spread to the gentile world. The messianic doctrine developed into one of otherworldly individual salvation, which, in turn, resulted in a remodelling of scripture to fit the facts. So, what started out as a sectarian messianic belief turned into a new religion with a new myth about Christ, the saviour. An entirely different structure was set up, which was dependent on Judaism, on the one hand, and repudiated its religious value, on the other.

Because the New Testament was compiled in Roman times – after the destruction of the second temple in 70 CE and the routing of the Jewish revolutionaries – the authors of the gospels made every attempt to distance themselves from their Jewish origins. This was not an unnatural reaction, since the Jews were justifiably seen as rebels. The early Christian movement wished to ingratiate itself with the ruling power, and blamed the Jews for the death of Jesus, absolving the Romans. The evangelists, as an embattled minority, felt the need to distort history to ingratiate themselves with their Roman overlords. Reorganising the historical events, they depicted the Romans favourably, while presenting the Jewish religious leadership as unscrupulous and blood-thirsty. Pontius Pilate – in reality cruelly opposed to the idea of Jewish messianism because of the insurrectionist activity it symbolised – is portrayed implausibly as Jesus' dithering supporter, easily manipulated by the Jews. As time went on, the layers of redaction became increasingly anti-Jewish, and the more so they became, the more they betrayed the Jewish Jesus. This was particularly ironic in that the early Christians had been protected under the umbrella of Judaism, which the Romans regarded as a licit, or franchised, religion. What had started out as a sect within Judaism eventually grew into a separate religion, based on the same tradition. With the emergence of Christianity as a gentile religion, a claim that it superseded Judaism now began.

Anthony Saldarini (1994) explains that some of the invective against the Pharisees may have been relatively early, while Matthew's community was still Jewish. He points out that Jesus' early followers and the Pharisees were the only Jewish groups to have survived the destruction of the second temple and were locked in battle for the heart of the traditions of Israel. Matthew's vitriol is addressed to the arch-rivals of the Jewish Christians, the Pharisees. With the later entry of a large number of gentiles into Matthew's community, however, the stage was set for the separation into two different religions and the insistence that Christianity now superseded Judaism.

The search for Jesus the Jew is not a trivial endeavour and should not be confined to the academic ivory tower. The Holocaust cannot be comprehended without taking into account the way people had been taught, within their own religious tradition, to view Jews. Nazi antisemitism, as Nicholls (1995, p. xxiv) points out, could never have arisen without a Christian past to draw upon, and Nazism was, itself, a secularised offspring of that past. All forms of modern antisemitism – whether secular, conservative, Marxist or liberal – though not identical with historical Christian anti-Judaism, "clearly sprang from it" and are "branches of the same tree". All of them have "inherited from the Christian past the conviction that Jews are bad". An initial disagreement between two groups on how the messiah should be recognised thus contained the seeds of the Holocaust. Nicholls affirms the view that antisemitism is a culturally taught paranoia that led ordinary men and women to convince themselves that the atrocities they committed were not directed at fellow human beings, but at agents of the devil.

RISKING THE TRUTH

Jesus of Nazareth was a faithful and observant Jew who lived by the Torah and taught nothing against his own people and their faith. The Jews neither conspired to kill him, nor were responsible for his death. Thus, the myth of the Jews as Christ killers and the profoundly opposed relationship between Jews and Jesus lack a basis in history. The prejudice that has arisen from this misrepresentation cannot, however, be divorced from the many antisemitic outrages against Jews in the history of Europe, up to and including the Holocaust.

The new scholarship is not without its dangers. It raises the question of whether the Jewish Jesus of history is a totally different being from the divine Christ of Christian orthodoxy. The difficulty of reconstructing the historical figure of Jesus is exacerbated by the fact that such reconstruction may make it impossible to preserve the credibility of the divine–human figure at the heart of the Christian myth. It presents us with a conundrum: "Christianity without Jesus is unimaginable", says

Michael Goldberg (1995, p. 373), but "Christianity *with* Jesus may be impossible." Only critical historical scholarship can disentangle Christianity from its antisemitism. The new scholarship is thus of moral import. According to Nicholls, it presents a double crisis for Christianity. Not only was the Jewishness of Jesus obscured, but the church failed during the Holocaust to stand up for the Jewish people. What is demanded now is an honest response. In the light of the terrible damage done, such study could be part of an act of repentance for historical Christian antisemitism. Nicholls sees it as a spiritual necessity for Christians themselves, whether or not it can earn forgiveness from Jews. Jesus is the only bridge across which the repentant church could walk back to its original home. It is now time to make a choice, the most revolutionary choice to face Christians since the church split off from Judaism. Not just Christianity's anti-Jewishness but also its non-Jewishness is now in question.

Convinced that Jews did not instigate Jesus' crucifixion, Nicholls asserts that Jesus was the victim of a ruthless occupying power. What killed him was the enthusiasm of his own followers and of the crowd, who insisted on treating him as the messiah despite his warnings of the danger for the people at large. The Romans would inevitably have regarded messianic agitation as subversive behaviour. As such, it was likely to culminate in widespread punishment of the people as a whole, and would risk the death of the claimant as well as many innocent people. The only connection that the Jews may have had with Jesus' death was the decision of the priestly officials to hand Jesus over to the Romans once the latter were already on the trail of the new movement. Jewish leaders might have had to make the tough choice of sacrificing one man rather than putting the whole nation in danger,[3] a political, not a religious, decision. With their teaching of reverence for all life, it is unlikely that the Pharisees – so maligned in the gospels – would have made this choice. By the time the gospels were written, the Pharisees' successors, the rabbis, had begun to proscribe Jewish Christianity in order to protect Judaism. The authors of the gospels identified them with the Pharisees of Jesus' time depicting them as Jesus' main enemies and, thereby, casting aspersions on all Jews.

Major areas in the reconstruction of Jesus' life remain uncertain. We do not know whether he was giving his message only to the "lost sheep of Israel", or whether he was giving it to the gentiles. Nicholls claims that his concern was with *Jewish* sinners. We know that the apostle Paul was given the mission to take the gospel to the gentiles. We also know that he did not feel it necessary for gentiles to observe the Torah. What we are uncertain about is whether Paul had a negative attitude to the Torah. Paul was convinced that the Jews were God's chosen people, but also that the gentiles could become part of the covenant people without being circumcised and following the minutiae of the law. The development of the new salvation myth is inseparable from the life and work of Paul of Tarsus, to which we now turn. The new myth retained the Jewish messianic idea in form only, replacing the content in such a way that the Christian myth eventually became directly opposed to Judaism.

THE INFLUENCE OF PAUL

According to Robert Wistrich (1991, p. 14), Paul is the person most responsible for detaching Jesus from his Jewish background, for shifting the guilt for the crucifixion from the Romans to the Jews, and for the stigmatisation of the Jews as the rejected people of God. Taking Paul's writings at face value, this is an almost inevitable conclusion, but there has been a great deal of debate about the role of Paul in laying the basis for Christian antisemitism. According to most scholars, he was the true founder of Christianity. Called upon to be the apostle to the gentiles, he had to reinterpret what the Torah meant for gentiles in the light of Christ, and he concluded that it was unnecessary for new converts to be circumcised or to observe the laws of the Torah. The views that he uttered for the exigencies of his own time ultimately formed the theological basis of Christianity, giving the impression that he was striking at the very heart of Judaism.

Scholars point out, however, that, since Paul had always identified himself as an Israelite[4] and loved his own people, his message must have been too subtle and complex to be easily understood. Nicholls suggests that Paul could not have been responsible for the radical nature of the break between Jews and Christians. His thought was easily misunderstood even in his own time, let alone in the sections of the New Testament that were written after his death. This misunderstanding is reflected in the later strata of the New Testament. Painstaking modern biblical scholarship is producing a new, more sympathetic, vision of Paul than the traditional one. As early Christianity developed and the conflict with the Jews grew, Paul's already misconceived message was distorted further. The New Testament was written over a long period of time, and there were probably several redactions before it was finally canonised in the fourth century.

According to tradition, Paul was born to a diaspora Jewish family in Tarsus in Cilicia, and was reared as a Pharisee. He was later educated in Jerusalem under Rabbi Gamaliel. Paul had been an avid persecutor of the early Jewish Christians, probably, Sanders (1991, p. 9) suggests, at the instigation of the Sadducees, or priestly sect, until his own call to spread the gospel to the gentile world, an event often called his "conversion" to Christianity. While on the road to Damascus, during one of these persecutory episodes, he was blinded by a vision of the risen Christ and charged with the mission of bringing Jesus' message to non-Jews. Though continuing to regard himself as an Israelite, he believed that God had given a new dispensation that would embrace all those who identified with the atoning death and resurrection of Jesus, now the Christ, or saviour. He spent the rest of his life spreading the gospel to the gentiles throughout Asia Minor, and founding and organising new churches. His letters were written to instruct the new communities on how to conduct their lives as Christians, and to counter the teaching of his "false brethren", but were not intended to be guidelines for the church two thousand years later. Paul expected the imminent return of Jesus and the inauguration of the Kingdom of God, whose arrival would make such instructions irrelevant. His letters reveal his complex theology and also the conflicts in which he found himself. His main activities were during the years 36–60 CE. According to most scholars he died in Rome in 62 or 64 CE.

THE TRADITIONAL UNDERSTANDING OF PAUL

The traditional understanding of Paul may be seen in the following summary of Paul's theology as outlined in W. L. Reese's *Dictionary of Philosophy and Religion* (1980, p. 418):

1. The era of the Mosaic Law had been replaced by a dispensation of the spirit. Henceforth, justification would occur through faith rather than by works. The dispensation of law had failed, merely revealing the weakness of the flesh.

2. This human weakness derives from the sin of Adam, which has determined the nature of human life and explains why human suffering and death are inevitable. People carry the consequences of the sin of Adam within themselves as "original sin".

3. God responded to the hopelessness of the human situation by sending Jesus Christ, the messiah and eternal Son of God. Through his death and bodily resurrection, he overcame sin and death and broke the hold of the law, making possible the salvation of all humanity. Just as, in Adam, all men sinned, so, in Christ, all can be saved. Paul seems to have believed that Christ's coming provided a substitute for deserved punishment, satisfying the divine standard of righteousness and providing for the vicarious atonement of all humanity.

4. Baptism was the manner by which people could enter the new order. Through it, they would share in Christ's death and resurrection and become one with the mystical body of Christ. Henceforth Christians would live no longer for themselves but for Christ. To help the individual in this new life, the power of the Holy Spirit, sent by God, enters his or her heart.

5. Paul frequently referred to divine predestination. The final salvation or damnation of each human being would rest on God's pleasure.

6. Offering a view of the last judgement that lay somewhere in between the Greek doctrine of the immortality of the soul, and the view that there would be a restoration of the earthly body, Paul argued that Christians would be provided with a heavenly body.

7. Paul's focus on faith, hope and charity (or love), as the summary of all values came to be known as the theological virtues and greatly influenced human thought.

The obvious shift in focus in Paul's teaching about Jesus transformed the latter, from the messiah expected by the Jews into a personal saviour, reminiscent of the pagan mystery religions. The spiritual replaced the carnal. Thus began what, with the Reformation, became a full-blown "law–gospel conflict". It was no longer adequate for Jews to go on serving God through observance of the laws of the Torah as the people of the covenant. The influential reformer Martin Luther experienced a profound struggle of conscience between the gospel of law and the gospel of freedom and grace, which he saw in terms of combat between Christ and the devil. The Jews had a role in this struggle, but not on the side of God. There was no place for the unconverted Jew in a world of grace. The law cannot save, Luther asserted, it can only condemn, for it imposes standards that unaided humanity cannot possibly reach.

Krister Stendahl, in a 1963 essay that has since become a classic, suggested, however, that Luther's views were later read back into Paul's writing, the Torah being viewed as a burden that revealed, rather than compensated for, sin. Luther, as Sanders (1991, p. 49) points out, was beset by guilt, seeing "righteousness" in judicial terms, and finding relief from sin in justification by faith alone. "But Luther's problems," he insists, "were not Paul's, and we misunderstand him if we see him through Luther's eyes." Paul probably never held these views. His main concern was to clear the way so that the gentiles could be brought into the covenant before Christ's imminent return. He was convinced that God had chosen Israel and that they remained chosen, but that they would ultimately be saved only through faith in Christ. He was mortified that his Jewish kin refused to recognise the new dispensation, and wrestled with the implications of his profound conviction and their apparent blindness, producing – in the ebb and flow of his anguish, hope and faith – partially contradictory assertions. These can be found in three classic chapters, Romans 9–11, to which we will return below.

REINTERPRETING PAUL

We misrepresent Paul if we see him as consciously setting down the foundations of Christian theology. Paul, as Sanders (1991, p. 1) emphasises, was not a systematic theologian, but an itinerant missionary. His thought is thus difficult to understand. He was a man beset by conflict, feeling both supremely successful and on the brink of failure, and regarding as enemies and a source of danger all who opposed his view. His letters were formulated in the cut and thrust of everyday problems as he urgently set about fulfilling his mission. In them, he reveals an uncannily agile mind as he parried the challenges and hardships that confronted him. It was Paul's passionate embrace of faith in Christ and the force of his writing, according to Sanders (1991, p. 18), that made him one of Christianity's foremost spokesmen and by far its most exciting and vigorous theologian.

Paul's letters have often served as the basis of major restatements of Christian faith, by Augustine in the fifth century, Luther in the sixteenth, and Karl Barth in twentieth. When Paul wrote his letters, however, he was embroiled in controversy, as were many of those who read them during the second and subsequent centuries. Of the people who cited him in their favour, some were branded as heretics, whereas others were seen as defenders of orthodoxy. Because Paul was polemical, his letters served other polemicists, each seeing him through their own spectacles; this was the case also with what Paul had to say about the Jews, their Torah and their chosenness, views that are difficult to ascertain with any certainty. Paul did not have one single theology of the law, and said different things about it, depending on circumstances. He also revised this theology on an *ad hoc* basis in terms of the behaviour he expected in his churches.

Paul's basic message was clear: God is good and merciful and holds history in his hands. He chose Israel and gave the Jews the law. Then, appointing Paul as missionary to the gentiles, he sent Christ to save the entire world. What is far from clear, however, is what now happens to the Jews, their Torah and their chosenness, and what the present dispensation implies about the previous one. Romans 9–11 has become a key passage both for providing clues about Paul's convictions and for Jewish–Christian dialogue, because, in it, he explicitly states that God has not cut the Jews off from grace.

As Sanders (1991, p. 98) points out, Paul, like anyone who believes in God's providence, read history backwards. This led him to ask: If God intended, ultimately, to save the entire world through Christ – Jew and gentile alike – why had he chosen Israel and given the Jewish people the law? Had God condemned them through the law, only to supersede it with a new dispensation? If such was the case, had God, as Sanders (1991, p. 118) puts it, been fair, honest, just, reliable, constant? Could God have allowed the law to be only an agent of condemnation and not one of atonement and grace? Paul was seeking a single master-plan that encompassed both the Mosaic Law and Christ. He had to hold them together in order to save God's reputation. This led him to pose the question of whether the law is sin, an idea so uncomfortable for him that he was forced, in Romans 7, to retract it.

Paul, as we have seen, was not opposed to Jewish law; it was from the law that he derived his proof texts. Brought up as a Jew, Paul loved the law as God's gift to Israel but, once God had sent Christ to redeem the entire world, it no longer seemed necessary, certainly not for gentiles. Paul did not even adopt the critique that moderns so often apply to the law, elevating its ethical dimensions and underrating its ritual ones. His view of salvation is rooted in the notion of sacrifice. He seemed particularly opposed, Sanders (1991, p. 90) observes, to those laws that separated Jew from gentile – the same laws that drew comment from pagan authors. Paul wanted faith in Christ from both gentiles and Jews in terms of a commitment to Christ, not just trust in God. But this inevitably forced him to question the law and Israel's election, and he was anguished about the implications, doing everything he could to try to avoid this conclusion. This resulted, as Sanders points out, in a modified dualism: Is the law good, and the flesh weak? Is sin the by-product of another power? Is sin an external power that can manipulate the law, or a power within the flesh?

Paul's underlying agony lay in that the Jews had refused to recognise that the old epoch had ended and a new one was underway, and he was forced to offer an explanation. He inferred that the Jews were temporarily hardened, or blinded, by God, but only until the full number of the gentiles had entered the covenant (Romans 11:25). Only then would the world be saved. As we will see below, this was to have terrible consequences in the development of Christian antisemitism, but it also provides the ground for dialogue if properly understood. Paul's affirmation that God has not repudiated the people of Israel undercuts any attempt to invalidate the meaningfulness of the Jewish covenant. According to John Pawlikowski (1986, p. 123), Romans 9–11 should be regarded, not as an end point, but as a challenge for further dialogue. It is, however, a problematic passage in that it appears to contradict Paul's apparently harsh rejection of the Jewish way, but, as Gager (1983, p. 223) points out, our fundamental attitude to the passage makes an enormous difference to its interpretation and what it may offer.

For those who assert that Paul has set aside Judaism, these chapters appear to be a digression from his belief in justification by faith, and to contradict his earlier statements that there is no room for the salvation of the Jews. Such an interpretation, however, leaves absolutely no way of reconciling these statements with Paul's unambiguous affirmation: "I ask then, has God rejected his people? By no means!" (Romans 11:1). The opposite interpretation, best exemplified by Krister Stendahl, suggests that Romans 9–11 is not an appendix and contradiction to the rest of the letter, but its climax. Paul is not disinheriting the Jews, but making room for the gentiles in God's promise of salvation.

Stendahl (1963) interpreted the passage in terms of Paul wanting to moderate unwarranted feelings of superiority on the part of gentiles over the people of Israel. Paul's idea about the mysterious coexistence of Jews and gentile Christians is, Stendahl says, designed to counter the haughty attitude Paul found in the spirituality of the new Roman Christians. There is not, Stendahl points out, one mention of Christ in this passage, and Paul was never reticent about mentioning him. Stendahl sees Paul as teaching coexistence with and love and respect for Jews.

The question, as Gager (1983, p. 223) puts it, is not "Since we are justified by faith, what remains of Israel?" Rather, it is "Given the constancy of God's righteousness, what are we to make of Israel's refusal to recognise and accept the obvious continuity between God's promise to Abraham and his act of redemption in Christ?" Paul's main motive, as established in the rest of the letter, seems to be to confirm that the gentiles can be incorporated into the company of the elect, and that this is fully consistent with God's righteousness as it was expressed in the promise to Abraham.

These efforts by New Testament scholars – a few among the many – all emphasise the need for reinterpretation against the backdrop of Paul's own times and his particular situation, an effort that is essential if we are to understand and counter Christian antisemitism. On the surface, however, Paul undoubtedly laid the basis for the law–gospel conflict by implying that Christ's saving death had rendered observance of the Torah secondary, if not inadequate. With baptism replacing circumcision, and the new covenant of the spirit replacing the old covenant of the flesh, observance of the law no longer seemed comparable to faith and inward obedience to Christ. God had revealed himself anew, and the Jews had to change their way of relating to God. Paul, it is argued, was not so much against the Torah as *for* the entry of gentiles into the covenant. He did not missionise among the Jews, but believed that they, too, should be baptised in order to be part of the new dispensation.

There was sharp conflict between Paul and those early Christians who felt that the laws of the Torah should still be observed. The latter were known as the "Judaisers". They were Christians who believed that, in order to be part of the covenant people, the gentile convert had to be circumcised and to observe Jewish law. Paul, in his urgent desire to bring in the gentiles, saw this, not only as unnecessary, but as possibly damaging. In Paul's doctrine, however, the conversion of the Jews is necessary before the second coming of Christ. As the Jews are the people chosen by God, they have to be part of the final drama of salvation, which will bring about the final ingathering of the elect. Paul, as we have already observed, saw this as imminent – within his own lifetime.

Paul's apparent ambivalence about Judaism is the subject of ongoing debate. He was speaking of individual salvation, a concept alien to Judaism, and seemed to believe that the requirements for entry into the people of God had changed in some radical way as a result of what God had done in Jesus. Paul was not, according to Nicholls, making converts to Judaism, but bringing gentiles into a new dispensation that would involve baptism for Jews as well. He must have known what the *halakahah* for conversion was and that it involved observance of the Torah. He obviously wanted to do something else. Had he been founding a new religion, it might have been different, but the Jews, understandably, saw him as bringing in converts improperly. They did not share Paul's particular ideas of the new age and the new form of the people of God. Thus, a great deal of friction ensued. His apparent ignorance of Judaism can be resolved only by asserting either that he was not a Pharisee and knowledgeable in the Torah, or that the traditional interpretation that sees him as ignorant of basic Jewish beliefs is wrong.

The key can be found in Paul's intentions rather than his actions. Paul seems to have thought that he was bringing converts into a new form of the same people of God, growing out of the latter in fulfilment of prophecy. Membership was open to Jews and gentiles on the same terms: faith and baptism. He did not intend to found a new religion because he did not expect history to last long enough for that to happen. When he admitted gentiles to the covenant people he was initiating them into the people of the age to come, beyond history, but at that moment overlapping with history. He was not asserting the superiority of a new religion over an old one, but the infinite superiority of the fulfilment of the end of days over ordinary history. Later, after the expectation of the return of Jesus and the imminence of the new age had died down, his ideas would be misunderstood. It would not take long before Christians would use them to claim Christianity's superiority over Judaism, a concept probably remote from his own mind. The earliest Christians – including Paul – did not think of themselves as belonging to a new religion. Rather, they saw themselves as a community living in the end time. As Nicholls (1995, p. 143) so aptly put it, "The powers of the age to come had been poured out upon them, and they lived in history as though beyond and outside history." It was not a time for making regulations that would govern an institution for centuries to come. *Ad hoc* decisions were made in the light of the overwhelming conviction of the imminent return of Jesus, who would usher in the new age in its fullness. Proper conversion to Judaism, viewed against this urgent reality, seemed irrelevant. Living, as Paul thought, in the last days, there was no time for non-essentials.

PAUL AND THE JEWS' BLINDNESS

If Paul's antisemitism was unintentional, as has been suggested above, how do we explain his views about the Jews' blindness? Did he see blindness as instrinsic to Jews, as a permanent part of their being? Joel Carmichael (1992) offers a plausible reconstruction of Paul, with specific reference to this blindness and its implications for the development of antisemitism. He sets the scene against the backdrop of widespread political turbulence, insurrection and fervent expectation of an imminent re-entry of God into history through a human messiah. Paul, he suggests, as a loyal Jew himself, never intended to give the world a permanent picture of Jews as blind rejecters of the truth. Ineffectual during his own lifetime, mainly because of the centrality of the temple in Jerusalem, it was only after Paul's death and the fall of the second temple in 70 CE that the image of the Jews as blind developed. Paul – believing that Jesus was the messiah – saw Jesus' resurrection as heralding the immediate arrival of the Kingdom of God. The fact that the Incarnation had already taken place meant that the coming of the Kingdom was already in process, but the delay in the final accomplishment of the Kingdom had to be explained. Paul's explanation led, unforeseen, to the transformation of the Jews into an otherworldly entity.

Jesus would return in glory to establish the Kingdom of God. When this happened, God would withdraw the Incarnation. Paul was trying to resolve the contradiction between Jesus as the messiah for the Jewish people and as saviour of the world. The final consummation would come about only after a huge cosmic battle between the negative devil forces and the positive God forces. But why, if the Jews were to play so central a role, were they so inexplicably blind to the true meaning of Christ? Their blindness must surely be temporary! Paul's remarks therefore referred not to what Jews intrinsically were, but to their mysterious behaviour at a given moment in time. "Israel has been blinded ... until the fullness of the pagans have gone in, then will Israel be saved" (Romans 11:25,26). Thus, for Paul, the messiah and Incarnation had meaning only in the context of this cosmic drama. Jesus was a human being, and the Incarnation was temporary – to bring about another state of the world, the eternal Kingdom of God. As there was to be only a short hiatus between the resurrection and the coming of the Kingdom, and the world had not come to an end, a new role had to be fashioned for the Jews to play.

The sacraments were merely a stopgap till the arrival of the Kingdom, and were part of the antechamber to the Kingdom. Their purpose would soon be obviated. When the Kingdom failed to replace the material world, however, the sacraments became central and, according to Carmichael, totally magical. The powerful myth Paul formulated, unlike the pagan myths, took on universal dimensions, the Incarnation becoming infinite. The collision between two opposing forces lost its dramatic power, and the idea that God would soon conquer the negative forces, became dissipated. After Paul's death, the Incarnation, crucifixion, sacraments, mystic body of Christ and mystic church became the substance of Christian theology. The preamble to their interaction – the real conflict between superhuman forces – was dropped. Only a single element was retained: the Jews' inexplicable blindness. But this mystery of their rejection of the Incarnation was to be brief. Their eyes had to be opened, because it was part of God's plan. Paul's view was to have fateful consequences for the Jews. Although they could be persecuted and reviled, they had to be kept alive as witnesses to the second coming of Christ.

Whatever Paul's original motives may have been, the message he gives in his letters is that faith in the risen Christ has superseded observance of the law. In his dualistic vision, the law now seems to separate humankind from the true, spiritual light of Christ and no longer has the capacity to absolve one from sin. The Torah becomes a sign of an inferior, this-worldly and therefore superseded Judaism. By the new covenant, gentile Christians – though only grafted on to the stem of Israel – qualify as the true elect of God. The "Old Testament" is now merely a witness to the coming of Christ. Carmichael's book *The Satanizing of the Jews* deals with the profound after-effects of Paul's ideas about the resurrection and glorification of Christ. These led ultimately to dangerous new notions that would underlie the installation of a new institution, the universal church. This leads to the question: can the New Testament be considered an antisemitic book?

IS THE NEW TESTAMENT ANTISEMITIC?

Having located the seeds of antisemitism in the New Testament, Ruether provoked a good deal of scholarly resistance. The question is not so much whether the New Testament has provoked antisemitism, but whether it is – in its essence – antisemitic in intention. The Jewish theologian Eliezer Berkovits (1978, p. 324) affirms, unambiguously, that it is. "The New Testament," he states, "has been the most dangerous anti-Semitic tract in history. Its hatred-charged diatribes against the 'Pharisees' and the Jews have poisoned the hearts and minds of millions and millions of Christians for almost two millennia now ... Without Christianity's New Testament, Hitler's *Mein Kampf* could never have been written. In its effect upon the attitude of Western man toward the Jew, this New Testament has been the spiritual progenitor of a vast library of international hate literature. To face this truth is the first condition of a meaningful Jewish–Christian dialogue." This kind of conclusion is deeply disturbing to Christians. As Lloyd Gaston (1979, p. 48) put it, "A Christian Church with an antisemitic New Testament is abominable, but a Christian Church without a New Testament is inconceivable." Thus, a number of theories have arisen to explain the New Testament's anti-Judaism.

John Pawlikowski (1986) has taken up this question and, under-standably, finds it impossible to answer with a simple "yes" or "no". We need to discuss the New Testament in the context of Christianity's emergence – against the backdrop of the historic situation of second temple Judaism. This context, as we have seen, is still being researched. Much more is needed than the New Testament text, and only by looking at the emergence of the New Testament historically may we be able to understand why it was written as it was. It is not easy to project ourselves into this past time without bringing in our present concerns, which may tempt us to read antisemitism back into the New Testament.

Starting his discussion with the deicide accusation – because it has had such tragic entailments – Pawlikowski points out that this cannot be separated from the broader issue of how Jesus related to the Jewish community of his times. If we knew more about the Judaism of Jesus' time, he argues, we would realise that it was marked by tremendous upheaval. There was a good deal of legalism and corruption, but this was a distortion of Judaism, condemned by Jews and Jesus alike. The Pharisees constituted a new movement, and would have shared Jesus' critique. Jesus was thus in concert with the progressive movements in Judaism. We have, therefore, to reassociate Jesus with the wider Jewish struggle to find an authentic Judaism among the various competing sects. The question therefore moves from "*Who* crucified Jesus?" to "*What* crucified Jesus?" According to Pawlikowski (1986, p. 109), the Romans were nailing to the cross human freedom. Jesus claimed to be the messiah who came to free human beings. The Jews themselves were so dissatisfied with Roman rule that they staged a revolt. A connection needs to be made, therefore, between the suffering of Jesus and the suffering of the Jewish people. If we had additional background – more than just the biblical text – we might be able to extend this reading and find that the New Testament is not as antisemitic as some claim.

John's gospel, with its frequent critical and derogatory mention of the "Jews", is often thought to be the most antisemitic of the gospels. But Pawlikowski shows that scholars are trying to determine exactly who John was referring to when he used that designation. Raymond Brown, one of the foremost scholars on the gospel of John, suggests that John used it as a technical term to denote all those who were opposed to Jesus. John's gospel is, above all, symbolic, and its characters symbolise the different faith responses to Jesus. If, as Brown suggests, the "Jews" are symbolic of those who reject Jesus, the evangelist is not condemning the Jews as a people, but opposition to Jesus. Scholars, like John Townsend and Nicholls, have observed several textual layers in the gospel of John which Ruether's work did not take into account. Townsend argues that John is not shifting the blame for the arrest of Jesus to the Jews. Rather, he avoids emphasising Jewish involvement in the trial and sentence. Pawlikowski suggests that if consensus could be reached on this issue, it would be of great help to the task of reconciliation. Townsend admits the anti-Jewish ethos in John, particularly in the passion narratives, but he insists that the negative is not the full story.

Allied to these questions is the question of whether Paul was antisemitic. Paul was, according to Pawlikowski, a biblical prophet to his own people, neither hating nor despising them. Jews remain as witnesses, and are not to be proselytised. Salvation will be realised at the end of history when the church and the synagogue are finally reconciled. Paul's denunciations against the Judaisers in Galatians are aimed not at Jewish Christians, but at pagan converts who had become ritualistic distorters of the gospel. Application of the term "antisemitism" with regard to the New Testament is problematic. The anti-Judaism of the New Testament is not, according to Pawlikowski (1986, p. 125), "a hatred unto death" like modern antisemitism. The New Testament is not embryonic Nazism. Our treatment of the subject needs nuance.

Lloyd Gaston (1979) offered an unusual, minutely argued, inter-pretation of Paul, suggesting that his central concern was the positive justification of the status of *gentile* Christians, and that the question of whether the Jews should continue to observe the Torah was irrelevant to him. The "law" meant different things to Paul, but he had only one Greek word *nomos*, by which to convey its complexity. He sometimes used the word *nomos* in the broader sense in which the rabbis understood it, namely that, for the Jews, faith and works were not separate and opposing issues, but part of the same covenant that God had entered into with them. At other times, Paul used it in the sense that God had offered the Torah to the other nations of the world, and only the Jews accepted it. To fulfil his broader promise to the world, God now revealed himself anew, in Jesus Christ, so as to bring the gentiles, too, to righteousness. Paul's phrase, "under the law", can thus be read in more than one way. It could refer to the pagan laws under which the majority of gentiles had lived, those being the laws that "revealed sin". It could also have been used to describe the gentile "Judaisers", who insisted that God required rigid observance of the Torah by all Christians if they were to qualify as belonging to God's elect. For Paul, the new dispensation enabled gentiles to participate in God's grace, without becoming Jews first, or being bound by the commandments. The Israelite, the *Mishnah* (Ber. 2:2) states, "first takes upon himself the yoke of the Kingdom of Heaven, and afterwards takes upon himself the yoke of the commandments". Paul's concern, according to Gaston (1979, p. 64) was to say that the gentiles in Christ are under the equivalent of the yoke of the kingdom (faith) but not under the yoke of the commandments (laws that only Jews were obliged to fulfil). Gaston (1979, p. 66) claims that Paul was not even asking the Jews to recognise Christ for themselves, but was accusing them of failing to become a "light unto the gentiles", or for not understanding that his mission to the gentiles was both valid and urgent. "Had all Israel followed Paul's example," says Gaston (1979, p. 66), "we could have had an Israel loyal to the righteousness of God expressed in the Torah alongside a gentile church loyal to the righteousness of God expressed in Jesus Christ and his fulfilment of the promises to Abraham." History was not consummated as Paul had predicted, however, and the emerging New Testament forced its readers to choose between the Torah and Christ. We need, suggests Gaston (1979, p. 67), to allow room in Pauline thought for two religions, two chosen people because, as long as Judaism is understood as a kind of Christian heresy to be combatted, there will never be an end to Christian anti-Judaism.

Though, with this type of argument, scholars are able to conclude that the New Testament is not *intentionally* antisemitic, some Christian scholars, like Gregory Baum, found it impossible, in the wake of Ruether's challenge, to maintain their previous defence of the New Testament. There is no final resolution in sight and this remains a hotly contested issue. Paul's views have been exaggerated by Ruether, but her challenge proves that there is a need in Christian belief for more theological space for Judaism. Otherwise, Pawlikowski suggests, we face the prospect of continuing antisemitism.

Whether scholars can prove that the New Testament was intentionally antisemitic or not, it is almost impossible for ordinary people to read it without imbibing negative images of the Jews and Judaism. Nuance and reconsideration may be effective for scholars, but for vast numbers of Christians the damage has already been done. For many Christians, *all* Jews are condemned in the New Testament. Not only are they demonic Christ killers, but they are seen as blind, legalistic hypocrites. For example, the text offers no hint that, in line with their prophetic tradition, Jews themselves would have been critical of empty observance. When reading anti-Jewish passages such as Matthew 23, Christians are often blind to how insulting such passages are to Jews. Mary Boys, a Catholic scholar who has done some exceptional work in promoting understanding between Christians and Jews, suggests, for example (2000, p. 28), that it is only when a Jew is physically present at such scriptural readings that Christians feel embarrassed. Whether it be in a teaching or congregational setting, the hearer is shocked into recognition of the falseness and negativity of the portrait of the Jew in their midst.[5] The presence of Jews affects one's hearing of the texts, and anti-Jewish verses, previously glossed over, become a source of deep discomfort.

THE LEGALISATION OF THE TEACHING OF CONTEMPT

In the fourth century CE, when Christianity became the official religion of the Roman Empire, a decisive period in the development of antisemitism began. It inaugurated the need for the final canonisation of the New Testament, and the fixing of Christian teaching into such doctrines as the Trinity and the Incarnation. It was also the time in which the teaching of the church fathers became dominant. They structured Christianity according to the opposition between Judaism and Christianity, emphasising the new, as opposed to the old, covenant. But it took until the end of the first millennium for the negative image of the Jew to reach its comprehensive form.

For the first three centuries of the common era, Jews and Christians were active rivals. This stopped with the rise of Christian imperialism after Constantine made Christianity the official religion of the Roman Empire. Whereas paganism was outlawed, Judaism was not. It was regarded as a *religio licita*, and, though Jews were protected, they and their religion were assigned a position of permanent legal inferiority. Imperial laws from the first half of the fourth century prohibited, on penalty of death, conversion to Judaism and intermarriage of Jews with Christians. In the early fifth century, Jews were excluded from government posts. The spirit of these laws was undergirded by religious contempt. Jews could not, for example, be given authority to administer or defend a city. "Indeed," said the 439 edict of Theodosius II, "we believe it sinful that the enemies of the heavenly majesty of the Roman Laws should become the executors of our laws ... and that they ... should have the power to judge or decide as they wish against Christians, yes, frequently even over bishops of our holy religion themselves, and thus, as it were, insult our faith."[6]

This approach to the legal rights of Jews was to predominate in most places until the end of the eighteenth century. Raul Hilberg (1961), in a now famous comparative table, has suggested that these laws set a precedent for the much later Nuremberg Laws, which removed all legal rights for Jews in Nazi Germany. According to Edward Flannery (1965, p. 45), the fourth century was, for Judaism, "a prelude to millennial misfortune". By its end, "the Jew's civil status was precarious, and his image had greatly deteriorated. At the close of the previous century, he was no more than a special type of unbeliever; at the end of the fourth, he was a semisatanic figure, cursed by God and marked off by the state."

Constantine, who reunited the eastern and western parts of the empire, was baptised as a Christian just before his death. His conversion began after he had had a vision of a cross in the sky on the eve of the battle of the Milvian Bridge, a critical battle on the outskirts of Rome in 327 CE. Above the cross were the words *"In Hoc Signo Vinces"* (Under this sign conquer). Having won the battle, Constantine subsequently ordered his soldiers to march to war under a standard shaped like a cross. He increasingly threw his support behind the church, legalising the privileges of the clergy, and standardising church doctrine by calling together a worldwide Church Council in Nicea, in 325, to resolve all doctrinal disputes in the Nicene Creed.

Before Constantine, James Carroll (2001) suggests, the cross was not Christianity's central symbol. The *life* of Jesus – rather than his death –

formed the basis of his followers' beliefs. The adoption of the cross was to have fateful implications for the Jews. When the death of Jesus – now rendered literally, in all its violence, as opposed to metaphorically or theologically – replaced the life of Jesus and the new life of resurrection at the heart of the Christian imagination, the balance shifted decisively against the Jews. That shifting balance is the subject of Carroll's book *Constantine's Sword*. Carroll offers a comprehensive study of the process by which Christianity – a religion that grew out of and originally existed side by side with Judaism – developed the conviction that it superseded Judaism. Though Jesus, throughout his life, saw himself as a Jew, supersessionism was to become the prevailing attitude of Christians toward Judaism. By using its power against the Jews, the church betrayed the essence of Jesus' faith and, itself, embodied the power that killed him, the power of state. Now, Judaism was permitted to survive, but only under conditions of reprobation.

This view was articulated by St Augustine of Hippo (354–430). Elaborating on Paul's views, he taught that the church now replaced the old Israel as God's chosen people, Israel having betrayed the true message of God – one that, according to Augustine's logic, they should have been the first to acknowledge. Because they killed Christ, and continue to live in blindness and error, the Jews bear the mark of Cain – the first murderer in human history. Like his, their guilt – and, in their case, their blindness – has condemned them to permanent exile. Though they may merit death for the crime of deicide, the Jews should be preserved – and indeed loved – as witnesses to Christian truth, but under conditions of reprobation and misery. Jews could not be dismissed entirely, because God's work of redemption had been enacted through their history, but they were enemies of the church. Their continued abject existence served to vindicate Christian claims.

Anti-Judaism was now a doctrinal necessity. Because Christianity shared a tradition with Judaism, the ongoing presence of Jews constituted a perpetual challenge to Christian truth. The teaching of contempt and the dissemination of anti-Jewish pronouncements found their most eloquent expression in the church fathers – of whom Augustine was the most influential. By this time – known as the Patristic period – the identification of the Jews with the devil was so strong that it could be said, as Moshe Lazar (1991, p. 40) put it, "The Devil is Jewish and the Jew is the Devil, or his servant, his mediator on earth." The church fathers developed what has become known as the *Adversus Judaeos* tradition.

The church fathers' demonisation of the Jews had far-reaching effects because the devil was very real to Christian believers during the Middle Ages. Haunting people's thoughts and deeds from cradle to grave, he was as much a part of their faith and mind as were the divine Incarnation of Christ and the Holy Trinity. The church fathers conceptualised the Jews as part of a demonic trinity. The Devil–Antichrist–Jew stood as a reverse image of, and in antagonism to, the Father–Son–Holy Spirit.[7] As the volume of writings on the nature of Christ grew, so did the volume of diabolical treatises. In addition to the diabolisation of the Jews, the church fathers articulated a series of other myths about them. Chief among these were that:

- Judaism was degenerate at the time of Jesus.
- The Jews were Christ killers.
- The Jewish diaspora was God's punishment of the Jews for the crucifixion.
- Israel had been rejected by God.

The identification of the Jews with the devil grew out of emerging gentile Christianity's need to differentiate itself from ancient Israel and its Torah. The church continued a relentless anti-Jewish campaign in which the literal meaning of both the texts and historical events was subverted. A body of literature was produced in which the "true Israel", Christianity, was seen as the realm of the sons of light whereas the Jews were represented as the sons of darkness. The church was defined as Godly, the synagogue as Satanic. As Lazar points out, the gospel of love towards gentiles became the gospel of hatred towards the Jews, and the two developed simultaneously. Lazar (1991, p. 42) sees "an abyss" separating pagan from Christian anti-Judaism, "both in content and intent". The defamatory rumours of pagan antiquity were very different from the anti-Jewish ideological elaborations that had developed by the time the gospels were edited and interpreted by the earliest church fathers. The way that Jesus' teachings were presented and the way they were elaborated progressively de-Judaised him. Jesus had neither opposed Jewish law, nor advocated the demonisation of his fellow Jews.

The more Jesus was de-Judaised, the more the Jews were demonised. Roman guilt for the crucifixion had already been transferred to Jews. The idea was now dramatically highlighted by the church fathers, who perceived it as a conspiracy. Origen, for example, presents as fact that the Jews "nailed Christ to the cross" (Lazar 1991, p. 44). In a number of medieval illustrations, Pilate himself was transformed into a Jew. John's gospel, branding the Jews as the sons of the devil, had opened the way for further elaboration, and the Jews became the incarnation of evil. Denigrated as liars, deceivers, agents of corruption and debauchery, horned beasts, treacherous poisoners and killers, the Jews were automatically associated with any new verbal or visual characterisation of the devil that came along in succeeding centuries. Lazar notes three phases in the demonisation of the Jews:

- John's gospel, which suggests that the devil is the father of the Jews;
- the identification of the synagogue as the house of Satan;
- the view that the messiah for whom the Jews are waiting is the Antichrist.

THE "GOLDEN" MOUTH

Works on the history of antisemitism generally quote the antisemitic diatribes of John Chrysostom, because his was the most extreme example of the vicious rhetoric of the church fathers, and because what he taught about Jews so belies the name he was given by later generations: Chrysostom, "the golden mouthed". But he was one of many. Gregory of Nyssa, for example, called the Jews murderers of the Lord, assassins of the prophets, rebels against God, God haters ... advocates of the devil, a race of vipers, slanderers, calumniators, dark-minded people, leaven of the Pharisees, a Sanhedrin of demons, sinners, wicked men, stoners, and haters of righteousness. St Jerome, who translated the Old Testament into the Latin Vulgate, and therefore needed frequently to consult with rabbis, used similar descriptions when speaking of Jews. They were serpents, in the image of Judas, and their praying was seen "as pleasant to God as a donkey's braying". Socrates, a continuator of Eusebius, was one of the first to spread the ritual murder libel, accusing Jews in Imnestar (Syria) of having crucified a Christian boy during the feast of Purim (Lazar 1991, p. 47).

The Jews' blood-thirsty role in Jesus' passion was portrayed with particular vividness by Melito (d. *c.* 190 CE), a leader, or even bishop, of the Christian community of Sardis, who is generally regarded as the originator of the charge of deicide. In a fragment, "*Peri Pascha*", "Concerning the Passover, or Easter", he compares the Exodus to the death of Jesus, and mounts a vicious attack on the Jews for crucifying

Jesus on the very day they were commemorating their liberation. He was a Quartodeciman, one who belonged to a community who observed both Good Friday and Easter on the same day as Passover and, in his contrast of the Jewish and Christian "Passovers", asserted the complete superiority of the latter. In the same way that a building supersedes the initial plan of it, Christianity, as the final construction, invalidates Judaism, the preparatory structure. The intensity of Melito's polemic testifies to the antagonism between Jews and Christians in Sardis (in Asia Minor) at the time. Unlike Justin Martyr, who still hoped to convert the Jews by using milder, more seductive, language in his polemic *The Dialogue with Trypho*, Melito, according to David Rokéah (1988, p. 56), had despaired of the Jews and wanted to neutralise their dangerous influence on both Christians and potential pagan converts.

John Chrysostom capped them all, however, contributing greatly to the formation of anti-Jewish propaganda imagery; he made the idea of the Jews as Christ killers, punished by dispersion, a cornerstone of his theology. Jews, he said in his *First Homily Against the Jews*, "are dogs, stiff-necked, gluttonous, drunkards. They are beasts unfit for work ... fit for killing, for slaughter.[8] There is no difference between the theatre and the synagogue ... The synagogue is a dwelling of demons ... a place of idolatry ... not only a brothel and a theatre, it is also a den of robbers and a lodging for wild beasts" (Lazar 1991, p. 48).

Some historians have tried to mitigate Chrysostom's inflammatory statements by pointing out that he was merely using the rhetoric of the late fourth century to cope with the threat of Judaising, or of Christians lapsing back into a kind of Judaism. Indeed, as Nicholls suggests, the unrestrained and hysterical nature of his outbursts may testify to the fact that Judaism was alive in Antioch, exercising profound fascination for the Christians there. "Is it not strange", Chrysostom asked, "that those who worship the Crucified keep common festival with those who crucified him? With those who shouted 'Crucify him, Crucify him' and 'His blood be upon us and upon our children?' All Jews are demons and all are guilty." Several centuries later, his dramatic and violent anti-Jewish propaganda found their equivalent in Martin Luther, whose ideas gained wide influence, not only because of his towering status in the church, but because the printing press was invented in his time. Luther, in turn, was quoted by Adolf Hitler.

Thus, the mythical Jews of Christian theology became superimposed on the real Jews, and medieval Christianity disseminated a grotesque and dehumanised image of Jews through masterful use of its mass media. In sermons, plays and visual arts, a canned image of the Jew and Judaism was disseminated as an integral part of the "literature of the illiterate" (Lazar 1991, p. 49). The Jew as devil was translated into popular imagery that could be exploited in times of crisis. Slight changes in style, technique or iconography occurred, but the effectiveness of the image remained the same. The medieval passion plays, for example, re-enacted the crucifixion. In them, Christ's suffering was vividly portrayed, the Jews being cast as the traitorous executioners, wearing contemporary dress, the yellow Jewish hat, and moneybags hanging from their belts, the people of Judas rather than the people of Jesus. The more the audience identified with Jesus' suffering, the more they hated the Jews. The world's most famous passion play has, since 1634, been performed every ten years or so in the Bavarian town of Oberammergau. It was banned for a while during the eighteenth century and, oddly enough, during the Hitler years, when the anti-religious policy of the Nazis was permitted to eclipse their hatred of Jews. In 1969 a few textual modifications were made to remove some of the more offensive anti-Jewish passages.

THE FIRST CRUSADE

By the eleventh century, these images were well integrated into the daily life of Europe's Christians. At that time the "millennium phenomenon" became important. In 1096, manipulated by zealous political leaders who exploited people's fear of the Antichrist and the devil, the First Crusade took place. People had been waiting for signs to herald the coming of the end of days. An increase in disasters – like the plague, famines, comets and sudden deaths – was evidence of the troubles that would precede the end time.

Jews had been separated from Christians by canon law, and the general lack of knowledge about them permitted credence of all sorts of horrible images. In the heated fervour to root out the "Muslim infidel" from the Holy Land, awareness was aroused of another "infidel" people close by, the Jews. Even before the official Christian armies assembled, gangs of would-be crusaders set out through the Rhineland, attacking whatever unbelievers they could find. In the late spring and summer of 1096, Jewish communities were besieged, pillaged and killed, unless they consented to baptism. Some communities survived, such as in Speyer, where the bishop acted quickly and effectively. In places like Worms and Mainz, however, almost the whole Jewish community was exterminated, even though they defended themselves. In the supercharged religious atmosphere at the time, many Jews chose to die as martyrs, *Kiddush ha-Shem* (for the holiness of God's name), rather than to convert. The authorities, as Seltzer (1980, p. 355) points out, did not condone the violence, and the emperor allowed those who had converted under duress to return to Judaism, extending protection to them in 1103. Out of this crucible East European Jewish pietism emerged.

In the face of all this negativity, one might have thought that Jews could not prosper in Christian society. Though this was not the case, their economic success had drawbacks. As a source of prosperity, they were protected by the governing powers, on the one hand, but hated and envied by the peasantry, on the other. After the First Crusade, their economic and social conditions deteriorated. They were increasingly denied a variety of occupations, and were restricted to banking and money lending. As the church had outlawed the earning of interest by Christians, money lending was one of the few occupations open to Jews. Jews were "owned" by princes who used the Jews' exemption from this law to make interest-bearing loans to non-Jews. In this way, members of the nobility enriched themselves at the expense of both the peasantry and the Jews, the latter subsequently being condemned as blood-sucking usurers.

Jews were portrayed as opposite to all that was good. A common theme was the juxtaposition of images of the church triumphant and the synagogue blinded. The first took the form of a proud, triumphant maiden, wearing a crown and holding an orb and sceptre, whereas the second was symbolised by a downcast maiden, blindfolded and carrying a broken staff.[9] Entire bestiaries of fantastic creatures were invented to depict Jews. For Christians, use was made of images like the dove, lamb, eagle or lion – all of them positive. For Jews, images of serpents, wolves, sows and dogs were employed. The positive imagery, according to Lazar (1991, p. 56), retained a metaphoric character, whereas the demonic imagery was interpreted literally. The identification of Christians with attractive animals served to humanise the animal world, whereas the identification of Jews with beasts served to animalise the Jews into nightmarish monsters.

From the twelfth century, as Christian devotion to Jesus' blood developed, Jews were frequently accused of ritual murder, the "Blood Libel". They allegedly murdered a Christian child and then drained its blood for ritual purposes, usually to mix into their unleavened bread for Passover – a ludicrous accusation, given Judaism's prohibition against the ingestion of blood. The Blood Libel, as a re-enactment of the Passion, became a potent literary device in the spread of antisemitism. The first recorded ritual murder charge occurred in 1146 in Norwich, England. Jews were accused of having crucified a Christian boy, William, during Passion Week. Despite the fact that, eight years later, Pope Innocent IV issued a bull proclaiming the falsity of ritual murder, the Jews of Lincoln were accused of killing an eight-year-old boy, called Hugh. Whole Jewish communities could be slaughtered as a result of the outrage that such accusations caused. Livia Bitton-Jackson points out that the slaughter of all the Jews in the town was the "happy ending" of Chaucer's "Tale of the Prioress" in *The Canterbury Tales* (1387–1400), which is centred on another such incident, briefly alluding to Hugh of Lincoln at the end. The tale offered gruesome details of the torture to which the child was subjected, and was embellished by minstrels and monastic bards. The Blood Libel became the most colourful and dangerous fiction of all time, providing a rationale for a protracted cycle of slaughter. As Bitton-Jackson (1994, p. 238) points out, a slander was circulated that Jews needed Christian blood to replace the blood that flowed steadily from their bodies – a peculiar, ostensibly genetic affliction, purportedly visited on Jews as retribution for deicide. The Blood Libel survived into the twentieth century, the most recent cases of it being the Beiliss trial in Kiev in 1912, and the post-Holocaust riots in Kielce, Poland, in 1946. Charles Lamb, who popularised Shakespeare's plays, once said

> I should not care to be in the habit of familiar intercourse with that nation. I confess, I have not the nerve to enter their synagogues. Old prejudices cling about me. I cannot shake off the story of Hugh of Lincoln.[10]

In the thirteenth century the Jews were accused of "desecrating the host", another re-enactment of the crucifixion. They would sneak into churches, it was alleged, and stab the consecrated wafer until it spurted blood. They were said to be exacerbating the pain that Jesus suffered, an agony that was dramatised over and over again by medieval passion, mystery and gospel plays, which also added the Jew in the guise of Judas, betraying Jesus for profit. This had the effect of combining money with blood in the popular mind. The desecration of the host had a high emotional impact on Christian believers, almost equal to the accusation of ritual murder. These, with the "pound of flesh" story – which first appeared in Italian and French narratives and found echoes in Shakespeare's *The Merchant of Venice* – depict Jews as torturing Christ once again. With ritual murder, Jews literally re-spill Jesus' blood. By stabbing the host, spilling the chalice of wine or demanding a pound of flesh they do so symbolically. These fictions stand for their historical "refusal" to convert to Christianity or to convert outsiders to Judaism, a stricture that, as we saw, arose out of canon law.

Because of their putative harmful influence, from 1555 Jews were confined to ghettos, walled-off areas in cities or towns where their occupations were severely limited and they lived in crowded poverty-stricken conditions. Instituted by Pope Paul IV, the first ghetto was in Rome, with others soon following.[11] The Jews' enforced separation was designed to keep their contagion away from Christian society.

MARTIN LUTHER

Martin Luther, the pioneer of the Reformation, condemned the Jews with extreme harshness. The Protestant Reformation, however, had ambiguous consequences for Jewish history. On the one hand, the break-up of Christian unity led to increased religious toleration for dissident Christians, which was extended to Judaism. Protestantism, especially Dutch Calvinism and English Puritanism, were more receptive to ideas and symbols of the Old Testament making possible greater respect for Jews. On the other hand, in Germany, Luther issued one of the "most vituperative denunciations ever" of Jewish perfidy (Seltzer 1980, p. 501), drawing extensively on the Satanic image of the Jew in medieval German folklore. Although Luther, at first, had favourable words for Jews, and identified with their rejection of the papacy, his attitude underwent a radical change when they refused to convert to his new reformed church.

In his *On the Jews and Their Lies* (1543), he recast the Jews as greedy blasphemers and murderers. With the Reformation, the idea of the "universal church" began to decline, and the Protestant Reformation served to strengthen the connection between religion and nationalism. After Luther, there was a specifically "Germanic" way of being Christian, nationalism later being linked with race, as we will see in chapter 8. It is sometimes argued, therefore, that Luther's antagonism verged on being racial. He deeply resented "Jewification", *Verjudung*, which tainted even the Jew who had converted to Christianity. Some scholars see this as introducing the idea of Jews as a race, whereas others see it as the old medieval antisemitism.[12] Rubenstein and Roth (1987, p. 268ff) argue that Luther was not a modern racist antisemite. Rather, there was a change in emphasis during his career. In his optimistic youth, he had hope for the Jews' conversion and advocated kindness to them, "for they have dealt with the Jews as if they were dogs and not human beings". In his deeply pessimistic old age, however, the Jews seemed obstinate and unconvertible, requiring, at best, a severe mercy.

"What shall we do with this damned, rejected race of Jews?" he said in *On the Jews and Their Lies* (47:267).

> We cannot tolerate them if we do not wish to share in their lies, curses, and blasphemy. In this way we cannot quench the inextinguishable fire of divine rage ... nor convert the Jews. We must prayerfully and reverently practice a merciful severity. Perhaps we may save a few from the fire and the flames. They are surely being punished a thousand times more than we might wish them ... Let me give you my honest advice.
>
> First, their synagogues should be set on fire, and whatever does not burn up should be covered or spread with dirt so that no one may ever see a cinder or stone of it ...
>
> Secondly, their homes should likewise be broken down and destroyed ...
>
> Thirdly, they should be deprived of their prayer books and Talmuds in which such idolatry, lies, cursing, and blasphemy are taught ...
>
> Fourthly, their rabbis need to be forbidden under threat of death, from teaching ...
>
> Fifthly, passport and travelling privileges must be absolutely forbidden to Jews ...
>
> Sixthly, they should be stopped from usury ...
>
> Seventhly, let the young and strong Jews ... earn their bread by the sweat of their noses ... for it is not proper that they should want us cursed *Goyim* to work in the sweat of our brow and that they, pious crew, while away their days at the fireside in idleness, feasting ...
>
> If however we are afraid that they might harm us personally ... then let us settle with them for that which they have extorted usuriously from us, and after having divided it up fairly, let us drive them out of the country for all time.[13]

As Alex Bein (1990, p. 524) points out, Julius Streicher, the editor of the scurrilous antisemitic weekly *Der Stürmer*, complained at his trial in Nuremberg after the Second World War, that it was not only he who should have been there arguing his case; Martin Luther, too, should have testified. Although Streicher's complaint may be exaggerated, in that Luther was not the racist antisemite he was, it leaves no doubt that Christian theological anti-Judaism was the precursor of modern antisemitism. Rubenstein and Roth (1987, p. 53) suggest that, though four centuries passed before the Nazis made public Luther's largely forgotten text, they did so in ways that Luther could not have anticipated, or even imagined. Yet those ways would not have surprised him altogether either.

THE STEREOTYPE IN LITERATURE

By the late sixteenth century in England, France and Spain, the image of the Jew had evolved into a literary stereotype of the blood-sucking usurer, which was later to be adopted by Russian and American *belles lettres* and, even later, by the Nazis. The first such villain to appear on the Elizabethan stage, suggests Bitton-Jackson (1994, p. 239), was Barabas in Christopher Marlowe's *The Jews of Malta* (*c.* 1588). More popular than Shylock, this portrayal helped to perpetuate the negative image of the Jews, who, by then, had been excluded from England for some three hundred years. So powerful was this stereotype, Bitton-Jackson says, that when Oliver Cromwell proposed, in 1655, to readmit Jews to England – to improve the country's commerce – the move was opposed. "Solid proof" was presented that the Jews of England "had crucified three or four children, at least, which was the main cause of their banishment".[14]

The ideas that Jews stabbed not only the host, but also humans and lived off human flesh also entered the antisemitic stereotype. They were accused of eating corpses, babies ripped from their mother's wombs, scorpions, serpents and other reptiles. In these horrible images the Jew was portrayed in the Western world, growing monstrously in the minds of the untutored masses. Though England had been without Jews for three centuries, the image of the Jew survived as a powerful mythical monster, and was useful in times of crisis and change. It was easier to project frustrations and guilt feelings on the Jew than for Christians to take responsibility for these emotions in themselves. In Shakespeare's *The Merchant of Venice*, according to Lazar, we are back in the genre and framework of the medieval miracle play. Antonio is Christ, Shylock is the

Antichrist, and Portia is the Virgin Mary. Many argue that Shakespeare's treatment of Shylock served to humanise Jews, because he portrays him as having the same characteristics as other human beings:

> Hath a Jew not eyes? Hath not a Jew organs, dimensions, senses, affections, passion? ... If you prick us do we not bleed?

Lazar, however, believes that Shylock is a combination of beast, blood-sucking usurer and the devil, and that Shakespeare's powerful theatrical talent brought a reinvigorated image of the mythical Jew into the modern world, fathering a rich lineage of monstrous Jews, including Dickens's Fagin.

WHY WAS THE "OLD TESTAMENT" RETAINED?

The need to retain the Jews as central actors in the drama of salvation has had devastating effects. The Hebrew Bible functions very differently for Jews and Christians. For Jews, the Hebrew Bible continues to reveal the faithfulness of Israel, who, though chastised and in exile, awaits messianic redemption with legitimate hope. For Christians, the "Old Testament" points to Jesus as the messiah and has been fulfilled in his life, death and resurrection. The Jews' failure to recognise Jesus both accounted for and justified their exile. They had been punished and rejected by God. All the Jews had left, then, were a scripture and tradition that they did not understand and, as a result, had turned into a system of arid legalism. Robert Chazan has pointed out that the Jews were in a unique category. Unlike all other non-Christians, they had been vouchsafed the truth, but had misread – and thereby lost – all claims to it. Jews were, therefore, seen as a notch above other religious minorities, but were doubly debased because they had squandered their blessing. Was it necessary, therefore, for Christianity to have maintained this link with the Hebrew Bible and to be at war with the Jews? Was the adoption of the Jewish philosophy of history inevitable? How might it have been if Christianity had decided to dispense with the Hebrew Bible, something a number of early Christians were keen to do?

There were movements in early Christianity, identified with the gnostics in general and Marcion of Pontus (c. 100–160 CE) in particular, that denied the link with Jewish salvation history and wanted to abandon the Jewish scriptures. They viewed Jesus as a redeemer consonant with

Hellenistic mystery religions, and rejected notions of his having been an earthly Jewish messiah of flesh and blood. The Jewish God, Marcion believed, was the Demiurge, the creator god of the *inferior* material world – a lesser god than Christ. Marcion wanted to go further than Paul, who had questioned the adequacy of the law for attaining salvation, and reject the Jewish connection entirely. This provoked heated controversy, since there were distinct advantages for the church in retaining the "Old Testament".

Although none of the advantages may, on its own, be compelling, in sum they were, as William Nicholls points out, decisive. The first was that, in an age that prized antiquity, Christianity was seen as a *nouveau* religion, with an unknown God. The pagan world respected national religions, particularly if their antiquity was recognised. Christian apologists could therefore rebut this charge by rooting their religion's origins in Judaism. Indeed, with the adoption of new ideas that amalgamated biblical religion with Greek philosophy – like the doctrine of Christ as the divine *Logos* – Christianity could be seen as even older than Judaism. The adoption of the "Old Testament" would be more effective if Christianity could disengage itself from those aspects of Judaism – like its exclusiveness and distinctive way of life – that pagans found objectionable.

Second, Nicholls argues, the controversy about the messiahship of Jesus may have already been too deeply embedded in both tradition and the New Testament for the Christians to consider abandoning the Jewish scriptures. The New Testament depended too much on the "Old", and dropping it would have involved the complete rethinking of Christology on gentile terms. Though theologians had already done much implicit rethinking, with ideas such as the divine *Logos*, total rejection would have been too revolutionary.

Third, there was the question of Jesus' humanity. The doctrine of the Incarnation is based on the idea that Jesus is fully divine and fully human, simultaneously. One part of the doctrine – that Jesus was a human being born into a historical nation – was preferable to the unhistorical saviour gods of Hellenistic and oriental mythology. For people like Marcion, however, Jesus' humanity was a problem. If Jesus had taken on human flesh, he would not only have been the product of a lesser god, but would have polluted the envelope of the spirit. Jesus' humanity was, therefore, an illusion. This grew into heresies, like Docetism, according to which Jesus only "appeared" to be human.

In order to reclaim the humanity of Jesus, the church had also to reclaim the creator, the God of the Jews. It had to assert God's unity and the goodness – within limits – of the created world and of human flesh. This could be achieved only by retaining the Hebrew Bible, but this carried the necessity of denying Jews the right to own and interpret it. The orthodox church finally decreed total acceptance of it as the "Old Testament", which could only be correctly read through a Christian *midrash*, the New Testament. Thus, the church, according to Ravitch, landed up adopting a semi-gnostic position that rejected much of the Hebrew Bible and the people to whom it belonged.[15] The Jews remained the secret centre of world history, chosen for their blindness and disobedience, not for their faith and covenant. Jews thus remained of permanent significance to Christian theology.

Ravitch (1982, p. 44) points out that Christianity always has the potential to go one way or the other in its ambivalence about the Hebrew Bible. For all its apparent advantages, there were dangers in retaining it. The "Old Testament" did not unequivocally foresee the type of saviour that Christians believed Jesus to be. The result was that Christianity was always in danger of lapsing into a kind of Judaism. Constant vigilance was needed to prevent Christians from becoming Judaised. The church fathers were on the front line in the struggle against heretics on the one hand and the Judaisers on the other. All their venomous statements about the Jews were designed to prove that the church was the "true Israel".

Forthright rejection of Jewish history and prophecy could have freed the church from unpopular ethnic identification with the Jews and from an equivocal national history. A Marcionite Christianity was, therefore, very tempting. When the church did battle against the gnostics, a two-fold process was involved. The "Old Testament", the creator God and whole Jewish tradition had to be defended, and the Christian faith had to be explained as something other than, better than, the religion of the Jews. This could be achieved only by simultaneously exalting the Jews of the Hebrew Bible and berating the Jews of the present age. The church's insistence on maintaining the connection with the Jewish scriptures thus fatally and necessarily led it to attack the living people of Israel.

The church, suggests Ravitch, adopted the prophetic view of history through which to edify its followers. But it could do this only at the price of excoriating the Jewish people. Disaster was interpreted not as a result of superior political or military power, but as divine punishment for, or divine warnings about, Israel's shortcomings. The genius of the prophetic interpretation of history was that it enabled the Jewish people to endure hardship and disaster, and helped to purge society periodically of injustice and immorality. Its danger was that it could be used to rationalise as the will of God even the most hateful of political and social reverses. The logic of the prophetic tradition led the church to see in Jewish catastrophes – in both past and present – the hand of an avenging God.

Christians turned traditional Jewish understandings of history into weapons against the Jews. The classic teaching about the reprobation of Israel came almost entirely from the Jewish tradition itself, but was used to confirm the view that Judaism had become irrelevant, Christianity being the only valid channel to salvation. A new people of God had been born. "From there to the theory of punishment, rejection and wandering is not a big jump. Every step followed Jewish models and categories even though the net result was a repudiation of Judaism."[16]

The Christian theological view of Jewish defeat never lost its persuasiveness. It simultaneously explained the mystery of Israel, while becoming a motive for cooperating with providence by making Jewish existence as precarious as possible. It was perceived as furthering God's will to persecute Jews, as part of God's judgement. Christian salvation history needed Jews, and Christians took care to moderate persecution just enough to permit them to survive in an appropriately debased condition.

WHAT IF MARCION HAD WON?

There are arguments suggesting that if Marcionite Christianity had won the day, the Jews would have been better off. For Marcion, the Jewish God, though regarded as inferior, was real. Marcion therefore gave the Jewish God concept a legitimacy denied it by orthodox Christianity. If the church had followed Marcion, it need not have adopted a position so opposed to Jews. Judaism could have remained an entirely different religion – albeit with an inferior god – instead of being the "false" version of the "true" religion. That would have permitted more tolerance of the Jews. Since Marcion did not see Jesus as predicted in the Hebrew scriptures, Jews were not to blame in rejecting him. Though Judaism would certainly have been seen as imperfect, the hostile, polemical relationship between Judaism and Christianity might have been avoided.

The close family relationship between Judaism and Christianity lies at the heart of the negative reading of Jewish history among Christians. Citing Arnold Toynbee, Ravitch points out that Jews and Judaism did not play a major part in the history of humankind before they gave birth to what Toynbee calls the two "deviationist" Judaic world religions, Christianity and Islam. If these had not been generated, Judaism would be surviving today in an environment of Hellenic paganism as Zoroastrianism survives today in the midst of Hinduism, a religion in which there is no dogmatic core. In that event, the Jews' position in the world today might have been more like the present position of the Parsees than like the actual position of the Jews themselves. "The Jews would have been more obscure than they now are, but they would also have been more comfortable." Ravitch feels that Toynbee, contrary to received opinion, is not insensitive to Jewish concerns. Toynbee admitted the permanent value of Jewish life and saw the religious schisms as unfortunate. He admitted the presence of antisemitism in the gospels themselves.[17]

In a moving and impassioned argument, however, the Jewish historian Yosef Hayim Yerushalmi defends the choice to retain the Hebrew Bible on historic grounds. Since Christianity has never been genocidal, what was it, Yerushalmi asks, that prevented the church from wiping out the Jews? He sees the answer to this as resting on a far more basic choice, the decision to retain the Hebrew Bible as the "Old Testament". Popes protected Jews and intervened on their behalf *in extremis*, he argues. It was the masses who attacked and murdered Jews. Religious leaders often intervened to stop the carnage. The church had made the fundamental decision to keep the Jews alive. Though Yerushalmi welcomes views like Ruether's, he warns that, in the light of the Holocaust, Jews cannot wait for the new revolution in Christian theology to be completed. But theology is not everything. He insists that there was always a human factor in the way individual leaders handled Jews. Despite the teaching of contempt, many Christians have treated Jews with decency. To say that Christianity promoted a particular image of the Jews is not to say that all Christians have shared this view. It is clear that the conflict arises out of complex interrelationships formed over a long period of time.

7

Islamic antisemitism

This much may be said with reasonable certainty ... that they [Jews under Islam] were never free from discrimination, but [were] only occasionally subject to persecution; that their situation was never as bad as in Christendom at its worst, nor ever as good as in Christendom at its best; and that while prejudice was always present, it was often muted, rarely violent, and mostly inspired by disdain and contempt rather than by the explosive mixture of hate, fear and envy that fueled the antisemitism of Christendom.

Bernard Lewis

Today there are no antisemites in the world, as you know. Nobody says, "I am antisemitic." You cannot, after Hitler. The word has gone out of fashion. You have to have a new word ... new words maybe ... new terminology. And the terminology has to be hygienic, sterile and not mention Jews. Anti-Zionism is very good terminology.

Yehuda Bauer

THE EMERGENCE OF ISLAM

Islam is the youngest of the three Abrahamic religions. From its inception in 622 CE, Jews began to live under Muslim hegemony where Islam had penetrated. It was in the interaction between Muhammad, the prophet of Islam, and the Jews of Arabia that the first negative attitudes to Jews in Islam are to be found. Jews lived as a minority people, under either Islam or Christianity, until the re-establishment of the State of Israel in 1948.

Jews and Muslims have, therefore, lived together over a large geographic area for fourteen centuries, sometimes symbiotically and at other times antagonistically. The long period and wide area make it difficult to trace one distinct line in Islamic attitudes to Jews, but they have, on the whole, been far milder than attitudes in Christendom. Jews were neither demonised nor cast out as pariahs in Muslim societies. Depending on one's definition of antisemitism, traditional Islamic attitudes may not qualify as antisemitism at all. This has changed in the modern era.

It is often argued, as we saw in chapter 2, that Arabs cannot be antisemitic because they, themselves, are Semites. But the word "Semite" is based on a fiction that was spuriously connected with ideas about race. As use of the word "antisemitism" applies only to Jews in practice, such arguments are disingenuous, signs sometimes of ignorance but more often of bad faith. Antisemitism is an option as open to Arabs as it is to everyone else, and many have chosen it. The modern period presents us with an acute paradox. In spite of the comparative mildness of historic Islamic attitudes, some of the Arab countries have been the only places in the world since the end of the Second World War where hard-core Nazi-style antisemitism is publicly and officially endorsed and propagated (Lewis 1988, p. 57). Whereas it is politically incorrect in the post-Holocaust Western world to openly express antisemitism, in the Muslim world a full-blown, demonising antisemitism, masquerading as anti-Zionism, has developed. A pertinent example of this was the United Nations' World Conference against Racism and Xenophobia that was held in Durban, South Africa, in August 2001.

THE 2001 UNITED NATIONS WORLD CONFERENCE AGAINST RACISM, DURBAN, SOUTH AFRICA

The conference happened to coincide with the eleventh month of the second *Intifada* in the Middle East, the collapse of negotiations for peace, and a polarisation of Jews and Muslims in South Africa and beyond. In the planning phase, there was a move to resurrect the long rescinded 1975 UN resolution equating Zionism with racism. After much wrangling, including threats by Israel and the United States to boycott the conference, the issue was taken off the official agenda. But this did not prevent the conference from being taken over by well-organised and well-funded Muslim groups, some more radical than others, and from being overshadowed by inflamed anti-Zionist rhetoric that soon degenerated into open antisemitism. Because of the genuine suffering of the Palestinians under Israeli occupation, this propaganda received wide sympathy. During the conference, vile caricatures of Israelis (or, more accurately, Jews) were distributed and Jewish delegates were harassed and intimidated. Though officially banned in South Africa, copies of *The Protocols of the Elders of Zion* were sold there on the pretext that the conference venue was technically "international territory". This aroused fears of a dangerous spread of Muslim antisemitism, fears exacerbated by the fact that children in Arab countries are routinely indoctrinated with negative images of Jews, and antisemitism in the Arab media has become part of "respectable" public discourse.[1]

In describing the conference – which he refused to attend because its planning promised anti-Israel rhetoric as a major part of its content – the Holocaust survivor Eli Wiesel labelled it an "enterprise of disgrace" and likened antisemitic hatred to a cancer. "It spreads from cell to cell, from organ to organ, from person to person, from group to group. We saw it in action in Durban ... The conference in Durban will be remembered as a forum that was governed not by anti-Israelites but by anti-Semites." He remarked on the way that people in the Arab world "preach hatred and violence, not against Zionists but against *Jews*. Their slogan, naked and brutal and identical everywhere, was keenly felt and even heard in Durban: 'Kill the Jews.' What is painful is not that the Palestinians and the Arabs voiced their hatred, but the fact that so few delegates had the courage to combat them. It is as if in a strange and frightening moment of collective catharsis, everyone removed their masks and revealed their true faces."[2]

Within three days of the end of the conference, the cataclysmic terror attack on the USA took place, an attack that is widely seen as arising out of Islamic extremism. It did not take long before conspiratorial explanations were offered, accusing the Jews and Israel of responsibility and suggesting that most of the Jewish employees who worked in the World Trade Centre presciently did not go to work on the fateful morning of 11 September 2001. Few will forget the widely televised pictures of people in Arab lands, particularly those in the Israeli-occupied West Bank and Gaza Strip, dancing in the streets, celebrating the substantial new chink in America's armour. We will consider, briefly, the antisemitic fallout of that event in the epilogue.

It must be emphasised that not all opposition to Israel is antisemitism. Bernard Lewis (1988) has distinguished three forms of antagonism to

Jews, only the last of which qualifies as antisemitism proper. The first is opposition to Israel in a situation of genuine political conflict. It may or may not be fuelled by prejudice, but it may also serve to generate prejudice. The hostility to which the conflict gives rise is not necessarily antisemitism, however, especially in a region where violent language is normal and accepted in the expression of political conflicts. The second is "normal" prejudice, the dislike of the unlike, or antagonism towards another tribe, nation, majority or minority. The third is antisemitism, a hatred unique in its persistence, universality, depth and, above all, its theological and psychological origins. This form of hatred attributes to its adversary a quality of cosmic and eternal evil, a form that did not exist in traditional Islam.

This chapter will examine the origin and development of the negative image of the Jew in Islam, and show how, in modern times, the fatal transformation to antisemitism came about. It will outline the fundamental difference between Christian and Islamic attitudes to Jews, which will involve a brief discussion of the basic features of Islam and its traditional perception of Jews.

ISLAM: THE YOUNGEST OF THE WORLD'S MAJOR FAITHS

Islam, like Judaism and Christianity, believes in prophecy, holding that there has been a long line of prophets, from Adam, through Jesus, to Muhammad, each of whom received a revelation from God, whom Muslims call Allah, *the* God, the one and only. The final, perfect, revelation was received by the prophet Muhammad, the sinless exemplar of Islam, in about 610 CE, through the agency of the angel Gabriel. Muhammad is thus the last prophet, the "seal" of prophecy, who delivered Allah's revelation first to Arabia and ultimately to all humanity. The holy book in which this revelation is recorded is the Qur'an (Recitation). Muhammad is charged with the mission to

> Recite in the name of your Lord who created,
> Created man from clots of blood!
> Recite ... for thy Lord is most beneficent ...
> who by the pen has taught man that which he knew not.
> (Qur'an 96:1–4)

Having been given Allah's most perfect instruction, humanity's response should be *submission* to his will, the word "Islam" meaning "to submit".

The term is also associated with the word, *salaam*, meaning "peace", and denotes the tranquillity that descends on the believer when life is lived according to God's will. Muhammad's message was, it seems, originally intended as a local Arabic one. Islam's holy book refers to itself as the Arabic Qur'an (Qur'an 42:7), so that Muhammad could warn "in plain Arabic language" (Qur'an 26:195) the mother of all cities, Mecca, of an impending day of judgement. It is suggested that the refusal of the Jews and Christians to heed his message is what led to Islam becoming a universal faith.

Receiving his first revelation in Mecca, his birthplace, Muhammad soon found his message violently opposed by its dominant pagan tribe, the Quraish, who objected to the new moral strictures imposed by monotheism, like the prohibition of gambling and idolatry. He was forced, in 622 CE, to flee to Yathrib, where his presence was eagerly sought because his diplomatic skills would help to control the city's warring factions. Yathrib was later named Medina, from *medinat an-Nabi*, the city of the prophet. This emigration from Mecca, known as the *hijra*, marks the official beginning of Islam.

Whereas he had been forced to live the life of a fugitive in Mecca, in Medina Muhammad was able to lay the basis for the later establishment of Islam as a world religion, and it was there that he achieved his status as a religious and political leader. The revelations were given to Muhammad over twenty-three years and were received in both cities. Historians of religion have noted that the Qur'an's Meccan passages are more urgent and clipped than those from Medina, where the prophet had the time to articulate a theological framework for Islam and to formulate a lifestyle that bears a strong resemblance to Judaism. Many attribute this similarity to Muhammad's encounters with the Jews of Medina, which became an important city only because Muhammad settled there, and which housed the largest concentration of Jews in northern Arabia at that time. Their origin and previous history are unclear, but they may have arrived there shortly after the destruction of the second temple.

Judaism, as we saw in chapter 3, is a way of life that is governed by divine law, the aim of which is to hallow the everyday act. Islam is very similar. As in Judaism, divine law determines every detail of personal and communal life, from how believers pray, to what they eat or wear. There is no priestly class in either religion and both have developed a system of certification whereby men learned in holy law can become the religious leaders of their communities. Unlike Judaism, however – which developed as a response to exile, or homelessness – Islam was characterised by political power and territorial expansion. Muhammad was both the religious leader of his people, the *ummah*, and a consummate political leader. Islamic law thus legislates on statecraft, as well as on individual and community activities. During his lifetime, Muhammad became, as Lewis (1997, p. 5) puts it, "a head of state, commanding armies, collecting taxes, administering justice, and promulgating laws. The resulting interpenetration of faith and power, of religion and authority, has remained characteristic of Islam throughout most of its history." Islam, therefore, is a unique amalgam of theology and politics.

Thus, Islamic attitudes to Jews are bound up with theology and politics and have to be studied in relation to the way these interact in time and space. This is particularly important with regard to the Arab–Israeli conflict in the Middle East today. Jews, as we will see, were *dhimmi*, or protected people, in Muslim lands. Their return to Israel, and their achievement of political sovereignty in 1948, contradicted Islamic theological verities and resulted in a complicated reversal of the traditional Islamic attitudes to Jews. The defeats suffered by the Arab world in the ongoing Arab–Israeli conflict served to reinforce this reversal.

Like Judaism and its Torah, Islam has a central scripture, the Qur'an, from which the laws for life are derived. Many of the laws that regulate the believer's life were formulated later, through oral interpretations of the central text. In the case of Islam, the oral tradition was developed in the *hadith*, which reports the sayings and actions of Muhammad. So, for example, though the Qur'an commanded Muslims to pray, it did not give the details of *how* to pray. Wherever the Qur'an was not specific, the words and actions of the prophet Muhammad became the model for how believers should comport themselves. While Muhammad was establishing the faith in Medina, he came into conflict with the Jews there because they refused to accept his new message. His negative appraisal of them also form part of the *hadith*.

There are various collections of *hadith*, or stories that developed around Muhammad, some more authoritative than others. Each report about a saying or action of Muhammad is preceded by a chain of authorities through whom the story has been passed down through the ages and through whom the original observer or hearer, an associate of Muhammad, can be identified. The more reliable the chain, the more authentic is the tradition. Islamic jurists used these traditions in conjunction with the Qur'an, to formulate the Sharia, the laws of Islam. In their formulation of laws to guide the lives of Islamic communities, other concepts, such as community consensus and human reason, were also used. Over time, commentaries on the various texts emerged. The Qur'an, itself, reveals an attitude of superiority over and disdain for Jews, so it is not surprising that the writings that developed out of it elaborated on this theme.

JEWS UNDER ISLAM

The Jews of Medina rejected Muhammad's message. Sharing the Abrahamic tradition, they were perceived as clinging insistently to an imperfect faith. The Muslim attitude to them was one of contempt for an inferior minority rather than the blend of hatred, awe and jealousy that characterised the relationship of Christians to Jews. Jews, as Bernard Lewis (1997, p. 12) puts it, "were never free from discrimination, but only rarely subject to persecution ... their situation was never as bad as in Christendom at its worst, nor ever as good as Christendom at its best". There is no parallel, in Islamic history, to the degradation of the Spanish Inquisition, the expulsion of the Jews from Spain, the Russian pogroms or the Nazi Holocaust. But there is also nothing to compare to the emancipation and acceptance of Jews in the democratic West. The Jews' experience under Islam, though no utopia, was not accompanied by the relentless persecution of Jews that pervaded Christendom.

Though Jews were treated unfavourably under both Christianity and Islam, there is, as Lewis (1984) suggests, something conducive to active Jewish life under either of them that is lacking in societies dominated by other religions. Jews managed to flourish under Christian and Islamic rule, which the small Jewish communities living in the more tolerant lands of the East failed to do. Lewis ascribes this positive development to the fact that, in both Christianity and Islam, the Jews have been given a cosmic role. Neither religion could simply ignore Jews. This cosmic role, as we have already seen, carries an inherent danger. Since all three religions trace their lineage back to the patriarch Abraham, there was an inevitable development of friction between them. Islam's image of the Jews was historically less damaging than that in Christianity, because the Jews' role was more peripheral under Islam than in Christian theology. The gospels played no role in Islamic education, and Arab children were not brought up on the notion of deicide. Islam, in fact, rejects Jesus' crucifixion, holding that no prophet of God could have died so ignominious a death. Jews tried to crucify him, Muslims believe, but God sent a substitute in his place. Although the evil intent of the Jews was retained, so was their impotence to succeed in it. Muslims also reject as blasphemous the notion of the Incarnation. Jesus is seen as no more than a prophet or messenger.

THE *DHIMMI*

Islam saw its mission in terms of territorial conquest, and divides the world into two domains: *dar al-Islam*, the domain of Islam, or peace, and the domain of war, *dar al-Harb*. In Islam's period of ascendancy, there was an obligatory and perpetual state of war, *jihad*, to extend its territorial domain. However, there was barely any forcible conversion and the spread of Muhammad's message was generally brought about through persuasion and inducement. Once the advance of Islam stopped, the fulfilment of *jihad's* victory was postponed to the end of days. As Lewis (1984, p. 23) points out, in the heroic age of Islam, loss of territory and populations to infidel rule was simply inconceivable. By the mid eighth century, it had become clear that the advance of Islam was ending, and the idea of accepted boundaries, accompanied by dealings with neighbours, had come to be accepted.

Jihad is, today, a problematic concept. On the one hand, it is being widely abused by Muslim radicals in acts of aggression that go against the spirit of Islam as a religion of peace. On the other, according to Edward Said in his 1997 book *Covering Islam*, "it has become the single most important motif in Western media representations of Islam", offering a grossly distorted picture of the religion. In the earliest days of Islam, when Muhammad was battling against enemies to establish the religion to which God had called him, he was forced to defend himself and his new community militarily. He needed also to ensure that his community did not stray back into paganism. The word *jihad* has always denoted a struggle in the cause of God, and refers to the inner struggle of the individual to live the life of submission. It is not necessarily associated with military war, nor was it ever meant to be aggressive. "Struggle in the cause of God against those who fight you, but do not be aggressors, for God does not like aggressors" (Qur'an 2:190).[3]

The fact that Islam is an amalgam of religion and politics enabled Muhammad to become, as Forward (1997, p. 63) points out, a more successful political leader than any other human founder of a world religion. Within a century of the prophet's death, the Islamic empire stretched from the Atlantic Ocean in the west, to the borders of India and China in the east, and many people came under its control. Islam thus had to establish a *policy* with regard to non-Muslims. Only the pagans were expected to convert to Islam. Jews and Christians had already received divine revelation through earlier prophets, and had their own scriptures. They were therefore called *ahl al-kitab*, or "people of the book", and categorised as *dhimmi* (protected people), having a provisional form of religious freedom.

Although Allah's earlier revelations were regarded as true and beyond question, they were seen as neither final nor perfect, and as having been appropriated and written down incorrectly. The Jewish and Christian scriptures are thus faulty records of an incomplete revelation. The Qur'an, as the literal word of God, assumes ultimate authority, holding that *all* the prophets had preached *one* religion, namely, Islam. The Qur'an recognises four scriptures: the *Tawreh* (Torah), which was given to Moses, the *Zabur* (Psalms), which was given to David; the *Injil* (*Evangelion*, the Greek word for "gospel"), which was given to Jesus, and, finally, the Qur'an, which was given to Muhammad. Muhammad was about forty years of age when he received his first revelation. Aware of previous revelations through God's prophets, he was convinced that he had been chosen as the prophet to the Arabs to warn them of an impending day of judgement, and proclaimed publicly the content of the revelations he had received.

He repeatedly emphasised that his message was to confirm and correct previous revelations, and that the Qur'an clarifies any ambiguities in the earlier ones and supersedes them. Thus, the earlier scriptures were not adopted as Christianity had adopted the Hebrew Bible. There were, therefore, no conflicting interpretations. Jews were seen by Muslims as stubborn and ungrateful, but not as blind or unable to understand the purport of their own scriptures. Muhammad quoted extensively – and from a Jewish perspective, sometimes wrongly – from the Bible.

The Qur'an recognises the kinship and cultural affinities between members of the three Abrahamic faiths, but it clearly enunciates Muslim political and religious superiority. As monotheists and recipients of prior revelation, Jews and Christians were free to practise their religions, under Islam's laws of protection, *dhimma*, provided that they acknowledged

Islam's superiority, kept a low profile and paid a special poll tax, *jizya*, under humiliating circumstances. There are accounts, for example, of *dhimmis* being seized by the scruff of the neck and shaken while paying the *jizya*, or of having to stand while the recipient of the tax sat. *Dhimmis* were to be overtly differentiated from Muslims. They had, for example, to ride on donkeys instead of horses, have places of worship more modest and less high and splendid than Muslim ones, and wear distinctive clothing. Patches of different colours distinguished Jews and Christians from Muslims. The yellow badge – which became infamous in Nazi Germany as the yellow star to demarcate Jews – was instituted in the ninth century by the caliph of Baghdad. Its use spread to Europe in the late Middle Ages. The disabilities suffered by Jews and Christians in Muslim lands were eventually systematised and were referred to collectively as the Pact of Umar, being ascribed retroactively to the caliph Umar I.

Although it cannot be judged by the norms of a modern democracy, the *dhimmi* system created a formula for religious pluralism in which Jews could survive and even prosper. But if they became too ostentatious in their success, there was no guarantee that the original contract of protection would be honoured. Although the notion of "toleration-protection cum humiliation" took on, as Jane Gerber (1986, p. 84) suggests, varied and sometimes outrageous forms, the radical isolation of the Jew as "outsider" in Europe was never approximated in the Muslim world. "Jews were objects of officially legislated contempt, but they were not intended to be objects of officially instituted hatred."

The precedent for legal discussions about the *dhimmi* was Muhammad's battle with the Jews of the oasis of Khaybar (ninety-five miles from Medina) when they rejected his message. After fighting bravely, they eventually capitulated to Muhammad's forces, and were allowed to stay on and cultivate the land, provided that they gave over half of their produce to the Muslim state. This was the first instance of submission to Islamic rule by non-Muslims. As Islam spread, it came into contact with many cultures among which Jews lived, and individual communities of Jews experienced different fates in different parts of the Muslim world. The variations are so wide that one could, suggests Jane Gerber (1986, p. 74), find evidence to support any thesis one proposed about Muslim attitudes to Jews. Moreover, there was often a gap between Islamic theory and practice, Muslim precept often being harsher than the actual treatment of Jews under Islamic governance. In any event, there have always been divergent attitudes within the Muslim world and, still today, different attitudes can be observed among the various branches of Islam. Of the two main branches of Islam, the Sunna and the Shia, the latter have tended to show a sterner attitude to Jews. More recently, Islamic fundamentalists have exploited the negative popular image of Jews. The Jews' political powerlessness supported what, for Muslims, was a stable worldview, the world order as it *should* be. Contrasted with Muslim success, it served to vindicate Islam's truth.

MUHAMMAD AND THE JEWS OF MEDINA

Muhammad's attitude to Jews was essentially ambivalent, but it is difficult to ascertain his exact relationship with them and how his attitude developed. As Muslim scholars have not yet opened Islam up to critical scholarship and modern historiographical methods – as those of Judaism and Christianity have done – there are many gaps in our historical knowledge about Muhammad's life. In his early days in pagan Arabia, when accompanying Meccan trade caravans, Muhammad came into frequent contact with Jews and Christians; scholars have long discussed their possible influence on his message, some emphasising Judaism's influence and others Christianity's. There is no certainty about the extent of the influence of either. What is generally agreed is that his message is intricately tied in with the day-to-day tribulations he experienced, first in Mecca, and then in Medina, and that his encounters with pagans, Jews and Christians helped to shape it. Jews in Medina certainly played a critical role in the way Islam developed.

On the one hand, Muhammad respected the Jews as recipients of previous divine revelation and, on the other, he faulted them for distorting it. When the Jews refused to accept Muhammad's message as the natural and logical successor to previous divine revelations, he was deeply disappointed and distanced himself from them as the enemies of Islam. The Qur'an and *hadith*, both of which developed over time, are the chief sources on these attitudes, and reflect Muhammad's changing interaction with Jews. The Qur'an refers to Jews sometimes favourably and at other times negatively. The favourable statements seem to derive from the earlier revelations when there was still hope of the Jews' conversion to the new message.

It is not certain at what point Muhammad's message developed into a distinct new form of monotheism that reaches out to the entire world.

According to Martin Forward (1997, p. 56), Muhammad's rift with the Jews and Christians led to the formulation of a specifically Arabian monotheism, which was based on Abraham but had universal aspirations. This new, reformed, Arabian monotheism was now self-consciously set against Judaism and Christianity. Jews and Christians were accused not only of rejecting Muhammad's ministry, but of failing to uphold the unity of God. The latter was a lot easier to charge against Christianity's Trinitarian doctrine than against Judaism. Ronald Nettler (1990) suggests that the negative image of the Jews that arose out of Muhammad's conflict with them played a useful role in the formation of Islam's self-identity. Citing Kenneth Cragg, Nettler calls it "the most abiding and massive example of an identity discovered out of an antipathy".

By Muhammad's time, there were three major Jewish tribes in Medina – the Banu Qunayqa, the Banu Nadir and the Banu Qurayza – and others in nearby oases. Their main occupation being the cultivation of palm groves, they were Arab in speech, culture and way of life, and were accepted and respected. The conflict between Islam and the Jews began with the *hijra*, when the Jews ridiculed Muhammad's apostolate and rejected his military leadership. It is generally believed that until then Muhammad had been well disposed towards the Jewish tribes. Once he realised that there was no possibility of winning them over, a complex and ambivalent attitude towards them emerged. Two of the tribes were expelled, but the third, the Banu Qurayza, was severely punished for alleged treachery.

The Banu Nadir had been accused of plotting to kill Muhammad, and surrendered only when the Muslims began chopping down their date palms. They were allowed to leave with all that their camels could carry, but without military arms. Some went to the oasis of Khaybar, from where they petitioned the Quraish, Muhammad's Meccan enemies, to avenge them. The Banu Qurayza, too, were suspected of being in league with the Quraish. The Muslims besieged the suburb of Medina where the Qurayza lived and fifteen days later the latter sued for peace. They wanted to emulate the earlier tribes and be allowed to leave, but were cruelly punished. Between six and nine thousand of their men were beheaded and thrown into a ditch, and their women and children were sold as slaves. No Jews have since been allowed into Medina. Elsewhere in Arabia, Jews were treated more leniently, probably for economic reasons. But they were associated with treachery, the breaking of treaties and conniving with the enemy.

In his initial attempts to win over the Jews, Muhammad adapted some of the rituals of his community to those followed by Jews. For example, he originally wanted believers to direct prayer to Jerusalem, and to fast on the tenth of Ashura, a day coinciding with the Jewish day of Atonement. When the Jews failed to acknowledge his mission, he introduced laws that emphasised the difference between Islam and Judaism, and adopted a hostile attitude to the Jews of Medina. It was then that Muhammad received the revelation that Abraham, with the aid of his son Ishmael, had built in Mecca the Kaba, the holiest shrine of Islam. Abraham, Muhammad was told, was neither a Jew nor a Christian, but a Muslim. Henceforth, Muslims were commanded to pray in the direction of the Kaba and to fast for the entire month of Ramadan.

Jews were seen as stubborn and perverse, and as rebelling against God and killing his prophets. The term *Banu Israil*, "the children of Israel", Forward (1997, p. 55) suggests, generally refers to the Jews in the sense of their having been called by God but having forgotten this privilege. Muhammad was merely reminding them of it. The word *Yahud* tends to have a more negative connotation, referring to those Jews in Medina who opposed Muhammad's message and conspired against him, colluding with his enemies. There is thus a tension between the Qur'an's reminder to the Jews to return to obedience to God, and its tendency to condemn all Jews as intrinsically hostile and malevolent. The Qur'an represents the Jews as corrupters of scripture (Qur'an 3:63). They were accused of falsehood (Qur'an 3:71) and were seen as enemies of Islam. "Thou wilt surely find that the strongest in enmity against those who believe are the Jews and the idolaters" (Qur'an 5:85).

According to Ronald Nettler, the idea of Jews being Islam's arch-opposers – who already in Muhammad's time aided and abetted his enemies – resulted in a negative archetype, that carried a potently positive message of Islam's own contrasted brilliance. As political success was a vindication of Islam's truth, the archetype was the flip-side of Muslim power. Any reversal of the Jews' powerless status would contradict the correct world order. Thus, the Jews' place in the scheme of things, according to Nettler (1990, p. 64), was central, and they became the chief enemies of Islam. As the first recipients of divine revelation, they should have been the first to accept the final revelation. Their stubborn refusal to improve their lot by openly recognising the new revelation led to them being seen in the Qur'an as the people most hostile to the Muslims. The time at which they refused Muhammad's message coincided with the beginning of the realisation of Islam's political and social destiny, and their obstinate resistance was an insult to both Islam and Muhammad. His harsh treatment of the Jewish tribes was, from an Islamic point of view, appropriate.

Jews were seen as having a tendency towards political incitement – and even rebellion – against Allah's truth. This, says Nettler, was a natural conclusion in the tribal milieu of the time, where "religion" often became embroiled in internecine conspiracies. But he takes the issue further, suggesting that the Jews' stubborn denial of the truth led to the idea that they possessed an "eternal" perfidious nature that impelled them to act with conspiratorial malevolence, the most extreme example of their perfidy being their desire to kill Muhammad himself. This notion reflects the Christian deicide accusation, and is nowhere more graphically illustrated than in the story of the Jewish woman Zaynab, who allegedly gave the prophet poison that led to his death. Appearing in a biographical text of Muhammad's life,[4] this story was seen as the ultimate Jewish assault on the apex of prophetic religion. Jewish obduracy made a permanent impression on Islamic doctrine.

Nettler makes the point that whether the events related in the literature are historically true or not is irrelevant. Islam's historic memory of these allegations has been long and strong, made permanent by the depiction of Jews in Islamic sources – long after Muhammad's problems with them – as anti-Islamic provocateurs and conspirators. Whereas the pagans had been defeated early on, the Jews remained a subversive threat. However, this archetype remained part of routine Islamic historiography and was devoid of hatred as long as the malevolent, conspiring Jews were humbled and could be treated with contempt.

Compared with their centrality in Christianity, however, the role of the Jews in traditional Islam is minor. Lewis (1997, p. 126) points out the peripheral nature of their role in the broader context of Muhammad's outstanding career. In the Qur'an, the really important point about the Jews is not their opposition to the prophet, but that he defeated and humbled them. "Shame and misery were stamped upon them, and they incurred the wrath of God; because they disbelieved God's signs and slew His prophets unjustly, because they were rebels and transgressors" (Qur'an 2:61). Words like "shame" and "humiliation" are used frequently in Islamic texts in relation to Jews. Their political impotence – between the mighty empires of Christendom and Islam – was seen as just punishment for their rebelliousness. As such, it was a condition to which they were perpetually condemned, the humbled Jew becoming another archetype in Islamic literature and folklore.

JEWS AS PERIPHERAL

Muhammad's encounters with the Jews, Lewis insists, were different, in both circumstance and outcome, from Jesus' depicted contact with them:

- Muhammad's companions were not Jews and he did not live in a predominantly Jewish society. The three tribes of Medina, though they constituted the largest concentration of Jews in northern Arabia, were a minority within a pagan community.
- In the Islamic world, Jews were one minority among several and, although the *Qur'an* favours Christians over Jews, the two groups received equal treatment under Islamic law. Jews were never free of discrimination, but were only occasionally subject to persecution.
- The Qur'an was a new revelation, not a fulfilment of Judaism. It superseded both the "Old" and the New Testaments, which were seen as distorted records of incomplete revelation.
- The Hebrew Bible was not retained as it was in Christianity. Thus, there was no clash of interpretations.
- Islamic society did not see itself as the "new" or "true" Israel, so was not threatened or impugned by the obstinate survival of the old Israel.
- Muhammad never claimed messiahship. Rather, he was God's apostle. Rejection of a prophet was less wounding, less significant, and less of a reproach than the rejection of an expected messiah.
- Muhammad's conflict with the Jews ended in the destruction of the Jewish tribes, not in his. In Christianity, the Jews are depicted as crucifying Jesus.
- Because there was no equivalent of the deicide myth in traditional Islam, the Jews were not demonised. This made it possible for Muslims to adopt a more relaxed and less embittered attitude towards their Jewish subjects than existed in Christendom.
- Rather than suffering an ignominious death, Muhammad triumphed within his own lifetime. He was head of state and of his religious community.
- Historically, the clash between Judaism and Islam was resolved by the victory of Islam.

With the return of the Jews to political sovereignty, the role of the Jews has been given pre-eminence, and Jewish enmity has gained a cosmic significance that it lacks in the classical texts. But this development took time.

ISLAM'S ASCENDANCY AND DECLINE

Being intimately involved in power politics, and having spread so widely, Islam was not untouched by political developments in the outside world. All religions go through stages, which the historian usually demarcates in relation to challenges from within and without. Though some scholars identify four phases against which to examine the development of Islamic antisemitism,[5] these can, for our purposes, be collapsed into two. The first may be called "classical Islam", which started with the life of Muhammad in the seventh century and lasted until the retreat of Islam in the face of Europe's advance in the nineteenth century. The second can be termed the "modern period". Beginning earliest in the western part of the Islamic empire, with the reconquest of Spain, Portugal and North Africa, the retreat of Islam was delayed in the Middle East by the existence of the Ottoman Empire, which, even while in decline, was a formidable military power. There the retreat did not begin until the eighteenth century.

The first period, though sometimes interrupted by local setbacks, was one of strength and confidence. Islam expanded territorially, while advancing in power. External factors exerted little influence and Islam was able to develop according to its own internal logic (Lewis 1997, p. 122). Though there were harsh words about Jews in the Qur'an and *hadith*, they were rooted in Muhammad's actual conflict with the Jews of Medina, and there was never any question about his consistent victory over them. Other passages were respectful of Jews and balanced the negative statements about them. Jews had limited rights as long as they knew their place in the world order. Their inferiority was accepted and their acceptance formalised within a legal system that could enforce their position to a greater or lesser degree. It was possible, as Emmanuel Sivan put it, to treat the Jews with "disdainful disregard".

We have seen that there was no tradition of guilt and betrayal as characterised Christian attitudes to Jews. Though Jews sometimes prospered and at other times were treated harshly, even the worst treatment was, according to Lewis, "normal" in that it was based on genuine differences and expressed within specific historic circumstances. There were no theological or psychological grounds for fears about a Jewish conspiracy or Jewish domination, nor were there charges of diabolical evil. Jews were not accused of poisoning wells or causing the plague. There was no evidence in the Muslim world of the Blood Libel, though it was introduced to the conquering Ottomans by some of their Greek Christian subjects in the fifteenth century and taken up seriously later. Before the penetration of nationalism and patriotism into Islamic culture, both of which were Western notions, people's main loyalty was to the religious community. Jews did not bear arms, as this was the privilege of Muslims only.

However negative the portrayal of Jews, their hostility was always seen as ineffectual. They had rebelled, the Qur'an relates, against Moses, but the revolt was quelled. They had tried to crucify Jesus, but failed, and were merely deluded into thinking they had succeeded. They opposed Muhammad, but he overcame and punished them, some with expulsion, others with enslavement or death. Whereas for the Christian the Jew was a dark and deadly power, capable of deeds of cosmic evil, for the Muslim the Jew was hostile, cunning and vindictive, but always weak and unsuccessful. He was an object of ridicule, not fear. The archetype of the humbled Jew was accompanied by one of Jewish cowardice. Whereas the Christian was in power in some parts of the world, the Jew was humbled everywhere. Archetypes, as Nettler argues, have a life of their own, and today, in very changed historical circumstances, the anti-Jewish archetype is used in a much more ominous way.

The change in Muslim perception of Jews began in the eighteenth century, and gathered momentum in the nineteenth. By then, most of the Islamic world had been brought under Christian empires and, thus, under European influence. With this, confidence changed to anxiety. At the same time, new notions and institutions, previously part of the European Christian world, were adopted, among them antisemitism. The once despised Christian infidel was now imitated; the trickle of foreign influence became a flood. With the Jews' return to sovereignty in the mid twentieth century, their preordained inferior status underwent a blatant turnabout, one whose impact was reinforced by each successive Israeli victory in the Arab–Israeli conflict. A master people had been transformed into a subject people and Jews, instead of being seen as contemptible, were now deemed dangerous. Christianity had always been a threat to Islam, both militarily and as a competing civilisation.

Judaism had been neither. Persecution, forced conversion and banishment had been rare under Islam. Only in times of stress and danger, when the Islamic world was threatened, either from within – as during a famine or religious division – or from without – as during foreign invasion – were they evident.

ISLAM INVADED

Islam was subjected to three major invasions: the crusaders, the Mongols, and the modern European empires.With each incursion into Muslim territory, there was increasing evidence of Muslim intolerance to minorities. The period of the Crusades saw the segregation of Muslims from non-Muslims for the first time, accompanied by harsh treatment of the latter. With the Mongol invasions of the thirteenth and fourteenth centuries came a wave of mistrust and polemics against non-Muslims. Though directed mostly at Christians, Jews too were targets, especially in North Africa, where, after the extinction of the indigenous Christian community, they became, as they had been in Christendom, the only religious minority, which made them more vulnerable. The final invasion – that of European imperialism – was the most deadly and lasting, and caused Muslim society to undergo profound changes.

As the Europeans became increasingly dominant, there was a growing sense of weakness and defeat. Accompanying the political changes came economic and social changes. Non-Muslim minorities were now viewed as disaffected and disloyal, their sympathies as lying with the European enemy. They were, therefore, a danger to Islam, a perception reinforced by the wealth and prominence of, especially, Christians, but also Jews. Both had achieved power that as *dhimmi* would have been impossible. The Jews were especially targeted because of the pre-existing anti-Jewish archetype, discussed above, and the entry into the Islamic world of European-style antisemitism, a virulent hatred that had hitherto been unknown even to the most prejudiced Muslims. Jews had, at times, been useful to Muslim rulers, because they were not thought to be sympathetic to the external enemy.

With one exception – the Muslim polemicist Ibn Hazm – there had been no attempt to refute Judaism, as Luther and other churchmen had tried to do. Whereas Christian philosophers had generally found it necessary to say something negative about Jews, this was not the case with Muslim thinkers. There were no Jewish "monsters" in Muslim literature, like Shylock in Shakespeare's *Merchant of Venice*, or Fagin in Dickens's *Oliver Twist*. Today, however, these stereotypes have invaded Arab fiction and drama. What had characterised Jews previously was their unimportance. They were not praised, but neither, according to Lewis (1997, p. 127), were they seen as inherently evil.

The real penetration of antisemitism began in the nineteenth century with Christian Arab minorities for whom Jews were the main commercial competitors. Along with calls for boycotts, ritual murder accusations began to be commonplace. In the latter half of the century, the first Arabic versions of European antisemitism were published. Translations, especially of French tracts, began to proliferate as a result of the Dreyfus trial. It was at this time that Auguste Rohling's *The Talmud Jew* appeared in Arabic. The Ottoman authorities tried to stop its circulation as a threat to public order, but to no avail. *The Protocols of the Elders of Zion* also began to take hold, but the influence of these texts had not yet become decisive. The situation deteriorated steadily, but worse was to come with emergence of the Zionist movement and the Jews' return to the land of Israel.

THE JEWS' RETURN TO SOVEREIGNTY

With the establishment of the State of Israel in 1948, the Jews had doubly defied their *dhimmi* status. Not only had they reoccupied their land, but they had become a military power to be reckoned with – a shocking reversal of the proper Islamic world order. Starting out as marginal to the main Arab struggle, antisemitism intensified after the 1956 Sinai War and was accelerated by the Six-Day War of 1967, both of which were swift and overwhelming Israeli victories. The War of Independence, in 1948–49, had been a hard-fought struggle, lasting many months, in which Israel won the prize of survival at high cost. The Jews had always been perceived as cowardly and lacking in the military virtues. "The Jew in his very soul and character has not the qualities of a man who bears arms. He is not naturally prepared to sacrifice for anything, not even for his son or wife."[6] How could they be so suddenly victorious? These humiliating defeats demanded recourse to an explanation that was beyond the normal processes of rational thought, one that invoked demonic, conspiratorial powers. Such an explanation had already been offered in Christendom – originally religious, and later overlaid with potentially murderous secular rationalisations – and had, by now, gained wide currency in the Arab world. Grafted on to the ancient Islamic archetype of the Jew, this allowed Islamic antisemitism to become more dangerous than its Christian counterpart had been.

Previously, even though Jewish obstructiveness had been seen as an inherent trait, "racism" had been absent from Islamic views about Jews. Jews and Christians had been seen as part of the Arab family, and could easily convert to Islam. Now Jews were seen as racially inferior, an idea that was imported with European antisemitism.[7] Though not comparable to their position in a modern democracy, the Jews' situation under Islam in the Middle Ages had been more favourable than that under Christianity. But new ideologies of hatred had been learned from Christendom. The old system of toleration and inequality was replaced with modern secular ideas like democracy, constitutional government and equal rights. With these came notions such as patriotism and ethnic nationalism, which soon turned into bigotry and racism and disturbed attitudes to non-Muslim minorities. All this boded ill for Jews in the Muslim world.

Today, antisemitism is generally disguised as anti-Zionism, which postulates a dangerous, shadowy, international conspiracy with its Jewish centre in the Middle East. Although the geographic focus has changed, the content of the mythology remains familiar. In the view of Robert Wistrich (1985), there is a continuity between Nazi antisemitism and current militant anti-Zionism. Hitler unleashed an attack on the Jews which is not yet fully spent in that it has been resuscitated by Arab nationalism. The problem today lies not so much in the resurfacing of antisemitism, but in the reintroduction of antisemitism as a legitimate ideological tool and its acceptance as part of "respectable" public discourse.

Hitler's Holocaust made the direct expression of hostility to Jews as a racial, religious or ethnic group unacceptable to most of Western public opinion. In the Arab world, an alternative intellectual framework and mode of expression had to be found for justifying a new goal – denial of the Jews' right to political sovereignty. As Wistrich (1985, p. 9) suggests, "anti-Zionism provided this post-war substitute, just as a hundred years ago 'antisemitism' itself replaced Jew-hatred (or anti-Judaism) in the European vocabulary".

ANTI-ZIONISM AND ANTISEMITISM

Difficult as it is to define antisemitism, it is even more difficult to decide whether anti-Zionism is an entirely new expression of antisemitism or the old beast in a new guise. It is often questioned whether it is antisemitism at all. The latter question is probably the one most easily laid to rest. Scholars widely agree that it is necessary to distinguish between opposition to Israeli policy as legitimate political criticism, and ideological anti-Zionism that persistently denies any legitimacy to a Jewish homeland in the Middle East. As Bauer (1988, p. 34) puts it, "When anti-Zionism takes the form of denying Jews the right to have their own national political entity, then we would define this as antisemitism." Criticism of individual Israeli policies, or even ideological disagreement about Zionism – a distinction between the dream and the reality – would not necessarily be antisemitic. Jews themselves have, at various times, opposed the idea of a Jewish state, such as in the early days of reform Judaism, when the new movement did not feel that Jews needed a home of their own. Putting a finer point on it, Shlomo Avineri (1988, p. 34) says that anti-Zionism is antisemitism when there is a refusal to accept a separate Jewish entity as understood by the Jews. It is precisely this non-acceptance that characterises previous forms of antisemitism, whether Christian or modern. Regarding Judaism as a religion only, and not permitting the idea of Jews as a nation, denies to Jews their existence as *they* understand it and is, therefore, antisemitism.

There is so much malevolence and malice in the attack on Zionism that it is hard to see it as part of legitimate political opposition to a political movement. The word "Zionist", Dan Segre (1986, p. 145) points out, has acquired an autonomous derogatory meaning of its own that transcends both time and space and is applied as an epithet for evil. The term has lost all rational connotations with history or geography, and Zionists have ceased to be seen as human beings. Zionism is thus perceived not merely as a bad political phenomenon, but as a cancerous growth. The ongoing state of war with the Arabs is not seen, therefore – in analogous contexts – as a situation of military occupation so much as one of colonial racism. Jewish involvement in the Middle East crisis serves to propel anti-Zionism, but does not explain its nature.

Anti-Zionism is antisemitism when it denies Jews their right to political sovereignty in the Middle East, refuses to accept their own definition of identity, and subjects Israel to moral expectations not demanded of any other sovereign state. So virulent is the denunciation of Zionism that scholars believe that it is not merely an extension of antisemitism but that some of its roots lie elsewhere and that anti-Zionism possesses a logic of its own. According to Segre, anti-Zionism can, in large part, be attributed to deep-seated psychological fears about developments with which rationality cannot cope. One of these is the strength of the separate Jewish identity not only in the past, but also now in the context of a nation-state. The dispersion of Jews was historically seen as divinely sanctioned, but, as rationalism and historical criticism took hold, this shielding interpretation was overturned. The gentile world has always seen Jewish survival as an enigma. With the establishment of the State of Israel, this enigma has been transferred from the individual to the political plane, and is exacerbated by the peculiar nature of Israeli nationalism. There is a widespread inability to come to terms with Israel as a transnational state – a state whose affiliates, or people who identify with it, live outside it. This results in deep fears about some kind of "pan-Judaism" with its focus in Israel, and is one of the dynamics underlying the accusation that Zionism is racism.

The charge that "Zionism is racism", though an outrageous canard, contains, according to Nathan Glazer (1986), a tiny node of meaning, which is based on the special relationship of Israel to the Jewish people. Because it was established as a home for the Jewish people, Israel must be a home for all the Jewish people. However, Israel accepts the orthodox Jewish religious definition of "who is a Jew", namely, either someone born of a Jewish mother, or someone who has undergone conversion to Judaism through the appropriate rituals and change of lifestyle. This results in a questioning of the Jewish status, for example, of the Beta Israel,[8] the black Jews from Ethiopia, who were airlifted to Israel some decades ago. Because their origins are obscure, and their religion developed differently from that of rabbinic Judaism, they had to undergo suitable conversion in order to qualify for Jewish citizenship. The issue is, therefore, not one of racism, there being Jews from all "races" – if we are, indeed, to assert any validity to the concept of "race", an issue that will be dealt with extensively in chapter 8, where it will be argued that race is an ideological construct. Rather, the charge that Zionism is racism results from the following chain of religious, historical and political circumstances: Zionism is an overwhelmingly secular movement for the national liberation of Jews, who are defined by religious criteria.

Strictly speaking, the very notion of a "Jewish" state conflicts with democracy in its modern sense, because the latter insists on equality of all citizens in a nation-state, irrespective of the ethnic or religious groups to which they belong. The same holds true for Muslim states. In any state governed by religious norms, whether it be Islamic or Jewish, the affiliates of the religion in question will be the "first class" citizens, all others being relegated to a secondary status. So, if modern democracy is used as the sole criterion, religiously governed states open themselves up to the charge that they are "racist". Factors, such as these, arouse widespread hostility to Israel, which is either fuelled by an existent antisemitism, or helps to give rise to it. It should be noted here that the orthodox rabbinate in Israel has sole religious authority. Reform and conservative, as well as reconstructionist Jews, have introduced other criteria to define Jewishness, such as patrilineal descent.

The identification of Zionism with racism opened the way for a cruel twist. Jews, previously victims of racism, are now, themselves, seen as racists. This serves to "exonerate" the world from any sense of guilt towards the Jews for the Holocaust, and from any sense of commitment to a Jewish state. It allows the Israeli Jews to be perceived as "Nazis", while the Palestinians are now perceived as the victims or "Jews", a situation that Wistrich calls the greatest inversion of history.

It is well known that the United Nations, in which Arab hostility was supported by the Soviet Union, has been one of Israel's greatest detractors. Irwin Cotler (1988, p. 44) has suggested that the way the United Nations has cast Israel, over the years, amounts to nothing less than antisemitism. Israel has been denounced as the enemy of everything that is good – labour, health, culture, human dignity, women, peace and human rights. It has been stigmatised as the present-day poisoner of wells, the contemporary equivalent of the traditional antisemitic stereotype, but with a more powerful and resonant ideological impact.

THIRD WORLD ATTITUDES

As Rivlin and Fomerand (1976) cogently argue, an important conduit of anti-Zionist sentiment is Third World ideology and its relationship with the Arab bloc. Though Third World countries differ from one another, they are united by certain psychological and social attitudes that have a critical bearing on their perception of Israel. Having been passive subjects of the policies of others, Third World countries have in common their recent emergence on the international scene as independent actors. Generally lacking in industrialisation and crippled by social and economic underdevelopment, their common experience of political subordination and economic poverty has implanted in them bitter memories of victimisation by foreign exploiters. Anti-colonialism and anti-imperialism were thus central in their struggle for self-determination, as were identification with, and a concern for, all the oppressed peoples of the world.

Originally sharing many attributes of the Third World states, Israel wanted to be perceived as part of the Third World, and initially hoped to pursue a policy of non-alignment with either the United States or the Soviet Union. Like in other Third World countries, Israel's people had long been oppressed, and had fought a war of national liberation in Palestine against the British colonial regime. Like countries of the Third World, Israel had to confront problems of economic development, social movement and modernisation, and most of its inhabitants – but not its leadership – were oriental Jews with a Third World background. Nonetheless, Israel was not accorded Third World status. Its inhabitants were not viewed as natives, but as foreigners who, as exponents of Western culture, were agents of Western imperialism. Israel's struggle against Britain was not accepted as that of an oppressed people, but was seen as thwarting another colonised people, the Arabs of Palestine, in their own fight for independence. The anti-colonialist and anti-imperialist lens of Third World countries directed them towards a pro-Palestinian and anti-Israeli position. This was reinforced by the bourgeois style of life that developed in Israel and by Israel's treatment of the Arab minority. Israel's dependence on the United States for military and economic aid after the Six-Day War of 1967 further honed this negative image of Israel.

Just as African and Asian colonies were beginning to attain independence, Islam experienced increased solidarity, reinforced by meetings of the Islamic elite at world Islamic meetings. Contact with the Islamic world, brought about through the *hajj* (the annual pilgrimage to Mecca) and the media, determined the pre-eminent place of Islam in the worldview of much of the Third World. People there had had little contact with Jews and were unfamiliar with their history of suffering and persecution. This helped to impede sympathy for the return of the Jews to their homeland.

Third World peoples who do not have large Jewish communities in their midst, say Rivlin and Fomerand (1976), do not share the guilt that the Western world may feel about the Holocaust. Major antisemitic events, including the Holocaust, were not part of their close experience. So it is not surprising that their reactions are different from reactions in the West. Given all these factors, it took a surprisingly long time for

Israel to become completely alienated from the Third World. Originally, there were positive attitudes to Israel. Sharing with Israel the challenges of nation-building and changing the face of the land, underdeveloped African countries turned to Israel for technical assistance, knowing little of the political problems of the Middle East or of the human tragedy involving the Palestinians.

The shift in black Africa's attitude to Israel was not abrupt and needed prompting from the Arab countries who wanted to cultivate African support without risking the loss of continental unity. Their goal was to loosen the African states' ties with Israel and persuade them to accept the Palestinian issue as a legitimate concern of black Africa. At the Casablanca Conference in 1961, the tide began to turn. Israel, in addition to being viewed as siding with apartheid because of an influential Jewish population in South Africa, was condemned as "an instrument in the service of imperialism and neo-colonialism", not only in the Middle East, but also in Africa and Asia. Concern was expressed about the Arabs of Palestine being deprived of their legitimate rights. But the Arab–Israeli dispute was still not a matter of direct concern to black African states, and only became so in 1967, with Israel's spectacular victory in the Six-Day War.

No longer perceived as a biblical David fighting against impossible odds, Israel was now seen as an invincible military power – just as the Third World was being transformed into a cohesive coalition of the underprivileged peoples of the world, fuelled by their growing frustration with their inability to bridge the gap between this coalition and the rich industrialised world. Anti-imperialism and anti-colonialism were now directed primarily against the United States and its allies, especially, Israel. Israel's friendly relations with white southern Africa at the time added to its dereliction. In 1973 the estrangement of Africa from Israel reached its nadir. Seventeen African countries broke relations with Israel, which was now seen to exhibit close parallels with the hated South Africa. Both were viewed as nations of alien settlers oppressing indigenous populations and serving as outposts of imperialism.

The Arab–Israeli conflict added fuel to all these developments. A vital part of the anti-Zionist picture, its outcome will have an effect on the development of antisemitism. The future prospects of Muslim–Jewish relations are inextricably tied in with peace in the Middle East. As Lewis (1988, p. 65) points out, "for Christian antisemites, the Palestine problem is a pretext and an outlet for their hatred; for Muslim antisemites, it is the cause. Perhaps," he suggests, "if that cause is removed or significantly diminished, the hostility too may wane, not disappear, but at least return to the previous level of prejudice." Jews, Arabs and indeed the world are confronted by an awesome choice. Will Israel and the Palestinians be willing to enter into genuine dialogue and, both of them, be prepared to make painful compromises? If no solution is found, Lewis avers, and the conflict drags on, there will be no escape from an unending spiral of mutual hate which will embitter the lives of Arabs and Jews alike. Whatever optimism we may have about Arab–Jewish relations must, however, be tempered by the possibility that the virus of a demonising antisemitism may already have "entered into the bloodstream of Islam to poison it for generations to come as Christendom was poisoned for generations past". If this is so, says Lewis, "Arab and Jewish hopes will be lost in the miasma of bigotry".

FUNDAMENTALIST ISLAM AND ANTISEMITISM

If resolution of the Middle East conflict depended on mainstream Muslims and Jews alone, there might be some hope. Several scholars have noted that Islamic anti-Jewish rhetoric tends to diminish with the success of peace efforts.[9] But extremists, or fundamentalists, on both sides have muddied the waters. "Fundamentalism" is a rather meaningless term that arose, originally, in a Christian context. It referred to the "fundamentals" of the Christian faith, like belief in the divinity of Jesus Christ, heaven and hell and the second coming. It is characterised by acceptance of the authority of the Bible and the literal interpretation of the text. More than this, however, it stresses the inerrancy of the Bible. Since both Jews and Muslims regard their texts as inerrant and immutable, and since both religions have formulated laws to guide the lives of believers that are often literal interpretations of the text, "fundamentalism" is an absurd and meaningless word to describe them. Moreover, many find the word offensive in that it is difficult to demarcate religious revivalism from fundamentalism. Nevertheless the name has passed into common use, so it is necessary to explain what is usually meant by it.

Of the characteristics that delineate "fundamentalists", the following may be the more obvious. They are subgroups who formulate a total lifestyle based on what they deem to be the pristine form of their particular religion. Intolerant of the beliefs of others – both within and outside their own religion – they seek immediate results and are militant in their attempts to achieve them. The term "fundamentalism" will be used here to denote a radical Islam that displays the above characteristics. From this sector the most virulent anti-Zionism and antisemitism emerge. The fundamentalists, or Islamists, constitute a small, but influential, minority of the world's Muslims, and refuse to consider any form of peace with Israel. Today, they are Islam's most vital and prospering branch; according to Emmanuel Sivan (1986), fundamentalism is one of the most important developments to have taken place in the Muslim world. Its members' perception of Jews seesaws between disdainful disregard and obsessive hatred.

For Islamic fundamentalists, the ultimate answer to the pressing problems of the world lies in a return to authentic Islam, which, they believe, is Islam as Muhammad himself practised it. In their quest for authenticity, no room is left for either interfaith or intra-faith dialogue. True reason is always Islamic reasoning. True tolerance is the medieval-type tolerance that held the world in its proper sacred order. Islam is perceived as being in mortal danger from both without and within, the more serious danger coming from modernised, secularising Islamic states, like Egypt, which have become "intoxicated" by poisonous Western ideas, such as democracy, nationalism, and development-at-any-price. Suffering "Westoxication" (as the late Ayatollah Khomeini put it), these post-colonial Muslim states threaten the sacred world order by willingly becoming prisoners of the West. Confrontation with America, the "Great Satan", was a secondary danger that could wait.

At the same moment that European imperialism had weakened Islam, the habitually plotting and rebellious Jews uncorked Zionism, the Jewish "genie in the bottle". Not only had Jews upset the world order by becoming a nation-state, they are now seen as conniving with Islamic leaders to secularise their countries, their ultimate aim being the overthrow of Islam. Jews are identified, therefore, as the underlying cause of Islam's deterioration within. Speedy return by these countries to authentic Islam is the only answer. Failing this, power must be seized forcibly. Peace with Israel is regarded as impossible because Jewish sovereignty symbolises an upset world order. Islamic states, Islamists believe, are being duped by America to enter into peaceful coexistence with Israel in return for economic aid, a carrot dangled in front of them to lure them into relinquishing their heritage. The Peace Process is part of the plot to undermine Islam, and to fight one enemy the Islamists also have to fight the other.

It had been arrogance, under Islam, for non-Muslims to ask for equality. But now non-Muslims have achieved supremacy in an area that, as part of *dar-al-Islam*, is regarded as Muslim territory in perpetuity. This has been followed by a succession of humiliating defeats imposed by the historically cowardly and timid Jews. The Six-Day War of 1967, in which Israel captured a swath of territory – including East Jerusalem – came as a tremendous shock. Jerusalem, the third most holy city in Islam, became the emblem of the fall of Islam itself, and many radicals started to pray in its direction, as had been the case in the earliest days of Islam. Disdainful disregard now turned to obsessive concern with the evils inherent in Jews and Judaism. The new Jewish "arrogance" had to be explained. This could only be done, as we have seen, by recourse to something outside traditional Islam, namely, the existing Christian-inspired stereotype of the Jew. This was amalgamated with Muhammad's old conflict with the Jews, which was now resurrected and expressed with all the bitterness of the seventh century, and projected ominously on to the current conflict. The idea of the Jews as Islam's most ancient enemy was revived, as was the idea that their goal was to destroy Islam. They were now seen to bear an eternal enmity to "true" revealed religion.

The watershed came in 1977 when Egypt's President Anwar Sadat visited Jerusalem as part of a peace initiative with Israel. Soon thereafter came the Iranian Revolution, which fired the Muslim imagination and served as a rallying point for the world's Muslims. The Shah, seen as a pseudo-Muslim tyrant, was toppled, and Khomeini became the model of "true" Islam. At this point the United States and Israel, the two external arch-enemies, were identified as *the* greatest danger, eclipsing the danger of internal foes. The position worsened with Israel's invasion of Lebanon in 1982. Described as the "tenth crusade", it was perceived as more serious even than the Soviet invasion of Afghanistan: whereas Afghanistan was distant, Lebanon was part of the Muslim heartland. This invasion, alongside the continued Israeli occupation of the West Bank and Gaza, resulted in Jews being seen as the enemies of resurgent Islam. The "rotten essence" of Judaism was equated with Zionism.

Vituperations about Jews were drawn from the Qur'an, and old medieval texts about Jews were amplified with new introductions. Jews were identified with the crusaders, and the Blood Libel was resurrected. Racist *Stürmer*-style caricatures were published in the fundamentalist press and the historical misdeeds of Jews against Islam were emphasised. As the main enemy of Islamic revival, Israel and Jews had to be eliminated. The liberation of the Holy Land now became a legal precept binding on all Muslims. Whereas before 1967 restoration of the proper Islamic world order was deemed possible, the fall of Jerusalem seemed now to have reversed this possibility. As Nettler (1986, p. 105) put it, Israel's triumphant presence, Islam's failures and fundamentalism's rise may have engendered a widespread revival of the earliest antipathy to the Jews, overlaid by the modern antisemitic stereotype. The current situation in the Middle East seems to bear out his prediction. Let us now turn to a discussion of secular antisemitism, which has been touched on in this chapter and which, as we have just seen, plays an important part in Islamic antisemitism.

Part IV

THE SECULARISATION OF ANTISEMITISM

8

The secularisation of antisemitism

Though initially the Jews had been symbolized by a theological concept, the symbol itself proved capable of dislocation to a nontheological sphere without loss of potency. Hatred thus became autonomous, its own justification, so to speak, and since it remained wholly phantasmagorical – Jews are not, after all, emanations of Satan – it proved a locus for true dementia.

Joel Carmichael

THE BACKGROUND

Modern antisemitism emerged in the late nineteenth century when the name "antisemitism" came into being to denote indelible *racial* characteristics that were attributed to Jews as part of their essential nature. This coincided with the development of another modern concept, ideology, which, as Lindemann (1997, p. 99) defined it, is a cluster of ideas, symbols and motifs used to mobilise the masses through the spread of propaganda. Ideologies like race and nation were used in active political programmes in which the negative image of the Jew was exploited. None of this, however, emerged out of a vacuum. Modernity found its roots in the European Enlightenment and the French Revolution and the new way of thinking that grew out of them. The modern worldview, and the changes in all aspects of life that accompanied it – scientific, religious, political, social and economic – led to the negative stereotype of the Jew taking on new forms. New layers were built on an ancient foundation.

The Enlightenment had emphasised the power of human reason, replacing the authority of religion with confident reliance on what human beings could achieve if they put their minds to it, released themselves from superstition and obscurantism and formed a brave new world based on shared human values. Changes came quickly and gathered momentum in the nineteenth century with the development of science and technology and, along with them, communications. In less than two centuries, the feudal world has been transformed and left behind for ever by the "global village".

In the meantime, new geographic frontiers were crossed, new peoples discovered, and disciplines like ethnology and anthropology emerged. But so did a sense of European superiority that, in conjunction with industrialisation and colonisation, was to express itself in racial terms. The emphasis on reason had resulted in the Bible being subjected to critical analysis, which regarded it as the product not of divine revelation, but of human agency. This led to a questioning of its moral authority. Along with the emergence of biblical criticism came modern historiography.

One of the major forces for change was the Industrial Revolution. The invention of power-driven machines, accompanied by the principle of maximum efficiency, led to the abandoment of inefficient traditional methods of production. There was an increase of wealth, which was now more accessible to the lower orders of society, and this gave rise to the emergence of social classes. More power was put into the hands of the masses. With factories now replacing the workshop, there was a need for independent financing and migration to the cities. Western Europe was transformed from a rural agricultural society to an urban industrial one. Religious bonds were now replaced with concepts such as race and nation. The nation-state was born and European territory was divided and redivided as military interventions – such as those under Napoleon – swept across the land.

This progress came at a price. A pervasive sense of alienation and loss brought a reaction in the form of Romanticism. Reason was dethroned by emotion, and a deep yearning was expressed for the intimacy of pre-modern life. This was a revolt against the impersonal cosmopolitanism of modern society. Community closeness became central to much thought and artistic expression of the time. The Grimms' fairytales, for example, tried to recapture the purity of the German soul and the essence of the German spirit. Blood bonds and rootedness in national territory were linked with the idea that only those born of a particular race had the capacity to share these. This Romantic nationalism naturally excluded outsiders, the most quintessential of whom were the Jews.

Simultaneous with these developments was the entry of the Jews into the wider European society, a process known as the emancipation of the Jews. Entering the modern world, for the most part with hope and optimism, Jews adapted to the changes wrought by modernity with striking success. They showed an explosion of talent as they became urbanised and entered fields such as science, medicine, literature, music, finance and commerce. Their role in the economy became more obvious and given their close social and religious cohesion, they were also perceived as more threatening, because they were no longer clearly identifiable as Jews. Because Jews were associated with all these modern trends, so was modern antisemitism. Jews had long been the butt of hatred, serving as a convenient explanatory device and safety valve for human anxiety and discontent. The modern period was no exception. But, as the negative image of the Jew was religiously inspired and religion was now losing its force, a new rationale had to be found. This was the concept of Jews as a "race". The term "modern antisemitism" is an oxymoron because the word "modern" usually denotes progress and reason. In the case of antisemitism, the very opposite prevailed.

This was the backdrop against which modern antisemitism developed. New myths about Jews arose, based on the foundations of Christian antisemitism, but fused, deliberately, with classical pagan antisemitism and emerging racial theories. This hybrid image of the Jew, unlike the negative images that preceded it, left no safeguard, since there was no longer any theological imperative to keep Jews alive, and there could be no escape through conversion to Christianity. The new myth was thus more destructive than any that had preceded it. It was, as Nicholls (1995, p. 277) puts it, "uncaused hatred", the only antidote to which is historical truth. Only historical insight into the developing situation of the Jews, and why and how the surrounding peoples responded to them in the way they did, can dissolve the myth and present the Jews to the world as they really are and not as the outside world imagines them. This history is, however, a complex subject to trace.

Where does one begin? Jews lived in many countries and in each different developments were taking place. Though virulent antisemitism was developing in both Germany and France, the outcome for Jews was different in the two countries. Modernity arrived in Russia much later than in Central Europe, and there were also more Jews living in the former area. Different strands of antisemitism developed in different arenas, mingling in such a way that within one-and-a-half centuries of the emancipation two-thirds of Europe's Jews were dead. A people that had approached modernity with so much enthusiasm and hope were cruelly murdered in the Nazi Holocaust.

Any attempt to organise the material is subjective and incomplete, all the more so in an introductory work like this one. The interested reader would do well to read Jacob Katz's 1980 book, *From Prejudice to Destruction: Anti-Semitism, 1700–1933*. Here, Katz gives the period a detailed and nuanced discussion. He shows how the process started by Christianity ended in the Holocaust, but is at pains to point out that a particular set of historic circumstances, and no single ideology, led to the destruction of the Jews. The Holocaust was neither inevitable nor predictable. As our starting point, let us turn to the emancipation of the Jews.

THE EMANCIPATION OF THE JEWS

The emancipation of the Jews was a political process that started with the French Revolution in 1790 and took over a century to accomplish. In its narrowset sense, emancipation brought Jews into the wider body politic by proclaiming them citizens of their lands of residence. Broadly, however, it brought far-reaching changes for Jews, both in the way the outside world perceived and treated them and in the way they saw themselves. One of the most important results, for our purposes, was the emergence of a new type of Jew hatred, which was now, for the first time, called "antisemitism"; the word was coined by antisemites themselves. The designation had a scientific ring to it, said nothing about Jews and was based on pseudo-scientific theories about race and biological inequality.

Until modern times, Jews lived on the fringes of society as self-governing communities. Their leaders were the rabbis, and their lives were regulated by the Torah, as interpreted by rabbinic Judaism. Unlike their position under Roman rule, where they could be granted citizenship, the Jews under Christianity or Islam were a tolerated community of aliens. With the changes wrought by modernity, however, and particularly with the French Revolution's new ideals of liberty, equality and brotherhood, discussion began about integrating the Jews into the wider Christian society, or "emancipating" them. But the emancipation of the Jews, who had always been a distinctive community, was grounded in an expectation of profound change in them, their culture, their socioeconomic behaviour and their fundamental beliefs about their position in the world. In the absence of persecution and enforced segregation, it was assumed, Jews would assimilate into the prevailing cultural norms, forgo any claims to Jewish particularity and redefine themselves.

Behind the emancipation lay the European Enlightenment, with its preference for secular thought and its antagonism to religion. The Enlightenment's main target was the dominant religion, Christianity. But Judaism, as its vehicle, had to be attacked first. While Christian practice may have receded by this time, the negative image of the Jew persisted. If Jews had been a thorn in the flesh of Christian society when they lived on its periphery asks Katz (1994, p. 55), how much greater would be their potential for harm if they were granted the status of full citizens and allowed to live in the midst of that society? This question lay at the root of modern antisemitism.

Just when religion seemed to be losing its hold on people's hearts and minds, and a process had been set in motion that should, logically, have led to the total equality of Jews, a new, more destructive, form of antisemitism began to develop. This coincided with the emergence of the secular state, in which emphasis was being placed on the individual within the community. The negative image of the Jew promoted under Christendom was now connected to new secular myths. Independent of the church, the state could develop a new image that made use of the religious myth, while shedding its connection with Christian belief. It was questioned whether Jews could be loyal citizens if they continued to observe Judaism as a group. Religion was now seen as a private matter, a matter of personal opinion. If Jews wanted to become equal members of society, it was argued, they had to lose their distinctiveness. They could be Jews at home, but had to be Germans, French, or other nationals in public, indistinguishable from their non-Jewish neighbours. They were to be compatriots, but of the "Mosaic persuasion". The classic formulation of this position came from the Frenchman, Count Stanlislas de Clermont-Tonnerre: "Jews as individuals deserve everything; Jews as a nation nothing ... There can only be the individual citizen ... it is inconceivable that there should be in the state a society of non-citizens, a nation within the nation" (Katz 1994, p. 109).

Acceptance of Jews as equal citizens was, therefore, conditional. For Jews to obtain the "ticket of entrance" to gentile society, as the young Heinrich Heine put it, they had to be made "better" in some way. This was the "emancipation contract" which, given the strong emphasis on peoplehood in Judaism, contained a profound contradiction. Jews were trapped. The more indistinguishable they became, the more threatening they seemed. The more they resisted modernity, the more they were seen as obscurantist.

Jews, as we saw in chapter 3, had never regarded themselves as "individuals", but as sharers in a communal way of life, the organic community being more than the sum of its parts. Always constituting a separate people, Jews were given their sense of identity through their own religious laws and their own set of loyalites. To remove this was to upturn the foundations of Jewish identity. In fact, as William Nicholls points out, questioning of the collective aspect of Judaism removed individual Jews from membership of the Jewish commonwealth and, in the process, transformed the tradition itself. New religious movements, like reform and later conservative and reconstructionist Judaism, were formed to fit the Enlightenment spirit and its emphasis on ethics. Whereas, before, ritual and ethics were equal and essential parts of a web of Jewish practices, excessive emphasis was now put on ethics, denigrating ritual as "embarrassing". This led to an over-emphasis, by the more traditional, on ritual practices, leading to them being seen as "different" from their fellow Jews. Judaism was being transformed, unbeknown to the Jews, to conform to Christian religious convention. Secularisation thus affected Judaism internally, making it more prone to assimilation into the wider society, and hence threatening its survival from within. But it also rebounded on the Jews catastrophically in the form of modern antisemitism.

Religion had been put under fire by the Enlightenment, but the emotional attitudes to religion remained. Nowhere was this more obvious than in Christianity's inherited attitude to Jews. Antisemitism thus developed along two contradictory paths: a religiously inspired image, overlaid with new secular rationalisations. "It was the image of the Jew that was inherited from Christianity that determined the secular perception of the Jew," said Jacob Katz (1994, p. 320). "The difference was that on the *cognitive* level this perception had to be supported by reasoning derived from the newly evolved systems of thought. It was this composite character of modern anti-Semitism – an absolute archaic image covered by a layer of justifications – that made it an irrational phenomenon inaccessible to overt, logically oriented argumentation" (emphasis mine).

INTERNAL CHANGES

The process of emancipation was not, at first, called "emancipation"; it was described as "the civic betterment of the Jews". Only in 1829, after the successful achievement of Catholic equality in Britain, did the campaign for equal rights for Jews become known as the "emancipation", a word that implies redemption. However, as Paula Hyman (1987, p. 166) points out, compared with the disenfranchised masses, Jews had not been in an inferior position. They had had rights of corporate self-rule, which, although they might not always have been deemed acceptable according to modern political tenets, were a potent guarantor of cultural self-determination. The rabbis had the right to enforce the religious law on all members of the community, provided they had not renounced Judaism, and these powers were upheld by the gentiles, both Christian and Muslim.

Before the emancipation, Jews and gentiles shared assumptions about the Jewish condition. Both saw the Jews as in exile (*galut*), though the perceived reasons for the exile differed. Jews saw themselves as having been punished for unfaithfulness to the covenant. By living according to God's law, as interpreted by the rabbis, their exile would end with the coming of the messiah, when their suffering would be vindicated and the entire world would come to recognise the one God. For the Christians, the Jews' exile was a punishment for having rejected the messiah and, more seriously, for having murdered him. These assumptions were now shattered. The new stress on individual rights undermined the power of the organised community. Communal affiliation was now a voluntary matter. If religion, as it was now regarded, was in the realm of "opinion", it could not be coerced either by the Jewish authorities or by gentiles. Thus, the Jewish community was transformed from a self-governing corporate body, with powers of coercion, into a voluntary association. Jews now saw themselves more as adherents of a religious faith than as members of a religio-ethnic polity (Hyman 1987, p. 167).

This facilitated the emergence of denominations within Judaism, particularly in America, where the voluntary nature of the Jewish community was most fully realised. Anyone, who could raise the necessary financial and communal resources could establish a synagogue of his own persuasion. The community now became pluralist, both ideologically and institutionally. As Jews integrated more fully into the surrounding societies in which they found themselves, modern interpretations of Judaism began to be coloured by trends in different nations and countries, and the hegemony of rabbinic Judaism was brought to a close. The Jewish concept of community had depended on self-government by an autonomous community and a consensus of belief in the authority of the rabbis.

Under the new conditions, with the loyalty to the country of residence that equal citizenship required, the idea of exile changed. The emancipation had been predicated on the Jews' presumed ability to renounce observances and beliefs that would impede the fulfilment of their role as citizens, a role that most Jews, tired of the limitations of exile, were eager to grasp. With this, they disavowed their wait for the messiah and accommodated Jewish practice accordingly. First in Germany, and later in America, France, England and Hungary, synagogue worship was revised to reflect the values of the bourgeoisie – to whose ranks most Jews aspired.[1]

In accordance with the Enlightenment's emphasis on reason, a new goal was set for Judaism, to spiritually edify modern Jews. This was accompanied by a need for decorum, for sermons in the vernacular and for translation and abbreviation of the liturgy. There was also a desire for modern scholarship and historiography, and so the science of Judaism, *Wissenschaft des Judentums*, developed. Reform Judaism – the first denomination in Judaism to emerge – rejected the rabbinic law (*halakhah*) in order to be more in tune with the modern age. "Orthodox" Judaism, as rabbinic Judaism now became known, values the opinion of the early rabbinic authorities over their successors, an outlook that, in the modern age, seemed to deny progress and fly in the face of reason. Jewish sources now had to be mined selectively for their wisdom, and were no longer seen as the authoritative guide for life. Reform Judaism changed Jewish theology radically, eliminating prayers for the restoration of Zion because it seemed absurd to persist in regarding emancipated Jews as being "in exile". *Galut* came to stand for the current imperfection of the world, which would be rectified by the realisation, in the messianic age, of global peace. Redemption was no longer to be accomplished by a personal messiah. Conservative Judaism took a more moderate line, arguing for the developmental nature of Jewish law and adapted *halakhah* by counterpoising rabbinic authority with public consensus.

A new concept of Jewish particularity emerged, the "mission theory", or the idea of the Jews as a light unto the gentiles. It was argued, as Hyman (1987, p. 168) describes, that dispersion of the Jews was the ground from which this could be achieved, thus legitimating the diaspora and giving a rationale for survival *as Jews*. Whereas, previously, autonomy and self-segregation had been necessary, now, through integration, Jews could fashion a model community in order to propagate God's teachings of ethical monotheism. Thus, says Hyman (1987, p. 169), there is a persistent tension in modern Jewish thought between restating Judaism in a modern idiom and the need to proclaim its superiority. This stimulated the drawing of a universal message out of Judaism, to allow it to be disseminated both to Jews and others. It is the universal dimension, which Judaism shares with other religions and intellectual traditions, that legitimates Judaism for modernising Jews. Every new form of Judaism has, however, had to strike a balance between the universal and particular, otherwise, what reason is there to remain Jewish and to suffer the stigma of minority status and deviation from the cultural norm? All forms of Judaism have, therefore, retained particularity in some form. They have done this by such means as modifying the chosen people doctrine, or asserting that Judaism is the noblest version of monotheism. At the same time, although most Jews have been enthusiastic about emancipation, they reject its most radical presumptions. Their particularity has been retained primarily in terms of ethnic solidarity. In this, even non-believers can assert their Jewishness. Zionism and the Holocaust strengthened the concept of peoplehood in all branches of Judaism. However, the emancipation also challenged the very survival of Judaism – in more than one sense. It led to acculturation, which exacerbated antisemitism, on the one hand, and helped to diminish it, on the other. In the modern Westernising world, it is argued, the absence of antisemitism serves to increase assimilation, thus dissipating the Jewish people.

The new notion of Jewish peoplehood proved to be problematic in another sense. As Seltzer (1980, p. 541) points out, the emancipation of the Jews was a logical consequence of the principle that a nation should have a uniform system of law for all its citizens, one that abolished the statutory rights and disabilities of feudal estates and other social enclaves. Once the political nation included not just the nobility but every citizen, other groups, previously called "nations", could no longer be called by that name without causing confusion (Seltzer 1980, p. 544). If Jews were a religious denomination only, how do we reconcile the nationhood of Israel? This ambiguity undoubtedly serves as a convenient pretext for much of the anti-Zionist sentiment that is so prevalent today.

THE PROCESS OF EMANCIPATION

Jews could only be emancipated by bringing them under the law of the state and eliminating discriminatory legislation. This was a slow and erratic process and differed in different parts of Europe. The map of Europe was very different then, and was to change again and again with the wars that rocked that continent. Napoleon Bonaparte, at one stage, assumed hegemony over almost the whole continent and, after his defeat, the Congress of Vienna reallocated various territories. The social position of Jews varied from area to area, but it was the French Revolution that reordered European society, making the emancipation of the Jews possible.

Ealier, the Jews of Holland and England had been the least burdened by economic restrictions, and had suffered little interference in their lives. This resulted from acknowledgement of the contribution of Jewish merchants who had settled there during the seventeenth century. The Jews' only limitation there was that they were outside the established church. At the other end of the continent, in Poland, Jews had also had freedom. They constituted a substantial sector of the middle class in a largely agrarian society with weak central government. A wide range of economic options were open to them – the export trade, crafts and village inn keeping, for example. They also ran their own affairs with minimal interference from the government. This changed with the partitions of Poland between 1772 and 1795, which brought the Polish Jews under Russian, Austrian or Prussian control.

The Jews were only one sector of the European community to be liberated from discriminatory legislation by the French Revolution. Previously, Europe had been more medieval than modern. There was an unequal distribution of rights and duties, with legal deference to a hierarchy of inherited prerogatives and honours. Most monarchs claimed sovereignty by divine right, and the nobility had certain privileges – like exemption from direct taxation – which they carefully guarded. Each country had an established church whose adherents had privileges that were denied to members of other faiths. Some of the more economically advanced countries allowed trade competition from newcomers, because it increased the country's wealth. In the more backward nations, however, merchant privileges were carefully guarded. The lower one's status, the more legal disabilities one suffered and the more obligations one owed to one's superiors. In Central and Eastern Europe, serfs were virtually chattel, forced to work on the estates of their lords.

Unlike the Jews of Holland or England, the Jews in central Europe were subject to complicated restrictive laws, some inherited from the later Middle Ages, when Jews were socially marginal, and others new. The latter were promulgated by the early modern state when the monarch in question wanted to tighten his control, enhance the prestige of his state, strengthen the army and civil administration and promote wealth creation. Jews who had previously been autonomous were now brought under increasing supervision, mainly so that they could not cause "harm" to Christians, for which reason they had to be identifiable by wearing a special badge or distinctive clothing. They were not allowed to compete freely. Some Jews, who were considered "useful", however, were granted privileges but were subject to extra taxes. Jewish residence was confined to ghettos, specific streets or even particular houses. Jews had to take a special oath in courts, which was worded to emphasise their untrustworthy nature. When travelling through cities or principalities, they had to pay the same body tax (*Leibzoll*) as livestock in transport. They were not allowed to employ Christian servants or to be on the streets during Christian religious processions. Changes in attitude only came about in the 1770s and 1780s.

It was at this time that Wilhelm Dohm wrote an essay, "Concerning the Amelioration of the Civil Status of the Jews" (*Über die bürgerliche Verbesserung der Juden*, Berlin, 1781). In it, he asserted that Jews were only a problem because of the conditions under which they lived. If discriminatory legislation were lifted, Jews could become patriotic and would no longer be a danger to the rest of society. He condescendingly believed that what Jews needed was benevolent government, which would allow them to acquire secular knowledge to better themselves and to open to them occupations other than commerce. This view was motivated by evidence from America, England and Holland that dissident religious groups were able to enrich a country.

As part of this wider effort to reorder society, in 1781 the Holy Roman Emperor, Joseph II (1741–90), embarked on a programme of reform in the Hapsburg territories – Austria, Hungary, Bohemia and Moravia. He wanted to limit the privileges of the nobility, improve the situation of the peasants, reduce the power of the Catholic clergy and broaden the rights of non-Catholics. Accordingly, in 1781, he abolished the Jewish badge and the body tax for travel. In 1782, he issued an "Edict of Toleration" for the Jews of Vienna and Austria, which granted more freedom in trade and industry and eliminated domicile restrictions and ghettos. Other petty restrictions were also lifted, such as Jews being prevented from leaving home before noon on Sundays and Christian holidays, or being barred from places of public amusement. They were encouraged to send their children to public schools, or to set up German-language schools of their own. In 1784 the autonomy of the Jewish community was abolished, and in 1787 Jews were inducted, for the first time, into the Hapsburg army.

Needless to say, these new measures were debated; they were opposed by the privileged, who felt their positions threatened. More thorough-going change came about with the French Revolution. However, though it wiped out traditional monopolies and inherited birth-rights, it left the Jews' status ambiguous – in spite of the Declaration of the Rights of Man and the Citizen. "All men," the Declaration proclaimed, "are born, and remain, free and equal in rights." Furthermore, "no person shall be molested for his opinions, even such as are religious, provided that the manifestation of those opinions does not disturb the public order established by the law" (Seltzer 1980, p. 522). For the Jews, this was going to play itself out in contradictory ways, revealing a deep-seated antagonism to them. In the general upheaval of the 1790s, French armies carried the revolutionary ideology abroad. Jews in Holland were granted full citizenship in 1796. In 1797 ghettos in Italy were abolished and in the Rhineland the Jews were liberated. But in France we see most clearly the dilemma that European society believed it faced.

The Jews in France were composed of two different groups. One group, made up of Sephardim, were like the Jews of England and Holland, living in relative comfort and security as respected international merchants. The other group, made up of the Ashkenazi[2] Jews of Alsace and parts of Lorraine, were more like the Jews of Central Europe. They were petty traders and money lenders, spoke Yiddish and had an autonomous communal structure. Although the Sephardi Jews were granted full citizenship rights, the "foreign" appearance, language and manners of the Ashkenazi Jews presented a problem. They were said to be "exploiting" the peasants, and it was alleged that the Jewish religion prevented them from becoming active citizens.

NAPOLEON BONAPARTE

In 1804 Napoleon Bonaparte became emperor of the French, and created a fairly efficient and centralised regime. A new code of civil law, in 1804, allowed equality for all, permitting ownership of private property, and guaranteeing entry into any trade. With Napoleon's escalating victories, the status of the Jews in Central Europe was to change. The Jews of Westphalia were put on equal footing. Frankfurt declared equal rights in 1811. In Prussia, reforms were introduced for Jewish citizens, but other German states did not change the Jews' status significantly.

But this did not end Jewish vulnerability, which came to a head in Alsace, where tension prevailed between the Jews and the peasants and was brought to the attention of Napoleon. As petty traders, the Jews were owed money by the peasants, who were unable to pay them. Napoleon suspended the debts to the Jews for a year, posing as the champion of the peasantry against "usury". Although he gave some attention to the status of the Jews, he had other ideas in mind. He wanted to reorganise the Catholic and Protestant churches and bring them under the state. And Jewish affairs, too, were to be regulated – another reason being that he wanted to enhance his reputation among East European Jews as "protector" and "regenerator" of the Jewish people (Seltzer 1980, p. 525).

To this end, he convened the infamous Assembly of Jewish Notables from France and Italy in 1806 to define the relationship of Judaism to the state and to establish a new set of Jewish institutions. The Assembly was presented with a set of cunningly devised questions, such as:

• Did Jewish marriage and divorce procedures conflict with French law?
• Were Jews permitted to marry Christians? (Napoleon wanted to encourage intermarriage.)
• Did Jews consider Frenchmen their brothers and France their country?
• What was the Jewish view of usury?

The "Notables", shocked that their loyalty and patriotism were put into question – since Jews had fought and died in recent wars – were forced to make cautious and tactful replies. They answered that Jewish law was unquestionably compatible with French law, and affirmed that Jewish marriage and divorce had no validity unless they were preceded by a civil act. Mixed marriage, they averred, was binding according to civil law, but could not be religiously sanctified. France was, indeed, their fatherland, and the French were their brothers. They condemned usury and other "discreditable occupations" as contrary to Jewish law. Napoleon had put them on the defensive and, in the process, cast suspicions on Jews in French society.

In February 1807, he called together the "Grand Sanhedrin" of rabbis and laymen to confirm the responses of the Notables as "Jewish doctrines". It pledged undying loyalty to the emperor, and declared as no longer binding any aspect of Jewish tradition that conflicted with the political requirements of citizenship. This was followed by two edicts, in March 1808, which were to be in force for ten years. The first set up a series of district consistories (boards of rabbis and laymen) to oversee Jewish affairs under a central consistory in Paris. They were to encourage changes in Jewish occupation and to maintain synagogues, but their chief function was to facilitate Jewish conscription. Jewish conscripts were not allowed to offer substitutes for themselves, a procedure permitted to Christians. The second edict introduced new restrictions and regulations. Among these, debts owed to Jews were postponed, cancelled or reduced, and Jewish trade and residence rights regulated. So prejudicial and humiliating was this new legislation that it became known as the *décret infâme* (infamous decree).

Napoleon's handling of the Jews was blatantly contradictory. He wanted the Jews to amalgamate with the wider society and to normalise themselves by eliminating those features that made them conspicuously different, but they were to be *compelled* to do so. He sought to retain them as a useful scapegoat, by blaming the Jews for exploitation of the peasants, and pretending to be on the peasants' side, while doing nothing to solve the economic problem at the root of their discontent. It was clear that legal acceptance of Jews was not enough. Where the negative image of the Jew persisted, their acceptance as legitimate constituents of Western civilisation would not be easily achieved.

The destruction of time-honoured monopolistic patterns had opened up a whole range of economic options for Jews, at the same time as destroying the means by which they had earned a living previously. The growth of the middle class, the development of new industries and the increased tempo of business activity occurred whether Jews were present or absent. But where they were present, they stepped into certain economic roles that replaced their old forms of livelihood. The competition they offered was to exert an extemely negative influence on the development of antisemitism. The emergence of some Jewish financiers – notably the Rothschilds in Germany – provoked enormous hostility, a hostility that cannot be separated from the negative teaching about the Jews that was laid down by the church.

THE LAST EMBERS OF THEOLOGICAL DENIGRATION

The German scholar Andreas Eisenmenger (1654–1704), represents the last flare-up of traditional Christian antisemitism in his – even then – controversial book *Entdecktes Judenthum* (*Judaism Unmasked*). Eisenmenger had as thorough a knowledge of Jewish sources as any Jewish scholar, but used it to discredit Judaism and, thereby, to "prove" to Jews the superiority of Christianity. Though he used the sources accurately, he was ignorant of the context in which those who lived by these sources understood them, and was deeply prejudiced. He actually believed the medieval calumnies about Jews – that they robbed their Christian neighbours, were guilty of ritual murder and desecrated the host. He pointed, for example, to statements in the Talmud about gentiles in order to demonstrate Jewish law's immoral attitude to them. What he failed to do, however, was to appreciate that the Talmud developed over a period of a thousand years and that, when later generations sanctified it, they did not change its content, but accommodated actual practice to changed circumstances. Laws that demanded separation from pagans, and that may have been necessary in pagan times, were regarded as merely theoretical after the development of Christianity and Islam. The literal reading of them had long been in disuse. Eisenmenger's study of the Talmud – isolated from the belief system that it nourished – resulted in a grave distortion. The conclusions he arrived at were no different from the assumptions with which he had started. Jews were to remain a degraded and inferior people until such time as they accepted the truth of Christianity.

Eisenmenger's vicious teaching on Jews was rooted in the medieval world, where theological terms had determined the Jews' negative character. The new critical, rationalist spirit suggested that everything – all natural and historical phenomena – could be examined and explained in the cold light of reason, and earlier views of the world were judged as imaginary delusions. It was now widely believed that there was a need for social change because, theoretically, all people were seen as equal, including the Jews. They were, therefore, to be emancipated in their lands of residence. As Milton Shain (1998, p. 53) points out, however, the idea that the Jews should be emancipated was based not on genuine respect for Jews as *Jews*, but on the idea that reason was irreconcilable with discrimination against them. The Jews had been viewed negatively for so long that it was difficult to abandon well-held notions. Christian theology had permeated the minds of untold multitudes and infused in them what Carmichael calls "a special psychic entity", a fusion of "symbol-idea-person", that withstood the collapse of theological authority. "Thus," says Carmichael (1992, p. 132), "all those within the Christian world view, even those hostile to Christianity as a religion – perhaps *especially* those – have inherited the mystical obsession with the Jews independently of theology" (emphasis original). Eisenmenger's views would be reinvoked again and again in more secular contexts.

RATIONALIST ANTISEMITISM

There was now a renewed esteem for the values and accomplishments of the ancient Greeks and Romans, to which the Bible was unfavourably compared. It was now denigrated along with the "revealed" religions it inspired. The latter were seen as fostering superstition, intolerance and bloodshed. Though criticism of Christianity lay at the root of the new rational process, Judaism, as its matrix, had to be struck first. Whereas, previously, the Bible had been regarded as sacred, and the questions and contradictions in it a challenge to be resolved, this was no longer the case. The Bible's divine origin had been denied and the introduction of historical criticism gave free rein not only to doubt, but to ridicule. What was missing, however, as Jacob Katz (1980, p. 26) points out, was "criticism of the criticism". While enthusiastic and inventive, the scholars of the time tended to be naïve. Though the Christian doctrinal justification for discrimination against Jews was removed, new weapons were created to cast aspersions on them and their religion.

Not all the rationalists were negatively disposed to Judaism – two of its supporters being Jean Bodin and John Toland – but they all believed that nothing could be revealed beyond that which human reason could conceive. This development was very obvious in a group of predominantly

English philosophers in the seventeenth and eighteenth centuries, known as the deists. Though they believed in a good God, they saw him as impersonal and detatched from creation, and thus dismissed the idea of a God who was open to human supplication – particularly one who would show favouritism to any one group of people by "choosing" them. The biblical Jews were judged as barbarous, superstitious and bigoted. This was based on the deists' reading of the Bible, which they saw as immoral and at odds with God's fundamental goodness.

The deist movement arose in England at the time when Jews were returning there for the first time since their expulsion at the end of the thirteenth century. Its ideas did not have much impact on public opinion about Jews at the time, but would come to fruition later, under circumstances very different from those of mid eighteenth-century England. Negative feelings about Jews had been nourished by the Christian tradition but, in order for these feelings to become serviceable, the deists' ideas had to be removed from their original context, given a new sting and directed at a concrete target. This was done by the most influential of the French *philosophes*, François-Marie Arouet de Voltaire (1694–1778), who called himself a deist, and who, despite his combination of scepticism and moral activity on behalf of all humanity, managed to focus antipathy specifically on the Jews.

VOLTAIRE

Much more militant than the English deists, Voltaire came to prominence as their views were declining in importance. Ironically, though he did more than any other single man to shape the rationalistic trend that moved European society towards improving the status of Jews, he was also the primary transformer of deistic thought into antisemitism. His main motivation was to eliminate prejudice, superstition and anything that contradicted common sense. Believing that it perpetuated false and infantile ideas and restricted free thought, he wanted to overthrow the authority of the Roman Catholic Church, the then foundation of society and state. His watchword being *Ecrasez l'infâme* (Crush the infamous thing), all his work, according to Jacob Katz (1980, p. 38), should be seen as a "polemic with Christianity". As such, it was subjective and his conclusions were arbitrary. In challenging the church and its biblical foundations, he reduced the stature of the Jews, denigrated their culture, ridiculed their character and mocked what he saw to be their hopeless dreams and unwarranted pride (Katz 1980, p. 43). According to Voltaire, Judaism was the worst form of religion, its intolerance and credulity had infected Christianity. Though he ridiculed the gospel, he was even more scathing about the Hebrew Bible, whose laws and customs he judged to be both meaningless and contrary to accepted morality.

The New World, the East and Africa had been opened up by voyages of discovery and human horizons were widening. The disciplines of ethnography and anthropology, as well as historical writing, were being born. Voltaire was one of the first ethnographers and historians, and began to speculate in uninhibited fashion about the origin of the many cultural manifestations in the world. All, he believed, were natural phenomena that could be understood according to definable laws. He refused to accept the Bible as the source of all the world's cultural patterns, or Adam and Eve as the parents of all humans; he put forward his own assumptions and principles of analysis, and allowed no room for the supernatural or for divine providence. Accordingly, he saw no special role in history for the Jews, Jewish history being important only in so far as it underlay Christianity. Peoples, he averred, had physical and moral characteristics that explained their cultural patterns, laws and customs. Thus, although he took away the underlying theological rationale for the Jews as a divinely forsaken community, he created a new system of concepts by which he could "prove", using the Bible as his source, that the Jews were despicable and that their negative qualities were permanent and deeply rooted in their spirit and character.

Voltaire put forward four criteria by which, he believed, any civilisation could be judged. These were their ethics, their reason-ableness, their cultural productivity and their political gifts. Jews, he argued, were deficient in all of these, and were, therefore, inferior from every point of view. Their poor ethics were proved by their ancient practices, such as polygamy. Their reasonableness had to be questioned in the light of their adherence to complicated ritual directed to a God whom Voltaire saw as aloof to human action. Jews showed no evidence of cultural or artistic productivity, and were ignorant of scientific laws, an example being their absurd story about the origin of the rainbow. They had neither a gift for politics nor any political experience. This was demonstrated, Voltaire averred, by their history of having twice been exiled from their land, and by the fact that they were traders and money lenders rather than soldiers or statesmen. With neither the theory nor the required practice, they were unsuitable ever to govern their own state.[3]

Having rejected the Hebrew account of creation, Voltaire went back to the classics to rediscover the Greek and Roman accounts. Here, he also found classical antisemitism, which he drew on heavily. It was through Voltaire that ancient pagan antisemitism passed into the mainstream of Enlightenment thought. According to Arthur Hertzberg (1968), Voltaire was the bridge between pagan antisemitism and modern European thought. By bringing classical antisemitism into the post-Christian rationalist thought of the eighteenth and nineteenth centuries, Voltaire enabled it to be grafted on to medieval Christian stereotypes, providing a new, international, secular anti-Jewish rhetoric in the name of European culture.

Voltaire claimed that the Jews had never been in Egypt and, echoing Apion, suggested that if they had, they were surely thrown out because they were leprous. He denied the existence of the patriarchs Abraham, Isaac and Jacob and the prophet Moses, denouncing the laws and actions associated with them as unethical. Using instances such as Abraham turning his wife over to Pharaoh for money, he "demonstrated" the low ethical level of the people who created these characters. He then proceeded to attibute to Jews of his own time the characteristics and situation of the Jews of the Bible, presenting them as tainted by the defects of their forebears. Although fully aware that historic situations differ, he ignored this and drew evidence from Jews in any time to apply to Jews in any other time. He derided what he saw as Jewish prophecies to master the world, equating desperate speculations about the messianic era from the Middle Ages with sentiments of Jews of his own time. He scoffed that the Jews had once possessed only a tiny corner of the world, and now had nothing.

In Voltaire's time, there was, as yet, no discussion of the emancipation of Jews, but, because he was considered the greatest of the rationalistic authors and philosophers of the eighteenth century, his venomous ideas about Jews were sure to influence such discussion when it came. Voltaire was one of a community of philosophers in France, a member of the "enlightened" few, the *philosophers*, that, through spreading their ideas, hoped to teach people to think independently, and so free themselves from superstition and obscurantism – an opportunity the masses would not have. Voltaire admitted that a few Jews had attained enlightenment, but they were the exception. In this way, he left a small opening for Jews, not because he valued them, but because logic demanded it. He believed, however, that they would ultimately assimilate "among the scum of other peoples" and be swallowed up by the despised masses. Prefiguring Karl Marx, he suggested that the Jews were doomed to disappear as soon as they were no longer economically necessary.

RACE AND ANTISEMITISM

The idea that Jews constitute a race, combined with previous religiously inspired slanders, found practical fulfilment in the Holocaust. Race, on its own, did not cause this. It was one – though perhaps the most destructive – of the channels through which prior hatred was transmitted. Race became especially dangerous when it was linked with Romanticism and nationalism, and was further entangled with social Darwinism. Having lost its theological rationale, antisemitism showed a tendency to link up with any system of thought or set of ideas that offered ideological shelter, and the theory of race is just one example of such ideological fusion.

Though sixteenth-century Spain saw the notion of *limpieza de sangre* (purity of blood) as a criterion for assessing the genuineness of the Jews' conversion to Christianity, the idea of "race" as a pseudo-science was a later development, though it occurred well before Jews became a factor in the discussion. Originally a neutral term, meaning "division" or "type", the term "race" possessed none of the moral opprobrium that is associated with the term "racism" today. As religion became less useful as the binding definition of peoples, "race" was used in its stead and by the mid nineteenth century had entered a variety of disciplines. Many leading scientists and other scholars – including liberals – used the term, and it was long taken for granted, even by Jews themselves, that the Jews constituted a separate race.

One of the main Jewish influences on the development of ideas of race – albeit an unwitting one – was Benjamin Disraeli, a baptised Jew who became a famous British statesman. In his novel *Tancred*, as Nicholls (1995, p. 323) points out, one of his characters pronounces, "All is race; there is no other truth." In another novel, *Coningsby*, Disraeli implied the superiority of the Jewish race, thus giving what Vamberto Morais (1976, p. 170) calls a "free gift" to the antisemites. Yet, Disraeli was probably responding to slurs against the Jews of his own time, especially Charles Dickens's ugly stereotype of Fagin in *Oliver Twist* – the novel itself being a product of the Industrial Revolution. At this stage "race" was beginning to take on the idea of unchanging, inherent characteristics, and a link was made between physical characteristics and moral or other attributes. But race did not necessarily imply a destructive attitude to Jews, though nearly everyone believed in racial determinism. It was not the aggressive and hate-filled racism that would become apparent later. Race did not have to be linked with antisemitism or hierarchical grading of people.

The genocidal tendency in German antisemitism, as Jacob Katz points out, did not depend on racial theory alone. Radical modern antisemites, like Paul Lagarde, were able to enunciate vile antisemitic ideas without using the word "race" or any related term. Yet Lagarde, along with Houston Stewart Chamberlain (of whom more later), was regarded by the Nazis as one of their ideological forerunners. A Bible scholar and orientalist, Lagarde called for a Germanic national revival without a Christian component and, more particularly, without a Jewish component, since this would pollute the national spirit. More than half a century before Hitler, his anti-Jewish exhortations amounted to an appeal for the physical removal or destruction of all Jews living in Germany. He and Houston Stewart Chamberlain were abundantly cited in Alfred Rosenberg's *The Myth of the 20th Century*, the semi-official compendium of Nazi ideology. It was only under Hitler, when race was amalgamated with an already existing antisemitic tradition and a unique cluster of historical circumstances, that it became a deadly political weapon.

Let us now trace the development of racial antisemitism. We will see that it evolved in a variety of countries and was constituted by a haphazard placement of one theory upon another, in which race was combined with other ideologies.

THE DEVELOPMENT OF RACIST ANTISEMITISM

European discoverers and colonists, identifying themselves with the Greek notion of physical symmetry and perfection, regarded themselves as "superior" to indigenous peoples, even though this contradicted the universality of the Enlightenment and Christianity's idea of human brotherhood. Once human equality was questioned, other refinements were put into action. The "superior" progress of European whites in the arts and sciences was explained by race, and this idea was later meshed with nineteenth-century nationalism. Each race, it was believed, deserved a nation-state made up uniquely of its members. Race became one important component of national identity, among others like language, history and culture. Romanticism suggested that only a "pure" race was capable of feeling real fidelity to the state. Focusing on intuition and the mystical religious feeling of the inner person, Romanticism bonded well with racism. Patriotism was now believed to be an inner experience that only those with the same inner nature could share. Not all Romantics were racist, but the inclination was there. Jews, like the Gypsies, were a "race" without a homeland, and were thus regarded as foreign everywhere. With the strengthening of European nationalism, Jews were increasingly perceived as alien.

The German philosopher Johan Gottfried von Herder (1774–1803), who inspired a whole generation of nationalist intellectuals, suggested that each nation has a *Volksgeist*, a national spirit, or genius, that is as much a product of nature as is a flower or plant, and that this inspired a culture's particular language, literature and art. Individuals within the nation were joined by spiritual bonds, so it was not possible for outsiders to become part of the nation. Each nation, Herder believed, could fulfil itself under its own sovereign government and, when this happened, there would be peace between the nations. He yearned for a politically unified Germany. Herder did not make a distinction between Aryans and Semites. This was to come later. He also did not rate nations as superior or inferior to one another, and held that there was only one race, the human race. Herder's ideas on the *Volksgeist* had a huge influence on nineteenth-century thought generally and inspired sophisticated philo-sophical systems, such as that of Georg Friedrich Hegel (1770–1831), in which individual national cultures played a central role. Herder's work was borrowed so extensively by others that it became commonplace. His concept of *Volk* was useful for defining who belonged to a culture and who did not (Schleunes 1972, p. 17).

Johann Gottlieb Fichte (1762–1814), who is known as the "prophet of German nationalism", drew on Herder's thought to rally Germans, through their unique culture, to fight a war of liberation against the Napoleonic occupation. Herder also influenced Friedrich von Schlegel (1772–1829), a leading German Romanticist who, in 1808, published a pioneering work on the Sanskrit language and the Aryan civilisation of ancient India. He found similarities between Sanskrit, Greek, Latin and German, and called them "Aryan" languages; the word, in its original context, meant "noble". But this notion was, for him, more than merely linguistic. He saw it as part of a larger cultural unity among the ancient

Aryan tribes, something akin to von Herder's *Volksgeist*. Only Aryan languages were dynamic and organic; other languages were static.

Schlegel's linguistic classification is still accepted today, the Aryan languages now being called "Indo-European", though his flights of Romantic fantasy concerning the superiority of the Aryan languages are not. But he laid the basis for the idea of Semitic inferiority: a pupil of his, Christian Lassen, made the specific connections. The Semites, Lassen held, had neither self-control nor social discipline. They were given to unbridled egoism and possessed no epic poetry or sense of beauty. This image was reinforced by negative evaluations of the Arabs that were forming among Europeans as they were busy conquering Arab territories. The Jews were, at the time, moving out of the ghetto and the religious similarity between Jews and Muslims resulted in the two peoples being lumped together as Semites, with shared racial character-istics, over and above their shared linguistic traits. The Aryans were conceived as the exact opposite of the Semites, but only later was this distinction applied specifically to Jews as opposed to gentiles.[4]

The work of the French scholar Ernest Renan (1823–92), was crucially important to the development of racist antisemitism. His whole life's work impinged on the image of the Jew, past and present. Educated as a theologian, he made scholarly contributions to a variety of fields, but particularly to the history of religion. He was regarded as a legitimate reinterpreter of Christianity and, by this token, as a competent judge on Judaism. His 1863 *Life of Jesus* was so widely read that it was rated second only to the Bible in popularity. Examining the life of Jesus through secular eyes, he gave support to traditional Christian denigration of Jews. Echoing Emmanuel Kant, the German philosopher, as well as German liberal Protestant theologians, he asserted that Christ had founded a genuinely universalistic religion, the "eternal religion of humanity", one whose spirit was "liberated from all priesthood, from all cult, from all observance". A religion accessible to all races and superior to all castes, it was "absolute". Judaism, by contrast, remained "tribal", containing principles of "narrow formalism", "exclusive fanaticism" and being "disdainful of strangers". He called this the "Pharisaic spirit", which later became the "Talmudic spirit" (Katz 1980, p. 133). Renan thus salvaged Christianity for his contemporaries by reinterpreting it to suit modern thought, at the same time as declaring Judaism obsolete.

Renan, who used the word "race" constantly but inconsistently, marks the point at which the alleged vices of the Jews' character began to be attributed to the Jewish racial heritage. In his linguistic studies, he hit on the distinction between the Semitic and Aryan races, and then proceeded to elaborate this distinction into a system. All positive qualities he attributed to Aryans, all negative ones to Semites. "I am the first to recognize," Nicholls (1995, p. 329) reports him as having said, "that the Semitic race, as compared to the Indo-European race, essentially represents an inferior store of human nature." Renan was, nevertheless, not clear whether he meant a cultural predilection or a biological determinism. In his specifically racial statements, he does not refer to Jews in particular, but the same characteristics that he attributed to Semites had been attributed to Jews by Voltaire and the deists a century earlier. The negative traits that the deists saw as collectively distinguishing the Jewish mentality – such as being morally insensitive, acquisitive, xenophobic, superstitious, irrational and lacking in social graces and cultural productivity – Renan transformed into racially conditioned characteristics common to all Semites, aware that the only relevant example was the Jews (Katz 1983, p. 42). When he formulated his theories, there was no programme for violence or for imposing disabilities on Jews. Lindemann (1997, p. 87) argues that Renan was repelled by the antisemitism that emerged in the last quarter of the nineteenth century and retreated from some of his earlier statements in the interests of civil equality.

Count Joseph-Arthur de Gobineau (1816–82), a contemporary of Renan, has often been called the "father of modern racism", but he, too, did not use the word "race" in a consistent way. He formulated ideas about Jews which were later used in a way that he did not intend. In his four-volume *Essay on the Inequality of Races*, published from 1853 to 1855, he pronounced racial mixing to be inevitable and to herald the end of European civilisation and its genius for freedom and creativity. Strictly speaking, de Gobineau, who had enormous influence on the development of racist thought, does not belong to the history of antisemitism. He was not anti-Jewish, and rated the contribution of the Jews to history and culture very highly. But his views linking racial mixing with the decline of civilisation were influential, as were his notions that the "purest" whites, the Teutons – whom he saw as the highest branch of the Aryans – were superior to both the Semites and the Hamites. The former had been infused with "black blood", and the latter were saturated with it (Morais 1976, p. 172). Even though de Gobineau turned race into a central concept in historical interpretation, his formulas did not yield any specific anti-Jewish animus. He did not see Jews as noble, but they did not receive the worst rating either. So, the notion of race, *per se*, did not automatically imply a derogatory judgement. His mythology was, however, enthusiastically taken over by the German composer Richard Wagner and the Germanised Englishman Houston Stewart Chamberlain, through whom de Gobineau unwittingly gave German racialism its ideological basis.

De Gobineau's work was not well received in France, where the values of the Revolution, like human equality, were still influential. But it was widely appreciated in Germany, where de Gobineau became friends with Richard Wagner. Wagner (1813–83) was one of the most famous antisemites of the nineteenth century and had a wide influence on educated Germans. His pamphlet *Jewry in Music*, which was published anonymously in 1850 and under his name in 1869, was a sweeping indictment of the Jewish spirit and its stultifying influence on Germany. Jews, he suggested, only wanted to steal art, and he questioned whether they were capable of real unity with the German people. Although he admitted that there were great intellectuals among the Jews, he believed that they could not become German. Only a minuscule minority might succeed, most being incapable of throwing off their commercial Jewish nature. Jews had gained a damaging hold on German arts, the most destructive of them all being the critics.

Another crucial link in the chain of racial antisemitism is Wilhelm Marr, the German journalist discussed in chapter 2, who wrote his bestselling antisemitic pamphlet, *The Victory of Jewry over Germandom*, in the wake of the 1873 crash of the Berlin stock exchange. Though not as severe as the 1929 financial crash that led to the Nazi seizure of power, this event nevertheless caused bankruptcy and suffering. Jews, now widely involved in German public life, were blamed. Marr's main contribution was to tie race to the "Jewish question", though he did not elaborate clearly on what distinguished the Jewish race from other races. That gap was filled by Eugen Duerhing, who, in 1881, claimed that blood was the distinguishing mark of race. He also advocated a type of "national socialism" that defined itself against Jewish "liberalism" and "capitalism". Germans could defend their racial honour by removing Jews from their positions in government, business or finance, and German blood could be protected by annulling racially mixed marriages. Duerhing's ideas about blood, according to Schleunes (1972, p. 27), later supplied the psuedo-scientific base for Nazi antisemitic propaganda.

Marr's short pamphlet purported to be from a rational and secular point of view, constituting a complete break with any religious or pseudo religious motivation. The Jewish "race", with its cunning and control of the press and finance, was gaining mastery everywhere. Marr blamed Jews for the loss of his job as a journalist and pessimistically saw the Jewish victory as almost complete. He blamed the Germans for being so ethically weak as to allow this, and warned that, unless the Jews were stopped, they would destroy Germany, *Finis Germaniae*. This new form of antisemitism, though abandoning some of the old slanders, was still buttressed by the old religiously inspired image of the Jew. It allayed people's feelings of envy and frustration by projecting a threatening minority whose danger was becoming ever more real as it grew in power and wealth. In this new myth, Jewish influence was magnified to cosmic proportions. The struggle with the Jews was to be a struggle unto death. Their assimilation was the cause of Germany's problems, and they could never integrate with the values of Germandom. Marr's pamphlet, which gave antisemitism its name,[5] was a bestseller: twelve editions appeared over six years.

Following on his success, Marr founded an antisemitic newspaper and in 1879 founded the Antisemitic League, the first organisation of its kind in the world. Before Marr's pamphlet, in 1871, the fanatical Roman Catholic priest Augustus Rohling had published a book called *The Talmud Jew* which was little more than a repetition of the old accusations and legends collected by Eisenmenger. On the Protestant side, Adolf Stoecker took the lead. A Lutheran court chaplain who claimed to be a socialist, he saw Jews as exploiting the capitalists, and founded the Christian Social Workers' Party. His antisemitism wooed many supporters among the middle classes. He was, in many ways, a forerunner of Hitler, whose Nazi party's full name was the National Socialist Workers' Party.

By the agency of these men, and others, a large body of antisemitic literature emerged, which, though it may have differed in detail, agreed on the following: Jews were a race, they threatened German cultural, biological and national purity, and they were incapable of becoming Germans. Part of the problem, as Schleunes points out, was that Germans had no clear idea of their national self-identity, the most articulate definition of which came from the historian Heinrich von Treitschke, a professor of history at Berlin University from 1874. He believed that the purpose of German history was to imbue the German people with pride and idealism. Bismarck's unification of Germany had supplied only the shell of the nation; only history could fill it with German identity.

As Treitschke was writing his multi-volume *German History of the Nineteenth Century*, a wave of antisemitism erupted, triggered essentially by the economic depression that followed the Franco-Prussian War, for which the Jews were blamed. Treitschke raised the Jewish question to the level of Germany's identity problem. Jews were an alien cosmopolitan element and were, therefore, dangerous to a society that still lacked firm traditions. This lack had enabled the Jews to take control of important aspects of life, including the economy. Treitschke coined the slogan "The Jews are our misfortune" (*Die Juden sind unser Unglück*), which was to echo fatally thoughout the Nazi years. Besides his lectures, which were very popular, he edited an influential periodical and was also a member of the Reichstag. Ironically though, his anger at the Jews resulted from their failure to take full advantage of the opportunities offered by emancipation. Jews, alien though they were, could, he believed, eventually become part of the German community. It was the *unassimilated* Jew that was the problem. For Hitler, it was the assimilated, or disguised, Jew.

Contributions to racist antisemitism came from many sources – professors, journalists, clergymen, statesmen, philosophers – and in Germany the antisemitic movement took to the streets, reaching a climax in 1881. This was also the year in which the first pogroms took place in Russia, and Jews began to emigrate in large numbers to the New World. The final brick in the structure of nineteenth-century German racist antisemitism was the 1899 book by Houston Chamberlain, *The Foundations of the Nineteenth Century*. This became the most renowned antisemitic treatise of the age. English by birth and German by choice, Chamberlain believed that there were forces at work that shaped history and that these need to be understood to be effectively countered. His book offered the diagnosis and cure of Germany's ills.

In his theory, race was the most central feature, but it was combined with a new Aryanised theory of Christianity which glorified Christ while totally severing him from his Jewishness. The basic philosophy of his book is that everything good in civilisation derives from the Aryans, particularly from the Teutons, everything negative from Semites. The Jews had made a predominantly negative contribution to civilisation and were a dangerous enemy of the Aryans. The quality of goodness or evil in a race, he averred, resulted from the blending of race with different virtues, the right combination of which resulted in excellence, as was the case in the Germans. The most bastardised combination thereof gave birth to the Jews. Using anthropological and historical data he had at his disposal, he also claimed that intuition – the immediate synoptic experience – was of far greater value than the findings of experts.[6]

Spending the major part of his book on the Jews, Chamberlain "explained" their physical and mental inferiority, quoting the many religiously inspired deprecations of Jews that had preceded his, as well as those emerging among the new biblical critics, like Julius Wellhausen and Renan. Jews, Chamberlain argued, were devoid of religious sensibility and unable to unite with Christ's mystical personality. Inherently destructive, the Jews had, he said, rejected Christ because of an unbridgeable chasm between him and themselves.

Chamberlain's book appeared ten years after the birth of Hitler and was destined to have a wide impact and lasting effect. By the end of the First World War, it had sold more than a hundred thousand copies, few people seeing it for the "ideological bunk" that it was (Katz 1994, p. 309). Its power lay in its weaving of Jewish inferiority into what looked like a total system, embracing all of history, while, at the same time, appealing to German racial pride. By making Christ the central symbol, it glorified Christianity, thus making it easy for Christians to embrace its message. Chamberlain's book filled the gap between 1900 and 1914, when antisemitism was at its lowest ebb. He had been inspired by his mentor, Richard Wagner, and later married one of Wagner's daughters. When Hitler came to power in 1933, Chamberlain's book assumed an unprecedented political importance. Building on earlier theories of race, like that of de Gobineau, which was not prejudicial to Jews, Chamberlain's work was amalgamated with corruptions of Charles Darwin's argument that evolution takes place through natural selection, or survival of the fittest, and Chamberlain, himself, became an ardent admirer of Hitler. It was through linking itself with the theory of evolution – particularly Darwin's biological illustration thereof – that racism came closest to acquiring "scientific" repute.

The publication of Darwin's ideas in 1859 had had an immediate impact in Germany. At a conference of German scientists in 1863, a young biologist, Ernst Haeckel, of the University of Jena, elaborated Darwin's views beyond biological evolution in order to extract a theory of human and social development. He suggested the elimination of Germany's unfit by mercy killing and was, for the next four decades,

Germany's chief apostle of social Darwinism, popularising Darwin's ideas by applying them to the development of civilisation. Haeckel was not a racist, but his ideas had a powerful bearing on the race question for those who saw it in hierarchical terms. The *Volk* was seen as a race, and, since race was now linked with culture, science had "established" the "fact" that there were inferior and superior races. Social Darwinism welded racism, the *völkish* movement and antisemitism together, supplying them with a "scientific" foundation that they could not have found on their own.

CZARIST RUSSIA AND *THE PROTOCOLS OF THE ELDERS OF ZION*

No other European state in the nineteenth century, according to Wistrich (1991, p. 171), pursued as repressive an anti-Jewish policy as did Russia under the Czars, who had tried to keep Jews out of the territory they ruled. The partitions of Poland at the end of the eighteenth century, however, brought nearly half a million Jews under their rule, and the Jewish population grew steadily so that by 1914 almost half of world Jewry was located in the huge area controlled by the Czar. Most of them were confined by law to the "Pale of Settlement", a territory of about a million square kilometres in western Russia, established by Catherine II in 1772, where they lived in poverty and deprivation. Jews in the Pale were humiliated by many decrees designed to "protect" the surrounding population from their "economic exploitation". Russian antisemitism there was still "medieval" in that it continued to be rationalised in religious terms. Russian Orthodoxy was an important part of Russian-ness, and had barred Jews from full acceptance into Russian society. However, by the end of the nineteenth century, all this was transforming into a set of modern myths that charged the Jews with an international conspiracy to destroy Russia. Anti-alienism was combined with the traditional Christian stereotype of the Jew.

Jews had been driven, by deliberate economic restrictions implemen-ted by the govenment, into insecure middleman occupations that forced them into contact with poorer peasants, furthering distrust and hatred of the Jews. When, in 1881, widespread pogroms occurred, the government did nothing to stop them. The murder and pillage of Jews were so severe that the word "pogrom" entered the English language. There had been sporadic pogroms in Russia in 1820, 1829 and 1871, all in Odessa, but those of 1881 were so much more severe that they led to the large-scale emigration of Jews to the New World. Emigration was also spurred by the famous "May Laws" of 1882, which tightened the already restrictive laws under which Jews lived. No new Jews were allowed into the Pale. They were not allowed to own or manage real estate or farms outside the cities of the Pale, and they were prohibited from doing business on Sunday or other Christian holidays (Morais 1976, p. 184). In the later 1880s the government imposed restictive quotas on the number of Jews entering various professions and into Russian schools and universities. Harrassment of Jews increased even further as the police expelled over twenty thousand Jews from Moscow in 1891–2 (Seltzer, 1980, p. 632). As the Russian revolutionary surge grew, the government deflected its problems on to the Jews and in April 1903 the bloody pogrom of Kishinev in southern Russia took place. Despite the large-scale emigration of Jews, many remained. Some of the most energetic and intelligent of these threw themselves into the various revolutionary movements that aimed to overthrow the backward and repressive Czarist regime.

The most influential revolutionary theory, as it was later to manifest itself in Russia, was proposed by the baptised Jew Karl Marx (1818–83), whose Jewish background did nothing to mitigate his hostility to Jews and Judaism. He saw history as a process of adaptation to the forces of production, a fierce struggle between the old and the emerging economic classes. The modern age, on the verge of a scientific and technological transformation, offered for the first time a prospect of the eradication of economic scarcity. Seeking a new world order, based on the overthrow of capitalism, Marx saw the Jews as embodying the worst attributes of mercenary civilisation. "What is the worldly cult of the Jew?" he asked in his 1843 pamphlet, *On the Jewish Question*. "Huckstering. What is his worldly god? Money." Marx's views exhibited both self-hate and hatred of the Christian society that had inflicted upon Jews their situation. The Enlightenment had made possible the liberation of Jews from their religious and communal traditions, but their roots remained suspect, and their socioeconomic position marginal and vulnerable. Marx was what Isaac Deutscher terms a "non-Jewish Jew". His writings were later used by the Soviet Union to legitimate its atheistic campaigns and to justify its antisemitism, supplying a rationale for antisemites of the radical left. For the extreme right, Marx, himself, became the symbol of Jewish revolutionary subversion, his rootless cosmopolitanism being seen as the enemy of all traditional values.

The involvement of Jews in revolutionary activity offered a convenient pretext to conservative government antisemites, like Konstantin Pobedonostsev, to deflect attention from the government and focus it on the Jews in the form of pogroms, of which the Kishinev pogrom of 1903 was one of the most brutal. Pobedonostsev offered a succinct prognosis of the Jewish problem: "One third will die out, one third will leave the country, and one third will be completely dissolved in the surrounding population." By 1905, the revolutionary movement so threatened the government that antisemitic propaganda was undertaken to rally the masses against the liberals and revolutionaries; for this purpose Czar Nicholas II subsidised the proto-fascist thugs called the Black Hundreds. Amidst the revolutionary activity of 1905 the most dangerous forgery the world has seen, *The Protocols of the Elders of Zion*, was first published under the auspices of the Russian secret police by the Czar's press, even though Nicholas judged them to be a fraud. Russia's propagandists had learned to use the new ideas that had originated in the West and by the time of the First World War they were fully conversant with modern antisemitic themes.

The *Protocols* were not uniquely Russian. They purport to describe no less than twenty-four secret meetings, held by "rabbis", to organise the takeover of the world by international Jewry in conjunction with the Freemasons. This would be achieved by domination of the world banking system and the world press. The *Protocols*, according to Carmichael (1992, p. 138), crystallise the main medieval theories about Jews, such as the idea that Jews have long conspired to wipe out Christians by well poisoning and spreading the plague. To a receptive audience, they present a seductive picture of scheming Jews, with their deep hostility to all humankind and their incredibly close-knit organisation.

The text of the *Protocols* was composed in Paris at the end of the nineteenth century, but was based on an original text that had nothing to do with Jews. A brochure called *The Dialogue in Hell between Montesquieu and Machiavelli*, written by a French critic of Napolean III, Maurice Joly, satirising the emperor's dreams of world conquest, was plagiarised and turned into something entirely different that pointed suspicion to "international Jewry". It was amalgamated with ideas from the novel *Biarritz*, written by a well-known German antisemite, Herman Gödsche, who used the English-sounding pen-name, "Sir John Retcliffe". The latter told of a fantastic meeting in the old cemetery of

Prague of representatives of the Twelve Tribes of Israel, who, under the chairmanship of Satan, planned to take over the world. The adapter of the *Protocols* is unknown, but seems to have worked for the Czsarist secret police. The first translation into Russian of the *Protocols* in 1905 is attributed to Sergei Nilus, who linked it with Theodor Herzl, "the Prince of Exile", who had called the First Zionist Congress in 1897 in Basel.

At first obscure, the *Protocols* were transplanted to the West by the 1917 Russian Revolution. Their message was, and still is, widely believed by avowed antisemites and the more gullible sectors of the world community in times of crisis and change – despite the fact that Philip Graves clearly established it as a forgery in three separate articles in *The Times* in August 1921. The Jews' ostensible "plotting" served as an "explanation" for the carnage and disruption of the First World War, and for the Russian Revolution by those who opposed it. The *Protocols* appeared, Carmichael (1992, p. 140) notes, "as Jews were fanning out through society as individuals, rapidly achieving distinction in countless activities. It would have been evident to any observer unbiased by ideology that so many individuals could not act in unison, especially since in any given activity they might ordinarily be competing with each other" (emphasis mine). But, the publication offered a summary of what antisemites had been saying for generations and confirmed what they already believed.

The Russian text was published in Europe in numerous translations; thirty-three editions appeared in Germany *before* Hitler came to power. The protocols were one of his most important sources of inspiration. In the United States of America, they were principally distributed by Henry Ford, under the title, *The International Jew* which he serialised in the newspaper, *The Dearborn Independent*. Their most enduring success, however, was to take place after the Second World War, in Soviet Russia, from where they became a bestseller in the Arab world, despite their obviously fraudulent origins and dangerous implications. What makes them particularly effective, according to Hadassa Ben-Itto (1993, p. 44), is that the original characters of Gödsche's myth – bearded and clad in flowing gowns with Satan hovering over them in an ancient cemetery – are now identified with well-known, highly intelligent Jewish leaders, wearing well-tailored suits, who are actually meeting in well-publicised international congresses. Applying the text of the *Protocols* to these real events there are many who infer that behind the scenes, these very same

Jews are meeting in secret sessions to plot, in frightening detail, their takeover of the world in the hope of realising their age-old dream of world supremacy.

What distinguishes the *Protocols* from all other antisemitic documents, according to Ben-Itto, is its violence and extremism, its cruelty of tone, and the sheer enormity of the criminal ideas it expresses. Its efficacy lies in its use of modern terms and simple language, and the fact that it clearly outlines not only ostensible Jewish aims, but the practical means by which Jews intend to attain them. Most importantly, it has an inbuilt explanation for any trouble that may afflict society at any given point in history. Everything can be blamed on the Jews, "from economic depression to crime, from epidemics to plagues, from revolutions to wars, from moral afflictions to violent crimes. There is a relevant chapter for everything" (Ben-Itto 1993, p. 44). Each edition of the *Protocols* comes with "proof" of how this "secret" document came into the hands of true believers, the "proofs" often being as imaginative and outlandish as the plot itself.

The turn of the twentieth century in Russia saw famine and an epidemic of cholera, in addition to the increasing threat of revolution. In this fevered atmosphere, the 1911 ritual murder trial of Mendel Beiliss occurred. Beiliss was accused of murdering a Christian boy to use his blood in the production of unleavened bread for Passover. After a two-year trial, in which both the accused and Judaism were besmirched, Beiliss was acquitted. His story was popularised in Bernard Malamud's *The Fixer*, which was subsequently made into a film. With events such as this, the situation looked so hopeless that some Jews gave up all hope of emancipation and sought a solution in Zionism. In 1882, Leo Pinsker published anonymously *Auto-emancipation: An Appeal to His People*. Diagnosing antisemitism as an incurable "demonopathy", he believed that Jews would continue to be persecuted as long as they did not have their own homeland.

SOVIET ANTISEMITISM

The twentieth century saw massive upheavals in Russian society. Its early years were marked by revolutionary activity, culminating in the 1917 Revolution that brought the Bolshevik Party, and Communist rule, to power. Its closing decades saw the collapse of the Soviet Union. Although antisemitism was always present in the Soviet Union as a convenient rallying point, it was relatively quiescent from 1917 to the early 1930s, when, under the rule of Josef Stalin, harsh antisemitism, combined with unrelenting anti-Zionism, was implemented, soon to take on paranoid proportions.

Ironically, incitement of racial or religious enmity was legally prohibited in the Soviet Union. Vladimir Lenin had outlawed antisemitism for two reasons. First, from an ideological perspective, he believed that antisemitism – like all forms of ethnic prejudice – should disappear in a classless society, and Communism was, in any event, opposed to religion generally. Second, the Bolsheviks' rise to power was followed by civil war in which White Russian reactionaries exploited the fact that some of the top Communist leaders were of Jewish origin, and Lenin wanted to disempower them. In the 1920s, there was stringent legislation, backed up by educational programmes, to suppress antisemitism. But the new economic policy helped to sharpen negative attitudes to Jews, which were exacerbated by the influx of Jews from the Pale to the industrial and administrative centres in search of jobs.

The White Russians carried out pogroms, especially in the Ukraine, manipulating the public through distribution of the *Protocols*. Over a hundred thousand Jews were massacred in what, according to Wistrich (1991, p. 174), was perhaps the worst Jewish disaster before the Holocaust. Demonisation of the Jews was facilitated by the fact that the Bolshevik armies were commanded by the Russified Jew Leon Trotsky. Born Lev Bronstein, he opposed all forms of religion, believing that salvation lay in the establishment of a new world order based on the principle of economic justice for all. Giving up his Jewishness and his Jewish name, he was, however, to remain forever Bronstein in the eyes of antisemites.

The turn of the tide came with Stalin's infamous purges, which, in addition to the murder of millions of people – including Jews – progressively paralysed Jewish cultural and religious life. The blackest years were between 1948 and 1953. There was a brief respite in Stalin's antisemitism during the later phases of the Second World War, after the breaking of the Nazi–Soviet Pact. Needing support in the West for the Soviet cause, Stalin even made overtures to Zionist leaders, which culminated in his vote at the United Nations in favour of the creation of a Jewish state in Palestine. Made solely for reasons of *Realpolitik*, this act did not change his underlying antisemitism, but was fateful for the Jews' subsequent history.

With the infamous "Doctors' Plot" of 1953, in which Stalin accused nine prominent physicians – of whom six were Jews – of wanting to poison the Soviet leadership at the instigation of Western intelligence agencies and the American Joint Distribution Committee, antisemitism reached new heights. All Jews came under suspicion. They were dismissed from institutions and randomly assaulted, including children in schools. Only Stalin's death, a few weeks after the announcement of the plot, averted a pogrom.

Under his successors, though the accusation was withdrawn, antisemitism continued apace, now blended with anti-Zionism. During the 1950s, Nikita Kruschev initiated a military alliance with Egypt's Gamel Abdul Nasser and the Arab world as part of an aggressive Third World anti-imperialist strategy. Anti-Zionism reached new heights with the Six-Day War in 1967, when the Arabs, who had been armed and supported by the Soviet Union, were decisively defeated. In 1971, at a United Nations Security Council debate on the Middle East, the Soviet ambassador called Zionism "fascist" and "racist", linking it with the doctrine of chosenness, and seeing Jews as plotting an international takeover. In the 1970s and 1980s, a great deal of hack literature appeared playing on themes of world conspiracy. Henry Ford's *The International Jew* was updated and the term "international Jewry" was replaced by "world Zionism".

As the Soviet Union began to crumble, these writings became the basis for the Pamyat organisation, a new nationalist right-wing party whose attitudes resembled German *völkish* antisemitism in the Weimar Republic that preceded Hitler. The image of Jews as the malevolent enemy in many guises papered over the cracks in a disintegrating society. With Gorbachev's coming to power in 1985, right-wing antisemitism flourished under the new uncertainties unleashed by his policies of *glasnost* and *perestroika*.[7] As the revolution had been blamed on Jews, so was the failure of Communism, and they were accused of wanting to destroy the Soviet Union. The new pluralism was blamed on the Jews' rootless cosmopolitanism, Jews being the conveyors of destructive Western values.

As is so often the case in times of spiritual, economic and political crisis, antisemitic mythology came to the fore and semi-official propaganda reinforced popular suspicion. Jews were blamed for all the worst catastrophes in Russian history – the collapse of Czarism, the cruelties of the Revolution, the Gulag labour system, Stalinist terror and, finally, the fall of Communism. Jews, as Wistrich (1991, p. 191) puts it, were the scapegoat for the Communist experiment that, after untold misery, ended in disaster.

POST-SOVIET ANTISEMITISM

Since the collapse of Communist rule, and the emergence of a number of independent republics in the former Soviet Union – now known as the Commonwealth of Independent States (CIS) – the largest number of former Soviet Jews find themselves in Russia. The second largest number are in the Ukraine, which shows interesting signs of more intense Jewish activity than in Russia. The third largest number are in Belarus. A large percentage of Jews from the region have emigrated, mainly to Israel, but also elsewhere. For those who remained, the end of Communist suppression of religion has allowed a resurgence of Jewish life. In Moscow there are now several synagogues, at least seven Jewish day schools, the first having been established in 1991, and at least nine Sunday schools for Jewish education. Writing in 1994, Alexander Lesser observed that the Jews of Russia did not yet constitute a community. Rather, some individuals had chosen to participate in Jewish life, and the Jews had not yet emerged as a political group able to defend its interests. This situation, judged by the *American Jewish Year Book 2000*, is improving: a number of Jewish organisational structures have been set up in the last few years, much of the acitivity sponsored from abroad. However, three-quarters of a century of assimilation have taken their toll on the Jewish community, and the more financially successful Jews have chosen, on the whole, to assimilate and become Russified (*rossiski*).

Russia is still in a state of flux – a process of transition from a centrally planned to a market economy – and there is a good deal of poverty. In 1997, about 23 per cent of the Russian population lived below the breadline.[8] The attendant social and political volatility has resulted in uncertainty and resentment. A high percentage of Russians have lost confidence in the existing system and the general instability has resulted in a rise of nationalism and feelings of ethnic exclusiveness and xenophobia, aimed primarily at dark-skinned people, but also at Jews. This tendency had been dormant for decades, lacking any means of expression under Communist rule, which classified it as "fascist". An aversion to Nazi-style fascism was inculcated into the public conscious-ness during the Soviet years, so it is predicted that Nazi-style groups are unlikely to gain wide popular support in the future (Hoffman 1995, p. 41). However, a message from the Simon Wiesenthal Center, entitled "Violent Antisemitism Sweeps across Russia" (February 2002),[9] warned specifically about high-profile neo-Nazi rallies, the possible growth of the movement through the distribution, in the Moscow subway system, of neo-Nazi recruitment leaflets, and the antisemitic violence that has already occurred.

Ephraim Tabori (1995, p. 9) points out that the emergence of new states in the former Soviet Union brought the question of national identity to the fore as they struggled against both Russia and one another for independence, power and security. Tension between the republics spilled over into antagonism between people of different nationalities and ethnic backgrounds, and the main targets were Russia and non-natives. The political vacuum left by the collapse of Communism proved to be fertile ground for the rise of a large number of political parties with a broad range of ideologies, one of which, Victor A. Shnirelman (1998) points out, is neo-paganism. Glorifying the pre-Christian Russian past, this ideology accuses Christianity of brutally destroying and obliterating it. Christianity is regarded as an evil ideology that was created by Jews in order that they may dominate the world and subjugate all other peoples. But there is also a strong Christian influence beneath some of the antisemitic movements. As Nicholls (1995, p. 389) points out, movements like Pamyat in Russia, the Arrow Cross in wartime Hungary, and the Iron Guard in Romania had united nationalism with a conservative Christianity in the mould of the old Catholic and Eastern Orthodox worlds. Untouched by modernity, and kept frozen for decades, these ideas could be grasped by people capitalising on the seething hostility to Communist rule. Nationalism in Eastern Europe, Nicholls suggests, has always gone hand in hand with antisemitism.

The harsh economic realities, the social uncertainty and loss of personal esteem, the deprivation, humiliation, and fear about loss of public safety that have arisen in this period of transition all encourage the search for a scapegoat, and, sadly, Jews have historically fulfilled that role. Consequently, there have been several antisemitic outbursts in the region, sometimes accompanied by violence – one of the worst was the bombing of a Moscow synagogue in May 1998, an attack that evoked little reaction from the Russian government. The attitude to antisemitism in Russia has not changed greatly, and little has been done to stop it. Many openly advocate it. Though Article 74 of the Russian Criminal

Code forbids the incitement of racial or ethnic hatred, its wording is so vague that it is not often implemented. At hearings in the Supreme Soviet of the Russian Federation, for example, Sergei Kovalev, a former prisoner of conscience, and then chairman of the Committee of Human Rights, opposed a ban on the publication or distribution of *Mein Kampf*, the *Protocols* and other antisemitic hate literature. His contention was that bans of this nature could lead to totalitarianism. Commentators in the newspaper *Moskovskie novotsi* did, however, voice their disagreement: "History knows no instance in which lawful prosecution of blatant extremists harmed democracy", they said. "On the contrary, connivance with extremists has always led to dictatorship" (Hoffman 1995, p. 34).

Given the current state of flux and uncertainty, it is not possible to predict the future of either Jews or antisemitism in Russia. Stefani Hoffman (1995, p. 29) avers that, in the present volatility, opposites – like democracy and totalitarianism, privatisation and state control, internationalism and chauvinism – tend to merge, to become blurred and to be magnified. Some commentators predict a greater danger in antisemitism. Others see it as diminishing. Hoffman (1995, p. 29) suggests that "an analogy for Russia today might be an amusement park house of mirrors, in which normal phenomena acquire grotesque shapes". We need, therefore, to distinguish between reality and distortion. Things that look large and threatening in a distorted mirror may ultimately be small and harmless. It is simply too early to tell. But antisemitism, and other forms of ethnic or religious incitement, cannot be ignored. Russia, as it democratises, needs to guarantee the individual freedom of all its citizens, irrespective of their ethnic, racial or national origin and, for this, it might need the aid of the West. Inaction, Hoffman (1995, p. 42) points out, will be detrimental not only to the West, but to the future of Russia itself.

FRANCE AND THE DREYFUS AFFAIR

France, though it was the birthplace of Jewish emancipation and the home of the Revolution and the Declaration of the Rights of Man, was also, from the nineteenth century, what Wistrich (1991, p.126) calls a "laboratory" for antisemitic concepts and slogans. What was produced then still finds echoes in the new right and Europe's largest fascist movement, *Le Front National*. The antisemitic tradition was strongest on the clerical right, but drew support also from the left. Although there were violent antisemitic riots in Alsace in 1848, there was no organised antisemitic movement until 1870, when Gougenot des Mousseaux, using a combination of traditional Christian ideas about Jews and new ideas drawn from contemporary antisemitic literature, denounced the Jews for Judaising France and conspiring with Freemasonry to rule the world.

In 1882, the French daily *Le Figaro* ridiculed the antisemitism that had presented itself in other countries. From the enlightened perspective, the anti-Jewish commotion that was taking place elsewhere looked ridiculous. At the same time, however, there was a tendency to emulate these countries. A number of attempts were made to start antisemitic weeklies, but they all failed. Jacob Katz attributes this to the fact that they used Voltairian antisemitism, which denigrated Christianity. This changed with Edouard Drumont's two-volume *La France juive*. Though it sold poorly for the first two months, it was reviewed in *Le Figaro* and soon became a bestseller, going through a hundred printings within a year.

La France juive was a vitriolic treatise that argued that Jews, who were members of an inferior race, and who follow a despicably primitive religion, are working to become the masters of modern France. Although Drumont's message looks similar to Marr's, he quoted from a variety of sources, including religious ones, thus combining traditional Christian accusations with racial antisemitism. He also identified the threat posed by the Jews with that posed by the Freemasons. Quoting Renan – whom he, in fact, despised – he accused the Jews of being culturally inferior and morally incorrigible. A skilled journalist, he produced a *pot-pourri* of scandal, gossip and antisemitic denunciations that appealed enormously to a mass audience. In 1889 Drumont founded the Antisemitic League and in 1892 he began to edit the antisemitic newspaper *La Libre Parole*, which would keep the antisemitic atmosphere at fever pitch during the 1895 Dreyfus trial. He relied on the legacy of French antisemitism, claiming that the great German antisemites were unknown in France because the press was in the Jews' hands.

From 1870, when France's Third Republic was established, the Roman Catholic clergy and monarchist groups – who were hostile to the liberal modernising trend that had entered French politics since the French Revolution – used antisemitism as a weapon against the Republic, which Jews were seen as supporting. French antisemitism had long been supported by the clerical right. Trying to find a way to recover political influence, the clergy played on the suggestion that Jews lay behind the

French defeat by Prussia in 1871. In 1882, the Catholic *Union Generale* Bank in Paris collapsed, and this was blamed on the Rothschilds, well-known Jewish bankers. In the 1890s, the cry "Death to the Jews" swept France. This formed the backdrop to the infamous Dreyfus trial, in which the clergy joined with the army to falsely accuse Alfred Dreyfus, an Alsatian Jew on the French general staff, of selling military secrets to the Germans. This was a tool for the army, the church and the ultra-nationalists to attempt to overthrow the Republic.

The trial divided French society down the middle for over a decade, exposing a seething antisemitism. Those who supported Dreyfus were known as the Dreyfusards, and those who opposed him were the anti-Dreyfusards. Antisemitism, or its absence, was an indication of a far wider set of attitudes. The writer, Emile Zola was one of the most noteworthy Dreyfusards: in his treatise *J'Accuse* he produced an impassioned defence of Dreyfus. The trial was actively debated in the press, which flourished as a result. After the trial, antisemitism was marginalised, but it remained as a vehicle for all kinds of grievances and in the Nazi years assumed a political, and physically destructive, form.

The vicious antisemitism surrounding the Dreyfus trial was the direct spur to Theodor Herzl, the founder of political Zionism. He despaired of Jews ever being integrated into gentile society as equals. Antisemitism seemed no longer to be a passing affliction, but a chronic condition inherent in the living conditions of the afflicted themselves. A stateless ethnic group living in the midst of a foreign people was the cause of the illness. The only remedy was surgery, the removal of the people to a state that had to be founded specifically for that purpose.

PRELUDE TO GENOCIDE

This chapter has by no means been exhaustive, since antisemitism was rife all over Europe. Vienna, Hitler's birthplace, had been a magnet for Jewish immigration from 1860 and, by 1910, the Jewish community had expanded by something like thirty times (Lindeman 1997, p. 188). They were heavily over-represented in the liberal professions, especially in journalism, law and medicine and seemed to be the "creators" and "managers" of German high culture, which led to accusations that they had "Judaised" the press, art, literature and the theatre. Their rise in a number of fields – the new science of psychoanalysis, music, literature and philosophy – and their high profile as critics offered "credibility" to theories that Jews were conspiring to subvert the Catholic faith. These slanders were delivered to mass audiences who received them eagerly. Artisans protested against the liberal capitalism that threatened to impoverish them. But it was not only the successful Jews that caused discontent. Impoverished migrant peddlars from Eastern Europe had entered Central and Western Europe as a result of the Russian pogroms. These *Ostjuden*, with their different language (Yiddish) and traditional black garb, provoked considerable resentment. As Shain (1998, p. 63) points out, anti-alienism merged with antisemitism from Berlin to Paris. The rich Jews and the poor ones were seen as two sides of the same coin.

The lower middle class felt threatened by the Jews and, although the government valued the Jews' contribution, ordinary Austrians resented their sudden ascent, within one generation, to wealth and high social status. They ascribed it to dishonesty, bribery and malevolent conspiracy. In Austria demagogic antisemitism was taken up in the 1880s by Georg von Schönerer, who became the main spokesman for the incorporation of all ethnic Germans into one Germanic state, even though this meant dismembering the Hapsburg empire. In the early 1890s, antisemitism was used by Karl Lueger, an opportunistic former democrat, to tap into the anti-liberal, anti-Jewish sentiment of the Catholic lower classes in Vienna. So successful was his harping on "Jewish influence" that he was elected mayor and the head of the Christian-Social Party, the first democratic politician to triumph anywhere in Europe on an explicitly antisemitic platform. Remaining in office till his death in 1910, he was the first political role model for the young Hitler, who admired him as "the greatest German *Bürgemeister* of all times" (Wistrich 1991, p. 63). Lueger used antisemitism to attack liberal rule in city politics and, later, to defend bourgeois interests against the rising Social Democrats, most of whose leadership was Jewish. Though holding an academic degree, he did not hesitate to use crude antisemitism, denigrating the universities and medical schools for being "Jew-infested" strongholds of atheism, free thinking and revolution, all of which undermined Christian morality. He wanted the German *Völk* to be the masters of their own country in Christian solidarity, and vehemently opposed the *Verjudung* (Judaisation or, more crassly, "Jewification") of Austrian culture. A pragmatic opportunist, he used Jews when he needed them, knowing the power of antisemitism, but also respecting its limitations once he was in office. He managed to implant in the younger generation the notion that antisemitic discourse was respectable and normal in public life, and did so by linking it with traditional, sentimental, religiously oriented Catholic patriotism. Lueger showed Hitler the possibilities of antisemitism as a method of mobilising the masses against a single, highly visible and vulnerable enemy. It was in Vienna that the young Hitler would discover the "Jewish question" and link it with the struggle for existence of the German nation.

Bismarck's creation of a unified German Empire in 1870 was followed by a decade of economic depression, which exacerbated tensions in Austria and Germany between Jews and non-Jews. At the same time as large numbers of *Ostjuden* were migrating to Berlin, Vienna and other major cities, Germans were emigrating to the United States (*Auswanderung*) in search of economic stability. Germany's capacity to produce exceeded its capacity to consume; it desperately needed foreign markets, or it would be faced with massive unemployment. "Germany," said Leo von Caprivi, the then German chancellor, "must export goods, or people" (Rubenstein and Roth 1987, p. 97). There was a population surplus that required a solution. The young Hitler had witnessed these migrations, and blamed the Jews for taking the place of those who rightfully belonged in the German homeland.

Having served in a Bavarian infantry regiment during the First World War, Hitler was badly gassed in October 1918. By the time he recovered, Germany had surrendered and the Weimar Republic was inaugurated. Shocked at this capitulation, and disdainful of the conditions imposed by the Treaty of Versailles, he believed Germany had been betrayed by Jewish self-interest and "stabbed in the back". In post-war Munich, the city that fostered the growth of National Socialism more than any other, his antisemitism intensified. There, he witnessed some bungled Jewish attempts to bring about a socialist revolution, and was introduced to the *Protocols* by White Russian refugees. The White Russians identified the Jews as fomenting the very conspiracy that the *Protocols* were articulating. This, according to Rubenstein and Roth (1987, p. 98), played a significant part in Hitler's linkage of antisemitism with anti-Marxism.

In 1923 Hitler attempted to overthrow the Weimar Republic and seize power. His *Putsch* failed, and he was sentenced to prison, where he wrote *Mein Kampf,* which, along with the *Protocols*, has been one of the most destructively influential books of our time. In chapter 1 we saw how Hitler viewed life in terms of struggle, and the Jews as the supreme pollutant of German racial purity. Poles, Russians, Ukranians and other

Slavic peoples, as well as "defective" Germans – like the mentally retarded or physically handicapped, or "asocials", like homosexuals and criminals – would be his targets. Topping the list, however, was the most unrelenting and dangerous enemy of all, the Jews. Whatever Hitler prized found its opposite in the Jews. His propaganda portrayed Jews in three ways at once: as international anti-German conspirators, criminals and life-threatening pestilence.

As Hitler was gaining influence, the Western countries were beginning to close their doors to the flood of Jewish immigration from Eastern Europe. In Poland – the country with by far the largest Jewish population in the period between the wars – the Jews' political and economic situation was steadily deteriorating; many wanted to emigrate, but entry was closed. At the same time, the Jews were being increasingly identified as unassimilable in Polish society. Jews were overwhelmingly urban, so were disproportionately represented in Polish cities, whereas the Poles were predominantly rural. Tens of millions of Polish peasants were unemployed or under-employed, and the Polish government, rather than trying to expand the economy, enacted measures that transferred what jobs there were from Jewish into Polish hands. These anti-Jewish measures were supported by Poland's Roman Catholic Church, which saw the Jews as agents of secularisation, liberalism and Bolshevism. Antisemitism in Poland attained a virulence, according to Rubenstein and Roth (1987, p. 102), unmatched by any other European country, including Germany. Neither modern nor secular enough to execute a systematic programme of mass extermination, few Poles could have even entertained such ideas. Under Hitler and the Nazis, however, any such dreams could, and did, become a reality.

After becoming naturalised as a German in 1932, Hitler campaigned for political leadership under the banner of "Freedom and Bread", in a Germany ruined by political instability and economic depression. Though he was defeated by Field Marshal von Hindenburg, whose victory brought neither peace nor unity, the latter was persuaded in January 1933 to invoke emergency dictatorial power to prevent the overthrow of democratic order. Hindenburg used his authority to appoint Hitler as chancellor, ironically ensuring the very situation he was trying to prevent. German industrialists, military leaders and right-wing politicians had been behind the appointment, hoping that they would be able to control Hitler, who, in turn, would control the labour unions and stem the Communist tide that seemed to have engulfed

German society. A covert Nazi act of arson that caused the Reichstag to burn down in February 1933 was blamed on the Communists. This resulted in the "Enabling Act" of 24 March 1933, which was ostensibly designed to curtail civil rights "for the potection of the People and the State", but became the foundation of Hitler's "leaderstate" in which any decisions he made now became law. Though the act soon expired, the Nazi regime had ensconced itself. Hitler pulled out of the League of Nations, and could now fulfil his aim of establishing a pure German race on German soil, making additional territory (*Lebensraum*) available through military conquest. The road to Auschwitz was probably a crooked one, as we saw in chapter 1, there being no clear plan, initially, on how to dispense with the Jews. But there is no doubt about Hitler's pervasive antisemitism and his aim to make Germany *judenrein*. The invasion of Russia in 1941 provided the necessary cover for genocide.

Modern antisemitism arose, on the one hand, out of Jewish success but, on the other, out of the Jews' failure to keep the emancipation contract, that is, to disappear as a distinct group. The Jews' success in permeating Western society made them extremely conspicuous, particularly, as Carmichael (1992, p. 136) puts it, after they had been "abstracted" from European society for so many centuries, and then spread with such rapidity throughout a bourgeois world that, itself, was expanding and changing. Classical church theory dictated that Jews should survive in "abject circumstances". Though most Jews were poor, those who had scaled the heights had obviously disproved the church's theory. The fact that their success was achieved against a background of upheaval, made racist antisemitism a satisfying outlet for frustration.

What made the new antisemitism so potent was the ironic fact that it was associated with democracy, or populist forms of social organisation and mobility. In the last quarter of the nineteenth century, populist antisemitism overtook that of the bourgeois elite, and the masses asserted themselves in new ways. The ultimate cause of the tragic end of Jewish emancipation was the fact that it was inherently contradictory – the granting of civil rights to a people in the hope that they would disappear. It would not be long before this began to exact its cost (Katz 1983, p. 43).

WAS THE HOLOCAUST INEVITABLE?

Despite all these negative factors, Jacob Katz (1975) insists, the Holocaust was not inevitable. A particular concatenation of events resulted in it and, with just one ingredient missing, may not have done. It was impossible for those living through it to predict the Holocaust's occurrence. It seemed unbelievable and impossible. Yet, today, it seems predetermined and unavoidable. How do we explain this contradiction? Were there signs that were overlooked? Historians trying to find clues have examined the prehistory of Nazism and Hitler's early years in search of early indications of Nazism. They have put the spotlight on German antisemitism in the context of Romantic nationalism. Some have analysed the German mentality as reflected in representatives of the German *Geist* to seek any innate tendency towards tyranny, totalitarianism or social intolerance. Some have gone beyond Germany's borders and looked at the teaching of the Christian church since the Middle Ages, and further back, to Jewish–gentile relations in antiquity, to find an answer. Though there are links, the contradiction persists.

Even the threats to the Jews in Hitler's speeches gave no certainty to predictions of catastrophe. Retrospectively, they seem to, but his real views at the time were not so clear-cut; his statements often carry, in retrospect, a weight they did not carry in their original setting. In a 1926 address in Hamburg, for example, Hitler spoke for two and a half hours on his political philosophy, giving indications of how he would implement it, but nowhere mentioning Jews. Today, one cannot help thinking of Auschwitz when reading this speech – particularly in the light of his remarks on the Darwinian struggle between the strong and the weak, and the "right" of the former to eliminate the latter. The speech shows all the radical elements of his programme, but listeners probably heard only what they *thought* he was saying, ignoring the rest. Hitler's potential seemed clear, but there was no certainty he would ever be given the chance to fulfil his intentions. Until 1933, all one could know was that Hitler might come to power – not that he would.

The economic crisis had passed its peak, and Hitler became chancellor because of divisions in other parties. Some Jews even recommended that Hitler be given the opportunity to fail, and thus to seal his own doom. Certainly, Nazism opened Germany to a non-democratic government by a self-appointed elite with allegiance to one man whose command was law. Certainly, Hitler had given indications of his irrational visions and passionate hatred of enemies, among whom, very clearly, were the Jews. But the declarations of even the most radical parties had never been taken as actual guidelines to be implemented. Hitler, it was hoped, would relinquish his more radical ambitions and become more restrained as he assumed responsibility for the affairs of state. There is a difference in announcing an intention and acting on it.

This does not mean there is no way of assessing the potential dangers of a situation, says Katz, but Jews cannot be judged for responding the way they did. Moral judgement can be pronounced on individuals only when we have fully imagined their plight. Nothing like the Holocaust had happened before, and all the old, familiar rationalisations – based on historical experience – had been transcended. It was a *novum*, unassimilable in any vocabulary at the disposal of the generation that experienced it. And it remains so to this day, despite determined efforts to uncover all its aspects – historical, philosophical and theological.

If the event is so radically transcendent, asks Katz (1975, p. 45), why do we study the history of antisemitism or Jewish–Christian relations in past centuries? Why rehearse the horrors of history? Is it not unproductive masochism? Christian denigration of Jews is not, in itself, enough to explain the Holocaust. Nor is the record of Jewish–German relations in modern times. But the fact that a later event is not the necessary result of earlier ones does not mean there is no relationship between them. The Holocaust, which was produced by unforeseen and unforeseeable historical processes, absorbed all these previous elements, without which it could not have happened.

Epilogue

Whenever the world goes crazy, the Jews pay the price.

Jacques Tarnero, French Jewish filmmaker,
quoted in *Ha'aretz*, 29 March 2002

*If the hard and fast evidence of the possibility of good on earth is
allowed to slip through our fingers and turn into dust, then future
generations will have only dust to build on.*

Pierre Sauvage, Holocaust survivor

During the Second World War, antisemitism and genocide tragically
came together in the Holocaust, and humanity's potential for evil was
obscenely paraded. Whether the Holocaust is seen as a Jewish problem
or a universal one, there is no denying the enormous role that
antisemitism played in its execution. Looming large in Jewish self-
understanding, the Holocaust's shadow also continues to hang over the
self-awareness of the rest of the world.

I write this epilogue at a moment that seems to presage apocalyptic
doom.[1] The second *Intifada* is spiralling into outright war as Israel's
prime minister, Ariel Sharon, besieges Palestinian-controlled towns in the
West Bank in an operation designed to destroy the Palestinians'
infrastructure of terrorism. Yesterday, 9 April 2002, was *Yom Hashoah*,
Holocaust Memorial Day, and Jews all over the world paid tribute to the
six million Jews who perished under Hitler's tyranny. Later, on the same
day, fourteen Israeli soldiers were blown up on active duty in the West
Bank town of Jenin. This morning, Sharon stated that Israel is fighting a

war for the survival of the Jewish state and, therefore, for the very survival of the Jews as a people – thus evoking the Holocaust.

The Israeli siege is a response to a spate of vicious attacks on innocent Israeli civilians. Palestinian suicide bombers have, over the years since the Peace Process began in 1993, blown themselves up one after another, intentionally taking scores of Jewish civilians with them. Today, near Haifa, a bus bomb killed ten Israelis. The stated reason for the bombings? Resistance to Israel's occupation of land it conquered during the Six-Day War in 1967. The bombers are lauded by their people – and much of the rest of the world – as freedom fighters, sacrificing their lives for the liberation of their territory. The question of what exactly that territory is, however, is where this lionisation takes on deeply troubling dimensions.

If the land to be won is the West Bank and Gaza, many, including Jews, would agree with the Palestinians' sentiment, though certainly not their methods. If, however, it is "Greater Palestine" – all of Israel – then the Israeli military may have little option. One cannot ignore the fact that Palestinian suicide attacks began to be used as a weapon when the Peace Process was at its height and Israel was negotiating with the Palestinian Authority to hand over land in exchange for peace. In other words, extremist Palestinians, for reasons outlined in chapter 7, could not accommodate in their theological worldview an independent Jewish state on what they believe to be Islamic territory. They also could not accept the upset world order implied by militarily powerful Jews. A rush of bus bombings immediately after Yitzchak Rabin's assassination led me to believe that peace will be extremely hard to achieve in the face of the radicals on both sides. Rabin was murdered by a fanatical Jew who regarded the handing over of territory as a traitorous act in opposition to God's will. On the other side, the suicide bombers seemed opposed to the very concept of peace with Israel. Their terrorism effectively served to replace Israel's then Labour government with a more hardline Likud one, an event that was repeated when Yasir Arafat, in September 2000, turned down Ehud Barak's offer of about 90 per cent of the occupied territory and control over parts of Jerusalem. On the cusp of peace, the second *Intifada* began, and Sharon won a landslide victory. No voice in Israel has been silenced more effectively than that of the left, the "doves", who sincerely hoped for a comprehensive peace based on genuine compromise.

This has been followed by increasingly harsh action from both sides, culminating in what quickly became known as the "Passover Massacre".

Twenty-six Israelis were blown up as they began the ritual recitation of the Exodus at the Passover *seder* ceremony. It was in Netanya, the heart of Israel proper, and it was the commemoration of the Exodus, the heart of Judaism. This resulted in a re-entry of the Israeli army into towns previously handed over to the Palestinian Authority, and a devastating humanitarian crisis. The freedom of movement of thousands of innocent Palestinian inhabitants has been halted and they are cut off from ordinary life-maintaining facilities, like food, water or health care. People on both sides continue to die, and the mutual suspicion and hatred seem intractable. The world stands in condemnation of Israeli action, evoking the Holocaust but this time with the Palestinians as its victims. The media is having a field day indicting Israel, with little attempt to convey the complexity of the conflict, and blindly ignoring the Arab rejectionism that so squarely underlies it. This inflames public passion and is seen by Jews the world over as antisemitic.

The Holocaust informs both sides. The re-establishment of the State of Israel constituted a reversal of the Jewish condition, from the total powerlessness of the Holocaust years, to independent political sovereignty. The survival of Israel became intimately linked to the survival of the Jewish people. The Palestinians argue that, since the Holocaust was a European tragedy, they should not have to pay the price. But there is often denial of the Holocaust within their ranks. When it is acknowledged, it is often to portray the Palestinians as its ultimate victims or to indict Jews for insensitivity to Palestinian suffering.

ANTISEMITISM NOW

The mass slaughter of Jews during the Second World War resulted in the expression of antisemitism becoming socially taboo. Over time, however, antisemitism was transmuted into anti-Zionism. But the Holocaust produced some genuine and far-reaching efforts on the part of Christian scholars and theologians to confront Christianity's tradition of antisemitism. As we saw in chapters 5 and 6, significant strides have been made to make amends for past injustices. The most important of these were the 1965 document, *Nostra Aetate*, that arose out of the Second Vatican Council, absolving the Jews of the crime of deicide, and the 1998 document *We Remember: A Reflection on the Shoah*. Though debate continues on the exact role of Pope Pius XII – the pope during the Second World War – in opposing the genocide of the Jews or acquiescing to it through silence, the Catholic Church's attitude to Judaism and the Jews has undergone, as Wistrich (1999, p. 22) put it, a "sea change".

This new attitude was cemented by the visit, in 2000, of Pope John Paul II to Jerusalem, a visit that is bound to have long-standing positive effects. As James Carroll (2001) so graphically put it, Pope Pius XII marked the lowest point in modern Catholic history, because he elevated Catholic self-interest over Catholic conscience. But, with the visit of the current Pope to Jerusalem's Western Wall, "the church was honoring the Temple it had denigrated. It was affirming the presence of the Jewish people at home in Jerusalem. The pope reversed an ancient current of Jew hatred with that act, and the church's relation to Israel, present as well as past, would never be the same."[2] On that very spot, says Carroll, the living Jesus can still be found, if we excavate the rubble that has buried him. The Catholic Church has begun to do this, thus repenting in Jesus' name.

During the Second World War, there were valiant Protestant Christians in the Confessing Church, which asserted that Christianity was incompatible with racism and opposed the Nazis; among its leaders Dietrich Bonhoeffer and Martin Niemöller. But they were unable to unshackle themselves from the idea that Jews should convert to Christianity. Some Protestant leaders, notably Franklin Littell, have done amazing work in persuading the Protestant church to face Christianity's complicity in the Holocaust and its resultant loss of credibility. Speaking through its representative body, the World Council of Churches, the Protestant church has made some valuable statements against antisemitism.[3] But, as Nicholls (1995, p. 372) points out, this body has tended to reflect current fashions in theology and, in recent years, has favoured liberation theology. A fusion of Marxist ideas with Christian theology, liberation theology stresses the traditional gospel picture of Jesus as the adversary of the Jews. Claiming that God is always on the side of the poor, a tenet that should inspire all Christians, it reinforces the picture of Jesus as a radical revolutionary, implacably opposed by the Jewish establishment and martyred by Jewish hostility. It thus fosters antisemitism, and also encourages anti-Zionism by placing one-sided emphasis on the plight of the Palestinians, without relating it to the terrible history of antisemitism.

Though antisemitism – as antagonism to Jews – has never disappeared, it seemed quiescent until the current deterioration in Israeli–Palestinian relations. Barry Rubin, suggested in 1995 that "the starting point for any honest discussion of anti-Semitism today is the phenomenon's unimportance". Never, since the time Christianity seized power over the Roman Empire, he said, "has anti-Semitism been less significant than at present".[4] This view can no longer be held. Not only has there been an enormous upsurge in anti-Israel rhetoric, but there has also been a resurgence of antisemitism, accompanied by an increase in violent attacks on Jews and Jewish institutions. Immediately before the Saudi-led Arab summit that offered a peace deal to Israel, an article appeared in a government-sanctioned Saudi newspaper resurrecting the medieval Blood Libel. An "expert", a university lecturer, recounted in gory detail how Jews go about torturing and killing Christian or Muslim children, so as to extract their blood, a necessary ingredient in their Purim pastries.[5]

The current antisemitic mood may be reflected by perusal of one recent issue of *Ha'aretz* (29 March 2002),[6] Israel's most liberal daily newspaper. It contains at least half a dozen articles on antisemitism, all of which were written within the present political context, namely, the rise of the *Intifada* in September 2000 and the terrorist attack on America on 11 September 2001. Two articles deal with the rise in antisemitism in Europe. One, "The New Anti-Semitism", discusses a highly insensitive and suggestive cover of the *New Statesman* which depicted the *Magen David* (Star of David), one of its points penetrating the British flag, over the caption, "A kosher conspiracy?" The editor later apologised for unwittingly creating the impression that the magazine sees Jews as a conspiracy piercing the heart of the nation. Two articles describe the increase of antisemitism, both leftist and Islamist, in Britain, one entitled "Jewish Angst in Albion". They point out how pervasive antisemitism has become, entering polite dinner party conversation where previously it had been anathema. There seems to be a blurring of the line between hatred of Jews and legitimate criticism of Israel. Two articles deal with antisemitism in France, and the breakdown of relations between Jews and Muslims, who had previously been symbiotic communities there. Increased identification of Jews with Judaism and Israel, and greater empathy on the part of French Muslims with the Palestinians, is causing tension, over and above local conditions, like poverty, the French Jews' upward mobility and the generally inhospitable attitude of France to its Muslims. Some of the hostility to Jews has been mitigated, since the atrocities of 11 September, by outrage against Islam, which is seen as militant and as promoting terrorism. In the current climate, though, this often rebounds on the Jews, and resurgent antisemitism in France has taken on alarming proportions. "Haunted by ill winds of the past", describes the fears of Belgian Jews that the *Intifada* has lit the fuse of a long-smouldering antisemitism in their country.

The fact that these all appear in an Israeli newspaper may lead one to respond that they could be a sign of Jewish perception of antisemitism rather than of an actual resurgence of antisemitism. However, popular mainstream magazines, like *Time* and *Newsweek*, as well as scholarly journals like *Commentary*, have also raised the issue. The general consensus is that antisemitism is now quite obvious, from the "genteel" forms practised by the chattering classes, to acts of overt violence against Jews and Jewish institutions, and that these must be taken seriously. Less consensus is evident when it comes to the question of how threatening the current rise in antisemitism ultimately is. *Time* places it in the wider context of unease about immigrants and crime. Under the title "How Bad Is It?" (*Time*, 17 July 2002) an article suggests that another Holocaust is unlikely, precisely because people are not sweeping antisemitism under the rug. They are talking about it and trying to understand it. Josef Joffe, in the same issue, calls the new upsurge "neo-antisemitism". It is, he says, "a disease that resembles athlete's foot. The ailment is smelly and painful, and it keeps coming back. But it is not life-threatening." However, Hillel Halkin, in his article "The Return of Anti-Semitism" (*Commentary*, February 2002), is deeply uneasy and, indeed, frightened. He argues that the ultimate goal of the new antisemitism is the moral undermining of Israel, without which the future of Jews will be in jeopardy. No other form of antisemitism, he believes, is as threatening. "Only the isolation of Israel to the point that it might one day have to stand alone against enemies stronger than it can possibly lead to another Jewish catastrophe."

It is not clear to what extent Israel's handling of the Israeli–Palestinian crisis has brought to the surface a long-standing simmering antisemitism, and to what extent the conflict is causing new antisemitism. The vitriol that poured forth against Israel – and Jews – at the UN Conference on Racism in September 2001 seemed more than merely a response to political oppression. Israel was unfairly singled out for racism and for trampling on human rights, whereas other countries even more guilty of such offences were ignored. Halkin called it "the largest and best-publicized international anti-Semitic rally in history". The conference ended only three days before the ghastly terrorist attack on 11 September by Muslim extremists, and several scholars have made a link between the two events.[7] It did not take long before the Jews were blamed for the

American tragedy, the "proof" being the suggestion that Jewish employees who worked at the World Trade Center presciently did not go to work that day.

The Holocaust has, unfortunately, not brought an end to antisemitism. For most people, it revealed antisemitism's deadly potential, but others have cynically contorted it so as to foster antisemitism in a new pseudo-scientific guise, in the form of Holocaust denial. This and anti-Zionism are the two channels through which people – often educated people – justify what is no less than Jew hatred. These two forms of antisemitism are linked, in that one of the Holocaust deniers' main aims is to delegitimise Israel. We have already looked at the dynamics of anti-Zionism in chapter 7, so I will turn now to a discussion of the nature and aim of Holocaust denial. Thereafter, we will consider the spread of antisemitism on the internet, and look at the place of the Holocaust in Jewish self-understanding and its role in the Middle East conflict. I feel it important, however, to end on a positive note because we are all individuals with choices at our disposal. Nobody, whatever his or her tradition, is doomed to antisemitism. I will therefore end with a suggestion as to how individual choices, and the promotion by all of us of the values – rather than the distortion – of our religious traditions can, in small ways, make a decisive difference.

DENIAL OF THE HOLOCAUST

Deborah Lipstadt, in her 1993 book *Denying the Holocaust: The Growing Assault on Truth and Memory*, has offered a detailed explanation of Holocaust denial, revealing its rationale and aims, as well as its peril. Holocaust deniers, she points out, resort to all the familiar antisemitic stereotypes, but place them in a new pseudo-scientific matrix that helps to obfuscate historical facts and give their views a veneer of respectability. The current intellectual climate, fostered by deconstructionism, a movement that arose in the late 1960s, makes Holocaust denial appear legitimate. It holds that all experience is relative, and thus renders the objective truth of any event, text, or legal concept uncertain. "It created," as Lipstadt (1991, p. 18) points out, "an atmosphere of permissiveness toward questioning the meaning of historical events and made it hard for its proponents to assert that there was anything 'off limits'." A sentiment was generated that made it difficult to disentangle ideas from bigotry.

This kind of thinking allows Holocaust denial to insinuate itself into otherwise respectable media channels by making people feel that they are permitting freedom of speech to those genuinely representing the "other side" of the Holocaust debate. As Lipstadt points out, however, there is no "other side" when it comes to denying an event that has left so much grim historical evidence in its wake. The debate is, itself, illegitimate. There are, as we have seen, many ways to interpret the Holocaust, but every legitimate debate must begin with the incontrovertible fact that it happened. It is certainly necessary continually to revise and revision the past, but we may not fly in the face of irrefutable evidence. As Lipstadt put it, "Slavery happened; so did the black plague and the Holocaust."

Holocaust denial fits our picture of antisemitism in that it shows the same irrationality, the same demonisation of the Jews, and the same idea that Jews have cosmic conspiratorial powers. The whole enterprise rests on a claim that the Jews/Zionists, in an attempt to rule the world, have duped it into believing the Holocaust took place. Israel, it is argued, derived multiple advantages from the world's credulous acceptance of the "Holocaust hoax". Underlying the deniers' claim are the following:

- Israel's creation was a result of guilt for atrocities that were never perpetrated.
- Israel continues to extort money out of Germany for these so-called atrocities in the form of reparations, Germany having become the perpetual "milk-cow for Israel".[8]
- This profitable fraud enables the Jews/Zionists to control the world's finances, by tricking the world into ongoing support for Israel.
- The Holocaust "myth" continues to blacken the Germans and whitewash the Jews, who never were victims themselves, but have become victimisers – both of the Palestinians and of the world, which has gullibly fallen prey to the hoax.

After the war, Lipstadt explains, certain movements in various parts of the world, alarmed by the influx of foreign workers into their countries, turned to fascism as offering the only answer to their problems. But fascism had been so irreparably damaged by the Holocaust that only denial of the Holocaust's occurrence could rehabilitate fascism as a respectable ideology. A necessary corollary was the need to rehabilitate Hitler, whitewash the Germans and impugn the Allies. Germany became the victim of war rather than the aggressor, and the cruelty of the Allies is exaggerated accordingly. The Nazis are vindicated by the claim that the

Jews really were the enemy of the Third Reich and deserved their fate. The Jews' constant harping about the Holocaust is intimidating the world into racial tolerance and all the ills that race mixing brings. Their "false" claims of victimhood have, furthermore, resulted in the displacement of the Palestinians from their legitimate land. Victims of genocide, suggests Lipstadt, are granted a level of moral authority. Once they are seen as victimisers, however, they are stripped of it and it is conferred upon their victims. The "hoax" out of which these problems sprang, the deniers aver, needs to be "exposed" in the interests of "truth". They offer the same circular argument as do most antisemites: one cannot, they claim, criticise Jews or Israel without being labelled an "antisemite".

Holocaust deniers like to refer to themselves as "revisionist historians". Their bastion organisation, in California, calls itself the Institute of Historical Review. Lipstadt insists that Holocaust deniers must be called just that – "deniers" – because they deserve no unwarranted titles or historical legitimacy. They distort history and use the name "revisionism" illegitimately. They are selective, giving undue weight to factors that affirm their views, and ignoring those that would point in a different direction. Revision of history, Lipstadt emphasises, is a necessary pursuit, and historical reinterpretation goes on all the time in respectable scholarly circles, but academic research allows the facts to determine the conclusion. Holocaust denial decides on the conclusion in advance, and then uses only those facts that will support it. One example is the deniers' taking seriously only selected details where genuine historians revise some of the facts, such as the number of Jews murdered by the Nazis. Twisting the broader picture, deniers assert that if even the mainline historians are questioning the numbers, they must obviously be an exaggeration. From this, it is not far to suggest that there were no victims at all.

ANTISEMITISM ON THE INTERNET

One of the more worrying indications of a resurgence of antisemitism lies in the increasing amount of it on the internet. The internet, as Karen Mock in the *Human Rights Forum* (Summer/Fall 1997) explains, is the fastest growing communication medium in the world today. It seems to be especially dangerous because, unlike other forms of communication – like telephone conversations – it reaches a potentially worldwide audience, and not just a single listener. Oblivious to international borders, it allows all sorts of objectionable material, such as pornography and hate speech, as well as antisemitism and Holocaust denial, to be spewed to a global audience at the click of a mouse. It is unquestionable, therefore – as Antony Lerner put it in the *Jewish Chronicle* (1 August 1997) – that the "vast, uncontrollable nature of the Internet conjures up images of dark, pernicious impossible-to-counter forces", and suggests to some that internet antisemitism presents a new and unique danger.

To counter this threat, international conferences have been held and some governments – Germany being the first, in June 1997 – have tried to patrol the information highway, denying that this is an infringement of the right to free speech. As the German Minister of Education and Technology who sponsored the law put it, "The internet is a means to transport and distribute knowledge ... just as the highways, there need to be guidelines for both kinds of traffic." But such attempts are not adequately effective because the internet is a medium that defies borders and encourages anonymity.

However, it is possible to see this new development in less pessimistic terms. Lerner suggests that, though extremists have a substantial presence on the net, and their websites are becoming increasingly sophisticated, the danger is vastly exaggerated. "Racists produce", he says, "but who consumes?" There are so many websites going up every week, and so many millions of people accessing popular topics – like pop stars, sport and sex – that racist material must occupy only a tiny corner of what is available on the web. Many who hit a site, he argues, may be doing so out of curiosity, quickly abandoning it for something more interesting. We have no idea whether these sites evoke any real sympathy. The fact that extremists have embraced the internet with such zeal, Lerner says, may even be, "perversely, a good thing", because it makes their activity that much easier to monitor.

Despite this more sanguine view, there is no doubt that there is an underlying danger, which is impossible to assess, and that a multi-pronged approach is necessary to deal with it. As Mock points out, the battle against racism and hate on the internet will be won only through increased efforts to implement Holocaust education, multiculturalism, anti-racism and human rights education, particularly in schools. "It is important to remember", she insists, "that just as hate can be transmitted over the Net, so can good education and positive messages of tolerance."

THE HOLOCAUST IN JEWISH SELF-CONSCIOUSNESS

No century has seen as radical a transformation of the Jewish condition as the twentieth. Within a few years, it witnessed the near destruction of the Jewish people and their return to political sovereignty in Israel. These are the two decisive moments, apart from which modern Jewish history cannot be understood. A people cannot have a third of its number cruelly eliminated without dire effects on its self-understanding; and the way Israel was conceived was intimately associated with the Holocaust. Jewish sovereignty was seen as a direct contrast to the absolute powerlessness that characterised the Jewish condition in Nazi Europe. With state power, the Jews re-entered history. Previously the objects of world history, living as unwanted guests at the mercy of their Christian or Muslim overlords, with no power to make decisions over their own destiny, Jews now became subjects of history, taking control of their fate within the wider world polity. This accorded with the generally accepted Zionist view of Jewish history that only by Jews living in their own state could antisemitism be ended. But, as David Biale, in his 1986 revisionist account *Power and Powerlessness in Jewish History*, points out, much of this has more to do with myth and memory than it does with accurate history.

Viewing the entire Jewish past through the prism of the Holocaust gives us a lachrymose view of it which limits the present by giving the impression that Jews were perpetually weak and passive. Their whole history is perceived as the chronicle of a surrounded people, battling for its life, and now prepared to commit suicide rather than surrender. This perspective obscures, according to Biale, the dynamism of Jewish life and the creative ways in which Jewish leaders have exercised power – albeit in a situation of landlessness – over their community's internal life and its relations with the outside world. The saga of unrelieved Jewish powerlessness makes the Holocaust into the inevitable outcome of Jewish history, a view that, as we have seen, is not justified historically. It creates an unnecessary level of fear, constraining current options for peace. It results in a focus on military power as the only bulwark between Jews and another Holocaust, an important factor in relation to the ongoing state of war in the Middle East.

Massada, a mountain in the Judean desert, became a powerful symbol of resistance after the re-establishment of the State of Israel. A remnant of the Zealots – the rebels in the Great War against Rome from 66 to

70 CE – held out against Roman might atop Massada for three more years. When the Roman legions at last stormed this stronghold in 73 CE, they found the entire community dead. The rebels had made the decision to commit suicide rather than to succumb to foreign dominance. Richard Rubenstein interprets this as an expression of the "lordly consciousness", the will to resist unto death, which has been little in evidence in two thousand years of diaspora existence. One notable exception was the Warsaw ghetto uprising against the Nazis, a modern-day symbol of resistance, which has been telescoped with Massada. But suicide was not the way of rabbinic Judaism. It sought life through adaptation of Judaism to landlessness. The rabbis, according to Rubenstein, were characterised by a "servile consciousness" in that they offered conciliatory responses to the host governments under which their communities lived. Although he is aware that such a response was the only viable course if Jews were to survive two thousand years of exile, he also suggests that this accommodation unwittingly aided the Nazis in their programme of annihilation. If the Holocaust was the inevitable culmination of the Jewish condition of powerlessness, Jewish survival now depends on the Jews' ability to wield power. As Rubenstein put it, "as long as there is a Massada, there can never be another Auschwitz".

This view was widely shared immediately after the establishment of the State of Israel in 1948. Holocaust metaphors were shunned because it was too soon to confront so painful a trauma. The dominant reaction, particularly of young Israelis, was one of revulsion for the weakness of the diaspora, and they dissociated themselves from it and its people, who were perceived as having "gone to the slaughter like lambs". Zionism was seen as a revolt against diaspora passivity. This situation began to change with the Eichmann trial, in 1961, when Israelis began to identify with the pain of the Holocaust's victims, thereby enabling the forging of bonds with the diaspora. It was during this time that Raul Hilberg and Hannah Arendt published their work suggesting that the Jews had been complicit, through their ingrained behaviour patterns, in their own annihilation. Had they written a decade earlier, Arye Carmon (1988, p. 80) suggests, they may not have received such an angry response.

Then came the Six-Day War of 1967, and the feeling of encirclement and fear of annihilation that accompanied it. This cemented the interdependence between Israel and the diaspora. Israel's spectacular victory, Biale points out, resulted in a sense of omnipotence in a vastly enlarged territory, and strong forces to annex territory were soon at work, a "new Zionism" seeking expansion and settlement. For some, notably the *Gush Emunim*, settlement of "Greater Israel" was seen as a preparation for the coming of the messiah. At the same time, there was a reversal in the world's perception of Jews and Israel. No longer were they seen as a waspish David fighting an overwhelming Goliath, but as imperialist expansionists. No longer were they perceived as a pitiful remnant desperately seeking refuge, but as victors with enormous military might.

This, along with ongoing Arab belligerence, resulted in an increased sense of insecurity. The fear that the Arab world was determined to destroy Israel was exacerbated by the 1973 Yom Kippur War and the world community's increasing isolation of Israel. Paradoxically, the more power the state possessed, the more vulnerable it felt. This found expression in increased use of Holocaust metaphors. Menahem Begin's term as prime minister, starting in 1977, propelled the Holocaust into the centre of Jewish consciousness. The first of Israel's leaders to have come from the Holocaust world, he implanted the sense of desperation of war-time Poland into Israel, accentuating the unreliability and hostility of the gentile world. Only Jews could be relied upon to defend the Jewish state, those in the diaspora being obligated by the sentiment that, whereas the Jews of Europe and the New World were enjoying a reprieve from antisemitism, Israel was carrying the full burden of Arab hostility.

Zionism, as Biale pointed out, became not so much a negation of the diaspora, as a continuation of its fate in a new way. Jews everywhere were united by the inevitable hostility of the outside world. With Begin, the experience of the Holocaust survivors became the ethos of the state. Israel was seen as condemned to repeat the experience of the ghetto, as a pariah among nations, the view of the ghetto having been shaped less by the medieval ghetto than by the Warsaw ghetto. Arabs were seen as reincarnated Nazis and the Holocaust increasingly became the justification for Israel's military actions.[9] Israel's utopian dreams had been replaced by an obsession to survive. This "ideology of survival", as Biale explains, arose out of the feeling that Zionism had failed to solve the problem of antisemitism because it is endemic among non-Jews. Whereas Zionism had been formulated to normalise the Jewish people, their actual experience was one of perpetual conflict and therefore abnormality, thus reinforcing their unique role in world history. The power of sovereignty is constantly contrasted with the absolute weakness experienced by the Jews of the Holocaust, and feelings oscillate between extreme power and exaggerated powerlessness.

These exaggerated self-perceptions, Biale suggests, have dangerous implications. There is a symmetry, he points out, in the way two sides to the conflict perceive both themselves and the other. Each side sees itself as impotent in the face of an omnipotent enemy, a perception not rooted in reality. Modern antisemites, particularly the Nazis, Biale points out, saw Jews as an overwhelmingly powerful threat; the *Protocols* being used to support their views. In fact, the Jews' political power at the time of the Holocaust was at its nadir. Biale warns (1986, p.164), that it is "out of such illusory perceptions of oneself and one's enemies that political conflicts become mythologized and their resolution grows increasingly remote".

The signing of the Oslo Peace Accords in 1993 seemed to herald the possibility of an end to the conflict between Israel and her neighbours, and views like Biale's exercised a considerable appeal. But, with the current state of war, it is difficult to assess how influential the emphasis on the need for power has been on the conflict, bearing in mind the Arab world's rejection of Israel. The Arab world has persistently refused to grant Israel formal legitimacy as an independent state in the Middle East. But both sides have negotiated, in my opinion, in bad faith. Israel, though claiming to offer land for peace, continued building settlements in the territories it occupied after the Six-Day War, and the Palestinian Authority could not bring itself to revoke its charter calling for the destruction of Israel. Arab countries that long ago signed peace treaties with Israel still do not include Israel on their maps of the Middle East, and there is considerable antisemitism in the Arab world. Neither side has prepared its population for peace by encouraging genuine acceptance of the other.

The ongoing belligerence from the Arab world has had catastrophic effects for both sides, and it is disingenuous to blame Israel alone for the current impasse. It is easy to understand why the Arab world identifies with the Palestinians as part of the worldwide Islamic community, the *ummah*, but they were, for a long time, of no concern to the Arab countries, and their plight has generally been exploited for other political ends. Arab rejectionism has resulted, Arye Carmon points out, in death becoming the centre of Israeli collective consciousness. The continuing threat the Israelis face led to the telescoping of the Holocaust with sovereign power. Death became the common factor of both, with debilitating results. There is a general pessimism that causes a focus on the past rather than on the future, and that past is observed through the prism of death, rational lessons that could be learned from it are obscured. As a result, there is an inability to envision the future. Citing Robert Kennedy, Carmon claims that this preoccupation with survival persuades Israelis to "look at things as they are and ask 'why?' rather than dream of things as they might be and ask 'why not?'" There is a profound link between the trauma of the Holocaust and the ethos of survival, says Carmon (1988, p. 82), which, although it may well have become a morally impoverished symbol, was the only way to deal with helplessness.

These two opposing modes of death are evident in the way Israel remembers its past. Holocaust Memorial Day (*Yom Hashoah*) and the Memorial Day for Israeli soldiers who have fallen in battle (*Yom Hazikaron*) are commemorated within days of one another, and culminate in the celebration of Israeli independence, *Yom Ha-atzmaut*, a day of joy and freedom. The placement of these events makes Jews everywhere painfully aware of the need for independent statehood, and of the considerable cost at which it has come.

WHAT CAN ANYONE DO?

As this book has attempted to do, we need to confront those aspects of our religions that evoke so intense a level of hatred and misunderstanding that genocide could even have been contemplated, let alone perpetrated. Genuine interfaith dialogue is not polite acquiescence about those factors that unite us, but an honest and soul-searching confrontation with the issues that divide us. One of the strategies so often used by individuals partisan in the Middle East conflict, for example, is to delegitimate the claim of the opposing side. Jews sometimes offer the spurious argument that the Palestinians never constituted a "nation" and that the Jewish settlements on the West Bank and Gaza are therefore justified. Many supporters of the Palestinians claim that Jews, too, do not constitute a "nation", that they never had any real link with the territory of Israel, and have no right to statehood. Political frustration is expressed with no recourse to the vastly opposing religious claims that Jews and Muslims make about the land. We have seen that both Judaism and Islam have intimate links to the land of Israel, and definite views about to whom it should belong. These need to be brought into any process of negotiation. Attempts to deny one another's religious claims are not only a waste of time, but are provocative and counter-productive.

Speaking of his deep distress at the way Durban's 2001 United Nations Conference had degenerated into an antisemitic hate-fest, and the ominous implications of 11 September, which followed so closely in its wake, Michael Melchior, Deputy Foreign Minister of Israel, wrote in the *Jerusalem Post* (22 March 2002),

> If the two dates I have mentioned gave me the greatest cause for despair this past year, there was one date at least that gave me some cause for encouragement and hope. On the 21st of January ... I was privileged to help organize and participate in the first ever Conference of Religious Leaders of the Holy Land, which took place in Alexandria, and which produced the Alexandria Declaration.
>
> This brief document contains little or nothing that is new. Yet it was produced by Muslim, Christian and Jewish leaders engaged in genuine dialogue. Meeting at a time when a Palestinian suicide bomber exploded in the heart of Jerusalem, and Israeli tanks entered the Palestinian town of Tulkarm, these leaders still found the courage to publicly declare their faith that we have to respect the integrity of each other's historical and religious inheritance, to call for an end to incitement and hatred, and to urge the creation of an atmosphere where present and future generations can coexist with mutual respect and trust.
>
> This remarkable encounter strengthened my conviction that things could indeed be different. That hatreds, even thousands of years old, may yet be overcome, and that our region, witness to so much blood, may yet become one of milk and honey.

Because of its terrible implications – both particular and universal – the lessons that the Holocaust may teach – to both Jews and non-Jews – need to be conveyed. First, the Holocaust needs to be remembered, and Jews are encouraged by the world's recognition of their trauma through the institution of national Holocaust memorial days, as is the case in Britain. Such commemorations warn of the dangers of antisemitism and what can happen when a specific group is targeted, at the same time as offering a more universal message of the human potential for barbarity. There are also permanent Holocaust memorials in several countries, generally surrounded by a debate about whether it is the Jewish or the universal dimension that needs emphasis. The Holocaust memorial in Berlin has not yet been built because of the manifold questions such a building will raise and the emotions it is bound to evoke.

But we need also to teach the Holocaust. Because of difficulties such as those outlined in chapter 1, there are wide-ranging problems in doing so. A valuable 1988 volume, *Methodology in the Academic Teaching of the Holocaust*,[10] offers a variety of scholarly perspectives on how to make meaningful for today an event that is fast receding into history. One is to bring it down to the human level and approach it from the perspective of the individual person within his or her life situation. Of specific importance in this regard – and to the subject of this book – is James Moore's essay "Crossing the Experience Barrier" (1988, p. 155–67). Moore discusses the difficulty of conveying the Holocaust to Christian students, some of whom may have little experience of Jews. They have not only to understand Jews' pain, but also morally to confront Christianity's negative teaching about them, while coming to the realisation that the Holocaust is not only their concern but *their* tragedy. Moore facilitates this by encouraging his students to study the diaries of victims, simultaneously keeping their own journals in which they record their changing responses. Two essays in the volume are particularly haunting, and I will use them in closing this book, because they give hope in a situation that seems so hopeless. They speak of the nobility of the human spirit and the importance of human choices in a world that is becoming increasingly mechanised. We are often intimidated by the technology, political and economic structures, and the mindset that characterise the modern world. They have undoubtedly led to progress, but also to great danger. Modernity has spawned both population surplus and a unique tendency to cruel problem-solving techniques, which include mass murder. The Holocaust, as John K. Roth (1988, p. 108) points out, showed that the modern political state may not flinch from putting its apparatus of destruction into action and that, when it does, the ordinary man or woman seems impotent.

Entitling his essay "What Can Anyone Do?", Roth points out that we are *not* powerless, and need not despair about what we, as individuals, can achieve in opposing evil. Personal decisions can change the course of events even in the face of mindless bureaucracy. He cites Gitta Sereny's interviews with the Nazi commandant of Treblinka, Franz Stangl, and his wife, for her 1983 book *Into That Darkness*. Stangl's wife, Roth insists, could have made a decisive difference. Had she spoken – but once – of her real revulsion for her husband's activity as head of Treblinka's extermination process, had she threatened to leave him if he continued, she could have caused a change in his life's development. Sereny asked Theresa Stangl, "What would have happened if at any time you had faced your husband with an absolute choice; if you had said to him: 'Here it is; I know it's terribly dangerous, but either you get out of this terrible thing, or else the children and I will leave you.' Which do you think he would have chosen?" After much painful thought, Mrs Stangl finally answered that he "would in the final analysis have chosen me". That would have forced him to take another path.

Roth argues that the web of human responsibility and of human frailty spreads out beyond those immediately concerned. If Stangl's wife could have made a difference, so could many others. The inevitable conclusion, then, is that when people – especially those who are nearest and dearest – do not help one another to oppose human weakness, despair shifts to self-fulfilment. It is human weakness that enables the powers that be to consign defenceless victims to misery and death; human decisions and actions are fatally interdependent. Roth (1988, p. 118) cites the survivor, and distinguished French filmmaker, Pierre Sauvage:

> If we do not learn how it is possible to act well even under the most trying circumstances, we will increasingly doubt our ability to act well even under less trying ones. If we remember solely the horror of the Holocaust, we will pass on no perspective from which meaningfully to confront, and learn from, that very horror. If we remember solely the horror of the Holocaust, it is we who will bear the responsibility for having created the most dangerous alibi of all: that it was beyond man's capacity to know and care. If Jews do not learn that the whole world did *not* stand idly by while we were slaughtered, we will undermine our ablility to develop the friendships and alliances that we need and deserve. If Christians do not learn that even *then* there were practicing [sic] Christians, they will be deprived of inspiring and essential examples of the nature and requirements of their faith. If the hard and fast evidence of the possibility of good on earth is allowed to slip through our fingers and turn into dust, then future generations will have only dust to build on.

Ruth Zerner, in her essay "Resistance and Submission" (1988), makes a similar point. Education and the home environment can mould people to resist evil. She cites the case of Dietrich Bonhoeffer, who participated in a plot to kill Hitler, and was arrested by the Gestapo and later executed in a concentration camp. Though he seemed unable to disentangle the error of the Jews in not accepting the truth of Christianity from his picture of them, he spoke up vociferously for them as a Christian and humanitarian. He had come from an enlightened family, that opposed the Nazis from the start and drew others into their circle. Strong women in his family had inspired in him and his siblings a concern for the weak and a sensitivity to the oppressed and less fortunate people around them. His mother, a teacher, did not allow her children to attend German public schools and be indoctrinated, but taught them herself at home. The family was a conventional upper middle class one in the centre of German social and academic life – but it genuinely cared about those on the edges of society and thus, very atypically, resisted societal pressures, balancing strategies of submission to society and resistance to the Nazis. Had many more followed them, the course of history could have been different.

People in Bonhoeffer's position had to balance strategies of resistance to the Nazis within structures to which they were forced to submit. There are many greys, and very little that is black or white. Teachers need, therefore, to balance their presentation of Jewish suffering with accounts of the actions of individual bystanders, whether supportive, undermining or inspired by indifference. An accurate picture of the Holocaust requires identification with individual human beings, and we need to rid ourselves of stereotypes like "Jewish sheep" and "cold-blooded Germans". Ultimately the Holocaust cannot be understood without the negative, antisemitism. But it also cannot be understood without the positive. Zerner ends her essay with a life-affirming vision of the mother of Isabella Leitner, a survivor of Auschwitz, who left a loving note to her children in a train as it hurtled toward the death camp:

> Stay alive, my darlings – all six of you. Out there, when it's all over, a world is waiting for you to give it all I gave you. Despite what you see here – and you are all young and impressionable – believe me, there is humanity out there, there is dignity ... I want you to live for the very life that is yours. And wherever I'll be, in some mysterious way, my love will overcome my death and will keep you alive.

Isabella concludes her memoirs with a response to her mother's vision:

I want to tell my mother that I kept her faith, that I lived because she wanted me to, that the strength she imbued me with is not for sale, that the God in man is worth living for, and I will make sure that I hand that down to those who come after me ... and children will someday plant flowers in Auschwitz, where the sun couldn't crack through the smoke of burning flesh. Mother, I will keep you alive.

This book has focused on the inter-religious causes of antisemitism, and the way antisemitism was used to perpetrate genocide. It shows how religious belief can lead to hatred of Jews, a problem that can only be overcome by genuine interfaith dialogue. We need to examine our religious myths to expose the way we tend to view one another. Only then will we be able to release the human being that lies at the centre of each one of us. We need to be able to see beyond those theological categories in Christianity and Islam that demand a demeaned existence for Jews. This demand, at present, has less influence in the Christian world because of its recognition of Christian responsibility for the Holocaust. Hopefully, Islamic scholars will also open Islam up to critical analysis, and so free it from some of its current distortions and allow it to fulfil its vision of a peaceful world and remain the noble faith that its prophet, Muhammad, intended it to be. It is also to be hoped that the fraught relationship between Jews and Muslims, particularly in the Middle East conflict, can be mended. Jews, too, need to get in touch with the God in each human being in order to remain true to their mission of being God's partners in mending the world.

Notes

INTRODUCTION

1. The word means "order", the ritual surrounding a festive meal following a distinct order.
2. Michael Goldberg, in his book *Why Should the Jews Survive?* (1995), uses the term "master story" to stand for the foundation myths that give people their orientation in life.
3. *Haggadah* is associated with the verb "to tell" and means "narrative".
4. Jules Isaac's phrase for Christianity's negative teaching about the Jews, which will be discussed later.
5. Rubenstein (1966b, p. 186).

CHAPTER 1

1. The word "gentile" refers to anyone who is not a Jew. As will be shown in some detail in chapter 3, it originated out of the Jews' understanding of themselves as the chosen people, chosen by God to live by a particular lifestyle that was not expected of the *goyim* (nations or gentiles). Jews believe, however, that gentiles who live a righteous life, will inherit the Kingdom of God.
2. See Young (1988).
3. Cited by Kühl (1998, p. 136). This expression was probably first used by Fritz Lenz in 1931.
4. "Pogrom" is a Russian word meaning to "wreak havoc or devastation". It came to denote an organised massacre, particularly of Jews.
5. "Survival of the fittest" is Herbert Spencer's phrase, not Darwin's. Darwin provided the notion of evolution by "natural selection". To previous theories Darwin added an account of the biological mechanism by which evolution occurs.
6. See, for example, Young (1988).

7. There is barely an account of Holocaust literature that does not mention this aphorism. Irving Howe (1988, p. 179) suggests that no single writer has exerted as strong and pervasive an influence on Holocaust literature as has Theo Adorno. During the 1950s Adorno offered not a complete text or a fully developed argument, but scattered remarks that had immediate and lasting impact.

8. The poem "I Never Saw Another Butterfly" in the book named after it: *I Never Saw Another Butterfly ... Children's Drawings and Poems from Theresienstadt Concentration Camp 1942–1944*, London: Neville Spearman, 1965.

9. One of the most valuable aspects of *Schindler's List* is the interviewing programme that emerged out of it. Spielberg established the Survivors of the Shoah Visual History Foundation in 1994, and accounts from 51,661 survivors, from all over the world, have been recorded on video film, constituting 117,000 hours of testimony in thirty-two languages.

10. First published in French, *Breviaire de la Haine*, in Paris in 1951, and in English in London in 1956.

11. See Friedländer (1988, p. 28).

12. He selects these to prove a point, fully aware that they are not the only historians who made an important contribution. Eberhard Jäckel and Yehuda Bauer, among others, helped lay a firm basis for current historiography of the Holocaust.

13. See, for example, Ruth Wisse, in Brown (ed.) (1994, p. 30).

14. See, for example, Jäckel (1998, p. 24ff).

15. See appendix 1 in Manvell and Fraenkel (1982, p. 231ff).

16. See Thomas (1991, p. 377).

17. See the 1987 Festschrift in Littell's honour: *Faith and Freedom*, R. Libowitz, Oxford: Pergamon.

18. It should be noted that, thirty years later, Hilberg has modified his view. See Hilberg (1995).

19. See Rubenstein and Roth (1987, p. 11).

20. Cited in Novick (2001, p. 197).

21. See Hoffman and Fischer (1988, p. 11).

CHAPTER 2

1. Michael Curtis (1986), borrowing the term from Jacob Talmon, heads his introduction with these words.

2. The word "gentile" is used to translate the Hebrew word *goyim*, which means the "nations" or anyone not a Jew. In its original context, it referred to pagans. When Christianity spread beyond the original group of Jewish messianists, who believed that Jesus was the promised messiah, the word lost its exclusive meaning as "pagan" and now simply means "non-Jew".

3. See Bauman (1989, p. 154).

4. See Fackenheim (1986, p. 24).

5. Note his 1991 book by that name, which arose out of a three-part BBC film with the same title.

6. Parkes in Davies (1979, p. v). My own translation.
7. On this subject see, for example, Maccoby (1992).
8. See Parkes's introduction to Davies (1979).
9. *Midrash* will be explained in more detail in chapter 3.

CHAPTER 3

1. Jews see the leaving of Israel as "going down". To go to (especially to live in) Israel is "going up", *aliyah*. This arose because of the geographical elevation of Israel compared with low-lying Egypt. Compare Genesis 12:10 with Genesis 13:1. The convention was extended to any country outside Israel, regardless of its relative elevation.
2. *Shema* is the imperative form of the verb to "hear" or "listen".
3. The central theme in Sacks' book is that Judaism, as the living embodiment of these ideas, needs to be kept alive, and that Jews are obligated to tell the story of their experience to subsequent generations.
4. The Holocaust theologian Emil Fackenheim categorised it as a root experience, in contrast to epoch-making experiences. Root experiences define Judaism for all time. Epoch-making experiences, among which he includes the Holocaust, merely challenge the root experiences, such as the Exodus and covenant.
5. Seven injunctions that, according to the rabbis, were given to Noah and are binding on both Jews and gentiles. Six prohibitions – of blasphemy, idolatry, sexual immorality, murder, robbery and eating a portion of a living animal – are followed by a positive commandment to set up courts of justice.
6. Chief among them were M. Goodman and S. McKnight. James Carleton Paget (1996) gives a review of the debate, concluding that the majority view – that Judaism was a proselytising faith at the time – is more consistent with the scanty evidence available.
7. He was Joseph ben Joshua ha-Kohen of Avignon.
8. Exodus 23:19 and 34:26 and Deuteronomy 14:21.
9. The *Mishnah*, a six-part book of laws, was the first major text of the oral Torah. It was later elaborated on in the two Talmuds (the word means "study"), one produced in Babylon and the other in Palestine. These reflect centuries of exegesis and discussion, and occupy many volumes.

CHAPTER 4

1. This, as well as the other quotations of pagan authors in this chapter, has been taken from Menahem Stern's comprehensive three-volume collection of writings of *Greek and Latin Authors on Jews and Judaism*, 1976–1984.
2. He, however, spells it with the hyphen, "anti-Semite".
3. Quoted by Feldman (1986, p. 32), from Origen, *Contra Celsum*, 5:50. Emphasis mine.
4. Feldman sees this accusation as emerging in Hellenistic Egypt, which Cohen (1986, p. 44) disputes.

5. The gnostics called the God of the Hebrew Bible the Demiurge, from the Greek *demiourgos*. The word was originally used by Plato in his poetic description of the creator/craftsman in his *Timaeus*. It later passed into Christian usage to denote the creator God of the Bible, but has long become discredited because of the gnostics' adoption of it.

CHAPTER 5

1. Lanzmann (1985, p. 31).
2. Lanzmann (1985, p. 99ff).
3. Ravitch is here using Irving Greenberg's phrase from "New Revelations and New Patterns in the Relationship of Judaism and Christianity", *Journal of Ecumenical Studies*, Spring 1979.
4. Isaac wrote a 1964 book with this name, but had started to articulate his position in earlier works: *The Conflict of the Church and the Synagogue*, first published in 1934, *Jesus and Israel* and *Genèse de l'antisémitisme*.
5. Discussion of these three foci has appeared in previously published essays of mine (Hellig 1999; 2000).
6. Cited by Gager (1983, p. 14).
7. Cited by Gager (1983, p. 17). Gager's translation.
8. See Hertzberg and Hirt-Manheimer (1998, p. 6).
9. Gager's book offers an excellent summary of the scholarship on Christian antisemitism, as do de Lange (1991) and Pawlikowski (1986) quoted above.
10. I have summarised this conversation in my own words. See Gager 1983: 3–5.

CHAPTER 6

1. I gleaned this observation from the novelist A. N. Wilson's 1992 biography of Jesus, *Jesus: a Life*, in a colourful chapter called "The Cooked Fish, or How to Read a Gospel". Though he offers here a sympathetic picture of Jesus as a Jew, he has recently been accused of antisemitism, because he suggests that Israel has no logical right to exist. See David Landau, "Jewish Angst in Albion"' *Ha'Aretz*, 29 March 2002, and Hillel Halkin, "The Return of Anti-Semisitm", *Commentary*, February 2002.
2. "Tetragrammaton" refers to the four Hebrew letters of God's name, *Yod He Vav He*, which appear as YHWH in translation, and later become vocalised as Yahweh, not Jehovah, which is a mistranslation. The name has been connected with the phrase, *ehyeh asher ehyeh*, (translated as "I am that I am"), which is interpreted as denoting God's eternal existence. Jews never utter the name of God and circumlocute it with titles like Adonai, "Lord", when used in a liturgical setting, or simply *Hashem*, "the Name", when used in the context of Torah study.
3. See John 11:49, 18:14.
4. Paul refers to himself as an Israelite. See Rom. 11:1 and 2 Cor. 11:22.

5. She points out the effect of a Christian student reading aloud Jesus' statement, "But you are not to be called rabbi", in an academic setting, in the presence of a rabbi. The student, in a state of profound embarrassment, was forced to stop reading.
6. Seltzer (1980, p. 255).
7. According to Lazar (1991), it was a thinking pattern not far removed from ancient gnostic and dualistic thought.
8. He quotes Luke 19:27. "But for these my enemies, who did not want me to be king over them, bring them here and slay them." Cited by Lazar (1991, p. 48).
9. On a regular boat trip on the canals of Strasbourg, for example, one of the last sights to be pointed out to the tourists is a portal of the cathedral which vividly depicts these two figures, Ecclesia and Synagoga.
10. Cited by Bitton-Jackson (1994, p. 239).
11. The name derives from one of the early ghettos in Venice, which was in the *geto nuovo*, or "new foundry".
12. See Shain (1998, pp. 49–51) for a brief presentation of the debate on these conflicting views.
13. Bein (1990, p. 142f) quotes Luther at length.
14. Cited from Montagu Frank Modder, *The Jew in the Literature of England* (1960).
15. Ravitch (1982, p. 43). Although eventually condemned as heretical, gnostic views survived in Christianity.
16. Cited by Ravitch (1982, p. 44).
17. It is significant that he cites Toynbee, because this historian was accused of antisemitism when he introduced the idea of Judaism being a "fossil".

CHAPTER 7

1. See, for example, Fiamma Niernstein, "How Suicide Bombers Are Made", *Commentary*, September 2001, pp. 53–5, for an account of antisemitism in the Arab world.
2. Emphasis mine. "On Durban", http:www.etni.org.il/tragedy/Durban.htm
3. The more radical Palestinians argue that terror attacks against Israelis are a response to the aggression of Israeli occupation of land conquered during the Six-Day War. Calls for *jihad*, with suicide bombings as a weapon, are thus given justification.
4. *Kitab Al-Tabaqat Al-Kabir*, by Ibn Sa'ad cited by Nettler (1990, p. 65).
5. See, for example, Gerber (1986).
6. This was the way Jews were represented in the Arab media. See Lewis (1988, p. 65).
7. Ibn Hazm had already implied this was a result of inbreeding. But this was an exception. See Lewis (1997, p. 131).
8. They are often referred to as the "Falashas", a derogatory word meaning "wanderers".
9. See, for example, Yadlin (1986).

CHAPTER 8

1. The word "bourgeois", as Rubenstein and Roth (1987, p. 70) point out, originally denoted "a citizen of a city or burgh, as distinguished from a peasant on the one hand, and a nobleman on the other". Jews became an overwhelmingly urbanised people, where modern conditions forced them to compete as individuals in those fields open to them.
2. The name "Ashkenaz" was first used in Genesis 10:3 for a descendant of Noah, and was later identified with Germany. It denotes the Jews of Eastern Europe, as opposed to the Sephardi, (from Obadiah 1:20), which denotes the Jews of Spain and the Levant.
3. Ironically, at one time, he half-heartedly suggested that the Jews should return to their own land.
4. The term "gentiles" here would, of course, now include Arabs.
5. Joel Carmichael (1992, p. 128) says that the word was coined by a Jewish scholar, Moritz Steinschneider, and was adopted by Marr in 1879.
6. "Synoptic" here means to offer an overall vision, a so-called "ahah" experience.
7. *Perestroika* (restructuring) in conjunction with *glasnost* (openness) was a new policy instituted in 1986 by Mikhail Gorbachev to relax repression on human rights within the framework of socialism.
8. *Antisemitism: World Report, 1997*, Institute for Policy Research and American Jewish Committee, p. 229.
9. Email sponsored by the Simon Wiesenthal Center, an international organisation promoting tolerance and combating antisemitism worldwide. http:www.wiesenthal.com

EPILOGUE

1. As I revise this epilogue some two months after I originally penned these paragraphs, the feeling of doom has not abated. I have left the original paragraphs intact because the circumstances described therein resonate so profoundly with the subject of this book.
2. Review of Carroll's book *Constantine's Sword*, by Andrew Sullivan in the *New York Times Book Review* January 14 2001, p. 5.
3. See Nicholls (1995, pp. 351–84)
4. Cited by Hillel Halkin "The Return of Anti-Semitism", *Commentary*, February 2002, pp. 37–44.
5. See "The Specter of a New Anti-Semitism", *Newsweek*, 1 April 2002, p. 11.
6. Internet edition.
7. See, for example, Hillel Halkin, quoted above, and Arch Puddington, "The Wages of Durban", *Commentary*, November 2001.
8. Lipstadt (1993, p. 56), citing the French Holocaust denier Paul Rassinier.
9. Despite Israel's considerable military might, Jews remained victims, but now, as Biale (1986, p. 161) wryly put it, "a victim with an army".
10. See Garber et al. (1988).

Bibliography

Adorno, T.W. with Frenkel-Brunswick, E., Levinson, D. and Sanford, R., 1950, *The Authoritarian Personality*, New York: Harper.

Almog, Shmuel (ed.), 1988, *Antisemitism Through the Ages*, Oxford: Pergamon.

Arendt, Hannah, 1951, *The Origins of Totalitarianism*, New York: Harcourt Brace.

—— 1963, *Eichmann in Jerusalem: A Report on the Banality of Evil*, New York: Viking.

Atlan, Henri, 1987, "Chosen People", in Cohen and Mendes Flohr (1987, pp. 55–9).

Avineri, Shlomo, 1988, "Antisemitism as a Political Tool", in Bauer (1988, pp. 33–42).

Avisar, Ilan, 1988, *Screening the Holocaust: Cinema's Images of the Unimaginable*, Bloomington, Indiana University Press.

Bankier, David, 1998, "The Use of Antisemitism in Nazi Wartime Propaganda", in Berenbaum and Peck (1988, pp. 41–55).

Bauer, Yehuda, 1982, *A History of the Holocaust*, New York: Franklin Watts.

—— 1984, "The Most Ancient Group Prejudice", in Eitinger (1984, pp. 13–19).

—— (ed.), 1988, *Present-Day Antisemitism*, Jerusalem: Vidal Sassoon International Center for the Study of Antisemitism.

—— 1990, "Antisemitism and Anti-Zionism: New and Old", in Wistrich (1990, pp. 195–208).

—— 1994, "In Search of a Definition of Antisemitism", in Brown (1990, pp. 10–22).

—— 1998, "A Past that Will Not Go Away", in Berenbaum and Peck (1998, pp. 12–22).

Bauman, Zygmunt, 1989, *Modernity and the Holocaust*, Oxford: Polity Press.

―― 1995, *Life in Fragments: Essays in Postmodern Morality*, Oxford: Blackwell.

Bein, Alex, 1990, *The Jewish Question: Biography of a World Problem*, New York: Herzl Press.

Ben-Itto, Haddassah, 1993, "The Protocols of the Elders of Zion", in Zilbershats (1993, pp. 40–51).

Berenbaum, Michael, 1990, "The Uniqueness and Universality of the Holocaust", in *A Mosaic of Victims*, ed. Michael Berenbaum, New York: New York University Press, pp. 20–36.

Berenbaum, Michael and Peck, Abraham J. (eds), 1998, *The Holocaust and History: The Known, the Unknown, the Disputed and the Reexamined*, Bloomington: Indiana University Press.

Berger, David (ed.), 1986, *History and Hate: The Dimensions of Anti-Semitism*, Philadelphia: Jewish Publication Society.

Berghahn, V.R., 1996, "The Road to Extermination", *New York Times Book Review*, April 14, p. 6.

Berkovits, Eliezer, 1978, "Facing the Truth", *Judaism*, Summer, pp. 324–6.

Biale, David, 1986, *Power and Powerlessness in Jewish History*, New York: Schocken.

Bitton-Jackson, Livia, 1988, "The Nazi 'Blood Myth' and the Holocaust", in Garber et al. (1988, pp. 309–20).

―― 1994, "Myths and Negative Jewish Stereotypes", in Brown (pp. 237–45).

Boys, Mary C., 2000, *Has God Only One Blessing?*, New York: Paulist Press.

Brown, Michael (ed.) 1994, *Approaches to Antisemitism: Context and Curriculum*, New York/Jerusalem: The American Jewish Committee and International Center for University Teaching of Jewish Civilization.

Brown, Robert McAfee, 1983, *Elie Wiesel: Messenger to All Humanity*, London: Notre Dame Press.

Browning, Christopher, 1992, *Ordinary Men: Reserve Battalion 101 and the Final Solution in Poland*, New York: HarperCollins.

Broszat, Martin, 1977, "Hitler and the Genesis of the Final Solution" (in German), *Vierteljahrshefte für Zeitgeschichte*, October, pp. 739–75.

Cargas, Harry James, 1988, "My Papal Encyclical", in Garber et al. (eds), pp. 301–8.

Carmichael, Joel, 1992, *The Satanizing of the Jews: Origin and Development of Mystical Anti-Semitism*, New York: Fromm International.

Carmon, Arye, 1988, "Teaching the Holocaust in Israel", in Garber et al. (1988, pp. 75–92).

Carroll, James, 2001, *Constantine's Sword: The Church and the Jews: A History*, London: Houghton Mifflin.

Cesarani, David, 1996, "The German Ideology", *New Statesman*, 5 April, pp. 36–7.

―― 2000a, "Battle for the Right to Assert or Deny the Holocaust Looms", *The Sunday Independent* (Johannesburg), 16 January.

―― 2000b, "A Body Blow to All Deniers of the Holocaust", reprinted from *The Sunday Times* (London) in *The Sunday Independent* (Cape Town), 23 April.

Chazan, Robert, 1986, "Medieval Antisemitism", in Berger (1986, pp. 49–65).

Chertok, Haim, 2001, "James Parkes: Christendom's Whitest Knight", *Midstream*, May/June, pp. 23–4.

Cohen, A.A. and Mendes-Flohr, R. (eds), 1987, *Contemporary Jewish Religious Thought*, London: Free Press.

Cohen, Shaye J.D., 1986, "Anti-Semitism in Antiquity", in Berger (1986, pp. 43–7).

Cohn, Norman, 1967, *Warrant for Genocide: The Myth of the Jewish World-Conspiracy and the Protocols of the Elders of Zion*, New York: Harper & Row.

The Condition of Jewish Belief, 1966, symposium compiled by the editors of *Commentary*, New York: Macmillan.

Cotler, Irwin, 1988, "The United Nations", in Bauer (1988, pp. 43–8).

Craig, Gordon A., 1996, "How Hell Worked", *New York Review of Books*, 18 April, p. 4.

Curtis, Michael (ed.), 1986, *Antisemitism in the Contemporary World*, Boulder: Westview Press.

Curtis, Michael and Gitelson, S.A. (eds), 1976, *Israel in the Third World*, New Brunswick, NJ: Transaction Books.

Davidowitz, Moshe, 1978, "The Psychohistory of Jewish Rage and Redemption as Seen through Its Art", *Journal of Psychohistory*, 6(2), pp. 273–84.

Davies, Alan T. (ed.), 1979, *Antisemitism and the Foundations of Christianity*, New York: Paulist Press.

Davis, Moshe, 1988, "Introduction", in Bauer 1988, pp. 3–4.

Dawidowicz, Lucy S., 1975, *The War Against the Jews, 1933–1945*, New York: Holt, Rinehart & Winston.

De Lange, Nicholas, 1991, "The Origins of Anti-Semitism", in Gilman and Katz (1991, pp. 21–37).

Eckhardt, Alice L., 1987, "The Holocaust and the Church Struggle: Some Christian Reflections", in *Faith and Freedom: A Tribute to Franklin Littell*, ed. R. Libowitz, pp. 31–44.

Eitinger, Leo, 1984, *The Anti-Semitism of Our Time*, Oslo: Nansen Committee.

Ettinger, Shmuel, 1988, "Jew-Hatred in its Historical Context", in Almog (1988, pp. 1–12).

Fackenheim, Emil L., 1986, "Philosophical Reflections on Antisemitism", in Curtis (1986, pp. 21–38).

Fein, Helen, 1984, *Accounting for Genocide*, New York: Free Press.

Feldman, Louis H., 1986, "Anti-Semitism in the Ancient World", in Berger (1986, pp. 15–42).

Flannery, Edward H., 1965, *The Anguish of the Jews*, New York: Macmillan.

Fleischner, Eva (ed.), 1977, *Auschwitz: Beginning of a New Era?*, New York: Ktav.

Flinker, Moshe, 1976, *Young Moshe's Diary: The Spiritual Torment of a Jewish Boy in Nazi Europe*, ed. Shaul Esh, Jerusalem: Yad Vashem.

Flusser, David, 1988, *Judaism and the Origins of Christianity*, Jerusalem: Magnes Press.

Forward, Martin, 1997, *Muhammad: A Short Biography*, Oxford: Oneworld.

Frank, Anne, 1974, *Anne Frank: The Diary of a Young Girl*, New York: Doubleday.

Freud, Sigmund, 1951, *Moses and Monotheism*, London: Hogarth.

—— 1960, *Totem and Taboo: Some Points of Agreement between the Mental Lives of Savages and Neurotics*, London: Routledge & Kegan Paul.

Friedländer, Saul, 1988, "Confrontations of Memory", in Bauer (1988, pp. 13–30).

—— 1997, *Nazi Germany and the Jews: Vol. 1, The Years of Persecution*, London: HarperCollins.

Frye, Northrop, 1982, *The Great Code: The Bible and Literature*, Toronto.

Gager, John G., 1983, *The Origins of Anti-Semitism: Attitudes Toward Judaism in Pagan and Christian Antiquity*, New York: Oxford University Press.

Garber, Zev, Berger, Alan and Libowitz, Richard (eds), 1988, *Methodology in the Academic Teaching of the Holocaust*, New York: University Press of America.

Gaston, Lloyd, 1979, "Paul and the Torah", in Davies (1979, pp. 48–71).

Gerber, Jane S., 1986, "Anti-Semitism in the Muslim World", in Berger (1986, pp. 73–93).

Gilbert, Martin, 1978, *The Holocaust*, New York: Hill & Wang.

Gilman, Sander L. and Katz, Steven T. (eds), 1991, *Anti-Semitism in Times of Crisis*, New York: New York University Press.

Glazer, Nathan, 1986, "Anti-Zionism: A Global Phenomenon", in Curtis 1986, pp. 155–63).

Goldberg, Michael, 1995, *Why Should Jews Survive?*, New York: Oxford University Press.

Goldhagen, Daniel J., 1996, *Hitler's Willing Executioners: Ordinary Germans and the Holocaust*, London: Little Brown.

Grynberg, Henryk, 1982, "Appropriating the Holocaust", *Commentary*, November, pp. 54–7.

Halkin Hillel, 2002, "The Return of Anti-Semitism", *Commentary*, February, pp. 37–44.

Hellig, Jocelyn, 1996, *Anti-Semitism in South Africa Today*, Tel Aviv: Project for the Study of Anti-Semitism, Tel Aviv University.

—— 1999, "Antisemitism and Proselytism", in *Sharing the Book: Religious Perspectives on the Rights and Wrongs of Proselytism*, ed. John Witte, Jr. and Richard C. Martin, New York: Orbis, pp. 17–44.

—— 2000, "Antisemitism in Sub-Saharan Africa with a focus on South Africa", *Emory International Law Review*, 14(2), pp. 1197–248.

Herr, Moshe David, 1988, "The Sages' Reaction to Antisemitism in the Hellenistic-Roman World", in Almog (1988, pp. 27–38).

Hertzberg, Arthur, 1966, Essay in *Commentary Symposium*, pp. 90–6.

—— 1968, *The French Enlightenment and the Jews*, New York: Columbia University Press.

Hertzberg, Arthur and Hirt-Manheimer, Aron, 1998, *Jews: The Essence and Character of a People*, San Francisco: Harper.

Hilberg, Raul, 1961, *The Destruction of the European Jews*, Chicago: Quadrangle.
—— 1995, *Perpetrators, Victims, Bystanders: The Jewish Catastrophe 1933–1945*, London: Secker & Warburg.
—— 1998, "Sources and Their Uses", in Berenbaum and Peck (1998, pp. 5–11).
Himmelfarb, Milton, 1984, "No Hitler, No Holocaust", *Commentary*, March, pp. 37–43.
Hitler, Adolf, 1939, *Mein Kampf*, New York: Stackpole.
Hoffman, Eva, 2000, "The Uses of Hell", *New York Review of Books*, 9 March.
Hoffman, Stefani, 1995, "More Puzzles, Fewer Answers", in *Russian Jewry in Flux: Two Reports*, Jerusalem: The Institute of the World Jewish Congress, Policy Studies 2–3.
Hoffmann, Tzippi and Fischer, Alan, 1988, *The Jews of South Africa: What Future?* Johannesburg: Southern Book Publishers.
Howe, Irving, 1988, "Writing and the Holocaust", in Lang (1988, pp. 175–99).
Huchet-Bishop, Claire, 1977, "Response to Palikowski", in Fleischner (1977, pp. 179–90).
Hyman, Paula, 1987, "Emancipation", in Cohen and Mendes-Flohr (1987, pp. 165–70).
Irving, David, 1977, *Hitler's War*, London: Hodder & Stoughton.
Isaac, Jules, 1964, *The Teaching of Contempt*, New York: Holt, Rinehart & Winston.
Jäckel, Eberhard, 1972, *Hitler's Weltanschauung: A Blueprint for Power*, trans. Herbert Arnold, Middletown, CT: Wesleyan University Press.
—— 1998, "The Holocaust: Where We Are and Where We Need to Go", in Berenbaum and Peck (1998, pp. 23–9).
Jick, Leon, 1998, "Method in Madness: An Examination of the Motivations for Nazi Mass Murder", *Modern Judaism*, May, pp. 153–72.
Johnson, Paul, 1982, *A History of Christianity*, Harmondsworth: Penguin.
Kaplan, Samuel W., 1996, "Hitler's Willing Executioners", *Judaism* 45(3), pp. 361–76.
Katz, Jacob, 1975, "Was the Holocaust Predictable?", *Commentary*, May, pp. 41–8.
—— 1980, *From Prejudice to Destruction: Anti-Semitism, 1700–1933*, Cambridge, MA: Harvard University Press.
—— 1983, "Misreadings of Anti-Semitism", *Commentary*, July, pp. 39–44.
—— 1991, "Accounting for Anti-Semitism", *Commentary*, June, pp. 52–4.
Katz, Steven T., 1994a, *The Holocaust in Historical Context: Vol. 1., The Holocaust and Mass Death Before the Modern Age*, New York: Oxford University Press.
—— 1994b, "The Holocaust as an Historical Event: What the *Shoah* is Not", in *Proceedings of the Eleventh World Congress of Jewish Studies*, June 22–29, Vol 3 "Modern Times" Jerusalem: World Union of Jewish Studies, pp. 235–42.
—— 1998, "The Holocaust: A Very Particular Racism", In Berenbaum and Peck (1998, pp. 56–63).

Kertzer, David I., 2002, *Unholy War: The Vatican's Role in the Rise of Modern Anti-Semitism*, London: Macmillan.

Kosinsky, Jerzy, 1978, *The Painted Bird*, New York: Bantam.

Kühl, Stefan, 1998, "The Cooperation of German Racial Hygienists and American Eugenicists before and after 1933", in Berenbaun and Peck (1998, pp. 134–51).

Lang, Berel (ed.), 1988, *Writing and the Holocaust*, New York: Holmes & Meier.

—— 1999, *The Future of the Holocaust: Between History and Memory*, Ithaca, New York: Cornell University Press.

Lanzmann, Claude, 1985, *Shoah: An Oral History of the Holocaust*, New York: Pantheon.

Lazar, Moshe, 1991, "The Lamb and the Scapegoat", in Gilman and Katz (1991, pp. 38–80).

Lerman, A. (ed.), 1997, *Antisemitism: World Report 1997*, Institute for Jewish Policy Research and American Jewish Committee.

Lesser, Alexander, 1994, "Tied to Mother Russia", *Jerusalem Report*, 17 November 1994.

Levin, Nora, 1968, *The Holocaust: The Destruction of European Jewry, 1933–1945*, New York: Thomas Crowell.

Lewis, Bernard, 1984, *The Jews of Islam*, Princeton: Princeton University Press.

—— 1988, "Antisemitism in the Arab and Islamic World", in Bauer (1988, pp. 57–66).

—— 1997, *Semites and Anti- Semites*, London: Phoenix.

Libowitz, R. (ed), 1987, *Faith and Freedom: A Tribute to Franklin Littell*, Oxford: Pergamon Press.

Lindemann, Albert S., 1997, *Esau's Tears: Modern Anti-Semitism and the Rise of the Jews*, Cambridge: Cambridge University Press.

Lipstadt, Deborah E., 1993, *Denying the Holocaust: The Growing Assault on Truth and Memory*, New York: Free Press.

Littell, Franklin H., 1975, *The Crucifixion of the Jews*, New York: Harper & Row.

—— 1997, Review of *Hitler's Willing Executioners*, *Modern Judaism*, May, pp. 190–3.

Loshitzky, Yosefa, 1997, *Spielberg's Holocaust: Critical Perspectives on Schindler's List*, Bloomington: Indiana University Press.

Maccoby, Hyam, 1982, "Theologian of the Holocaust", *Commentary*, December, pp. 33–7.

—— 1987, "Anti-Judaism and Anti-Semitism", in Cohen and Mendes-Flohr (1987, pp. 13–18).

—— 1992, *Judas Iscariot and the Myth of Jewish Evil*, New York: Free Press.

Manvell, R. and Fraenkel, H., 1982, *Hitler: The Man and the Myth*, London: Granada.

—— 1982, "The Theory and Practice of Anti-Semitism", *Commentary*, August, pp. 38–42.

Marrus, Michael, 1987, *The Holocaust in History*, Harmondsworth: Penguin Books.

—— 1994, "Good Scholarship and Good Teaching: Holocaust History as an Exemplary Model", in Brown (1994, pp. 121–33).

—— 1998, "Where We Are, Where We Need to Go – A Comment", in Berenbaum and Peck (1998), pp. 30–34.

Mayer, Arno J., 1988, *Why Did the Heavens not Darken? The "Final Solution" in History*, New York: Pantheon.

Mendes-Flohr, P.R. and Reinharz, J. (eds) 1980, *The Jew in the Modern World: A Documentary History*, New York: Oxford University Press.

Michman, Dan, 1995, "'The Holocaust' in the Eyes of Historians", *Modern Judaism*, October, 233–64.

Milgram, Stanley, 1974, *Obedience to Authority: An Experimental View*, London: Tavistock.

Modder, Montagu Frank, 1960, *The Jew in the Literature of England to the End of the Nineteenth Century*, New York: Meridian Books.

Moore, James F., 1988, "Crossing the Experience Barrier: Teaching the Holocaust to Christian Students", in Garber et al. (1988, pp. 155–70).

—— 1994, "Teaching about Antisemitism in a Christian Setting", in Brown, (1994, pp. 161–70).

Morais, Vamberto, 1976, *A Short History of Anti-Semitism*, New York: W.W. Norton.

Moran, Gabriel, 1992, *Uniqueness: Problem or Paradox in Jewish and Christian Traditions*, Maryknoll, NY: Orbis.

Nettler, Ronald L. 1986, "Past Trials and Present Tribulations", in Curtis (1986, pp. 97–106).

—— 1990, "Islamic Archetypes of the Jews: Then and Now", in Wistrich (1990, pp. 63–73).

Neusner, Jacob, 1989, *The Ecology of Religion*, Nashville: Abingdon Press.

Nicholls, William, 1995, *Christian Antisemitism: A History of Hate*, Northvale, NJ Jason Aronson.

—— 1998, "Comprehending Antisemitism", *Judaism*, Summer, pp. 371–9.

Noakes, Jeremy D., 1996, "No Ordinary People", *Times Literary Supplement*, 7 June.

Novick, Peter, 2001, *The Holocaust and Collective Memory: The American Experience* London: Bloomsbury.

Oliner, Samuel P. and Pearl, M., 1988, *The Altruistic Personality: Rescuers of Jews in Nazi Europe*, New York: Free Press.

Ostow, Mortimer, 1989, "Judaism and Psychoanalysis", in *The Blackwell Companion to Jewish Culture*, ed. Glenda Abramson, Oxford: Blackwell, pp. 612–16.

Paget, James Carleton, 1996, "Jewish Proselytism at the Time of Christian Origins: Chimera or Reality?", *Journal for the Study of the New Testament*, 62, pp. 65–103.

Parkes, James. 1934, *The Conflict of the Church and the Synagogue: A Study of the Origins of Antisemitism*, New York: Hermon Press.

—— 1963, *Antisemitism*, London: Vallentine Mitchell.

Pawlikowski, John T., 1974, "Judaism in Christian Education and Liturgy", in Fleischner (1974, pp. 155–78).

—— 1986, "New Testament Antisemitism: Fact or Fable?", in Curtis (1986, pp. 107–27).

Peli, Pinchas Hacohen, 1991, "Responses to Anti-Semitism in Midrashic Literature", in Gilman and Katz (1991, pp. 103–14).

Poliakov, Léon, 1974, *The History of Anti-Semitism*, 3 vols, London: Routledge & Kegan Paul.

—— 1979, *Harvest of Hate: The Nazi Program for the Destruction of the Jews of Europe*, New York: Holocaust Library.

Prager, Dennis and Telushkin, Joseph, 1983, *Why the Jews?* New York: Simon & Schuster.

Ravitch, Norman, 1982, "The Problem of Christian Anti-Semitism", *Commentary*, April, pp. 41–52.

Reese, W.L., 1980, *Dictionary of Philosophy and Religion: Eastern and Western Thought*, Atlantic Highlands, NJ: Humanities Press.

Reitlinger, Gerald, 1953, The Final Solution: The Attempt to Exterminate the Jews of Europe, 1939–1945, New York: Beechhurst Press.

Richardson S. and Bowden J. (eds), 1983, *A New Dictionary of Christian Theology*, SCM Press.

Rivlin, B. and Fomerand, J., 1976, "Changing Third World Perspectives and Policies Towards Israel", in Curtis and Gitelson (1976, pp. 325–60).

Rokéah David. 1988, "The Church Fathers and the Jews", in Almog (1988, pp. 27–38).

Rosenbaum, Alan, S. (ed.) 1998, *Is the Holocaust Unique? Perspectives on Comparative Genocide*, Oxford: Westview Press.

Rosenbaum, Ron, 1998, *Explaining Hitler: The Search for the Origins of His Evil*, London: Macmillan.

Roth, John, K., 1988, "What Can Anyone Do?", in Garber et al. (1988, pp. 107–28).

Rubenstein, Richard L., 1966a, *After Auschwitz*, Indianapolis: Bobbs-Merrill.

—— 1966b, Essay in *Commentary Symposium*, pp. 192–200.

—— 1974, *Power Struggle: An Autobiographical Confession*, New York: Charles Scribner's Sons.

—— 1975, *The Cunning of History: Mass Death and Its American Future*, New York: Harper & Row.

—— 1990, "Modernization and the Politics of Extermination", in *A Mosaic of Victims*, ed. Michael Berenbaum, New York: New York University Press, pp. 3–19.

Rubenstein, Richard L. and Roth, John K., 1987, *Approaches to Auschwitz: The Legacy of the Holocaust*, London: SCM Press.

Rubin, Barry, 1990, "The Non-Arab Third World and Anti-Semitism", in Wistrich, (1990, pp. 85–92).

Ruether, Rosemary R., 1974, *Faith and Fratricide: The Theological Roots of Anti-Semitism*, New York: Seabury Press.

—— 1977, "Anti-Semitism and Christian theology", in Fleischner (1977, pp. 79–92).

Sacks, Jonathan, 2001, *Radical Then, Radical Now: The Legacy of the World's Oldest Religion*, London: Harper Collins.

Said, Edward, 1997, *Covering Islam: How the Media and the Experts Determine How We See the Rest of the World*, London: Vintage.

Saldarini, Anthony J., 1994, *Matthew's Christian–Jewish Community*, Chicago: University of Chicago Press.

Sanders. E.P., 1991, *Paul*, Oxford: Oxford University Press.

Sartre, Jean Paul, 1948, *Anti-Semite and Jew*, New York: Schocken.

Schafer, Peter, 1997, *Judaeophobia: Attitudes Toward the Jews in the Ancient World*, Cambridge, MA: Harvard University Press.

Schleunes, Karl, 1972, *The Twisted Road to Auschwitz: Nazi Policy Toward German Jews 1933–39*, London: André Deutsch.

Schwarz, Daniel R., 1999, *Imagining the Holocaust*, New York: St Martin's Griffin.

Segre, Dan V., 1986, "Is Anti-Zionism a New Form of Antisemitism?", in Curtis (1986, pp. 145–54).

Seltzer, Robert M., 1980, *Jewish People Jewish Thought*, New York: Macmillan.

Sereny, Gitta, 1983, *Into That Darkness: An Examination of Conscience*, New York: Vintage.

Shain, Milton, 1998, *Antisemitism*, London: Bowerdean Briefings.

Shnirelman, Victor A., 1998, *Russian Neo-Pagan Myths and Antisemitism*, Analysis of Current Trends in Antisemitism, no. 13, Jerusalem: Vidal Sassoon International Center for the Study of Antisemitism.

Simon, Marcel, 1948, *Verus Israel: A Study of the Relations between Christians and Jews in the Roman Empire* trans. H. McKeating, New York: Oxford University Press (Litman Library).

Singer, D. and Grossman, L. (eds), 2000, *American Jewish Year Book 2000*, Philadelphia: American Jewish Committee.

Sivan, Emmanuel, 1986, "Radical Islam and the Arab–Israeli Conflict", in Curtis (1986, 61–9).

—— 1990, "Islamic Fundamentalism, Antisemitism and Anti-Zionism", in Wistrich (1990, pp. 74–84).

Smart, Ninian, 1984, *The Religious Experience of Mankind*, 3rd edn, New York: Charles Scribner's Sons.

Smith, Huston, 1958, *The Religions of Man*, New York: Perennial.

Steiner, George, 1967, "Jewish Values in a Post-Holocaust Future", *Judaism*, Summer, pp. 276–81.

—— 1983, *The Portage to San Cristobál of A. H.*, New York: Washington Square Press.

Stendahl, Krister, 1963, "The Apostle Paul and the Introspective Conscience of the West", *Harvard Theological Review*, July.

Stern, Menahem, 1976, *Greek and Latin Authors on Jews and Judaism*, vol.1, Jerusalem: Israel Academy of Sciences and Humanities.

—— 1980, *Greek and Latin Authors on Jews and Judaism*, vol. 2. Jerusalem: Israel Academy of Sciences and Humanities.

—— 1988, "Antisemitism in Rome", in Almog (1988, pp. 13–26).

Stillman, Norman A., 1986, "Antisemitism in the Contemporary Arab World", in Curtis (1988, pp. 70–85).

Tabori, Ephraim, 1995, "Post-Soviet Jewry: Present and Future Prospects", in *Russian Jewry in Flux: Two Reports*, Jerusalem: The Institute of the World Jewish Congress, Policy Studies 2–3.

Tal, Uriel, 1975, *Christians and Jews in Germany: Religion, Politics and Ideology in the Second Reich, 1870–1914*, Ithaca, New York: Cornell University Press.

Thomas, Laurence, 1991, "Characterizing and Responding to Nazi Genocide: A Review Essay", *Modern Judaism*, 11(3), pp. 371–9.

Vermes, Geza, 1983, *Jesus the Jew: A Historian's Reading of the Gospels*, London: SCM Press.

Volavková , Hana (ed.), 1965, *I Never Saw another Butterfly ... Children's Drawings and Poems from Theresienstadt Concentration Camp 1942–1944*, London: Neville Spearman.

Volkov, Shulamit, 1988, "Western Antisemitism Today", in Bauer (1988, pp. 67–78).

Whitfield, Steven J., 1987, "Jewish History and the Torment of Totalitarianism", *Judaism*, (Summer, pp. 304–19).

Wiesel, Eli, 1970, *Night*, New York: Avon Books.

Wilson, A.N., 1992, *Jesus: A Life*, New York: W.W. Norton.

Wilson, Marvin R., 1989, *Our Father Abraham: Jewish Roots of the Christian Faith*, Grand Rapids, MI: William B. Eerdeman's.

Wistrich, Robert S., 1985, *Hitler's Apocalypse: Jews and the Nazi Legacy*, London: Weidenfeld & Nicolson.

—— 1988, "Anti-Zionism as an Expression of Antisemitism in Recent Years", in Bauer (1988, pp. 175–88).

—— (ed.), 1990, *Anti-Zionism and Anti-Semitism in the Contemporary World*, London: Macmillan.

—— 1991, *Anti-Semitism: The Longest Hatred*, London: Thames Methuen.

—— 1996, "Helping Hitler", *Commentary*, July, pp. 27–31.

—— 1999, "The Pope, the Church, and the Jews", *Commentary*, April, pp. 22–8.

Wohlgelernter, Elli, 2000, "No Denying Her Now", *The Jerusalem Post*, 16 June, p. 9.

Wyman, David S., 1984, *The Abandonment of the Jews: America and the Holocaust 1941–1945*. New York: Pantheon.

—— 1987, "Synthesizing a Nightmare", *New York Times Book Review*, November 22, p. 38.

Wytowycky, Bohdan, 1980, *The Other Holocaust: The Many Circles of Hell*, Washington: Novak Report on the New Ethnicity.

Yadlin, Rivka, 1986, "Arab Antisemitism in Peacetime: The Egyptian Case", in Curtis (1986, pp. 86–96).

—— 1994, "On the Significance of Textual Antisemitism in the Arab World", in Brown (1994, pp. 95–105).

Yahil, Leni, 1990, *The Holocaust: The Fate of European Jewry, 1932–1945*, Oxford: Oxford University Press.

Yerushalmi, Yosef Hayim, 1977, "Response to Rosemary Ruether", in Fleishner (1977, pp. 79–92).

—— 1999, *Zakhor: Jewish History and Jewish Memory*, Seattle: University of Washington Press.

Young, James E., 1988, *Writing and Rewriting the Holocuast: Narrative and the Consequences of Interpretation*, Bloomington: Indiana University Press.

Zelizer, Barbie, 1997, "Every Once in a While: Schindler's List and the Shaping of History", in Loshitsky (1997, pp. 18–40).

Zerner, Ruth, 1988. "Resistance and Submission: Teaching about Responses to Oppression", in Garber et al., (1988, pp. 93–106).

Zilbershats, Yaffa (ed.), 1993, *The Rising Tide of Anti-Semitism: Déjà-Vu?*, Tel Aviv: Bar Ilan University.

Index